The Eighteenth-Century Town
A Reader in English Urban History
1688–1820

Edited by
Peter Borsay

LONGMAN
London and New York

Longman Group Limited,
Longman House, Burnt Mill, Harlow,
Essex CM20 2JE, England
and Associated Companies throughout the world.

*Published in the United States of America
by Longman Publishing, New York*

First published 1990
Second impression 1995

BRITISH LIBRARY CATALOGUING IN PUBLICATION DATA
The Eighteenth-century town: a reader in English urban
  history 1688–1820. — (Readers in urban history).
  1. England. Towns, history
  I. Borsay, Peter II. Series
  942'. 009'732

ISBN 0-582-05135-5 CSD
ISBN 0-582-05134-7 PPR

LIBRARY OF CONGRESS CATALOGING-IN-PUBLICATION DATA
The eighteenth-century town: a reader in English urban history,
  1688–1820/edited by Peter Borsay.
      p.   cm.
  Includes bibliographical references.
  ISBN 0-582-05135-5. —ISBN 0-582-05134-7
  1. Cities and towns — England — History — 18th century. 2. England —
Social conditions — 18th century. I. Borsay, Peter.
HT133.E36   1990   89–29172
307.76'0942'09034 — dc20   CIP

Set in Linotron Times 10/11pts

Produced by Longman Singapore Publishers (Pte) Ltd.
Printed in Singapore

CONTENTS

Contents

PREFACE

The aim of this reader – one of a series of four volumes on urban history covering the late twelfth to early twentieth centuries – is to gather together in an easily accessible form, and place in a clear and comprehensible context, a number of key contributions to the study of the eighteenth-century town. In choosing the items for inclusion I have avoided the contents of readily available urban history collections. In general, weight has been given to more recent publications and an attempt has been made to provide a reasonably broad coverage of the various aspects of town life. Though I am conscious that in practice the pieces selected are concentrated in certain fields, this reflects the way the subject has developed and the need in a collection like this to allow for some common ground between the contributions. The reader opens with a specially written Introduction (Chapter 1), surveying the results of recent research on the history of the English town between 1688 and 1820, and locating the later essays in a broad contextual framework. Each piece (chapter) itself is prefaced by a brief editorial introduction, highlighting its central features, indicating other published work (occasionally of a critical nature) relevant to it, and sometimes raising questions about its methodology or conclusions. A select list of further reading is provided, which is supported by more detailed bibliographical references in the footnotes to the Introduction. In editing this volume I am grateful to the authors and publishers who have permitted me to reproduce their work, to Peter Clark and Anne Borsay for their valuable comments on my text, and to the trustees of the Pantyfedwen Fund at Saint David's University College, Lampeter, for their financial assistance in preparing the book.

ACKNOWLEDGEMENTS

We are grateful to the following for permission to reproduce copyright material:

the editors for the extract 'Bath: ideology and utopia 1700–1760' by R S Neale in *Studies in the Eighteenth Century III* edited by R F Brissenden and J C Eade (Australian National University Press, 1976); Cambridge University Press and the author, R J Morris for the article 'Voluntary societies and British urban elites 1780–1850: an analysis' in *Historical Journal*, 26 (1983); Jai Press Inc for the chapter 'Urban Improvement and the English economy in the seventeenth and eighteenth centuries' by E L Jones and M E Falkus in *Research in Economic History: Vol 4* (1979); the editors of *The Journal of Interdisciplinary History* and The MIT Press, Cambridge, Massachusetts, for the article 'Urban Growth and Agricultural Change: England and the Continent in the Early Modern Period' by E A Wrigley in *The Journal of Interdisciplinary History*, XV (1985), (c) 1985 by The Massachusetts Institute of Technology and the editors; the editor of *Midland History* and the author, J Money for the article 'Birmingham and the West Midlands 1760-1793: politics & regional identity in the English provinces in the later eighteenth century' in *Midland History*, Vol 1, No 1 (1971); The Royal Historical Society for the article 'Country, county and town: patterns of regional evolution in England' by A M Everitt in *Transactions of the Royal Historical Society*, 5th series, 29 (1979); the editors of *Social History* and the authors for the articles 'The English urban renaissance: the development of provincial urban culture c. 1680–c. 1760' by P Borsay in *Social History*, 2 (1977), 'Money, land, and lineage: the big bourgeoisie of Hanoverian London' by N Rogers in *Social History*, 4 (1979) and 'Social class and social geography: the middle classes in London at the end of the eighteenth century' by L D Schwarz in *Social History*, 7 (1982); The University of Chicago Press and the author, R B Shoemaker for the article 'The London "mob" in the early eighteenth century' in *Journal of British Studies*, Vol 26 (1987); The Voltaire Foundation and the author, R Porter for the article 'Science, provincial culture & public opinion in Enlightenment England' in *British Journal for Eighteenth-Century Studies*, 3 (1980).

Chapter 1
INTRODUCTION

Peter Borsay

The study of English urban history between 1688 and 1820, what may conveniently be called the long eighteenth century, was, until the last decade or so, relatively neglected. Attention focused on the more overtly 'eventful' periods before the Civil War and after the inception of the Industrial Revolution. This pattern of research had the effect of accentuating the differences between the pre-industrial and industrial town, and encouraged the view that the transformation of the one into the other was a dramatic, even revolutionary, event. However, notions of this type have now come under critical scrutiny. At a general level, the nature and significance of the Civil War[1] and the Industrial Revolution,[2] two of the corner-stones of post-war British historiography, are being reappraised. In the field of urban history pioneering volumes, such as Penelope Corfield's (1982) *The Impact of English Towns 1700–1800* and the collection of essays edited by Peter Clark, (1984) *The Transformation of English Towns 1600–1800*, have redirected attention to the long eighteenth century and emphasized the deep roots of economic and social change. In Britain and across the Atlantic, evolution rather than revolution is coming to seem the more appropriate concept to describe the transition from pre-industrial to industrial urban society,[3] and with this change in approach the stereotyped images

1. See, for example, J. C. D. Clark, *Revolution and Rebellion: State and Society in England in the Seventeenth and Eighteenth Centuries* (Cambridge, 1986), *passim*; P. Jenkins, *The Making of a Ruling Class: the Glamorgan Gentry 1640–1790* (Cambridge, 1983), pp. 132–3.
2. D. Cannadine, 'The present and the past in the English Industrial Revolution 1880–1980', *Past and Present*, 103 (1984), pp. 159–67; N. F. R. Crafts, *British Economic Growth during the Industrial Revolution* (Oxford, 1985); J. V. Beckett and J. E. Heath, 'When was the Industrial Revolution in the East Midlands?', *Midland History*, 13 (1988), pp. 77–94.
3. G. B. Nash, 'The social evolution of pre-industrial American cities 1700–1820', *Journal of Urban History*, 13, no. 2 (1987), pp. 115–45.

of the modern and pre-modern town are beginning to crack. Central to this reassessment are two questions. To what extent do traditional features of town life persist during the Industrial Revolution? And how far can the new urban trends associated with this economic transformation be detected in the century or so preceding it?

The issue of continuity is one of the key themes examined in this Introduction. The second major issue addressed will be that of urban identity. Though much has been written which touches obliquely upon English towns between 1688 and 1820, it is doubtful to what extent the majority of this constitutes urban history. More often than not towns are treated as the accidental spaces in which interesting processes and incidents happen to occur; not as a special type of place which, by virtue of its generic qualities, moulded experiences and instigated events. Such a lack of urban sensitivity is partly due to the tendency to investigate towns individually rather than collectively. But it may also reflect the fact that historians themselves often seem unclear as to what constituted a town. In their attempts to measure urbanization, C. M. Law, Penelope Corfield and Anthony Wrigley have excluded settlements of below either 5000 or 2500 people. Yet the clear majority of towns explored in the recent work of R. W. Unwin, John Marshall and Margaret Noble fall well below either of these thresholds.[4] The extent to which the mass of small settlements that formed the bedrock of the urban system were fully-fledged towns remains an unresolved problem. There is also doubt among some historians whether it is meaningful during the early modern period to distinguish between town and country, and therefore valid to isolate a specifically urban variable.[5]

Though continuity and identity are the two central issues investigated in this Introduction, it is also intended to touch upon other

4. C. M. Law, 'Some notes on the urban population of England and Wales in the eighteenth century', *Local Historian*, 10, no. 1 (1972), p. 18; P. J. Corfield, 'Urban development in England and Wales in the sixteenth and seventeenth centuries', in D. C. Coleman and A. H. John (eds), *Trade, Government, and Economy in Pre-industrial England* (London, 1976), pp. 221–3; P. J. Corfield, *The Impact of English Towns 1700-1800* (Oxford, 1982), p. 6; E. A. Wrigley, 'Urban growth and agricultural change: England and the Continent in the early modern period', *Journal of Interdisciplinary History*, 15, no. 4 (1985), pp. 684–90; R. W. Unwin, 'Tradition and transition: market towns of the Vale of York 1660–1830', *Northern History*, 17 (1981), p. 75; J. D. Marshall, 'The rise and transformation of the Cumbrian market town 1660–1900', *Northern History*, 19 (1983), pp. 154, 162–3; M. Noble, 'Growth and development in a regional urban system: the country towns of eastern Yorkshire 1700–1850', *Urban History Yearbook* (1987), pp. 4–5.
5. M. J. Daunton, 'Towns and economic growth in eighteenth-century England', in P. Abrams and E. A. Wrigley (eds), *Towns in Societies: Essays in Economic History and Historical Sociology* (Cambridge, 1979), pp. 272–7; N. R. Goose, 'In search of the urban variable: towns and the English economy 1500–1650', *Economic History Review*, 2nd ser., 39, no. 2 (1986), pp. 165–85.

problems which have come to the fore in recent research. With these concerns in mind, nine broad areas of urban life will be examined: the urban system, demography, the economy, social structure, standards of living, the environment, politics, religion, and culture. Exploration of these subjects will place the readings reproduced in this collection in a general context, though each contribution will also be prefaced by a brief comment intended to highlight its special significance.

One of the most important features of recent work in early modern urban history has been the determination to view towns as a whole rather than as solitary entities. Critical to such an approach has been the need to establish a typology and system of settlements. The most common solution has been the concept of an urban hierarchy, with many commentators adopting a four-tiered model: country or market towns at the base, regional centres on the next rung, provincial capitals on the next, and London, in a division all of its own, at the apex.[6] A town's place within this hierarchy depended on the depth and range of influence it exerted over its hinterland, and the sophistication of its economic, social, political and cultural organization. Few attempts have yet been made to evaluate precisely the type of interaction that existed between towns within the hierarchy, or to apply the idea of an urban system to a local context. However, the regional studies of Margaret Noble and John Marshall have pointed the way forward. The former detects an increasingly differentiated hierarchy of towns in eastern Yorkshire; while Marshall divides Cumbria into five groups of urban settlements, each possessing its own head town, with the constituent members of each group holding markets on separate days and the leading towns servicing the shopkeepers of their satellite centres with goods.[7] The links established through wholesale trading, such as Ian Mitchell has uncovered in Cheshire,[8] were probably a crucial factor in determining the composition and working relationships of a regional urban network.

On a grander canvas, the most cogent case for an early modern urban system has been that proposed by Jan De Vries. He argues that between 1500 and 1800 there emerged an integrated European network of towns, bound together by economic rather than political

---

6. P. Clark and P. Slack, *English Towns in Transition 1500–1700* (London, 1976), pp. 8–10; Corfield, 'Urban development', pp. 221–3; J. Patten, *English Towns 1500–1700* (Folkestone, 1978), pp. 52–4; and also C. W. Chalklin, *The Provincial Towns of Georgian England* (London, 1974), pp. 4–17.
7. Noble, 'Regional urban system', p. 15; Marshall, 'Cumbrian market town', pp. 133–53.
8. S. I. Mitchell, 'Retailing in eighteenth-century and early nineteenth-century Cheshire', *Transactions of the Historic Society of Lancashire and Cheshire*, 130 (1981), p. 52.

3

or administrative forces. These three centuries were themselves only one stage in a longer term process of urbanization, in which the medieval period represented a formative phase (as many new towns were established), and the early modern years an era of consolidation. The latter trend was particularly evident between the early seventeenth and mid-eighteenth centuries, 'the age of the rural proletariat', when town populations generally stagnated or declined, and the component parts of the urban hierarchy became increasingly differentiated. Only with the economic transformation of the late eighteenth century did a new creative period emerge, and with it a major restructuring of the urban hierarchy.[9] The problem for English historians, as Anthony Wrigley has made clear in an important article reproduced in this volume (Chapter 2), is that the shake up of the urban system was underway long before the mid-eighteenth century.[10] The rise of Birmingham can be traced back at least to the sixteenth century and it, along with Manchester and Liverpool, was experiencing dynamic growth from the late seventeenth century. By 1750 these three centres are among the top seven towns in the country, having rapidly ascended the urban ladder to join the élite club of provincial capitals.[11] England's 'urban revolution' of the nineteenth century therefore has deep roots, a consequence of it diverging from the European pattern of urbanization at some point during the early modern period. Indeed, the extent of change in the eighteenth century has led Penelope Corfield to question the whole notion of an urban hierarchy, and to suggest that during these years a more modern and pluralist system was emerging, in which towns were defined in terms of their 'leading economic functions' rather than their regional influence.[12] The development of thoroughfare towns, dockyards and resorts, and the migration of industrial production into the town, even before the rise of steam power, meant that many centres displayed a growing economic independence from their local hinterlands.

A striking feature of the English urban system was, as one observer of the continental scene has put it, 'the paltry size of all the towns outside of London prior to the eighteenth century'.[13] In 1700 over four-fifths of England's towns had a population of less than 2000 people.[14] It could be argued that this is something of a ter-

9. J. De Vries, *European Urbanization 1500–1800* (London, 1984), pp. 255–65.
10. Wrigley, 'Urban growth and agricultural change', pp. 705–12.
11. V. Skipp, *A History of Greater Birmingham — down to 1830* (Birmingham, 1980), pp. 38–54; A. McInnes, *The English Town 1660–1760* (London, 1980), p. 6.
12. Corfield, *English Towns*, pp. 15–16.
13. P. Benedict, 'Late medieval and early modern urban history à l'Anglaise: a review article', *Comparative Studies in Society and History*, 28 (1986), p. 169.
14. Chalklin, *Provincial Towns*, p. 5.

minological mirage, since any serious demographic definition of an urban centre would exclude the mass of petty settlements that masqueraded as towns, and demote them instead to the status of villages. However, such an approach flies in the face of several studies which suggest that communities of well under 1000 people, and even under 500, could display distinctly urban characteristics.[15] To add to the peculiarities and paradoxes of the English urban system, it was dominated by a capital city which had grown dramatically from about 120 000 people in 1550, to around half a million in 1700, containing almost one in ten of all Englishmen, and constituting the largest city in Western Europe.[16] England, therefore, had an extraordinarily bottom- *and* top-heavy urban hierarchy. It is difficult to avoid the conclusion that the two features were related. In a relatively compact and centralized state, linked together by good water and road communications, a highly differentiated and simplified network of towns made the greatest sense. During the eighteenth century, under the impact of a more diversified and regionally oriented pattern of economic development, the middle of the hierarchy was to fill out, foreshadowing the shape of the urban system in the following century. Whereas in 1700 there were only 67 towns of between 2500 and 100 000 inhabitants, accounting for a mere 7½ per cent of the nation's population, by 1801 there were 187 such centres, containing 20 per cent of the country's people. Not that London's ascendancy necessarily diminished: at the beginning of the nineteenth century, with about 1 million inhabitants, it still contained 10 per cent of the total population.[17]

If the metropolis retained its dominant position in the hierarchy, what was the fate of the smaller centres during this period of change? A number obviously climbed into the middle ranks. But it is argued that for the majority the eighteenth century was a bleak period, as the urban system was subject to a widespread process of rationalization or 'shake out'. Alan Everitt has suggested that by 1770 perhaps as many as one-third of the market towns of Tudor and early Stuart England and Wales had become extinct, and John Chartres has argued that in the century after 1690 the number of marketing centres fell by about one-fifth among a group of sixteen 'metropolitan Western England' counties. Competition from the

15. See C. W. Chalklin, 'A seventeenth-century market town: Tonbridge', *Archaeologia Cantiana*, 76 (1961), pp. 152–62; P. Styles, 'Henley-in-Arden in the seventeenth century', in P. Styles, *Studies in Seventeenth Century West Midlands History* (Kineton, 1978), pp. 205–12.
16. R. Finlay and B. Shearer, 'Population growth and suburban expansion', in A. L. Beier and R. Finlay (eds), *London 1500–1700: the Making of the Metropolis* (London, 1986), p. 48; De Vries, *European Urbanization*, pp. 270–8.
17. Corfield, *English Towns*, pp. 8–9.

prosperous middling towns, partly as a consequence of improved transport facilities, was squeezing the lesser and weaker centres out of the system.[18] However, detailed studies of the North of England have challenged the universal validity of this thesis. Only five of the twenty-three country towns of eastern Yorkshire between 1700 and 1850 could be described as 'declining centres'; only three of the nineteen market towns of the Vale of York in the late seventeenth century had 'virtually ceased to function as markets' by the 1830s; and John Marshall's extended study of Cumbria calls the years 1760 to 1830 'a high noon of the more substantial small market town, in the North of England and probably in the country at large'.[19] Persistence and continuity rather than serious decline is the message which emerges from these studies. Even at the beginning of the twentieth century there were still almost 700 urban centres with populations of under 10 000 people.[20] The future debate on the fate of the small town in the eighteenth century will clearly need to focus on two issues. First, how great was the degree of regional variation? For example, was the North a more conducive environment for the tinier centres than the South? Second, to what extent were there differences of status within the small town category itself? It is probable that the semi-small market centre, with good external communications, prospered at the expense of the more marginal and isolated towns.

The long eighteenth century was a period of substantial demographic urbanization. Between 1700 and 1801 the proportion of the people of England and Wales living in settlements of over 2500 increased from just under one in five to almost one in three.[21] The principal motors of change were the metropolis and the larger centres – Liverpool, for example, grew spectacularly from over 5000 people in 1700 to almost 90 000 by the end of the century – but it

18. A. M. Everitt, 'Urban growth 1570–1770', *Local Historian*, 8, no. 4 (1968), p. 120; J. Chartres, 'Markets and marketing in metropolitan western England in the late seventeenth and eighteenth centuries', in M. A. Havinden (ed.), *Husbandry and Marketing in the South West 1500–1800* (Exeter, 1973), p. 64; and also R. Davis, *The Rise of the English Shipping Industry* (Newton Abbot, 1972), p. 37; P. Clark (ed.), *Country Towns in Pre-industrial England* (Leicester, 1981), pp. 30–1; P. J. Corfield, 'Small towns, large implications: social and cultural roles of small towns in eighteenth-century England and Wales', *British Journal for Eighteenth-Century Studies*, 10, no. 2 (1987), pp. 130–2; Corfield, *English Towns*, pp. 20–1; J. Chartres, 'The marketing of agricultural produce', in J. Thirsk (ed.), *The Agrarian History of England and Wales*, vol. V, 1640–1750, part 2, *Agrarian Change* (Cambridge, 1985), pp. 409–14.
19. Noble, 'Regional urban system', pp. 16–17; Unwin, 'Tradition and transition', pp. 114–15; Marshall, 'Cumbrian market town', p. 131; and also D. Hey, *Packmen, Carriers, and Pack-horse Roads: Trade and Communications in North Derbyshire and South Yorkshire* (Leicester, 1980), pp. 163–70.
20. P. J. Waller, *Town, City, and Nation: England 1850–1914* (Oxford, 1983), p. 6.
21. Corfield, *English Towns*, p. 9.

is possible in some areas that even small country towns increased their share of their regional populations.[22] What caused this urban growth? At a national level the study of demography has been dominated by a debate over the relative influence of fertility and mortality on population change. However, in the case of towns critical attention has focused on the role of migration, since (given the high mortality rates found in towns) it was only this that could have instigated the level of urban increase achieved during the eighteenth century. In the case of London, where the death rate exceeded the birth rate and yet the population grew by more than 50 per cent between 1650 and 1750, it has been suggested that 'the birth surplus of . . . about half the total population of England at that time was earmarked to meet' the city's needs. Even in Nottingham, where natural increase played a significant part in growth from the mid-1740s, immigration was responsible for nearly 60 per cent of the 11 000 rise in the town's population between 1779 and 1801.[23] Early modern England was a remarkably mobile society, and it is clear that many of those on the move found their way to towns. Peter Clark has suggested that between 1660 and 1730 roughly two in every three people changed their parish of domicile at least once during a lifetime, and David Souden that one-half to two-thirds of the inhabitants of late seventeenth-century towns were newcomers. Though Jan De Vries argues that in late seventeenth- and eighteenth-century Europe towns lost much of their attractiveness to migrants because of rural proto-industrialization, there is little evidence that this was the case in England, doubtless because industrial growth affected both town and country.[24]

The substantial majority of migrants came from a relatively short distance away, a tendency that increased after the Restoration, in part because the dynamic new provincial centres provided alternative destinations to London. About four-fifths of migrants (with Poor Law settlement certificates) moving to Birmingham between the late seventeenth and mid-eighteenth centuries were from the surrounding counties of Warwickshire, Staffordshire and Worcestershire. Most of those entering the towns were young and women, in search of

---

22. Chalklin, *Provincial Towns*, pp. 20, 49; Noble, 'Regional urban system', p. 4.
23. E. A. Wrigley, 'London and the great leap forward', *The Listener*, 6 July 1967, p. 7; J. D. Chambers, 'Population change in a provincial town: Nottingham 1700–1800', in D. V. Glass and D. E. C. Eversley (eds), *Population in History: Essays in Historical Demography* (London, 1965), p. 347; Corfield, *English Towns*, pp. 109, 113.
24. P. Clark, 'Migration in England during the late seventeenth and early eighteenth centuries', *Past and Present*, 83 (1979), pp. 65–7; D. Souden, 'Migrants and the population structure of later seventeenth-century provincial cities and market towns', in P. Clark (ed.), *The Transformation of English Provincial Towns 1600–1800* (London, 1984), p. 139; De Vries, *European Urbanization*, pp. 238–40.

service-based employment (though industrial towns may have recruited more heavily among males), giving many of the larger centres a distinctly female-biased sex structure. Unlike the Tudor and early Stuart period, newcomers were generally attracted to the town in hope of personal betterment rather than being driven from the countryside by subsistence pressures.[25] Given the numbers involved, the interaction between the migrant and resident populations must have played an important role in shaping the demographic regimes of towns. John Landers has suggested that variations in the flow of rural migrants to London, with their relatively high vulnerability to disease, played a major part in determining long- and short-term fluctuations in the city's mortality level.[26]

The principal reason why country dwellers migrated to towns, and did so in such large numbers, was the attractive employment opportunities available. This was indicative of the generally buoyant and expanding nature of the urban economy. In the search for an urban variable there has been some debate as to whether towns spearheaded national economic growth, or were simply carried along in its wake, even, perhaps, inhibiting it. Martin Daunton has taken a mildly negative view, Anthony Wrigley and John Chartres in the case of London, and Penelope Corfield on a broader canvas, a more positive one.[27] Arriving at an answer to this problem is complicated by the fact that urban and rural economies in the period interlocked closely together. However, this does not mean that towns failed to perform a specific and identifiable role, and one through which they could exert a positive influence within the economy as a whole.

25. Clark, 'Migration in England', pp. 64–75, 81–90; Corfield, *English Towns*, pp. 99–106; Souden, 'Migrants and the population structure', pp. 141–61; M. J. Kitch, 'Capital and kingdom: migration to later-Stuart London', in Beier and Finlay (eds), *London*, pp. 228–48; R. A. Pelham, 'The immigrant population of Birmingham 1686–1726', *Transactions of the Birmingham Archaeological Society*, 61 (1940), pp. 49–50; A. Parton, 'Poor Law settlement certificates and migration to and from Birmingham 1726–57', *Local Population Studies*, 38 (1987), p. 25; E. J. Buckatzsch, 'Places of origin of a group of immigrants into Sheffield 1624–1799', *Economic History Review*, 2nd ser., 2, no. 3 (1949–50), pp. 303–6; E. G. Thomas, 'The Poor Law migrant to Oxford 1700–1795', *Oxoniensia*, 45 (1980), pp. 300–5.
26. J. Landers, 'Mortality, weather, and prices in London 1675–1825: a study of short-term fluctuations', *Journal of Historical Geography*, 12, no. 4 (1986), pp. 359–61; J. Landers, 'Mortality and metropolis: the case of London 1675–1825', *Population Studies*, 41, no. 1 (1987), pp. 75–6.
27. Daunton, 'Towns and economic growth', pp. 245–72; E. A. Wrigley, 'A simple model of London's importance in changing English society and economy 1650–1750', *Past and Present*, 37 (1967), pp. 55–70; J. Chartres, 'Food consumption and internal trade', in Beier and Finlay (eds), *London*, pp. 168–96; Corfield, *English Towns*, pp. 91–8.

Central to this role is the concept of a matrix of urban economic functions – based upon industry, commerce, services and administration – one, or normally several of which, a town could exploit.

Though in the eighteenth century industry was a phenomenon of both the urban and rural spheres, the two sectors performed different but complementary roles. The countryside tended to concentrate on the earlier stages in the production chain, towns on the later phases and on marketing. For example, Exeter and Leeds would take in cloth produced in their surrounding areas for finishing, and Norwich captured the product even earlier, importing local yarn for weaving.[28] In the long term this mutually advantageous division of labour laid the basis for greater rationalization and specialization. Agricultural areas de-industrialized and concentrated on food production, while there emerged an increasingly centralized manufacturing core of towns and satellite industrial villages, which themselves slowly coalesced into more substantial urban settlements. Peter Large has detected such a pattern in the West Midlands as early as the mid-eighteenth century; and John Marshall has noted in nineteenth-century Lancashire the existence of small industrial settlements which provided a staging post for migrants on the move into the textile towns, before some of these villages were themselves absorbed by the larger centres. The trend towards urban industrial concentration pre-dates the late eighteenth-century arrival of factories and steam power, though in the Lancashire cotton towns the widespread introduction of power looms after the Napoleonic wars rapidly accelerated the process.[29]

The urbanization of many industrial processes should not be taken to imply the emergence of an exclusive category of industrial towns. Manufacturing had been, and continued to be widely dispersed throughout the urban system, located in ports as well as in industrial centres, in 'old' as well as 'new' towns. Between 1792 and 1810 Warwick, a traditional county centre, established an iron foundry together with separate cotton weaving, cotton spinning, lace, and worsted spinning manufactories (the last powered by a Bolton and Co. steam engine); and in the early nineteenth century Bath, the acme of Georgian urban elegance, underwent its own

28. *The Journeys of Celia Fiennes*, ed. C. Morris (London, 1947), pp. 245–7; D. Defoe, *A Tour through the Whole Island of Great Britain*, ed. G. D. H. Cole and D. C. Browning (London, 1962), vol. 1, pp. 61–3, 72; vol. 2, pp. 203–4.
29. P. Large, 'Urban growth and agricultural change in the West Midlands during the seventeenth and eighteenth centuries', in Clark (ed.), *Provincial Towns*, pp. 169–89; J. D. Marshall, 'Colonization as a factor in the planting of towns in North-West England', in H. J. Dyos (ed.), *The Study of Urban History* (London, 1968), pp. 222–3; Corfield, *English Towns*, pp. 23–4; J. Walvin, *English Urban Life 1776–1851* (London, 1984), pp. 44–5.

'incipient industrialization'.[30] The widespread presence of manu-facturing in towns is particularly noticeable if it is defined to include not only staple industries, such as textiles, but also the processing of agricultural goods, and the kaleidoscopic craft sector, which was expanding and diversifying so rapidly in the eighteenth century under the impact of a 'consumer boom'.[31] Alan Everitt proposes in his essay in this collection (Chapter 3) that 'in a very real sense the craftsman's shop was the hallmark of the Hanoverian county town', and argues that such places were 'vital nurseries of skill' and 'fertile seedbeds of discovery'.[32] The highly diffused craft economy, based upon the workshop, persisted well into the nineteenth century, and may even have been strengthened during the early stages of in-dustrialization. Not until at least the 1830s did steam power and factories begin to make a substantial impact on Birmingham's metal-wares industry, and Gareth Stedman Jones has contended that 'the effect of the Industrial Revolution upon London was to accentuate its "pre-industrial" characteristics'.[33]

During the first half of the eighteenth century many so-called in-dustrial towns were as much market centres for rural–industrial regions as places of manufacture. Commerce, indeed, was of key importance to virtually every urban economy. After the Restoration internal and external trade expanded rapidly due to the growth of overseas markets, the increasing trend towards regional economic specialization (generating huge counter-flows of goods), improved transport facilities, and urbanization itself, particularly the growth of London. Most affected by these changes were ports and market towns, since they were the engines of the commercial system, pump-ing goods to and fro along the arteries of trade. Not all centres benefited equally, nor, given the increasingly integrated and com-petitive nature of the urban hierarchy, was success easily achieved. Small market towns, especially those without good water and road

---

30. W. Field, *An Historical and Descriptive Account of the Town and Castle of War-wick* (East Ardsley, 1969), pp. 76–8; *Victoria County History: Warwickshire*, Vol. VIII (London, 1969), p. 508; R. S. Neale, *Bath 1680–1850: a Social History* (London, 1981), p. 270.
31. N. McKendrick, 'The consumer revolution of eighteenth-century England', in N. McKendrick, J. Brewer and J. H. Plumb, *The Birth of a Consumer Society: the Commercialization of Eighteenth-Century England* (London, 1983), p. 9.
32. A. M. Everitt, 'Country, county, and town: patterns of regional evolution in England', *Transactions of the Royal Historical Society*, 5th ser., 29 (1979), pp. 100, 103.
33. V. Skipp, *The Making of Victorian Birmingham* (Birmingham, 1983), pp. 38–9, 65; D. A. Reid, 'The decline of Saint Monday 1766–1876', *Past and Present*, 71 (1976), pp. 84–6; G. Stedman Jones, *Outcast London: a Study in the Relation-ship between Classes in Victorian Society* (Harmondsworth, 1976), p. 26; R. Samuel, 'Workshop of the world: steam power and hand technology in mid-Victorian Britain', *History Workshop*, 3 (1977), pp. 6–72.

communications, were vulnerable to the predatory instincts of their larger neighbours.[34] Ports could face powerful rivalry for access to lucrative overseas markets, as Paul Clemens has shown in the case of Liverpool, which due to the challenge of London and Bristol still 'occupied an insecure position' in 1713.[35] Within towns there was a shift away from public towards private marketing, and this was accompanied by a change in the location of commercial activity away from the open street towards the more ordered and convenient surroundings of inns, shops and civic buildings.[36]

Inns and shops linked the urban economy's commercial and service sectors. The latter, perhaps because it embraced such a diffuse body of activities located in the interstices of the economy, has never received the sort of attention that it deserves from economic historians. Yet in the eighteenth century its development was of vital significance. General economic growth, the expansion in personal income and the emergence of a more complex political and social system instigated a leap forward in the demand for transport, legal, financial, administrative, cultural, residential and consumer services. Because these were predominantly situated in towns, their impact on the shape and fortunes of the urban economy was considerable. Some centres, such as resorts and thoroughfare towns, concentrated on providing specialized facilities: others, particularly the county towns and provincial capitals, offered a wider range of provision. For a number of major towns which had experienced economic decline or stagnation at some point during the early modern period – like York, Winchester, Salisbury, Warwick, Gloucester, Chester, Colchester, Exeter and Worcester – the development of a broader service- and consumer-based economy cushioned the impact of change, and provided the foundation for recovery and prosperity.[37]

34. S. Rudder, *A New History of Gloucestershire* (Cirencester, 1779), pp. 269, 289, 518, 562, 750, 825.
35. P. G. E. Clemens, 'The rise of Liverpool 1665–1750', *Economic History Review*, 2nd ser., 29, no. 2 (1976), p. 216.
36. A. M. Everitt, 'The food market of the English town 1660–1760', in *Third International Conference of Economic History* (Munich, 1965), pp. 69–70; A. M. Everitt, 'The English urban inn 1560–1760', in A. M. Everitt (ed.), *Perspectives in English Urban History* (London, 1973), pp. 104–8; T. M. James, 'The inns of Croydon 1640–1840', *Surrey Archaeological Collections*, 68 (1971), p. 124; S. I. Mitchell, 'The development of urban retailing 1700–1815', in Clark (ed.), *Provincial Towns*, pp. 264–78; Mitchell, 'Retailing in . . . Cheshire', pp. 49–56; J. Chartres, 'Marketing of agricultural produce', pp. 416–18.
37. J. Hutchinson and D. M. Palliser, *York* (Edinburgh, 1980), pp. 46–8, 56, 67–70; A. Rosen, 'Winchester in transition 1580–1700', in Clark (ed.), *Country Towns*, pp. 155–62, 170–84; *Victoria County History: Wiltshire*, Vol. VI (London, 1962), pp. 129–31, 141–3; A. L. Beier, 'The social problems of an Elizabethan country town: Warwick 1580–90', in Clark (ed.), *Country Towns*, pp. 48–53; *Victoria County History: Warwickshire*, Vol. VIII, pp. 507, 511–13; P. Clark, 'The civic leaders of Gloucester 1580–1800', in Clark (ed.), *Provincial Towns*, p. 313; *The*

The victualling and catering trades were central to the operation of the tertiary sector, since they provided or accommodated so many of the services available. The coffee house, of which there were 600 in London by the early eighteenth century, first emerged in the 1650s; and Alan Everitt and Peter Clark have revealed the remarkable development of the urban inn and alehouse from the reign of Elizabeth, with the post-Restoration years witnessing a growth in the comfort and sophistication of these establishments.[38]

The range of occupations generated within the urban economy gave towns a more varied and complex social structure than that to be found in the village. Not that there existed an archetypal urban social order. Towns differed too much from each other for this to be possible. Fashionable residential and social centres, like the resorts and county towns, displayed a more gentrified profile than industrial and commercial centres (where social leadership rested in the hands of professional, manufacturing and trading families), and this was a pattern still very much apparent in the mid-nineteenth century.[39] The nature of the middling stratum could vary considerably from place to place. Robert Morris has suggested that a new town like Merthyr Tydfil possessed a relatively small and immature middle class when compared with that of a long-established industrial centre such as Leeds.[40] One common difficulty which towns faced as a consequence of their high immigration rates and comparative social diversity was that of integrating a large and sometimes heterogeneous body of people into a viable community. It was a problem that was exacerbated by the decline of traditional forms of association, such as the parish and guild, and by the emergence of

British Courant or the Preston Journal, no. 289, 17 August 1750; Mitchell, 'Development of urban retailing', pp. 261–2, 275–7; A. F. J. Brown, *Essex at Work 1700–1815* (Chelmsford, 1969), pp. 111–12; P. King, 'Newspaper reporting, prosecution practice, and perceptions of urban crime: the Colchester crime wave of 1765', *Continuity and Change*, 2, no. 3 (1987), pp. 434–5; R. Newton, *Eighteenth-Century Exeter* (Exeter, 1984), pp. 23–7, 65–71; G. Talbut, 'Worcester as an industrial and commercial centre 1660–1750', *Transactions of the Worcestershire Archaeological Society*, 10 (1986), pp. 91–102.

38. A. Ellis, *The Penny Universities: a History of the Coffee-Houses* (London, 1956); B. Lillywhite, *London Coffee-Houses* (London, 1963); A. M. Everitt, 'English urban inn', pp. 91–137; P. Clark, *The English Alehouse: a Social History 1200–1830* (London, 1983), especially pp. 195–249.

39. Everitt, 'County and town', pp. 94–6; J. D. Marshall, 'Kendal in the late seventeenth and eighteenth centuries', *Transactions of the Cumberland and Westmorland Antiquarian Society*, new ser., 75 (1975), pp. 246–51; A. D. M. Phillips and J. R. Walton, 'The distribution of personal wealth in the mid-nineteenth century', *Transactions of the Institute of British Geographers*, 64 (1975), pp. 35–48.

40. R. J. Morris, 'The middle class and British towns and cities of the Industrial Revolution 1780–1870', in D. Fraser and A. Sutcliffe (eds), *The Pursuit of Urban History* (London, 1983), pp. 292–3.

a more class-oriented society. The pressing need, as one historian of the eighteenth-century American city has put it, to 'stitch together urban centres',[41] led to the development of some predominantly, if not uniquely, urban forms of social organization. Robert Morris (in his essay included here, Chapter 12), Peter Clark and Gary Nash have demonstrated that among the most important of these were clubs, societies and voluntary groups. Though one of the bed-rock features of nineteenth-century town life, their rise dates back to the late seventeenth century. From this point in time they played an increasingly important role in absorbing newcomers into urban society, providing specific groups with a meaningful collective life, and, to a more qualified extent, bridging the gaps between the different social strata. The institutions and organizations involved, which were often based around inns, taverns, alehouses, coffee-houses, churches and chapels, served a vital function in developing the informal web of association that gave urban society a measure of coherence and community.[42]

The concept of community, with its cosy connotations of equality and harmony, has to be used with caution. Eighteenth-century urban society was far from homogeneous, and substantial divisions, even fissures, existed within it. Heading many towns would have been a small circle of power brokers and social leaders, able to wield influence quite disproportionate to their number. In incorporated towns the most visible manifestation of this élite was the council (particularly its inner core of aldermen), whose membership would be drawn from wealthy merchants, tradesmen and, increasingly, the professions.[43] However, the governing body of a town was not

---

41. Nash, 'Pre-industrial American cities', p. 141.
42. R. J. Morris, 'Voluntary societies and British urban élites 1780–1850: an analysis', *Historical Journal*, 26, no. 1 (1983), pp. 95–118; P. Clark, *Sociability and Urbanity: Clubs and Societies in the Eighteenth-Century City*, 8th H. J. Dyos Memorial Lecture (Leicester, 1986); Nash, 'Pre-industrial American cities', pp. 138–42; B. Harrison, *Drink and the Victorians: the Temperance Question in England 1815–1872* (London, 1971), pp. 52–3; J. Money, 'Birmingham and the West Midlands 1760–1793: politics and regional identity in the English provinces in the later eighteenth century', *Midland History*, 1 (1971), pp. 14–16; J. Money, 'Taverns, coffee-houses, and clubs: local politics and popular articulacy in the Birmingham area, in the age of the American Revolution', *Historical Journal*, 14, no. 1 (1971), pp. 15–47; Marshall, 'Cumbrian market town', pp. 185–7; I. McCalman, 'Ultra-radicalism and convivial debating-clubs in London 1795–1838', *English Historical Review*, 102, no. 403 (1987), pp. 309–33.
43. R. Newton, 'The membership of the chamber of Exeter 1688–1835', *Devon and Cornwall Notes and Queries*, 33 (1977), pp. 282–6; F. E. Sanderson, 'The structure of politics in Liverpool 1780–1807', *Transactions of the Historic Society of Lancashire and Cheshire*, 127 (1977), pp. 65–6; Mitchell, 'Retailing . . . in Cheshire', pp. 48–9; Clark, 'Civic leaders of Gloucester', pp. 322–37; J. W. Kirby, 'Restoration Leeds and the aldermen of the corporation 1661–1700', *Northern History*, 22 (1986), pp. 123–74.

necessarily synonymous with its economic and social élite. In early Hanoverian London Henry Horwitz has identified a group of very wealthy businessmen who avoided civic office, and whose values differed in important respects from those of the city's aldermen: indeed, he argues that by the 1730s businessmen and merchants as a whole were becoming less and less involved in civic life and government.[44] In the developing resorts and social centres there existed a substantial body of prestigious leisured visitors and residents, many of them women, who though not holding civic office could exert considerable influence. In addition, the gentry and aristocracy frequently exercised a powerful brief over their local towns. It was no accident that the commission which controlled the rebuilding of Warwick after its devastating fire in 1694 was dominated not by the corporation but by the county élite.[45] The leadership of urban society could, therefore, be diffuse and pluralist, but this did not necessarily weaken the underlying coherence of the town's leaders. There was a growing tendency for all those of wealth, power and status, whether townspeople or countrymen, to meet and fraternize together.[46] Nicholas Rogers suggests in an article on the 'big bourgeoisie' of London which forms part of this reader, that by the mid-eighteenth century 'the great merchants . . . formed part of the heterogeneous but unified ruling class of the Hanoverian era'. This may be indicative of a trend among the leaders of urban and rural society to amalgamate into a more broadly based and diverse élite.[47] However, it must be emphasized that this ruling group could be racked by deep political and religious divisions, and that by the early nineteenth century its unity was being threatened in certain regions by the rising power and independence of a new breed of industrialists.

44. H. Horwitz, ' "The mess of the middle class" revisited: the case of the "big bourgeoisie" of Augustan London', *Continuity and Change*, 2, no. 2 (1987), pp. 275–83; H. Horwitz, 'Party in a civic context: London from the Exclusion Crisis to the fall of Walpole', in C. Jones (ed.), *Britain in the First Age of Party 1680–1750* (London, 1987), pp. 191–2; and also D. T. Andrew, 'Aldermen and big bourgeoisie of London reconsidered', *Social History*, 6, no. 3 (1981), pp. 359–60.
45. P. Borsay, 'The English urban renaissance: landscape and leisure in the provincial town c. 1660–1770', unpublished Ph.D. thesis (Lancaster, 1981), pp. 181–2.
46. J. Money, *Experience and Identity: Birmingham and the West Midlands 1760–1800* (Manchester, 1977), pp. 99–102; Clark, 'Civic leaders of Gloucester', pp. 326–7, 330–1.
47. N. Rogers, 'Money, land, and lineage: the big bourgeoisie of Hanoverian London', *Social History*, 4, no. 3 (1979), p. 454; P. Borsay, *The English Urban Renaissance: Culture and Society in the Provincial Town 1660–1770* (Oxford, 1989), pp. 230–1, 254–5, 282, 317. For criticism of Rogers see Andrew, 'Aldermen and the big bourgeoisie', pp. 363–4.

Forming an ever-deepening penumbra around the town élite, and constituting the pool from which it recruited most of its members, were the expanding middling groups. Their development represents the most fundamental long-term change in the shape of the urban social structure, accentuating the town's identity *vis-à-vis* the village, and laying the foundations for the dominant, and increasingly sexually differentiated role, Robert Morris, and Leonore Davidoff and Catherine Hall, have shown a self-conscious middle class played in the nineteenth-century city.[48] Four developments contributed to the growth of the urban middle orders. First, the rising numbers and affluence of the professions, which for the years 1680 to 1730 has been so ably charted by Geoffrey Holmes;[49] second, the emergence of a leisured, residential and quintessentially urban group of what Alan Everitt has called 'pseudo-gentry';[50] third, the increasing body of merchants, manufacturers, financiers and wealthy tradesmen; and finally, the development of a distinct petty bourgeoisie of prosperous shopkeepers, craftsmen and victuallers.

A larger and more diverse middling stratum would seem to fill the space between rich and poor, and lead to the emergence of a less polarized society. Whether in reality this was the case is debatable. The bourgeoisie had an obvious interest in emphasizing and reinforcing the gap between themselves and those beneath them. Moreover, the depth of this divide may have been strengthened by working people's own economic and social experiences. The standard of living of the common people has been

---

48. Corfield, *English Towns*, pp. 130–3; Clark (ed.), *Provincial Towns*, pp. 32–3; Morris, 'Voluntary societies', p. 96; Morris, 'The middle class', pp. 286–306; L. Davidoff and C. Hall, 'The architecture of public and private life: English middle-class society in a provincial town 1780 to 1850', in Fraser and Sutcliffe (eds), *Pursuit of Urban History*, pp. 327–45; L. Davidoff and C. Hall, *Family Fortunes: Men and Women of the English Middle Class 1780–1850* (London, 1987). For criticism of 'the rise of the middle class' thesis see Clark, *Revolution and Rebellion*, pp. 24–33, 158–60.

49. G. S. Holmes, *Augustan England: Professions, State, and Society 1680–1730* (London, 1982), especially pp. 11–12; G. S. Holmes, 'The achievement of stability: the social context of politics from the 1680s to the age of Walpole', in J. Cannon (ed.), *The Whig Ascendancy* (London, 1981), pp. 14–17; Clark (ed.), *Country Towns*, pp. 23–4; A. M. Everitt, *Ways and Means in Local History* (London, 1971), pp. 36, 38–9; M. Reed, 'Economic structure and change in seventeenth-century Ipswich', in Clark (ed.), *Country Towns*, pp. 102–3, 110–14; Rosen, 'Winchester in transition', pp. 177–8; S. McIntyre, 'Bath: the rise of a resort town 1660–1800', in Clark (ed.), *Country Towns*, pp. 221, 228; R. W. Unwin, 'Tradition and transition', p. 81; E. Baigent, 'Economy and society in eighteenth-century English towns: Bristol in the 1770s', in D. Denecke and G. Shaw (eds), *Urban Historical Geography: Recent Progress in Britain and Germany* (Cambridge, 1988), p. 115.

50. A. M. Everitt, 'Social mobility in early modern England', *Past and Present*, 33 (1966), pp. 70–2; Everitt, 'County and town', pp. 95–6.

relatively little investigated by post-Restoration urbanists, who, the present author included, have displayed greater interest in the expanding comforts of the well-to-do. For historians of the Industrial Revolution period quite the opposite has been the case, and the issue of whether the living standards of the working class declined or improved has provoked one of the fiercest and most enduring of historical controversies.[51] For many 'pessimists' the immiseration of the majority of workers, under the impact of industrialization, is closely linked to the emergence of an identifiable working class, and with it a major realignment of the social structure. The 'optimists' share neither the economic nor social analysis embodied in this view, and little common ground has emerged between the two camps. Apart from differences of ideological perspective, there has been no agreement over which factors should be taken into account in measuring the standard of living, over what period changes in these should be calculated and how local and occupational variations should be accommodated. More recent contributions have no more resolved the debate than earlier ones, though it is now less 'politicized'. John Landers and Anastasia Mouzas have suggested that early eighteenth-century London witnessed a rise in typhus mortality as a consequence of deteriorating economic and social conditions, whose decline has been underestimated because of the misinterpretation of real wage indices. On the other hand Leonard Schwarz has argued that in the metropolis there was a rise in real wages up to the mid-eighteenth century, followed by a sharp fall until 1800, and J. Söderberg has confirmed this downward trend for European cities as a whole. Peter Lindert and Jeffrey Williamson, using a broader range of criteria, claim there was a considerable improvement in workers' living standards between 1781 and 1851, but suggest that the majority of gains were made after 1820, before which date the 'pessimists' might still have a case, and for J. Mokyr this case may extend as far as the 1840s. Michael Flinn wished to push back the take-off point for real wages to 1810/14, and F. W. Botham and E. H. Hunt feel that the whole debate has focused too much on London, and argue for rising wages in the industrial Midlands and North from as early as the mid-eighteenth century.[52] One

51. For a valuable survey of the debate up until the mid-1970s see A. J. Taylor (ed.), *The Standard of Living in Britain in the Industrial Revolution* (London, 1975).

52. J. Landers and A. Mouzas, 'Burial seasonality and causes of death in London 1670–1819', *Population Studies*, 42 (1988), pp. 77–9; L. D. Schwarz, 'The standard of living in the long run: London 1760–1860', *Economic History Review*, 2nd ser., 38, no. 1 (1985), pp. 24–41; J. Söderberg, 'Real wage trends in urban Europe 1730–1850: Stockholm in a comparative perspective', *Social History*, 12, no. 2 (1987), pp. 155–76; P. H. Lindert and J. G. Williamson, 'English workers' living standards during the Industrial Revolution: a new look', *Economic History Review*, 2nd ser., 36, no. 1 (1983), pp. 23–5; J. Mokyr, 'Is there still life

suspects that this is one of those historical debates that will never be, and perhaps never can be, settled.

Of particular interest to urban historians is the influence of the environment on the living standards of the working class. The growing number of people living in towns, and – more importantly – in very large towns, allied to the impact of industrialization, placed severe pressure on public and private facilities, and generated a range of new environmental problems. However, at what point these difficulties escalated to a level where they led to a serious deterioration in the standard of urban health must remain an open question. Christopher Chalklin has suggested that the *per caput* provision of working-class housing held up remarkably well in the late eighteenth- and early nineteenth-century town, and may even have improved. In Carlisle a substantial rise in mortality levels, the most important cause of which was declining living conditions, occurred only after 1813, and in London, where it has been argued that there may have been an improvement in the environment during the second half of the eighteenth century, there was no serious diminution in the quality of the Thames water supply until after about 1816.[53] On the other hand, the origins of Liverpool's infamous court and cellar dwellings can be traced back to the late eighteenth century, and already by 1820 fashionable Brighton had developed its own slum areas. In some towns health problems specifically induced by industrialization were evident from an early stage. The debilitating grinders' asthma emerged in Sheffield from the mid-eighteenth century, as workers became increasingly exposed to dust due to the growth in dry grinding, the increasing specialization of the trade and the movement of the mills or wheels into the town: by 1794 about 1800 workers suffered from the disease, a figure which by 1819 had risen to 2500.[54] Industrial pollution was certainly a feature of English

in the pessimist case? Consumption during the Industrial Revolution 1790–1850', *Journal of Economic History*, 48, no. 1 (1988), pp. 69–92; M. W. Flinn, 'English workers' living standards during the Industrial Revolution: a comment', and P. H. Lindert and J. G. Williamson, 'Reply to Michael Flinn', *Economic History Review*, 2nd ser., 37, no. 1 (1984), pp. 88–94; F. W. Botham and E. H. Hunt, 'Wages in Britain during the Industrial Revolution', *Economic History Review*, 2nd ser., 40, no. 3 (1987), pp. 380–99.

53. Chalklin, *Provincial Towns*, pp. 304–8; W. A. Armstrong, 'The trend of mortality in Carlisle between the 1780s and the 1840s: a demographic contribution to the standard of living debate', *Economic History Review*, 2nd ser., 34, no. 1 (1981), pp. 104–8; Landers, 'Mortality, weather, and prices', p. 359; A. Hardy, 'Water and the search for public health in London in the eighteenth and nineteenth centuries', *Medical History*, 28 (1984), pp. 262–3.

54. I. C. Taylor, 'The court and cellar dwelling: the eighteenth-century origin of the Liverpool slum', *Transactions of the Historic Society of Lancashire and Cheshire*, 72 (1970), pp. 67–90; S. Farrant, *Georgian Brighton 1740 to 1820* (Brighton, 1980), pp. 28, 38; M. P. Johnson, 'The history of grinders' asthma in Sheffield', *Transactions of the Hunter Archaeological Society*, 11 (1981), pp. 65–75.

towns before the late eighteenth century, but it probably remained at relatively tolerable levels so long as much basic manufacturing was located in the countryside, and the majority of the filthiest urban industrial plant was situated on the edge of the town.

The urban environment, and inhabitants' different experiences of it, both reflected and reinforced divisions in the social structure. Eighteenth-century towns, especially the larger ones, were often subdivided into a number of social zones. In itself there was nothing novel about this. Throughout the early modern period there was a tendency for the more powerful and affluent citizens to live close to the centre, and the poorer ones near the periphery.[55] This pattern could be overlaid by other types of spatial organization, which to some degree mitigated the impact of social class. Occupational groupings in eighteenth-century towns were quite common, creating micro-communities embedded within the larger whole. Such was the case with the fishermen, bargemen and canal boatmen of Fisher Row in Oxford, and with the 'tightly knit . . . dense industrial society' of the weavers in the 'Over the Water' district of Norwich.[56] In many towns zoning occurred not so much between areas as within the structure of the street, with the wealthier and more prestigious inhabitants occupying the front premises, and the less well off the myriad of lanes, yards and alleys tucked away to the rear.[57] Such a close proximity of rich and poor could even be seen in the fashionable West End of London, where the presence of luxury craft

55. J. Langton, 'Residential patterns in pre-industrial cities: some case studies from seventeenth-century Britain', *Transactions of the Institute of British Geographers*, 65 (1975), pp. 7–11; Clark and Slack, *Towns in Transition*, pp. 114, 122; Patten, *English Towns*, pp. 37–9; *Victoria County History: York* (London, 1961), p. 165; R. Howell, *Newcastle-upon-Tyne and the Puritan Revolution* (Oxford, 1967), pp. 11–12; W. G. Hoskins, *Industry, Trade, and People in Exeter 1688–1800*, 2nd edn (Exeter, 1968), p. 116; A. Dyer, *The City of Worcester in the Sixteenth Century* (Leicester, 1973), p. 178; J. Hindson, 'The marriage duty acts and the social topography of the early modern town – Shrewsbury 1695–8', *Local Population Studies*, 31 (1983), pp. 25–7.
56. M. Prior, *Fisher Row: Fishermen, Bargemen, and Canal Boatmen in Oxford 1500–1900* (Oxford, 1982), pp. 10–12; U. Priestley, ' "The fabric of stuffs": the Norwich textile industry c. 1650–1750', *Textile History*, 16, no. 2 (1985), p. 197; and also Langton, 'Residential patterns', pp. 16–18; Hindson, 'Marriage duty acts', pp. 25–6, 28; J. M. Triffit, 'Politics and the urban community: Parliamentary boroughs in the South West of England 1710–1730', unpublished D. Phil. thesis (Oxford, 1985), pp. 75–81; M. J. Power, 'The social topography of Restoration London' in Beier and Finlay (eds), *London*, pp. 212–21.
57. Marshall, 'Kendal in the late seventeenth and eighteenth centuries', pp. 225–7; Power, 'Social topography of Restoration London', pp. 206–12; Baigent, 'Economy and society', p. 120.

workers, service personnel and criminal elements created a surprisingly heterogeneous population.[58]

If eighteenth-century towns reflected traditional forms of urban geography, they also displayed signs of the more rigid, class-oriented patterns of zoning associated with the nineteenth century. It is argued by Leonard Schwarz in his contribution in this volume that by the 1790s in London 'middle-class, or rather upper-middle-class *domination*, had not yet taken place, but a tendency towards *segregation* . . . was becoming a reality', and Paul Laxton that 'the strongly differentiated patterns . . . in the landscape of Victorian Liverpool are well established, though at a different scale, in late Georgian Liverpool'.[59] The middle-class flight to the suburbs, which completely reversed the traditional social arrangement of urban space, can be detected in several towns from an early stage – a point Jonathan Barry makes in his introduction to the early modern volume in this series. It was not uncommon for the leading merchants of Jacobean London to own a small country retreat within a few miles of the city, and by the time of Defoe the sprawling rural hinterland of the metropolis was studded with elegant suburban villas.[60] By the 1730s the principal inhabitants of Newcastle-upon-Tyne had abandoned the once prestigious centrally located Close for the more salubrious districts on the edge of the city, and from the Restoration the gentlemen merchants of Leeds began to vacate the main commercial thoroughfare and migrate outwards in a series of phased movements which carried them into the town's rural belt.[61]

58. Corfield, *English Towns*, pp. 78–9; M. Reed, *The Georgian Triumph 1700–1830* (London, 1983), pp. 113–17; N. Rogers, 'Aristocratic clientage, trade, and independency: popular politics in pre-radical Westminster', *Past and Present*, 61 (1973), pp. 89–94.

59. L. D. Schwarz, 'Social class and social geography: the middle classes in London at the end of the eighteenth century', *Social History*, 7, no. 2 (1982), p. 172; P. Laxton, 'Liverpool in 1801: a manuscript return for the first national census of population', *Transactions of the Historic Society of Lancashire and Cheshire*, 130 (1981), p. 87; and also Nash, 'Pre-industrial American cities', pp. 130–1.

60. R. G. Lang, 'Social origins and social aspirations of Jacobean London merchants', *Economic History Review*, 2nd ser., 27, no. 1 (1974), p. 41; Defoe, *Tour*, vol. 1, pp. 6, 165–9; vol. 2, pp. 2–4, 12–13; P. Morant, *The History and Antiquities of the County of Essex* (London, 1768), vol. 1, p. 1.

61. H. Bourne, *The History of Newcastle-upon-Tyne* (Newcastle-upon-Tyne, 1736), pp. 126, 151; Howell, *Newcastle-upon-Tyne*, pp. 4, 350–2; J. Ellis, 'A dynamic society: social relations in Newcastle-upon-Tyne 1660–1760', in Clark (ed.), *Provincial Towns*, pp. 198–9; R. G. Wilson, *Gentlemen Merchants: the Merchant Community in Leeds 1700–1830* (Manchester, 1971), pp. 195–8; R. Thoresby, *Ducatus Leodiensis*, 2nd edn, ed. T. D. Whitaker (Leeds, 1816), p. 76.

Social differentiation within the urban landscape was reinforced by changes in architectural fashions. From the later seventeenth century in the provinces, and rather earlier in London, the classical idiom began to exert a significant influence on the design of English towns. Because it was adopted far more rapidly by affluent citizens, and because it represented a major departure from the traditional vernacular style, its arrival visually highlighted the differences between rich and poor areas in the town. Hand in hand with the introduction of classicism, and closely linked to its architectural ethos, there emerged a growing interest in urban planning. This also accentuated social divisions, since new planned units, such as squares, were often situated away from the old centre of the town, and were deliberately conceived, constructed and maintained as exclusive residential areas.[62]

With its emphasis on large-scale physical and social integration, planning can play a vital part in enhancing the 'urban feel' of a town. One of the principal differences between the modern and pre-modern city in Britain is often taken to be a serious commitment to planning, which it is argued only emerged at the very end of the nineteenth century. Research on the post-Restoration town has to some extent confirmed this view. The failure of the authorities to grasp the golden opportunity provided by the Great Fire of London (1666) to introduce a radical rebuilding scheme suggests a pre-industrial culture highly unconducive to planning. England's fulsome supply of towns (which reduced the need to create new settlements), the fragmented pattern of landholding and ownership within urban cores, the diffuse nature of the construction process and the absence of any native post-medieval planning tradition tended to discourage large-scale urban design. Christopher Chalklin's detailed investigation of the urban building process suggests that for much of the seventeenth and eighteenth centuries, even where new towns or substantial additions to old ones were constructed, planning controls were minimal. Outward appearances can be deceptive. 'The regularity in the general street plan in West Dockfield' (Portsea), argues Chalklin, 'came not from any overall scheme' but simply reflected the prior agricultural use of the land; and he suggests that Georgian Bath – the example *par excellence* of eighteenth-century

62. Borsay, *English Urban Renaissance*, pp. 41–59, 294–5. For studies of the impact of classical architecture on individual towns see J. Summerson, *Georgian London* (Harmondsworth, 1962); D. Cruickshank and P. Wyld, *London: The Art of Georgian Building* (London, 1975); W. Ison, *The Georgian Buildings of Bristol* (Bath, 1968); W. Ison, *The Georgian Buildings of Bath* (Bath, 1969); I. and E. Hall, *Historic Beverley* (York, 1973); I. and E. Hall, *Georgian Hull* (York, 1978/9); A. Gomme, M. Jenner and B. Little, *Bristol: an Architectural History* (London, 1979).

town planning – 'is a unity, but it is a unity created by its building material, stone, and the classical uniformity of its architecture, not by its general planning'.[63]

Yet we should be cautious about underestimating the achievements of the long eighteenth century in the field of urban design. Four points are critical in this connection. First, it is important to judge developments by the standards of the time rather than those of today. To modern urban planners the post-fire rebuilding of London might appear a wasted opportunity, but given the virtual absence of town planning in England for three centuries before the 1660s, the simple but influential legislation governing the reconstruction could be considered something of a watershed. Similarly, detailed research on the creation of Whitehaven (particularly from the 1680s) and the rebuilding of Warwick after its fire in 1694, has produced evidence of planning, which though modest by twentieth-century standards, is impressive in the context of the period.[64] Second, if the history of planning is to be properly understood it is important not to focus exclusively on 'grand designs', but also to explore smaller scale projects. The widespread introduction of classicism into the town from the later seventeenth century stimulated a subtle but significant shift in emphasis away from the individual dwelling towards unit development. This was especially noticeable in the rise of uniform street architecture and the construction of squares: between the 1680s and 1770s at least fifteen of the latter had been introduced into provincial towns, not to mention the many examples built in the West End of London.[65] Third, to appreciate the contribution of the eighteenth century it is necessary to escape from the twentieth-century's heroic, professionalized view of planning history. The early achievements in England were the product not so much of inspired individuals, as of thousands of small developers and builders operating in the context of an architectural culture that encouraged a more uniform and 'sociable' approach to

63. A. Sutcliffe, *Towards the Planned City: Germany, Britain, and the United States 1780–1914* (Oxford, 1981), pp. 1–18, 47–87, 202–9; T. F. Reddaway, *The Rebuilding of London after the Great Fire* (London, 1951), pp. 40–67; C. W. Chalklin, 'The making of some new towns *c.* 1600–1720', in C. W. Chalklin and M. A. Havinden (eds), *Rural Change and Urban Growth 1500–1800* (London, 1974), p. 245; Chalklin, *Provincial Towns*, p. 80.

64. M. Turner, 'The nature of urban renewal after fires in some English provincial towns *circa* 1675–1810', unpublished Ph.D. thesis (Exeter, 1985), pp. 114–63, 215–29, 272–84; Chalklin, 'Making of some new towns', pp. 239–41; J. V. Beckett, *Coal and Tobacco: the Lowthers and the Economic Development of West Cumberland 1660–1760* (Cambridge, 1981), pp. 179–200; Borsay, 'Landscape and leisure', pp. 123–98.

65. Borsay, *English Urban Renaissance*, pp. 60–2, 74–9, 323–4; Summerson, *Georgian London*, passim.

building. Therefore, the absence of professional theorists, planners and formal controls should not of itself be taken as evidence of lack of planning. Fourth, the definition of planning needs to be as wide as possible so as to detect the true extent to which the urban environment was subject to the forces of organization and innovation. During the eighteenth century, as Eric Jones and Malcom Falkus demonstrate in their essay included here, there was a substantial growth in investment in public buildings, and considerable advances were made in street paving, cleansing and lighting, and in the installation of piped-water supplies – all areas which contributed to the general enhancement of the urban environment. Taken together these points suggest that the origins of modern town planning substantially pre-date the birth of the Garden Cities Movement, and even the Industrial Revolution.[66]

The involvement of town authorities in civic improvements raises the broader topic of the operation and effectiveness of local government. Research on this subject is surprisingly thin and has given rise to no modern survey.[67] In such circumstances it is tempting to follow the traditional line and assume that before municipal reform in the nineteenth century, town administration was unsophisticated, inefficient and corrupt. Though this picture may contain elements of truth, it is one which is almost certainly exaggerated. John Triffit, for example, finds little evidence of serious political or financial abuses in his study of seven south-western boroughs in the early eighteenth century.[68] A central problem is that it is difficult to establish a satisfactory definition of 'corruption' which is neither anachronistic nor misleading. Civic expenditure on fashionable leisure and corporate junketing might appear to modern eyes like

---

66. Borsay, *English Urban Renaissance*, pp. 68–74, 101–2; K. Grady, 'The provision of public buildings in the West Riding of Yorkshire c. 1600–1840', unpublished Ph.D. thesis (Leeds, 1980); C. W. Chalklin, 'The financing of church building in the provincial towns of eighteenth-century England', in Clark (ed.), *Provincial Towns*, pp. 284–310; M. E. Falkus and E. L. Jones, 'Urban improvement and the English economy in the seventeenth and eighteenth centuries', in P. J. Uselding (ed.), *Research in Economic History*, vol. 4 (Greenwich, Conn., 1979), pp. 203–20; M. E. Falkus, 'Lighting in the dark ages of English economic history: town streets before the Industrial Revolution', in Coleman and John (eds), *Trade, Government, and Economy*, pp. 248–73; F. Williamson, 'George Sorocold, of Derby: a pioneer of water supply', *Journal of the Derbyshire Archaeological and Natural History Society*, new ser., 10 (1936), pp. 65–93; E. Hughes, 'The new river water supply for Newcastle-upon-Tyne 1698–1723', *Archaeologia Aeliana*, 25 (1947), pp. 115–24; P. Borsay, 'The English urban renaissance: the development of provincial urban culture c. 1680–c. 1760', *Social History*, 2, no. 2 (1977), p. 588; C. and R. Bell, *City Fathers: the Early History of Town Planning in Britain* (Harmondsworth, 1972).
67. Corfield, *English Towns*, ch. 9 is the nearest modern approach.
68. Triffit, 'Politics and the urban community', pp. 158–69.

the urban élite using public money to finance their private pleasures. However, it could also represent a highly astute form of investment, designed to attract wealthy visitors and residents to the economic benefit of the town as a whole. The issue of definition apart, there are many signs of urban administration (in the broadest sense) being diligent and innovative. As we have seen, there was mounting activity, supported by a gathering tide of local Acts of Parliament, in the fields of street improvement and public amenities. The record in the sphere of social administration is also far from dismal. Peter Ripley has concluded that between 1690 and 1740 the 'responses of the decision-makers in Gloucester and its hinterland to the problem of poverty in the city was creditable', Philip Anderson stressed the 'high standard of proficiency' demanded by the committee overseeing the operation of the workhouse in mid-eighteenth-century Leeds, and F. H. W. Sheppard argued of the infirmary opened in the London parish of St Marylebone in 1776 that it provides 'an admirable example . . . of the ability of a large, rich, and well-run parish to discharge its duties under the Poor Law with a fair degree of efficiency'.[69]

Throughout the period there were attempts to improve the organization of poor relief by the introduction of new administrative bodies, such as the controversial 'Corporations of the Poor' of the 1690s and early eighteenth century.[70] Such schemes are indicative of the way in which the internal organization of local government could change even though its formal structure remained apparently moribund. The most important example of this process was the rise of the improvement commissions (explored in the piece by Eric Jones and Malcom Falkus in this reader), the first of which was established for St James's Square in London in 1725, and of which 160 had been created by the end of the century. They enjoyed a wide range of powers to control and reorganize the urban environment and, most critical of all, to raise revenue to execute their duties. The result was that many incorporated towns acquired a valuable additional regulatory body, and many of the dynamic

---

69. P. Ripley, 'Poverty in Gloucester and its alleviation 1690–1740', *Transactions of the Bristol and Gloucestershire Archaeological Society*, 103 (1985), p. 197; P. Anderson, 'The Leeds workhouse under the old Poor Law 1726–1834', *Thoresby Society Miscellany XVII*, 56, no. 2 (1980), p. 82; F. H. W. Sheppard, *Local Government in St Marylebone 1688–1835: a Study of the Vestry and the Turnpike Trust* (London, 1958), p. 180.

70. P. Slack, *Poverty and Policy in Tudor and Stuart England* (London, 1988), pp. 195–200; S. Macfarlane, 'Social policy and the poor in the later seventeenth century', in Beier and Finlay (eds), *London*, pp. 252–77; Ripley, 'Poverty in Gloucester', pp. 194–7.

unincorporated centres a vital new organ of self-government.[71] In the development of urban administration no less important than these public bodies were voluntary agencies and institutions, in fields such as health and education, whose numbers expanded swiftly to fill the gaps left in town government. Such organizations permitted the problems generated by a rapidly changing urban society, at least as they were perceived by the middle and upper classes, to be tackled with a flexibility and speed that would have been difficult for the more formal organs of authority to match.[72] Finally, in defence of the eighteenth-century record in urban local government, it should be stressed that when the town fathers appear to be unduly conservative and self-interested, there were often good reasons for this. In particular, there were the major problems of financing improvements from limited revenues, and of ensuring that any changes introduced did not damage the legitimate interests of the various economic and social groupings within the town.[73]

Despite an outward show of unity, local government was often something of a battlefield, as individuals and interest groups jockeyed for influence and power. Control of poor relief, or of specific institutions like the workhouse and infirmary, could generate bitter conflict, which on occasions acquired a distinctly partisan flavour.[74] Party affiliations and tensions were a crucial factor in the politics of London's local government in the late seventeenth and early eighteenth centuries. Up until the 1690s the Tories controlled the senior body of the corporation, the Court of Aldermen, and the Whigs, who at this stage espoused 'reformist' views and attracted much popular support, its junior body or Common Council. But with the heavy involvement of the wealthier London Whigs in the financial revolution, and their growing presence on the Court of Aldermen, the situation completely reversed, so that the Tories became the 'popular' party and acquired control of Common Council. This so frightened Walpole that in 1725 he legislated to give the aldermen the right of veto over the decisions of the Council.[75]

71. Falkus and Jones, 'Urban improvement', pp. 213–17; C. Gill, 'Birmingham under the street commissioners 1769–1851', *University of Birmingham Historical Journal*, 1 (1947–8), pp. 255–87; Sheppard, *Local Government*, pp. 131–64; Farrant, *Georgian Brighton*, pp. 51–3.
72. Morris, 'Voluntary societies', pp. 112–13.
73. McIntyre, 'Rise of a resort town', pp. 222–8.
74. Slack, *Poverty and Policy*, pp. 196–200; Macfarlane, 'Social policy and the poor', pp. 266–70; Anderson, 'The Leeds workhouse', p. 80; J. V. Pickstone and S. V. F. Butler, 'The politics of medicine in Manchester 1788–1792: hospital reform and public health services in the early industrial city', *Medical History*, 28 (1984), pp. 242–7.
75. Horwitz, 'Party in a civic context', pp. 173–94; G. S. De Krey, *A Fractured Society: the Politics of London in the First Age of Party 1688–1715* (Oxford, 1985), especially pp. 177–212. I. G. Doolittle, 'Walpole's City Elections Act',

The impact of local and national politics on towns is not a subject about which there is yet a clear picture. The study of eighteenth-century political history is in a fluid state. Moreover, though towns figure in many individual pieces of research, with a few notable exceptions there has been no concerted attempt to identify the specifically urban element in the political process. However, one point which clearly emerges is that towns were not political islands, but were themselves keen to foster their outside connections. Visiting royalty, aristocrats and assize judges were treated with lavish pomp, and influential local gentry would be regularly wined and dined by the urban patriciate, invested with the town's freedom, and – in increasing numbers – invited to sit on corporations.[76] Behind such largess lay not so much deference, though it may appear like this, as an intelligent awareness of the economic and political value of prestigious external contacts. Towns needed the support of Crown, government, MPs and county patrons to represent their interests at the centre of power, and to assist or resist the passage of vitally important local Acts of Parliament.[77] Urban élites might also use such connections to sustain their status and authority within their own communities. In addition, cultivating the gentry made excellent commercial sense at a time when many towns were developing their consumer and service sectors. For their part the rural élite freely reciprocated by providing a range of time-consuming political services, such as obtaining government appointments for their urban clients,[78] by sitting on town councils or special local commissions, and by making generous benefactions towards the provision of public amenities and buildings. In such actions patrons and MPs were motivated not only by a craving for flattery and influence, but also by a desire to capture and control the valuable wider political power which was vested in towns.

Four-fifths of Parliamentary constituencies were located in boroughs. Though a number of these were scarcely more than villages, it is reasonable to argue that control of the composition of the House of Commons rested with urban centres and their electors.

English Historical Review, 97, no. 384 (1983), pp. 504–29, disputes the view that the 1725 Act was a partisan measure, arguing that it was 'framed in a spirit of accommodation and equity'; but N. Rogers, 'The City Elections Act (1725) reconsidered', *English Historical Review*, 100, no. 396 (1985), pp. 604–17, challenges this interpretation.

76. Clark (ed.), *Country Towns*, pp. 19–20; Clark, 'Civic leaders of Gloucester', pp. 322–6; Rosen, 'Winchester in transition', pp. 183–4.
77. P. Langford, 'Property and "virtual representation" in eighteenth-century England', *Historical Journal*, 31, no. 1 (1988), pp. 83–4, 104–15.
78. C. Brooks, 'Interest, patronage, and professionalism: John, 1st Baron Ashburnham, Hastings, and the revenue services', *Southern History*, 9 (1987), pp. 51–70.

In theory this gave towns a powerful voice in the political system. To what extent this influence was realized, and therefore it is possible to distinguish an urban factor in politics, depends on the degree to which towns were able to act independently of the rural élite. Naturally the gentry supplied the majority of candidates in elections, and cases appear to abound of boroughs whose representation, in whole or part, was under, or came to be under, the effective control of local patrons.[79] However, it would be dangerous to exaggerate the extent of rural hegemony. There could be no simple and universally applicable pattern of manipulation, since the size and nature of borough franchises, and the economic and social structure of their electorates, varied enormously. John Triffit's study of seven southwestern urban constituencies emphasizes the growth and economic independence of the town's middling ranks, and finds little evidence of ductile and deferential voters, or of government, aristocratic, or gentry domination. A number of the bigger towns possessed large electorates which were difficult to 'manage', allowing these constituencies to develop an independent political voice, such as is reflected in the distinct brand of 'urban antiministerialism' which Nicholas Rogers detects in the mid-eighteenth century.[80] The narrowing of borough electorates, the decline in contested elections after the 1720s and the apparent growth in patron control towards the mid-eighteenth century potentially weakened the political position of towns. But J. A. Phillips has suggested that the impact of these developments should not be overstated. The number of boroughs contested at elections actually increased after 1760 despite growing patron power; where a local overlord held one seat in an urban constituency a ballot could still occur for the other; and even where a poll failed to take place this did not prevent a good deal of wrangling between potential candidates which the urban electorate could exploit to their advantage.[81] In general, it would be a foolish MP and patron who failed to minister to the needs of his borough, however 'pocketed' it may appear. Finally, it should be

79. P. Styles, 'The corporation of Warwick 1660–1835', *Transactions of the Birmingham Archaeological Society*, 59 (1935), pp. 53–4; R. Carrol, 'Yorkshire Parliamentary boroughs in the seventeenth century', *Northern History*, 3 (1968), pp. 103–4; W. A. Speck, 'Brackley: a study in the growth of oligarchy', *Midland History*, 3 (1975–6), pp. 30–41; J. V. Beckett, 'The making of a pocket borough: Cockermouth 1722–1756', *Journal of British Studies*, 20, no. 1 (1980), pp. 140–57.
80. Triffit, 'Politics and the urban community', especially pp. 13, 26–8, 36–7, 83–4; N. Rogers, 'The urban opposition to Whig oligarchy 1720–60', in M. and J. Jacob (eds), *The Origins of Anglo-American Radicalism* (London, 1984), p. 145.
81. J. A. Phillips, 'The structure of electoral politics in unreformed England', *Journal of British Studies*, 19, no. 2 (1980), pp. 76–100; Beckett, 'Making of a pocket borough', pp. 146–51.

recognized that a town, even if it was formally unrepresented, could exert considerable impact on the electoral and political process. As John Money reveals in his essay in this volume, many of Birmingham's expanding population were qualified to vote in the Warwickshire county constituency (by 1774 the town had established virtual direct control over the return of one of the two members), and many as immigrants retained votes in neighbouring boroughs or counties. In the Westmorland elections of 1818 and 1826 Kendal voters were able to mount a distinct challenge to the Lowther domination of the county seat, thereby preparing the ground for the acquisition of their own MP after 1832. Towns were also able to influence Parliament outside the electoral arena. MPs often possessed residences or owned property in places beyond their own constituencies, and would diligently represent the interests of these other communities. So powerful was this factor that during the campaign for Parliamentary reform in 1783 the great manufacturing towns were notable absentees among those petitioning for change.[82]

Modern research on the seventeenth- and eighteenth-century political system has challenged the notion that the unreformed electorate was grossly unrepresentative, and that the mass of people had no voice in the formal political system. Frank O'Gorman has stressed the 'indispensable political role' played by 'the middling orders', and the extent of 'communal involvement', in the electoral process. Geoffrey Holmes has suggested that in 1722 the true size of the electorate was around one-third of a million, representing 'not far short of one in four of the adult males'.[83] James Bradley and J. A. Phillips have shown how in the mid- to late eighteenth century those without votes were able to input into the political process by petitioning the Crown and Parliament on key issues: including such people Phillips estimates the political nation to be at least 425 000 to 475 000, or one-quarter of the adult male popula-

---

82. Money, 'Birmingham and the West Midlands', p. 10; Money, 'Taverns, coffeehouses, and clubs', pp. 32–6; J. D. Marshall and C. A. Dyhouse, 'Social transition in Kendal and Westmorland *c.* 1760–1860', *Northern History*, 12 (1976), pp. 139–40; Langford, ' Property and "virtual representation"', especially pp. 114–15.

83. F. O'Gorman, 'The unreformed electorate of Hanoverian England: the mid-eighteenth century to the Reform Act of 1832', *Social History*, 11, no. 1 (1986), pp. 49, 52; G. S. Holmes, *The Electorate and the National Will in the First Age of Party*, inaugural lecture, University of Lancaster (Lancaster, 1975), p. 23; D. Hirst, *The Representatives of the People? Voters and Voting in England under the Early Stuarts* (Cambridge, 1975); J. H. Plumb, 'The growth of the electorate in England 1600 to 1715', *Past and Present*, 45 (1969), pp. 90–116; W. A. Speck, *Tory and Whig: the Struggle in the Constituencies 1701–1715* (London, 1970), pp. 13–20.

tion.[84] It appears, therefore, that a substantial number of ordinary townsmen were able to participate in and influence the outcome of national affairs. But to what extent did there exist a genuinely 'popular' urban politics? Here the Industrial Revolution has been taken by many historians to be a watershed, with the emergence, under the impact of economic and social change, of a coherent, ideologically conscious and politically committed working class. Edward Thompson sees 'the making of the English working class' as having a relatively protracted gestation between the 1780s and the eve of the Great Reform Bill. For Harold Perkin the birth pangs were shorter, compressed into the years between the end of the Napoleonic wars and the Peterloo 'massacre' of 1819.[85] The whole subject has generated a huge debate which revolves around a series of questions. Were the political radicals of the period the vanguard of an industrial working class or merely the disgruntled remnants of a dying artisan culture? Was radical activity sustained and organized continuously from the 1790s – as F. K. Donnelly and J. L. Baxter argue for Sheffield, and Iain McCalman for London [86] – or did it merely erupt at opportune intervals? How widespread were subversive political ideas? – they do not appear to have been significant in the major cities of Bristol and Liverpool in the late eighteenth century.[87] Was radicalism democratic and revolutionary, or was it simply self-interested trade unionism, or even an exercise in nostalgia and conservatism? And finally, was there one or many working classes, divided along lines of employment, status, religion, ethnicity and so on? The very different responses of historians to these questions suggests that there can be no clear-cut answers.[88]

Disagreements about the chronology of working-class politics during the early Industrial Revolution prompts the further question,

84. J. Bradley, 'Religion and reform at the polls: nonconformity in Cambridge politics 1774–1784', *Journal of British Studies*, 23, no. 2 (1984), pp. 66-7; J. A. Phillips, 'Popular politics in unreformed England', *Journal of Modern History*, 52, no. 4 (1980), especially pp. 616, 624.
85. E. P. Thompson, *The Making of the English Working Class* (Harmondsworth, 1968), p. 12; H. Perkin, *The Origins of Modern English Society 1780–1880* (London, 1969), pp. 208–13.
86. F. K. Donnelly and J. L. Baxter, 'Sheffield and the English revolutionary tradition 1791–1820', *International Review of Social History*, 20 (1975), pp. 398–423; McCalman, 'Ultra–radicalism', pp. 309–33.
87. Sanderson, 'Structure of politics', p. 73; M. Harrison, '"To raise and dare resentment": the Bristol Bridge Riot of 1793 re-examined', *Historical Journal*, 26, no. 3 (1983), pp. 564–5.
88. For recent surveys of the debate as a whole see R. J. Morris, *Class and Class Consciousness in the Industrial Revolution 1780–1850* (London, 1979); J. Rule, *The Labouring Classes in Early Industrial England 1750–1850* (London, 1986), pp. 379–93; D. G. Wright, *Popular Radicalism: the Working-Class Experience 1780–1880* (London, 1988), especially pp. 1–22.

of central significance to this Introduction, to what extent do the late eighteenth and early nineteenth centuries actually represent a point of major social and political disjunction? In his study of crowd activity in several leading cities between 1790 and 1835, Mark Harrison contends that traditional patterns of mass political behaviour (which were generally orderly and structured) continued to operate throughout the period. On a different tack, it could be argued that since there is now a tendency to trace back the origins of industrialization and urbanization (key inputs into political change) to an earlier date, the same could be done for 'new' political attitudes. Edward Thompson, in one of his later contributions to the debate, develops the notion of a polarized 'field-of-force' to describe social relations in the eighteenth century, and accepts the concept of class struggle before the 1790s, though not that of a class society.[89] This would appear to raise the possibility of strong elements of continuity in popular politics. The work of George Rudé, John Money and John Brewer has revealed clear evidence of urban radicalism in the 1760s and 1770s. Rudé argues that 'For all its immaturity and lack of definition, the cry of "Wilkes and Liberty" was a political slogan and stirred the political passions of not only freeholders and freemen but of the unenfranchised craftsmen and journeymen . . . This was something new in the nation's political life'. Similarly, Money maintains that in Birmingham 'the escapades of John Wilkes and the dispute with the American colonies provided for the first time a series of issues on which the emerging self-consciousness and nascent radicalism of the seaport towns and the new manufacturing districts could concentrate their energies. This concentration produced a downward extension of articulacy. . . .'[90] Nicholas Rogers, Harry Dickinson and Gary De Krey have traced back a brand of urban radicalism and popular politics even further, through the 1740s to the years after the Glorious Revolution.[91]

However, in exploring the nature of popular politics before the 1790s, and in particular its radical content, a great deal of caution is necessary. Work on the subject tends to concentrate on London, which for a variety of reasons might be considered an exceptional political environment, more responsive to libertarian ideas than else-

---

89. E. P. Thompson, 'Eighteenth-century English society: class struggle without class?', *Social History*, 3, no. 2 (1978), pp. 148–51.
90. G. Rudé, *Wilkes and Liberty: a Social Study of 1763 to 1774* (Oxford, 1972), p. 197; Money, 'Taverns, coffee-houses, and clubs', p. 16; J. Brewer, *Party Ideology and Popular Politics at the Accession of George III* (Cambridge, 1976).
91. Rogers, 'Aristocratic clientage', especially pp. 71, 105; H. T. Dickinson, 'Popular politics in the Age of Walpole', in J. Black (ed.), *Britain in the Age of Walpole* (London, 1984), pp. 45–68; H. T. Dickinson, 'The precursors of political radicalism in Augustan Britain', in Jones (ed.), *First Age of Party*, pp. 63–84; De Krey, *Fractured Society*, especially p. 7.

where. Moreover, much of the evidence for popular attitudes is drawn from riots and demonstrations, which appear to be precisely the sort of primitive, pre-literate activism which it is argued a genuine class politics was destined to supersede. By their nature riots were sporadic and focused on very specific short-term goals; most were not overtly political but dealt with 'economic' issues such as the distribution and sale of grain; few aimed to subvert the traditional structure of authority, and some may even have been manipulated from above;[92] and most were ideologically conservative, aimed at supporting Church and King, or at defending traditional rights. On the other hand, demonstrations and 'disorders' appear to have been growing in number in the eighteenth century, and they continue to be an important phenomenon long after the emergence of class politics. There is evidence of crowds becoming increasingly self-motivated and independent. Robert Shoemaker argues in his article on the metropolitan 'mob', reproduced in this collection, that 'the early eighteenth century appears as a crucial period in the long process in which the political élite lost control of popular disturbances in London'.[93] There is also a risk of underestimating the political content and significance of riots, by failing to place them in their proper historical context, and neglecting to decode adequately their non-literate forms of protest. In a society increasingly imbued with capitalist market values, the defence of traditional economic norms could acquire an unexpected radical potential; patriotic, anti-Jacobite and anti-Catholic riots might represent not a conservative reflex but an attempt to safeguard English liberties and libertarian values in general; and in the vocabulary of radicalism the theatrical props of riot could possess a more powerful subversive message than many reams of print. It is, therefore, possible to see the manifold disorders of the eighteenth century not as evidence of an undeveloped, backward-looking popular politics, submerged beneath the weight of deference and paternalism, but of an evolving independent political consciousness which was to flower into overt class conflict at a later date.[94]

92. See, for example, G. S. Holmes, 'The Sacheverell riots: the crowd and the church in early eighteenth-century London', *Past and Present*, 72 (1976), pp. 78–81.
93. R. Shoemaker, 'The London "mob" in the early eighteenth century', *Journal of British Studies*, 26, no. 3 (1987), p. 304; and also N. Rogers, 'Popular protest in early Hanoverian London', *Past and Present*, 79 (1978), pp. 99–100; Rogers, 'Aristocratic clientage', pp. 94–5.
94. The literature on riots and demonstrations is considerable. For a general survey see J. Stevenson, *Popular Disturbances in England 1700–1870* (London, 1979). Studies of particular interest to urban historians include, along with those referred to above, P. B. Rose, 'The Priestley riots of 1791', *Past and Present*, 18 (1960), pp. 68–88; G. Rudé, *Paris and London in the Eighteenth Century:*

Inextricably woven into the fabric of eighteenth-century politics was religion. Gary De Krey has stressed the 'remarkable impact' in the 1690s and early eighteenth century of dissent 'on the tempestuous political society of which London was a part', a view reinforced by the work of Geoffrey Holmes and Henry Horwitz. In the same period John Triffit has discovered among a group of towns in the South West that 'the social dimension of church membership [was] so great that the churches found themselves at the centre of local struggles for authority'. James Bradley had demonstrated the striking link between dissent and the politics of reform in Cambridge in the 1770s and 1780s, John Pickstone and Stella Butler revealed the impact of religious divisions on the politics of medicine in Manchester in the late eighteenth century, and John Marshall and Carol Dyhouse pointed to the part played by dissenting masters in developing middle-class radicalism in Kendal in the late 1810s.[95] Such examples could be multiplied many times. The close links between religion and politics partly derived from the considerable power and influence the Church exercised in education, social policy and the formation of ideological attitudes. It also reflected the common economic and social roots of secular and spiritual divisions, and the fact that religion and politics did not occupy mutually exclusive compartments in people's consciousness. An all-embracing Anglican church stood as symbol and instrument of a unitary state, which legitimated both town and county élites' monopoly of local power. Dissent, on the other hand, with its inherent assumption of a pluralist society, represented a fundamental threat to that monopoly. For the lower orders religious diversity might have its libertarian attractions: alternatively, it could constitute a threat to the integrity

---

Studies in Popular Protest (London, 1970); E. P. Thompson, 'The moral economy of the English crowd in the eighteenth century', *Past and Present*, 50 (1971), pp. 76–136; P. Linebaugh, 'The Tyburn riot against the surgeons', in D. Hay *et al.*, *Albion's Fatal Tree: Crime and Society in Eighteenth-Century England* (London, 1975), pp. 65–117; A. Booth, 'Food riots in the North West of England 1790–1801', *Past and Present*, 77 (1977), pp. 84–107; J. Ellis, 'Urban conflict and popular violence: the Guildhall riots of 1740 in Newcastle-upon-Tyne', *International Review of Social History*, 25 (1980), pp. 332–49. For two different interpretations of the Bristol Bridge riot of 1793, see P. D. Jones, 'The Bristol Bridge riot and its antecedants: eighteenth-century perceptions of the crowd', *Journal of British Studies*, 19, no. 2 (1980), pp. 74–92; and Harrison, '"To raise and dare resentment"', pp. 557–85. Harrison develops his critique of the Rudé–Hobsbawm–Thompson approach to crowd activity in *Crowds and History: Mass Phenomena in English Towns 1790–1835* (Cambridge, 1988).

95. De Krey, *Fractured Society*, p. 112; Holmes, 'Sacheverell riots', pp. 62–6; Horwitz, 'Party in a civic context', p. 184; Triffit, 'Politics and the urban community', p. 91; Bradley, 'Religion and reform', pp. 55–78; Pickstone and Butler, 'Politics of medicine', pp. 242–5; Marshall and Dyhouse, 'Social transition in Kendal', p. 138.

of the local community, and to those bonds of social responsibility through which the prosperous were duty-bound to protect the poor as a whole. Therefore, popular support of the Anglican church, as evinced in Church and King, anti-Methodist, and anti-Catholic disturbances, was not necessarily a sign of unreasoning deference, but reflected the defence of interests which the populace perceived as their own.

In exploring the specifically urban dimension of religion two factors are of considerable significance. First, there were the serious difficulties faced by the established church as the rapid growth in towns placed mounting pressure on the supply of spiritual facilities and services. The problem was to be highlighted during the urban explosion of the nineteenth century, but signs of the difficulties ahead can be discerned in the previous century. Coping with the expansion in London's huge population, for example, was one of the motivations behind the 'Fifty New Churches' Act of 1711. Though there was a resurgence in the construction of Anglican churches and chapels after 1700, many of these buildings were erected to satisfy the requirements of fashionable society, so that provision for the poorest townspeople probably deteriorated during the century.[96] Second, and for some contemporaries a clear consequence of the failure of the Anglican church to meet the needs of its growing urban constituency, there was the evident strength of nonconformity, which was particularly associated with towns. Of the 1238 Presbyterian, Independent and Baptist congregations known to have existed between 1715 and 1718, over half met in places referred to as towns; moreover, urban congregations were generally larger than rural ones.[97] In the decades immediately after the Glorious Revolution nonconformity probably experienced 'a moderate, steady growth'.[98] Subsequently its vitality and strength appear to have declined, though the rise of Methodism from the 1730s both compensated for this, and in the long term revitalized certain branches of old dissent, especially the Congregationalists and Baptists.[99] The

96. K. S. Inglis, *Churches and the Working Classes in Victorian England* (London, 1963), especially p. 57; A. D. Gilbert, *Religion and Society in Industrial England: Church, Chapel, and Social Change 1740–1914* (London, 1976), pp. 109–10; Corfield, *English Towns*, pp. 139–40; H. M. Colvin, 'Fifty new churches', *Architectural Review* (March 1950), p. 189; Chalklin, 'Financing of church building', pp. 284–5, 288–9.
97. M. R. Watts, *The Dissenters: from the Reformation to the French Revolution* (Oxford, 1978), pp. 285–9.
98. G. S. Holmes, *The Trial of Doctor Sacheverell* (London, 1973), p. 37; and also Triffit, 'Politics and the urban community', pp. 18–19, 93-116.
99. Watts, *Dissenters*, pp. 382–464; Corfield, *English Towns*, pp. 140–1; Bradley, 'Religion and reform', pp. 59–60.

response of towns to these changes varied from place to place. During the late eighteenth and early nineteenth centuries the market towns of the Vale of York became the 'nerve centres' of the Methodist revival in the area, but the new dissent had comparatively little impact on Kendal which remained wedded to Quakerism and Unitarianism.[100] One of the reasons for the urban bias of dissent was that it tended to draw its membership from the small-scale, economically independent producer often found in towns. Within urban communities nonconformists came from a relatively broad cross-section of society, though this probably excluded the very poor. Among dissenters themselves certain denominations possessed a distinctly higher social profile than others. John Seed has shown how in many commercial towns in the 1770s and 1780s, rational dissenting congregations (some of which became Unitarians) had an élite of wealthy merchants and professionals, who could wield considerable political influence, and who shared the worldly values and pleasures of the Anglican gentleman.[101]

That prosperous urban dissenters should be seduced by the secular delights that surrounded them is hardly surprising, given the remarkable extent to which fashionable culture had expanded in the towns since the late seventeenth century. The availability of classical architecture, plays, concerts, lectures, bookshops, circulating libraries, clubs, assemblies, walks and a wide range of luxury shopping facilities must have made the temptations, for those who could afford them, difficult to resist. The development of a sophisticated cultural regime in many of the larger towns is a major feature of the eighteenth century, and is explored in this reader in the essays of Alan Everitt, Ronald Neale, Roy Porter and Peter Borsay, and also elsewhere in the work of J. H. Plumb and Angus McInnes.[102] Its widely varying impact on nonconformists prompts the broader question, to what extent did it accentuate divisions in society as a whole? Peter Burke has argued that at the beginning of the early

---

100. Unwin, 'Tradition and transition', pp. 88–91; Marshall and Dyhouse, 'Social transition in Kendal', pp. 132–3.
101. Watts, *Dissenters*, pp. 346–66; Marshall, 'Kendal in the late seventeenth and eighteenth centuries', pp. 236–42; Unwin, 'Tradition and transition', pp. 91–2; Bradley, 'Religion and reform', p. 61; Triffit, 'Politics and the urban community', pp. 99–102; J. Seed, 'Gentlemen dissenters: the social and political meanings of rational dissent in the 1770s and 1780s', *Historical Journal*, 28, no. 2 (1985), pp. 301–14.
102. J. H. Plumb, 'The commercialization of leisure in eighteenth-century England', in McKendrick *et al.*, *Birth of a Consumer Society*, pp. 265–85; A. McInnes, 'The emergence of a leisure town: Shrewsbury 1660–1760', *Past and Present*, 120 (1988), pp. 53–87, which, while accepting the growing influence of leisure and luxury on urban life, argues that the impact of this development was focused on a particular category of centres, the 'leisure towns'.

modern period a dual cultural model operated, consisting of an élite element (or great tradition) and a popular one (or small tradition). Though the common people enjoyed only the second of these elements, the higher ranks participated in both, thus mitigating the potentially divisive influence of the model on society. However, at some point in the period the better-off began to withdraw from the small tradition, attacking it as irreligious and uncivilized.[103] In England the emergence of a large-scale, commercialized and snobbish leisure culture, focused on the town, accelerated this process, both by stigmatizing popular pastimes, and by removing the need for the well-off to share in them. Roy Porter, in an essay on provincial science which forms part of this reader, and Harry Payne have specifically interpreted the eighteenth-century Enlightenment in terms of increased cultural and social differentiation.[104] In parallel with these changes, popular culture may itself have become more sharply defined and autonomous, as with élite withdrawal the populace were forced themselves to sustain and defend their traditional values and customs, and to recognize the reality of deepening divisions in society. Edward Thompson has written of the 'remarkable dissociation between the polite and the plebeian culture in post-Restoration England', stressing the independence and 'robust' nature of the latter; Charles Phythian-Adams argued that during the eighteenth century May Day celebrations in London were transformed from a socially cohesive ceremony into an 'occasion for ritualized social separatism . . . in compliance with the working realities of class-segregation in the world's first "modern city"'; and Iain McCalman maintained that the radical debating clubs of late eighteenth- and early nineteenth-century London developed a quite specific 'plebeian–populist rhetoric and theatre'.[105]

The thesis of eighteenth-century urban society becoming increasingly polarized along cultural lines raises several problems. First, where do the growing middling groups, particularly associated with towns, fit into the picture? Surely their presence would bridge the

---

103. P. Burke, *Popular Culture in Early Modern Europe* (London, 1979), pp. 23–9, 207–43, 270–81.

104. R. Porter, 'Science, provincial culture, and public opinion in Enlightenment England', *British Journal for Eighteenth-Century Studies*, 3 (1980), pp. 28–30; H. C. Payne, 'Elite versus popular mentality in the eighteenth century', in R. Runte (ed.), *Studies in Eighteenth-Century Culture*, vol. 8 (Wisconsin, 1979), pp. 13–24.

105. E. P. Thompson, 'Patrician society, plebeian culture', *Journal of Social History*, 7 (1974), pp. 393, 397; C. Phythian-Adams, 'Milk and soot: the changing vocabulary of a popular ritual in Stuart and Hanoverian London', in Fraser and Sutcliffe (eds), *Pursuit of Urban History*, p. 104; McCalman, 'Ultra-radicalism', p. 321.

polite–plebeian divide. Second, it has been argued, notably by Jonathan Barry in the case of Bristol, that traditional popular customs and values continued to appeal to the town's higher ranks long into the eighteenth century, and that the new fashionable urban culture was not a narrowly exclusive one, but was available to a surprisingly broad range of society. Accessibility was encouraged by the manner in which the commercialization of polite leisure reduced its price and increased its supply, and by the higher levels of literacy that existed among town dwellers. One pertinent example of the impact of commercialization was the buoyant trade in fashionable secondhand clothes, centred on London, which gave the less well off easy access to the status symbols of their superiors.[106] Third, it is clear that there existed substantial divisions *within* élite and popular cultures. Douglas Reid has shown how in late eighteenth- and early nineteenth-century Birmingham there developed 'a new artisan sub-culture . . . characterized in varying measure by rationalism, evangelicalism and political radicalism', and at odds with the licence associated with traditional popular pastimes. Hugh Cunningham has also suggested that during the early Industrial Revolution popular culture was opposed by 'two minority cultures', which none the less 'drew their impetus from the people'.[107] Fourth, the polite–plebeian antithesis tends to ignore other types of cultural divisions, of a less socio-economic kind, that may have been of greater significance, such as those of region, religion and politics.[108] Fifth, it may be argued that historians have directed too much attention to what divided eighteenth-century townspeople, and too little to what united them, perhaps because conflict is a more visible phenomenon. There may have been a core of beliefs, in fields such as the family, which were shared by the majority, and which silently underpinned social stability. For urban historians of particular interest is the extent to which there existed a common notion of civic consciousness and community, which might be used to express a genuine altruism, and help hold social and political tensions in check. However, the concept of the civic ideal is fraught with difficulties. It could be, and often was, exploited to further sectional

106. J. Barry, 'The cultural life of Bristol 1640–1775', unpublished D.Phil. thesis (Oxford, 1983), especially pp. 37–41, 140, 182, 221, 339; B. Lemire, 'Consumerism in pre-industrial and early industrial England: the trade in secondhand clothes', *Journal of British Studies*, 27, no. 1 (1988), pp. 1–24.
107. D. Reid, 'Interpreting the festival calendar: wakes and fairs as carnivals', in R. D. Storch (ed.), *Popular Culture and Custom in Nineteenth-Century England* (London, 1982), p. 132; H. Cunningham, *Leisure in the Industrial Revolution c. 1780–c. 1880* (London, 1980), p. 38.
108. Barry, 'Cultural life of Bristol', pp. 115–28, 173–81, 227–44, 275–82, 324–36, 339–44.

and personal interests, and – as Mark Harrison has argued in the case of Bristol – differing perceptions of it could divide as much as unite a town.[109]

The two underlying themes of this Introduction have been urban identity and continuity. These concepts are as important in understanding cultural aspects of town life, as – it has been argued – they are its demographic, economic, social, environmental, political and religious facets. Throughout the eighteenth century there was a specific and vital urban culture. It may be simplistic to argue that this was *more* urban in 1820 than it had been in 1688, but at the later date it was stronger and exerted greater influence on society as a whole. Growing public and private investment in the civic ideal – through ceremonies, buildings, artefacts, printed histories and pictorial representations – defined and asserted the special nature of towns.[110] Urban domestic material culture, developing rapidly under the influence of a 'consumer revolution', appears to have been more sophisticated than that in the countryside, at least to judge from the greater ownership of household goods like pictures, looking-glasses, linen, window curtains, china and silverware. Lorna Weatherill has suggested that this pattern of consumption may be due to 'a greater desire' on the part of more densely packed townspeople 'to look inwardly to the living space', and to their better access to consumer facilities.[111] The impact of the expansion of fashionable architecture and leisure on urban identity may appear less clear cut. Its presence increased the sophistication and status of urban life, but it also seemed to impose on the town the culture of the rural gentry, with the adoption of country-house building styles, and of recreations like hunting and horse racing. However, urban classicism developed physical forms, such as streets, squares and planned units, which were particularly associated with towns and their large-scale, collective style of life. Moreover, urban leisure and recreational activities, with their public, commercial and cosmopolitan character, also evolved in a manner which was quite different to similar pastimes in the countryside.

Cultural continuity is a feature many urban historians have stressed. James Walvin has written of the degree to which, even in

109. Harrison, *Crowds and History*, pp. 196–201, 260–7.
110. P. Borsay, ' "All the town's a stage": urban ritual and ceremony 1660–1800', in Clark (ed.), *Provincial Towns*, pp. 228–58; Borsay, *Urban Renaissance*, pp. 80–5, 101–13; P. Clark, 'Visions of the urban community: antiquarians and the English city before 1800', in Fraser and Sutcliffe (eds), *Pursuit of Urban History*, pp. 114–24; R. Hyde, *Gilded Scenes and Shining Prospects: Panoramic Views of British Towns 1575–1900* (New Haven, Conn., 1985), pp. 61–131.
111. McKendrick, 'Consumer revolution', *passim*; L. Weatherill, *Consumer Behaviour and Material Culture in Britain 1660–1760* (London, 1986), pp. 70–90.

the mid-nineteenth century, 'the people of urban England seemed remarkably addicted to rituals that were recognizably those of their forbears and which formed a complex cultural inheritance from one generation to another', and Douglas Reid, and John Walton and Robert Poole have demonstrated the resilience of traditional popular holidays in Birmingham and the Lancashire textile towns during the Industrial Revolution.[112] Civic culture during the years 1688 to 1820 remained a vital and highly ritualized phenomenon, invigorated by the growing wealth and aspirations of towns and their citizens. Preston continued throughout the period to celebrate its medieval Guild Merchant (held every twenty years) on a scale, if anything, of increasing magnificence. It could be said of the 1802 meeting that it 'was kept with not inferior ceremony and civic hospitality to what had been practised at any former Guild Merchant, in ancient or modern times', and of the 1822 Guild that it was held 'with unabated ardour'.[113] In future years the meaning of the Guild was to change substantially under the pressure of intensifying class divisions, but it is highly significant that, in what Dickens in *Hard Times* was to take as his model of an industrial town, this apparently archaic celebration was not abandoned.[114]

The history of the Preston Guild emphasizes the importance of the relationship between change and continuity in the development of English towns between 1688 and 1820. Change there certainly was. Individually towns were larger and collectively they contained a much higher proportion of the nation's population. The hierarchy in which they were organized was substantially restructured by the rapid growth of once small ports and industrial centres. Manufacturing processes were becoming increasingly focused in towns, and the urban economy as a whole was growing in scale and sophistication, responsible for a rising share of the country's wealth. Demographic and economic expansion created new environmental and administrative problems, prompting the building industry and urban government to evolve – by no means wholly unsuccessfully – to meet these demands. The urban social structure became more heterogeneous and complex as a consequence of the critical growth of the middling groups, whose accumulating strength and wealth en-

112. Walvin, *English Urban Life*, p. 171; Reid, 'Interpreting the festival calendar', pp. 133–4, 137–8; Reid, 'Decline of Saint Monday', pp. 81–4, 91–3; J. K. Walton and R. Poole, 'The Lancashire wakes in the nineteenth century', in Storch (ed.), *Popular Culture*, pp. 100–24.
113. W. A. Abram, *Memorials of the Preston Guilds* (Preston, 1882), pp. 108, 120.
114. R. D. Parker, 'The changing character of Preston Guild Merchant 1762–1862', *Northern History*, 20 (1984), pp. 108–26; C. Dickens, *Hard Times*, ed. D. Craig (Harmondsworth, 1972), pp. 16, 30–3, 36.

sured that political participation, religious pluralism and cultural
refinement became a permanent feature of town life. But a more
varied social structure did not necessarily prevent political and cultural polarization, and by the early nineteenth century mounting
tensions led to a society in which class divisions played a growing
part. So the years 1688 to 1820 were for towns years of transformation. However, it should be stressed that this change was not
exclusively focused on the late eighteenth and early nineteenth centuries, but was a feature of the *whole* period; and that running in
harness with change – in a way checking and containing it – were
powerful elements of continuity, as exemplified in urban ritual.
Paradoxically, it was the persistence of the past in some aspects of
urban life, which permitted towns to undergo rapid change in other
areas, without suffering the sort of major disjunctions that would
have threatened their underlying stability. And it was because there
was a long eighteenth century, and not a short one, that England
witnessed a peaceful transition from a semi-urbanized pre-industrial
society, to one dominated by the industrial city.

Chapter 2

URBAN GROWTH AND AGRICULTURAL CHANGE: ENGLAND AND THE CONTINENT IN THE EARLY MODERN PERIOD

E. Anthony Wrigley[1]

[*Journal of Interdisciplinary History*, 15, no. 4 (1985)]

Anthony Wrigley is one of the leading historical demographers working today: his major achievement, co-authored with Roger Schofield, is the monumental The Population History of England 1541–1871: a Reconstruction *(1981). His work displays a particular interest in the interrelationship between demographic, economic and social change, and is marked by the use of imaginative and lucid models to develop his arguments. These models are often built on a number of crucial assumptions, which the author makes evident, but which it is important for the reader to be critically aware of. The article reprinted here places English urban growth since the late seventeenth century in its all-important wider temporal and geographical context. From this emerges the exceptional nature of the English experience relative to Europe, and the significance of the long eighteenth century in Britain's emergence as the 'first industrial nation'. Wrigley is also keen to explore the close interaction between growth in agricultural productivity, of which he finds striking evidence in early modern England, and urbanization. That this was a two-way process, in which urban expansion itself stimulated agricultural innovation, can be further explored in Wrigley's influential study, 'A simple model of London's importance in changing English society and economy 1650–1750',* Past and Present, *37 (1967).*

---

1. E. Anthony Wrigley is Professor of Population Studies at the London School of Economics and Associate Director of the Economic and Social Research Council Cambridge Group for the History of Population and Social Structure.

The author is grateful to Penelope Corfield, Jack Goldstone, and Tony Sutcliffe for comments on an earlier version of this article.

The complexity and contingency of any relationship between economic growth and urban growth should need no stressing. It is clearly hazardous to undervalue, still more to ignore, the difficulties attending any examination of this topic. In the early part of this article I prefer to sketch out an initial thesis rather starkly at the risk of oversimplifying 'reality'. Later the limitations of the initial formulation become clear.

A rising level of real income per head and a rising proportion of urban dwellers, other things being equal, are likely to be linked phenomena in a pre-industrial economy. If income elasticity of demand for food is less than unity, then, with rising real incomes, demand for secondary and tertiary products will grow more rapidly than that for primary products, and will therefore cause employment in secondary and tertiary industries to rise more rapidly than in agriculture. Such employment is likely to be higher in towns, especially in the case of tertiary employment, and will result in an increase in the proportion of the total population living in towns. There may be an important feedback element in this relationship, since the growth of towns may help to further agricultural investment and specialization and so carry forward the rising trend in real incomes. Declining real incomes will have an opposite effect.[2]

In an economy which meets its own food needs, urban growth may not only be a symptom of rising real incomes: it may also be a rough measure of the level of productivity per worker in the agricultural sector of the economy. If productivity per head in agriculture is sufficiently low, the surplus of food available after meeting the needs of the agricultural population may be enough to sustain only a tiny urban sector. At the other extreme, if agricultural productivity is high, the economy may be able to support a third or a half of the population in towns without prejudicing nutritional levels elsewhere. In a closed economy, therefore, a substantial rise in the proportion of the population living in towns is strong presumptive evidence of a significant improvement in production per head in agriculture, and may provide an indication of the scale of the change.

Sufficient information is now available to justify an initial application of this line of thought to early modern England.

2. Adam Smith stressed the mutual stimulus which urban growth and agricultural improvement might afford each other in *An Enquiry into the Nature and Causes of the Wealth of Nations* (Edinburgh, 1863), 181–187. He included a chapter entitled, 'How the commerce of towns contributed to the improvement of the country'.

THE PACE OF URBAN GROWTH IN ENGLAND

Table 1 sets out some estimates of the size of the populations of leading English towns in about 1520, 1600, 1670, 1700, 1750, and 1800. Table 2 provides estimates of the total population of England at each of these dates and of the population of London and other urban centers with 5000 or more inhabitants.

As the notes to the tables make clear, all of the data given are subject to a substantial measure of uncertainty. Their sources are various and, apart from those taken from the 1851 census, most have been obtained by inflating and adjusting the raw data because the latter cover only a proportion of the total population. Some figures were originally suspiciously rounded and many incorporate alterations made in the light of subjective assessments of their deficiencies. Moreover, it is entirely arbitrary to draw a dividing line between urban and non-urban at 5000. It was done on the supposition that only a tiny fraction of the inhabitants of towns larger than 5000 would have been principally engaged in agriculture, but a plausible case might be made for a significantly lower dividing line.

To add still further to the crudity of the exercise, it is questionable whether the same dividing line should be used over a long period of time, during which the population increased greatly. For example, a moderate-sized market town with a population of, say, 3000 at the start of the period, serving a hinterland in which the population doubled, would itself grow in size and at some point exceed 5000 in population even though the functions it discharged did not alter. If this pattern were widely repeated, it would result in an upward drift in the overall urban percentage, but such movement would have occurred only because the total population had risen. It would not imply any structural change in the economy. Nevertheless, certain features of change over time are so prominent that they would remain clear cut, or might even be more pronounced, if less crude information were available.

During the sixteenth century, urban growth, relative to national population trends, was largely confined to London, the population of which quadrupled. London's share of the national total rose from 2.25 to 5 per cent. The percentage of the population living in other towns, however, rose only modestly from 3 to 3.25 per cent. Even this rise was largely because ten towns crept over the 5000 mark (Plymouth, King's Lynn, Gloucester, Chester, Hull, Great Yarmouth, Ipswich, Cambridge, Worcester, and Oxford). Most large provincial centers were growing *less* quickly than the national population as a whole, as appears to have been true of Norwich, Bristol, Exeter, Canterbury, Coventry, Colchester, and Salisbury. Of the initial list of towns above 5000 in population, excluding Lon-

TABLE 1 Urban populations ('000s)

c. 1520	c. 1600	c. 1670		c. 1750	1801
London 55	London 200	London 475	London 575	London 675	London 959
Norwich 12	Norwich 15	Norwich 20	Norwich 30	Bristol 50	Manchester 89[a]
Bristol 10	York 12	Bristol 20	Bristol 21	Norwich 36	Liverpool 83
York 8	Bristol 12	York 12	Newcastle 16	Newcastle 29	Birmingham 74
Salisbury 8	Newcastle 10	Newcastle 12	Exeter 14	Birmingham 24	Bristol 60
Exeter 8	Exeter 9	Colchester 9	York 12	Liverpool 22	Leeds 53
Colchester 7	Plymouth 8	Exeter 9	Gt Yarmouth 10	Manchester 18	Sheffield 46
Coventry 7	Salisbury 6	Chester 8	Birmingham *(8–9)*	Leeds 16	Plymouth 43[b]
Newcastle 5	King's Lynn 6	Ipswich 8	Chester	Exeter 16	Newcastle 42[c]
Canterbury 5	Gloucester 6	Gt Yarmouth 8	Colchester	Plymouth 15	Norwich 36
	Chester 6	Plymouth 8	Ipswich	Chester 13	Portsmouth 33
	Coventry 6	Worcester 8	Manchester	Coventry 13	Bath 33
	Hull 6	Coventry 7	Plymouth	Nottingham 12	Hull 30
	Gt Yarmouth 5	King's Lynn 7	Worcester	Sheffield 12	Nottingham 29
	Ipswich 5	Manchester 6	Bury St Edmunds *(5–7)*	York 11	Sunderland 26
	Cambridge 5	Canterbury 6	Cambridge	Chatham 10	Stoke 23[d]
	Worcester 5	Leeds 6	Canterbury	Gt Yarmouth 10	Chatham 23[e]
	Canterbury 5	Birmingham 6	Chatham	Portsmouth 10	Wolverhampton 21[f]
	Oxford 5	Cambridge 6	Coventry	Sunderland 10	Bolton 17
	Colchester 5	Hull 6	Gloucester	Worcester 10	Exeter 17
		Salisbury 6	Hull		Leicester 17
		Bury St Edmunds 5	King's Lynn		Great Yarmouth 17
		Leicester 5	Leeds		Stockport 17
		Oxford 5	Leicester		York 16
		Shrewsbury 5	Liverpool		Coventry 16
		Gloucester 5	Nottingham		Chester 16
			Oxford		Shrewsbury 15
			Portsmouth		
			Salisbury		
			Shrewsbury		
			Sunderland		
			Tiverton		

Notes:
a Including Salford.
b Including Devonport.
c Including Gateshead
d Stoke and Burslem
e The Medway towns: Chatham, Rochester, and Gillingham
f Wolverhampton, Willenhall, Bilston and Wednesfield

Sources: The following sources were used in compiling the table. (1) Penelope J. Corfield, 'Urban Development in England and Wales in the Sixteenth and Seventeenth Centuries', in Donald C. Coleman and Arthur H. John (eds.), *Trade, Government and Economy in Pre-industrial England* (London, 1976), 214–247; (2) Corfield, *The Impact of English Towns, 1700–1800* (Oxford, 1982); (3) Frank V. Emery, 'England circa 1600', in H. Clifford Darby (ed.), *A New Historical Geography of England before 1600* (Cambridge, 1976), 248–301; (4) Charles Phythian-Adams, *Desolation of a city, Coventry and the Urban Crisis of the Late Middle Ages* (Cambridge, 1979); (5) John Patten, *English Towns 1500–1700* (Folkestone, 1978); (6) idem, 'Population Distribution in Norfolk and Suffolk during the Sixteenth and Seventeenth Centuries', *Transactions of the Institute of British Geographers*, LXV (1975), 45–65; (7) 1851 Census, Population tables 1, Numbers of inhabitants 1801–51, I, II, *Parliamentary Papers* (1852–3), LXXXV, LXXXVI; (8) C. M. Law, 'Some Notes on the Urban Population of England and Wales in the Eighteenth Century', *The Local Historian*, X (1972), 142–147; (9) Roger Finlay, *Population and Metropolis. The Demography of London, 1580–1650* (Cambridge, 1981); (10) 1801 Census, Enumeration, *Parliamentary Papers* (1802), VII.

The data were abstracted as follows with the numbers given in brackets relating to the sources listed above. London 1520, 1600: (1) 217. London 1660: (9), 60. London 1700, 1750: (2), 8. Other towns 1520: (4), 12 and (1), 222. Other towns 1600: (3), 294–298 and (5), 115. Other towns 1670: (5), 106; 109–110; 114, 116, 120 and (1), 239, 241. Other towns 1700: (1), 223. Other towns 1750: (8), 22–26. All towns 1801: (7).

Some of the estimates may refer to dates a dozen or more years away from the date at the head of the column, except in 1750 and 1801. Often different scholars suggest different totals, or the same scholar may present more than one estimate for the same place and period. An element of judgment and selection is therefore unavoidable in compiling a table of this type. In one instance a quoted estimate seemed improbable and has been changed: (5), Table 9, 109 gives a figure of 9000 for Cambridge in the 1670s, which seems implausibly high in view of the estimates for 1600 and 1700. In one or two cases (for example, Plymouth, 1670), I could find no figure for a year close to the target year and the total was therefore estimated.

don, only Newcastle increased its share of the national total (Table 1). Its surge in growth was no doubt partly due to London's extraordinary rise, since the coal trade down the east coast flourished as London grew and brought with it prosperity to Newcastle.[3]

The effect of the artificial boost given to urban growth outside London by the inclusion of several new towns which had reached 5000 in population between 1520 and 1600 can be estimated either by ignoring the new entrants on the 1600 list, or by basing the calculation on the full 1600 list. The group of nine provincial towns on the 1520 list displayed a collective growth of only about 15 per cent, sluggish growth during a period when the national total population rose by about 70 per cent. If, alternatively, the list of nineteen large provincial towns in 1600 is made the basis of measurements, a rather higher percentage growth figure results. In 1520 these towns housed a total population of about 107 000 (see Table 1, sources). By 1600 the total had risen to about 137 000, a rise of 28 per cent. Both calculations underline the point that the doubling of the population living in provincial towns shown in Table 2 is misleading, since it was preponderantly due to the recruitment of new towns into the category, and not to growth within the individual towns.

If London's growth is ignored, the urban growth pattern elsewhere conforms well to expectation. In the course of the sixteenth century, real incomes in England fell substantially. If the Phelps Brown and Hopkins index of real wages is used as a guide to the extent of the fall in living standards, it suggests a decline between 1520 and 1600 of over 40 per cent. Even if the index overstates the change, a significant deterioration is nonetheless probable and ought, in conformity with the model sketched earlier, to have acted as a brake on urban growth and to have reduced urban population in percentage terms. London remains an exception so important as to outweigh in aggregate faltering urban growth elsewhere, but its overall dominance should not be allowed to obscure the significance of trends in the provinces.[4]

3. The modesty of urban growth outside London may be overstated by concentrating on places with 5000 or more inhabitants. There is evidence to suggest that the smaller towns were growing more rapidly than the provincial centers. Using a total of 2000 rather than 5000 inhabitants to divide urban populations from the remainder would probably have resulted in an impression of greater buoyancy for the urban population in the sixteenth century. Charles Phythian-Adams, 'Urban Decay in Late Medieval England,' in Philip Abrams and Wrigley (eds.), *Towns in Societies. Essays in Economic History and Historical Sociology* (Cambridge, 1978), 171–172.
4. E. Henry Phelps Brown and Sheila V. Hopkins, 'Seven Centuries of the Price of Consumables, Compared with Builders' Wages', *Economica*, XXIII (1956), 296–314. The construction of a slightly modified version of the Phelps Brown and Hopkins index is described in Wrigley and Schofield, *Population History*,

TABLE 2   National, London, and other urban population estimates (thousands)

	c. 1520	c. 1600	c. 1670	c. 1700	c. 1750	1801
Population of England	2400	4110	4980	5060	5770	8660
London	55	200	475	575	675	960
Other urban population in towns with 5000 or more inhabitants	70	135	205	275	540	1420
Total urban	125	335	680	850	1215	2380
Urban population as a percentage of the national total						
London	2.25	5.0	9.5	11.5	11.5	11.0
Other urban	3.0	3.25	4.0	5.5	9.5	16.5
Total urban	5.25	8.25	13.5	17.0	21.0	27.5

Notes: The population totals and percentages have been rounded to emphasize the approximate nature of the calculations. National population totals refer to England, excluding Monmouth, and those for *c.* 1600, *c.* 1670, *c.* 1700, *c.* 1750 relate to the years 1601, 1671, 1701, and 1751.

All the estimates of urban populations given in this table are subject to substantial margins of error. This is true even for those for 1801 derived from the 1801 census. For example, Law's careful examination of the 1801 material in the general context of nineteenth-century censuses led him to suggest a total urban population in England and Wales of 3 009 260 (in towns of 2500 inhabitants or more) compared with Corfield's estimate of 2 725 171, using the same definition of urban. The former figure is 10% larger than the latter. All earlier totals are subject to far wider margins of error. Law, 'The Growth of Urban Population in England and Wales, 1801–1911', *Transactions of the Institute of British Geographers*, XLI (1976), 141; Corfield, *Impact of English Towns*, 8

Sources: English population totals 1600 to 1801: Wrigley and Roger S. Schofield, *The Population History of England, 1541–1871: A Reconstruction* (Cambridge, Mass., 1981), 208–209. The figure for 1520 is an estimate based on the discussions in ibid., 565–568.

London totals: Table 1.

Other urban totals: 1520, 1600, 1670, Table 1; 1700, 1750, and 1801, Corfield, *Impact of English Towns*, 8. The totals have been rounded and, in the case of the 1801 total, slightly reduced to reflect the fact that Corfield's estimates refer to England and Wales (by this date 3 Welsh towns exceeded 5000 in population).

In the seventeenth century circumstances changed greatly. England's population grew by less than a quarter over the century as a whole and was falling gently during its third quarter. The Phelps Brown and Hopkins index suggests that real wages bottomed out early in the century and had risen substantially by its end.[5] Urban growth went on apace whether judged in absolute or percentage terms. London continued to dominate the picture. By 1700 the capital housed about 11 per cent of the total national population, more than double the percentage of a century earlier. It had become the largest city in Western Europe and continued to dwarf all local rivals. But other towns also began to grow vigorously. They grew rather slowly in the first half of the century, but after 1670 their relative growth was at least as rapid as that of London. The smaller urban centers were now increasing far faster than the country as a whole. Their population more than doubled during the century, a rate of growth more than four times that of the national aggregate.

Measurement of urban growth is less bedevilled in the seventeenth century than it was in the previous century by the problem of 'drift' across the arbitrary 5000 dividing line between urban and rural. In the sixteenth century, the increase of population in towns of 5000 or more was about 95 per cent, judged crudely, but the increase in the towns on the 1600 list was only 28 per cent and only 15 per cent on the 1520 list. The comparable figures for the seventeenth century were more closely bunched at about 105, 60, and 46 per cent respectively.[6] Several major provincial centers, notably Norwich, Bristol, Newcastle, and Exeter, increased by between 50 and 100 per cent. A striking portent for the future was the appearance on the list for the first time of towns never previously of

---

Appendix 9. The 25-year centered moving average of the annual figures given in Table A9.2 fell by 44% between 1520 and 1600. David M. Palliser, 'Tawney's Century: Brave New World or Malthusian Trap?', *Economic History Review*, XXXV (1982), 349–351. Palliser suggests reasons to suspect that the Phelps Brown and Hopkins index overstates the extent of the fall in real incomes.

5. The centered 25-year moving average suggests a rise of 27% between 1600 and 1700. Both the extent of the rise and the timing of the end of the long fall in Tudor and early Stuart times are debatable. Bowden's index of the purchasing power of agricultural wages in southern England suggests that the beginning of a recovery may have been as late as the 1640s. From a stable plateau in the 1520s and 1530s (the index figure is 80 in both decades where 1460–9 = 100), his index falls by 35–40% by the 1590s and shows no subsequent decisive trend until the series ends in 1640–9. Peter Bowden, 'Statistical Appendix,' in Joan Thirsk (ed.), *The Agrarian History of England and Wales: IV, 1500–1640* (Cambridge, 1967), 865.

6. In order to calculate the 60% figure some town populations had to be estimated (i.e. for some of the towns appearing on the 1700 list but not the 1600 list in Table 1).

much note but later to herald a new age. In 1670 Birmingham, Manchester, and Leeds appear for the first time, and in 1700 Liverpool.

If the seventeenth century saw a notable acceleration of growth within an urban system still consisting largely of towns with long-familiar names, the eighteenth brought radical reordering of the urban hierarchy and further rapid urban growth. London, moreover, although still vastly larger than any other city, no longer stood out because of its rate of growth. In 1800 it comprised much the same proportion of the national population as it had 100 years before. Meanwhile, the share of other towns larger than 5000 in population increased dramatically, rising from 6 to 17 per cent of the national total, and for the first time surpassing London's share.

Growth was widely but very unevenly spread. London's old rivals fared less well than London in the main. Bristol grew rapidly, riding on the back of buoyant Atlantic trade, but several cities which had once figured prominently in the English urban hierarchy, including Norwich, Exeter, and York, grew less quickly than the population overall and ended the century with smaller fractions of the national total than at the beginning. For many centuries such towns had exchanged places in the premier urban league, but the league's membership had not greatly altered. By 1800, however, only Bristol, Newcastle, and Norwich of the old major regional centers remained among the country's ten largest towns. Manchester, Liverpool, and Birmingham stood second, third, and fourth after London. They ranged between 70 000 and 90 000 in population, having grown fiftyfold or more since the early sixteenth century.

Lower down the list a host of new names appeared. Several were the seats of new industry – Leeds, Sheffield, Stoke, Wolverhampton, Bolton, and Stockport; but others reflected changing social customs and new forms of expenditure. Bath, for example, with 33 000 inhabitants, was the twelfth largest town in England, a gracious monument to the new ways in which the wealthy and well born found it convenient to make or maintain contacts with each other or to pass their hours of leisure. Ports and dockyard towns also enjoyed vigorous growth. Plymouth and Portsmouth were among the country's largest towns, and Hull, Sunderland, Chatham, and Great Yarmouth all exceeded 15 000 in population at the time of the 1801 census (although not all of the towns in this category were new names).

The simplest model connecting real income and urban growth will no longer 'save the phenomena' for the eighteenth century. The sustained momentum of urban growth, accelerating toward the century's end, would suggest a parallel rise in real incomes, but in some parts of England the long-sustained rise in real wages had ceased before the middle of the eighteenth century: It had probably halted nationally by 1780, to be succeeded by a substantial fall lasting about thirty years.[7]

By the eighteenth century the assumption of a closed economy is even more unrealistic than for the sixteenth. External demand represented a substantial fraction of total demand in many industries, although it is easy to exaggerate the importance of overseas markets. Any increase in the relative importance of overseas trade, however, would stimulate urban growth, conspicuously in the case of ports like Bristol and Liverpool, but in a lesser degree also elsewhere. Equally, transport improvements within England increased the scale of internal trade. The average distance travelled by goods between producer and consumer probably also increased. Both trends must have stimulated employment in the urban centers through which goods passed.[8] The pattern of urban growth suggests that the deceleration in urban growth which might have been expected on the simplest possible view of the link between real incomes and urban growth affected the older centers in the expected fashion, but that the new features of the English economy imparted impetus to those towns most caught up in the new developments. London, affected by all of the various and conflicting influences on urban growth, occupied an intermediate position.

The extent of the contrast among the fortunes of different types of towns in the course of the early modern period is illustrated in Table 3. The choice of towns in each group is inevitably arbitrary, both in the sense that other sets might have been made up to represent the type in question, and in the sense that 'pure' types are rare in large towns since size and complexity of function are closely linked. The balance of market functions, craft industry, administrative services, and professional employment varied considerably among the set of ten historic regional centers, and two of them, Chester and Exeter, also had important port functions. Nevertheless, the contrast among the groups is sufficiently marked to make

7. The behavior of wages and prices and, *a fortiori*, of real wages, both regionally and nationally between 1700 and 1850 has been the subject of much controversy. There have been several valuable surveys of the issues recently, and also some new empirical work. Michael W. Flinn, 'Trends in Real Wages, 1750–1850,' *Economic History Review*, XXVII (1974), 395–411. G. Nicholas von Tunzelmann, 'Trends in Real Wages, 1750–1850, Revisited,' ibid., XXXII (1979), 33–49. Peter H. Lindert and Jeffrey G. Williamson, 'English Workers' Living Standards during the Industrial Revolution: A New Look', ibid., XXXVI (1983), 1–25.

8. On overseas trade see, e.g., R. P. Thomas and Donald N. McCloskey, 'Overseas Trade and Empire, 1700–1860,' in Roderick Floud and McCloskey (eds.), *The Economic History of Britain since 1700* (Cambridge, 1981), I, 87–102. An excellent summary of knowledge about inland transport may be found in John A. Chartres, *Internal Trade in England, 1500–1700* (London, 1977), 13–46.

TABLE 3 Patterns of growth. Urban growth in early modern England (thousands)

	Population totals					Percentage growth			
	c. 1520	c. 1600	c. 1700	c. 1750	1801	1600/1520	1700/1600	1750/1700	1801/1750
England	2400	4110	5060	5770	8660	71	23	14	50
London	55	200	575	675	960	264	188	17	42
10 historic regional centers[a]	62	73	107	126	153	18	47	18	21
8 established ports[b]	38	53	81	128	190	39	53	58	48
4 'new' manufacturing towns[c]	6	11	27	70	262	83	145	159	274

Notes:
a Norwich, York, Salisbury, Chester, Worcester, Exeter, Cambridge, Coventry, Shrewsbury, Gloucester.
b Bristol, Hull, Colchester, Newcastle, Ipswich, Great Yarmouth, King's Lynn, Southampton.
c Birmingham, Manchester, Leeds, Sheffield.
Sources: see source note to Table 1.

it unlikely that other choices made with the same distinction in mind would have produced a very different result.

The historic regional centers did not keep pace with national population growth over the early modern period as a whole. In the two middle periods, when real wages were rising, they experienced a faster population growth than the national average; in the sixteenth and later eighteenth centuries, however, when real wages were probably declining, their rate of growth fell well below the national average. Thus they exhibited what might be termed the classic pattern of relative growth in terms of the model of the relationship between income and urban growth described earlier.

At the other extreme, the four towns which in 1801 were the largest manufacturing towns in England were always growing faster than any other groups in the table, apart from London until 1700. Their rate of growth accelerated steadily throughout the three centuries, becoming so hectic in the last half-century that their population almost quadrupled in fifty years.

The established ports also grew with increasing speed, except in the last period, outstripping the national growth rate, except in the first and last periods. The slight fall in growth rate in this group in the later eighteenth century was due in part to the extraordinarily rapid growth of Liverpool. If Liverpool were included in the group, the percentage growth of population in the group would rise to 72 between 1700 and 1750 and to 82 between 1750 and 1801.

London contrasts sharply with each of the other three groups, growing far more quickly until the end of the seventeenth century. It became so large that in 1700 it housed more than two-and-a-half times as many people as the other three groups combined. Thereafter, however, London was outpaced by both the ports and the new manufacturing towns, and did not even match the national average growth rate.

The foregoing is both compressed and simplistic. Uncertainties of definition, estimation, and periodization have been dealt with summarily or ignored. Nor has the nature as opposed to the quantity of urban growth been explored. It is possible, for example, that much of the growth of sixteenth-century London was a 'push' phenomenon linked to the scale and depth of rural poverty, and due to what Clark termed 'subsistence' migration. Later, in contrast, movement to the capital may have had a greater 'pull' element as living standards rose and 'betterment' migration came to predominate.[9]

It remains reasonable to argue, however, that there were important links between some types of urban growth and real income

---

9. Peter Clark, 'The Migrant in Kentish Towns, 1580–1640,' in *idem* and Paul Slack (eds.), *Crisis and Order in English Towns, 1500–1700* (London, 1972), 117–163.

trends in early modern England, although urban growth is not to be explained solely in this way. Neither the headlong growth of London in the sixteenth and early seventeenth centuries, nor the acceleration of urban growth in the new manufacturing towns in the later eighteenth century, is easily explicable in terms of the behaviour of domestic real income per head, yet both were developments of massive importance.

URBAN GROWTH AND AGRICULTURE

Even if the causes of urban growth are elusive, the fact of growth remains, and some of its implications can be examined. In any pre-industrial community, agriculture is the dominant form of economic activity and the levels of productivity per head achieved in agriculture necessarily govern the growth opportunities of other industries. This point was so well known to those living in pre-industrial economies as scarcely to warrant remark, and, when political economy reached its first great statement in the *Wealth of Nations*, Smith made the examination of this issue one of his chief concerns.[10]

But agricultural productivity has proved difficult to measure directly. One way of measuring it indirectly is to consider the extent of the rise in agricultural productivity suggested by the course of urban growth in England, while also taking into account changes in the occupational structure of the rural component of the total population.

To simplify calculations I have assumed that consumption of food per head did not vary between 1520 and 1800 and that England was neither a net importer nor a net exporter of food. The first assumption is doubtful and the second is demonstrably false, especially during the eighteenth century. In its early decades England was a substantial net exporter of grain, and toward the century's end large quantities of meat and grain reached the English market

---

10. Smith's chapter, 'Of the Different Employment of Capitals', includes a strong plea for agricultural investment as the ultimate basis of national productive capacity. 'The capital employed in agriculture, therefore, not only puts into motion a greater quantity of productive labour than any capital employed in manufactures, but in proportion, too, to the quantity of productive labour which it employs it adds a much greater value to the annual produce of the land and labour of the country, to the real wealth and revenue of its inhabitants. Of all the ways in which a capital can be employed, it is by far the most advantageous to the society.' Smith, *Wealth of Nations*, 161–162.

from Ireland. Yet it is convenient to begin with such simple assumptions.[11]

In 1520 the urban percentage was 5.25: in 1801, 27.5 (Table 2). This movement in itself suggests a useful gain in agricultural productivity. In 1520, 100 rural families fed 106 families in all; in 1801, 138 $(100 \times 100/[100 - 5.25] = 106: 100 \times 100/[100 - 27.5] = 138)$. The level of productivity in 1800 was 30 per cent higher than in 1520, far from a negligible increase, even if scarcely sensational. But any such exercise must understate the extent of the increase in agricultural productivity if there also is a decline in the proportion of the rural labor force engaged in agriculture.

There can be no reasonable doubt that such a decline occurred. In certain rural areas in the eighteenth century the growth in non-agricultural employment was so great as to dwarf the remaining agricultural population. Framework knitting became the dominant source of employment in many Leicestershire villages. In parts of Warwickshire and Staffordshire there was very rapid growth in the manufacture of small metal wares – nails, chains, buckets, etc. In much of south Lancashire and the West Riding of Yorkshire, the textile industry, whether cotton or wool, provided income for many more men and women than did agriculture. The steady growth of coal production in Northumberland and Durham produced the same result in substantial tracts of these counties. Even in more strongly agricultural counties in the south, lace making, straw plaiting, and the like provided much employment for women.

Moreover, in areas which attracted little industry there was often a growth in employment in service industries. In the rare cases where parish registers provide data on occupation over long periods of time, it is a commonplace to note a growth in specialist employments not previously encountered, especially during the eighteenth

---

11. Brinley Thomas has recently estimated the relationship between the value of imports of grain, meat, and butter and the income of British agriculture. From 1814 to 1816, total imports of the three commodities represented 6.4% of British agricultural income and of these imports 70% came from Ireland. See his article in this issue, 'Escaping from Constraints: The Industrial Revolution in a Malthusian Context', Table 2. Jones recently estimated that 90% of the population of Great Britain was fed from domestic agricultural production in 1800. Eric L. Jones, 'Agriculture, 1700–80', in Floud and McCloskey (eds.), *Economic History of Britain*, I, 68. In contrast, in the first half of the eighteenth century, English net grain exports were a substantial fraction of total production, reaching perhaps 6% of gross domestic grain output about the mid-century. Phyllis Deane and W. A. Cole, *British Economic Growth, 1688–1959* (Cambridge, 1962), 65; David Ormrod, 'Dutch Commercial and Industrial Decline and British Growth in the Late Seventeenth and Early Eighteenth Centuries', in Frederick Krantz and Paul M. Hohenberg (eds.), *Failed Transitions to Modern Industrial Society: Renaissance Italy and Seventeenth-Century Holland* (Montreal, 1975), 36–43.

century. A small town like Colyton, for instance, even provided a living for a peruke maker in the 1760s.

Almost everywhere the proportion of men described as laborers, husbandmen, yeomen, or farmers declined as a proportion of all the occupations mentioned. Many craftsmen also owned scraps of land and their produce was of crucial significance in their domestic economy. Even those who worked no land might nevertheless have been drawn into the labor of harvest. However, the reverse was often also true. Those to whom an agricultural occupation was attributed might turn their hands to craftwork during the seasonal slack periods on the farms.

Ideally, it would be preferable to measure hours worked in different forms of employment rather than to treat each member of the work force as uniquely engaged in a single occupation, but for the present purpose it is enough to show that there was a major fall in the proportion of the rural labor force in agricultural occupations.

By 1800 a tolerably accurate picture of rural employment structure can be drawn. Deane and Cole estimated that 35.9 per cent of the labor force in 1801 was engaged in agriculture, forestry, and fishing. If we assume for simplicity's sake that none of these workers was living in towns, then it follows that only some 50 per cent of the rural population were engaged in agriculture, given that the rural population comprised 72.5 per cent of the whole ($35.9/72.5 \times 100 = 49.5$). The comparable figure at earlier periods is difficult to establish, although useful clues may be found in the work of King and Massie. In order to make revised estimates of the changes in agricultural productivity, I have assumed that 80 per cent of the rural labor force was in agriculture in 1520; that this figure declined very slowly to 70 per cent by 1670, with the bulk of the fall occurring

---

12. Deane and Cole's estimate of the percentage of the labor force, quoted above, may be found in their *British Economic Growth*, 142. The first serious attempt to quantify the occupational and social structure of England before 1801 was that carried out by Gregory King in 1688. King, *Natural and Political Observations and Conclusions upon the State and Condition of England, 1696*, reprinted in *The Earliest Classics*, with an introduction by Peter Laslett (London, 1973), 48–49. When Deane and Cole considered King's estimates they suggested that 'between 75 and 80 percent of the occupied population was primarily engaged in agriculture'. Deane and Cole, *British Economic Growth*, 3. This figure is implausibly high. Having regard to the total national populations in 1688 and 1801 (4.90 and 8.66 millions) and the proportions in agriculture (say 75% and 35.9%), such a high proportion in 1688 would imply a fall in the absolute scale of agricultural employment of more than 15% over the intervening century.

Lindert has recently reexamined changes in English occupational structure in the eighteenth century, but the results, at least for agriculture, do not appear convincing. The percentage of the male labor force employed in agriculture is estimated at 22.3 in 1700, 26.1 in 1740, and 13.7 in 1811. Lindert, *English Occupations, 1670–1811* (Davis, 1980), 46–47. See also note 14 below.

TABLE 4 Urban, rural agricultural, and rural non-agricultural populations (millions)

	(1) Total population	(2) Urban population	(3) Rural population	(4) Proportion of rural population in agriculture	(5) Rural agricultural population (3) × (4)	(6) Rural non-agricultural population (3) −(5)	(7) Total population per 100 rural agricultural (1)/(5)	(8) Column (7) 1520 = 100
1520	2.40	0.13	2.27	0.80	1.82	0.45	132	100
1600	4.11	0.34	3.77	0.76	2.87	0.90	143	108
1670	4.98	0.68	4.30	0.70	3.01	1.29	165	125
1700	5.06	0.85	4.21	0.66	2.78	1.43	182	138
1750	5.77	1.22	4.55	0.58	2.64	1.91	219	166
1801	8.66	2.38	6.28	0.50	3.14	3.14	276	209

Percentages of total population in major categories

	(1) Urban	(2) Rural agricultural	(3) Rural non-agricultural	(4) Total
1520	5.5	76.0	18.5	100
1600	8.0	70.0	22.0	100
1670	13.5	60.5	26.0	100
1700	17.0	55.0	28.0	100
1750	21.0	46.0	33.0	100
1801	27.5	36.25	36.25	100

Populations relative to 1800 total (1800 = 100)

1520	5.5	58	14	28
1600	14	91	29	47
1670	29	96	41	58
1700	36	89	46	58
1750	51	84	61	67
1801	100	100	100	100

Relative population growth by period (100 × total at later date/total at earlier date)

1600/1520	262	158	200	171
1670/1600	197	105	143	121
1700/1670	127	92	111	102
1750/1700	144	95	134	114
1801/1750	195	119	164	150

Source: For population totals in top panel see Table 3 and discussion in text.

after 1600; that it fell more quickly to 66 per cent in 1700; and then moved linearly in the eighteenth century to 50 per cent in 1801.[12]

These assumptions allow the population to be subdivided into three groups rather than two: the urban population, the rural population engaged in agriculture, and the rural population dependent on employment other than in agriculture. At the same time, changes in output per head can be calculated. The results are set out in Table 4.

The table suggests that the rural agricultural population scarcely changed in size for a century and a half between 1600 and 1750 and that even in 1800 it was only a tenth larger than 200 years earlier. It is not surprising, therefore, that the table should show a striking rise in agricultural productivity, and indeed, to the degree that the assumptions which have been made in constructing the table are justified, the conclusions are inescapable. The crucial assumptions are that England was not a significant net importer or exporter of food; that the growth of the percentage of the population living in towns followed the pattern set out in Table 2; and that the proportion of the rural population engaged in non-agricultural production rose from 20 to 50 per cent between 1520 and 1800. For the second and third assumptions the central issue is the extent of change over the period as a whole; the question of its timing, although fascinating, is of lesser importance.[13]

Precision about any of the three basic assumptions is beyond reach. Regarding the first, it is worth noting that because England was a substantial food exporter in the early eighteenth century, agricultural productivity was probably understated at that period. Equally, by the end of the century, England had become a net importer, especially from Ireland, which implies the opposite. The second set of assumptions concerning urban growth is probably sufficiently accurate to avoid significant error. The third assumption relates to the agricultural proportion of the rural population. The figure for 1800 is fairly firmly grounded in the evidence of the early

---

13. In connection with the argument of this paragraph it may be noted that Jones estimated that the agricultural population of England and Wales increased by 8.5% in the eighteenth century. Jones, 'Agriculture, 1700–80,' 71. Crafts' recent calculations produce results broadly similar to those implied by Table 4 in relation to agricultural productivity. He estimated that agricultural output rose at the following percentage rates per annum over the periods 1710–1740, 1740–1780, and 1780–1800: 0.9, 0.5, and 0.6. This change implies a total increase in output of almost exactly 80% over the 90-year period as a whole. Assuming that the agricultural labor force grew by 13% over the century, as Table 4 suggests, the increase in output per man, at 59%, is closely similar to that which may be calculated from column 7 of Table 4 (52%). Nicholas F. R. Crafts, 'The Eighteenth Century: A Survey,' in Floud and McCloskey (eds.), *Economic History of Britain*, 1, Tables 1.1, 1.2, 2–3.

censuses, but earlier estimates become increasingly fallible. Any figure for the early sixteenth century must be largely guesswork. A lower figure would reduce the apparent gain in agricultural productivity, but only a radically lower figure would greatly change the general picture.[14]

Other assumptions could be used to construct Table 4. For example, if one were to assume that 15 percent of English food requirements were met by imports in 1800, and that agriculture

14. It is possible to use the work of King and of Joseph Massie to test how far the estimates made by contemporaries agree with those in Table 4. In 1760, out of a total of 1 472 000 families, Massie supposed that 210 000 were freeholders, 155 000 farmers, and 200 000 husbandmen, making a total of 565 000 clearly engaged in agriculture. In addition he estimated that there were 200 000 families of laborers outside London. Not all of these would be agricultural laborers. Massie reckoned that there were 20 000 laborers in London, only slightly short of the number to be expected on the assumption that laborers were as numerous per 1000 population inside cities as in the countryside. We may assume, therefore, that a further 15 000–20 000 were to be found in other urban centers, and it is probable that a further group, although living in the countryside, were employed outside agriculture, especially in the building trades (which were not separately itemized by Massie). Assume that these, too, were about 20 000 in number; then the overall total of those families engaged in agriculture would be *c*.730 000, or fractionally less than one-half of the national total. The comparable figure in Table 4, that for 1750, is 46%, a broadly similar figure.

A comparison with King (1688) is more difficult to make because of the form in which he drew up his famous table. King's totals for families of freeholders and farmers are not greatly different from Massie's (180 000 and 150 000 respectively), but he gave no separate figure for husbandmen. Instead, all other families which might be engaged in agriculture appear in two categories: laboring people and out servants (364 000); and cottagers and paupers (400 000). Most of those engaged in industrial crafts – weavers, glovers, knitters, tanners, carpenters, coopers, sawyers, thatchers, smiths, wrights, cordwainers, and so on – must have been included in one of these two categories (King lists only 60 000 families of artisans or handicraft workers in the entire country), together with all laboring families living in London or other towns. Assuming that half of the cottars were what Massie would have termed husbandmen and half were engaged in industrial crafts – a split similar to that found in Massie's separate tabulation of the two categories; that 15% of all laborers were in towns (where at this date about 15% of the population lived); and that of the remaining 309 000 laborers, 25 000 were employed outside agriculture – the total of families employed in agriculture is 814 000 or 60% of the national total of 1 361 000 families. The comparable figure in Table 4 is about 58% (1670, 60.5%; 1700, 55.0%). There is a convenient reproduction of both King's and Massie's tables and a discussion of the difficulties in comparing them in Peter Mathias, 'The Social Structure in the Eighteenth Century: A Calculation by Joseph Massie,' in *idem, The Transformation of England. Essays in the Economic and Social History of England in the Eighteenth Century* (London, 1979), 171–189. See note 12 for the provenance of King's table. Massie's table is derived from a broadsheet dated Jan. 10, 1760, entitled *A computation of the money that hath been exorbitantly raised upon the people of Great Britain by the sugar planters in one year from January 1759 to January 1760; shewing how much money a family of each rank, degree or class hath lost by that rapacious monopoly.*

employed 55 percent of the rural labor force rather than 50 percent, while other assumption were unchanged, the estimated overall rise in agricultural productivity would be reduced from 109 to 61 per cent. If one were to go still further, reducing the 1520 figure in column 4 from 0.80 to 0.70 and retaining the modified assumptions for 1801, the figure would drop even more to 41 percent, but this figure is improbably low. On present evidence, therefore, although the particular figure given in Table 4 is arbitrary, there is a strong likelihood that the true figure lies between 60 and 100 percent.[15]

The phasing of changes in the proportion of the rural labor force engaged in agriculture, no less than their scale, is also largely a matter of judgment, rather than a demonstrable pattern. The same pressures which kept urban growth outside London at such modest proportions in the sixteenth century are likely to have restricted employment opportunities outside agriculture. It therefore seems appropriate to make only a small reduction in the proportion of the rural population in agriculture between 1520 and 1600. Thereafter the pace of change probably accelerated.

One further implicit assumption deserves discussion. Individual intake of food measured in calories varies within fairly narrow limits. There is little evidence of widespread malnutrition so extreme as to cause death in early modern England. With rare and usually local exceptions even severe harvest failure did not provoke heavy mortalities. It is improbable (although also undemonstrable) that mean personal daily calorie intake varied in a manner which would significantly undermine the line of argument followed above. Nevertheless, periods of rising real income must have been periods in which food consumption per head rose, with the opposite happening in times of declining living standards. In addition there were changes in the composition of individual diet as incomes rose or fell. Meat was a luxury to the pauper but a commonplace to more prosperous members of society, and there were secular shifts in the

15. Sixteenth-century estimates of occupational structure are inevitably insecurely based, and the dominance of agriculture is probably overstated. The muster roll taken in 1608 for Gloucestershire, excluding Bristol, for example, suggests that only 46.2% of the adult male population between the ages of 20 and 60 were engaged in agriculture. The comparable figure when the 1811 census was taken was virtually the same at 45.8%. The economic history of Gloucestershire is far from typical of the country as a whole, but Gloucestershire affords an example which should caution us against assuming too readily that rural non-agricultural employment was always very limited in Tudor or early Stuart England. A. J. and R. H. Tawney, 'An Occupational Census of the Seventeenth Century,' *Economic History Review*, V (1934), 25–46. 1811 Census, Enumeration, *Parliamentary Papers* (1812), XI, 121.

relative prices of grain and meat which reflected the long-term trends of the average real income.[16]

Since such foods as meat and dairy produce needed larger inputs of labor, as well as land and capital, to produce the same number of calories of food as grain, it might seem that an allowance should be made for the impact of secular real income trends in attempting an individual measure of agricultural productivity. This consideration in turn would imply that agricultural productivity per head was rising faster during the seventeenth and early eighteenth centuries than suggested by Table 4, but less quickly during the later eighteenth century. It also suggests that it may have been falling in the sixteenth century, a finding in keeping with common sense, since the rural agricultural population is estimated to have risen by almost 60 percent between 1520 and 1600, a scale of increase likely to have involved a falling marginal productivity of labor and much concealed or overt underemployment.

Making an explicit allowance for real income changes, however, presents problems. At present, real income data are based on slender foundations and involve wide margins of uncertainty. Little is known about any changes which may have occurred over time in the income elasticity of demand for food. The only existing real wage series covering the whole period, that of Phelps Brown and Hopkins, stood higher in 1800 than it had two centuries earlier. The apparent gains in agricultural productivity over the seventeenth and eighteenth centuries as a whole are therefore unlikely to be overstated because of a failure to take real income explicitly into account.[17]

16. On harvest fluctuations and mortality, see Wrigley and Schofield, *Population History*, 320–340, 370–382, appendix 10. The principal exception to the rule that harvest failure did not provoke big mortalities was northwestern England in the sixteenth and early seventeenth centuries. Andrew B. Appleby, *Famine in Tudor and Stuart England* (Stanford, 1978). Estimating income elasticity of demand for food in eighteenth-century England presents great difficulties because of lack of relevant data. In a recent review of the limited evidence, Crafts concluded that the most probable figure for the late eighteenth and early nineteenth centuries was 0.7. Crafts, 'Income Elasticities of Demand and the Release of Labour by Agriculture during the Industrial Revolution', *Journal of European Economic History*, IX (1980), 154–159. Kussmaul provides a convenient graph of the relative prices of grain and meat. It bears a strong resemblance to an inverted graph of the Phelps Brown and Hopkins real wage series, although the match is by no means perfect, especially in the early seventeenth and late eighteenth centuries. Ann Kussmaul, *Servants in Husbandry in Early Modern England* (Cambridge, 1981), Fig. 6.3, 104. Real wage data based on Phelps Brown and Hopkins are set out in Wrigley and Schofield, *Population History*, appendix 9, and shown graphically in ibid., Fig. 10.5, 414.
17. The Phelps Brown and Hopkins index stood at 409 on average for the 11 harvest years 1595–96 to 1605–06 compared with 507 in the period 1795–96 to 1805–06. Ibid., 642–644.

Labor released from agriculture is available to increase other forms of production. The gross changes were striking. The rural agricultural population in 1520 was 76 percent of the total population in 1520 but only 36 percent in 1800 (Table 4). Non-agricultural employment therefore grew from 24 to 64 per cent of the whole. This difference may overstate the extent of the change in that some of the growth of non-agricultural employment represented jobs created by increased specialization of function. A carter, for example, making his living by moving to market goods previously taken there by local farmers, may be placed outside agriculture in an occupational breakdown, but undertakes a task previously performed by the farmer.

Yet the change was great. Smith argued that a surplus of agricultural production over the food needs of the farming population might either be consumed unproductively by, say, retinues of servants, or productively, if the surplus maintained an army of 'manufacturers' whose output added to the wealth of the community as a whole. In early modern England the growth of employment in industry and commerce is a testimony to the predominantly 'productive' use to which the growing relative surpluses in the agricultural sector were put. Smith considered that the scale of such growth was largely conditioned by the extent of the rise in agricultural productivity. He did not envisage the much more radical type of change which has come to be called an industrial revolution, nor is there any compelling reason to suppose that even increases in agricultural productivity as striking as those achieved in England between 1600 and 1800 must necessarily engender an industrial revolution. Yet the scale of change in early modern England bears stressing. It stands out more clearly if comparison is made with other countries.[18]

URBAN GROWTH ON THE CONTINENT

De Vries has recently published an informative analysis of urban growth patterns between 1500 and 1800 for Europe as a whole and for some major regional subdivisions. In it he makes use of an em-

18. On Smith's views on productive and unproductive labor, see the chapter in the *Wealth of Nations*, 'Of the accumulation of capital, or of productive and unproductive labor'. An attempt to clarify the contingent nature of the circumstances which preceded and accompanied the industrial revolution may be found in Wrigley, 'The Process of Modernization and the Industrial Revolution in England', *Journal of Interdisciplinary History*, III (1972), 225–259.

pirical relationship between the sizes of the towns and their position in a rank ordering whereby the difference in their populations is proportional to the difference in their rank orders. Thus $p_i = p_1/i$ where p_1 is the population of the largest town and i refers to the rank order of a town after all towns have been arranged in descending order of size. The population of the fifth largest town may therefore be expected to be a fifth of that of the largest, and so on. If logarithmic scales are used to plot the population and rank coordinates of each town, the resulting distribution in the archetypal case will fall on a straight line with a slope of 45 degrees. In practice the slope of the line may vary somewhat from the 45-degree slope suggested by the strictly proportional relationship, and the first few points plotted are sometimes aberrant, as when the largest settlement is much bigger than the second largest. But regularities in town size distributions are often impressive, and any anomalies within a data set or changes in the angle of the plotted slope over time may prove illuminating.[19]

By compiling rank-size data for European towns at intervals over a three-century period starting in 1500, de Vries was able to establish changes in the slope and shape of the urban hierarchy sufficiently pronounced and consistent to distinguish three major periods, as shown in Figure 1. At the beginning of the sixteenth century the slope was gentle and there was a flat 'top' to the distribution. He attributed the latter to the still strongly regional character of the European economy, which was insufficiently articulated to produce leading urban centers of the size implied by the slope of the lower part of the distribution. During the sixteenth century the rank-size plot gradually straightened. The continent-wide economy was becoming more integrated, and cities such as London, Paris, and Amsterdam grew rapidly as they assumed urban functions over wide hinterlands.

A second period then supervened, running from about the early seventeenth to the mid-eighteenth century. In general, in this period, the larger the town, the more rapidly it grew, so that a disproportionate part of the overall rise in urban population took place in the larger towns. The rank-size line pivoted slowly round a point close to its lowest reading and thus grew steadily steeper. After about 1750, however, urban growth changed in character again and a third period started. The rank-size line moved outward from the origin of the graph, implying a rise in the number of towns in all size categories, but there was more rapid growth in the number of

19. Jan de Vries, 'Patterns of Urbanization in Preindustrial Europe, 1500–1800', in H. Schmal (ed.), *Patterns of European Urbanization since 1500* (London, 1981), 77–109.

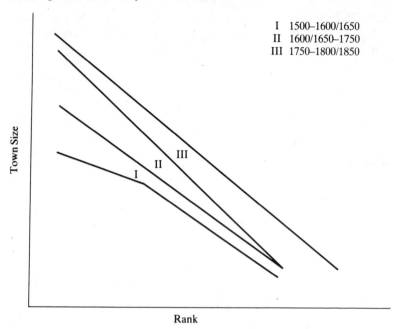

Fig. 1 Urbanization in Europe (source: de Vries, 'Patterns of Urbanization')

TABLE 5   Urbanization in England and the Continent. Percentage of total populations in towns with 10 000 or more people

	1500	*1600*	*1650*	*1700*	*1750*	*1800*
England	3.2[a]	6.1	10.8[b]	13.4	17.5	24.0
North and West Europe[c]	6.0	8.1	10.7	13.0	13.8	14.7
Europe[d]	6.1	8.0	9.3	9.5	9.9	10.6

Notes:
a *c.* 1520
b *c.* 1670
c Scandinavia, Netherlands, Belgium, England, Scotland, Wales and Ireland.
d The countries included in Europe are Germany, France, Switzerland, Italy, Spain, and Portugal together with those listed in note c.
Sources: For England see source notes to Tables 1 and 2. Other data from de Vries, 'Patterns of Urbanization,' 88.

TABLE 6 Urbanization in England and the Continent (revised).
Percentage of total population in towns with 10 000 or more people

	1600	*1700*	*1750*	*1800*
England	6.1	13.4	17.5	24.0
North and West Europe minus England	9.2	12.8	12.1	10.0
Europe minus England	8.1	9.2	9.4	9.5

Notes: De Vries provides estimates of population totals for north and
west Europe and for Europe as a whole for 1600, 1700, 1750, and 1800 in
the work listed below (although not for the other dates in Table 5). This
information and the urban percentages given in Table 5 make it possible
to calculate the size of the urban populations. The English totals can
then be removed from both the urban and total populations and the
percentages recalculated.
Sources: For England see source notes to Tables 1 and 2. For other data
see source notes to Table 5; de Vries, *The Economy of Europe in an
Age of Crisis* (Cambridge, 1976), 5.

smaller towns than in the number of larger ones. The slope became
less steep once more. The sequence of changes was shared by the
major subdivisions of Europe used by de Vries, although the timing
of the changes varied somewhat. The pattern of change in England,
however, was unlike that on the continent.

As Table 5 shows, England began the period with an unusually
slight proportion of her population living in large towns, but passed
the European average in the mid-seventeenth century and the
northwest European average by 1700. By the beginning of the nineteenth century England was relatively heavily urbanized. Events
there, however, were so different from those elsewhere as to distort patterns of change when England is included in some larger
grouping.

It is instructive to remove England from both the urban and the
overall population totals used to generate urban percentages for continental areas. The result is shown in Table 6. Urbanization in
northern and western Europe recedes rather than advancing substantially in the eighteenth century, although the scale of advance in the
seventeenth century is little altered. In Europe as a whole the exclusion of England slows the increase in urbanization in the
seventeenth century and brings it almost to a halt in the
eighteenth.[20] Over the full 200-year period the urban percentage

20. This finding might be thought spurious if de Vries' estimates of the population
    of English towns and those shown in Table 1 were widely divergent. But a
    detailed comparison of his data with those of Table 1 suggests that this is a
    groundless fear.

quadrupled in England, scarcely changed in the rest of north-western Europe, and advanced rather modestly on the continent as a whole. The English experience appears to be unique.

The extent of the contrast also comes home forcefully if de Vries' estimates are reworked to permit another comparison to be made, as in Table 7. The urban population of Europe more than doubled between 1600 and 1800, but the total population rose by almost 60 percent, so that much of the rise in urban population was caused by the rise in overall numbers rather than by an increase in the proportion of the population living in towns. Column 4 shows how the urban population would have grown if the urban percentage had stayed at the level prevailing in 1600. The totals in column 5 show the net gain in urban population at each later date compared with 1600: that is, the number by which the urban population exceeded what would have obtained had the urban percentage not changed in the interim. The second panel of the table repeats the calculation for England.

By combining information from the two upper panels, the proportion of total European urban growth that occurred in England can be calculated for the periods 1600 to 1700, 1700 to 1750, and 1750 to 1800. The proportion rises steadily from a third in the seventeenth century to 70 percent in the second half of the eighteenth. Over the two-century period as a whole the proportion exceeded one half. Since England contained only 5.8 percent of the population of Europe in 1600 and only 7.7 percent even in 1800, these proportions are an extraordinary testimony to the extent of the difference in urban growth between the island and the continent.

De Vries placed particular emphasis on the absence of growth in the smaller towns between 1600 and 1750, a period which he defined as the age of the rural proletariat. He argued that urban growth was almost entirely confined to very large cities, with 80 percent of all growth taking place in towns with 40,000 inhabitants or more. These towns were almost all capital cities or large ports, the development of which was stimulated by the growth in administrative, military, and legal employment in both absolutist and constitutional states, or by the development of long-distance, often extra-European trade. Smaller towns stagnated or lost population, afflicted by loss of political autonomy and by the 'abandonment of cities as locations for many of the most labour-absorbing industries'.[21] The balance of advantage favored protoindustrial development in the countryside.

There was unquestionably much growth in industrial employment in rural England during this period. At the same time London, combining administrative, commercial, and trading dominance, enjoyed

---

21. De Vries, 'Patterns of Urbanization', 101.

TABLE 7 The English share of European urban growth, 1600–1800 (populations in millions)

	(1) Total population	(2) Urban population	(3) Urban total (1) × (2)	(4) Urban total at 1600 proportion	(5) Net gain on 1600 (3) − (4)	(6) Net gain on last date (difference between successive totals in (5))
EUROPE[a]						
1600	70.6	0.080	5.65	5.65	0.00	
1700	75.0	0.095	7.13	6.00	1.13	1.13
1750	86.6	0.099	8.57	6.93	1.64	0.51
1800	111.8	0.106	11.85	8.94	2.91	1.27
ENGLAND						
1600	4.11	0.061[b]	0.249	0.249	0.000	
1700	5.06	0.134[b]	0.680	0.309	0.371	0.371
1750	5.77	0.175[b]	1.012	0.352	0.661	0.290
1800	8.66	0.240[b]	2.079	0.528	1.551	0.890

English percentage of total European net urban gain

1600/1700 100(0.371/1.13) = 33
1700/1750 100(0.290/0.51) = 57
1750/1800 100(0.890/1.27) = 70
1600/1800 100(1.551/2.91) = 53

Notes: a For a list of the countries comprising 'Europe', see notes to Table 5.
      b These proportions are derived from the column (3) totals rather than vice-versa as in the top panel.

Sources: For England see source notes to Tables 1 and 2.
         For Europe see source notes to Table 5.

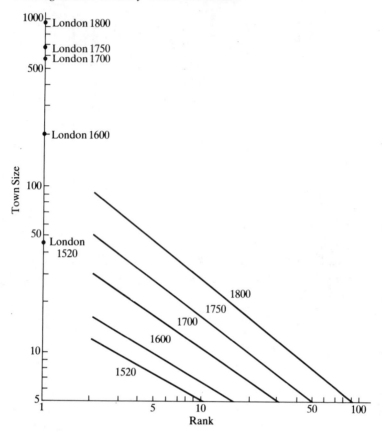

Fig. 2 Urbanization in England

an astonishing expansion. But neither the development of rural industry nor the growth of London precluded an equally remarkable surge of urban growth elsewhere in England. Other towns grew by much the same absolute amount as London between 1600 and 1750 and proportionally were growing even faster than London (Table 2). Towns with between 5000 and 10 000 inhabitants doubled in number from fifteen to thirty-one, while over the same period the number in Europe minus England fell from 372 to 331. Figure 2 shows rank-size plots for England. Like Figure 1 it is schematically drawn: empirical data plots would show points falling on either side of the straight lines for each date. Although the number of towns is small and the presence of London severely distorts the top of the distribution, the lines emphasize how different England was from the continent (compare Figure 1).[22]

De Vries' study has the admirable virtue of providing a framework of comparison for smaller units by epitomizing the characteristics of Europe as a whole. This framework helps to bring out the distinctiveness of English history, and it may be further examined by considering comparative data about England's two greatest rivals, Holland and France.

HOLLAND AND FRANCE

Even in 1800 England was a less urbanized country than Holland. Already in the early sixteenth century many Dutch people were town dwellers and their numbers increased rapidly as the century wore on. In this period the course of real wages in Holland was almost the reverse of the comparable pattern in England: real wages rose to a peak around 1610, the date when the English series approached its nadir, and urbanization continued. The percentage of the population living in towns grew from about 21 to about 29 percent, and since the total population of Holland was rising moderately quickly at the time, the absolute number of town dwellers rose even faster, from about 260 000 to about 435 000. There followed a period of half a century during which Dutch real wages fell back somewhat, just as a recovery was starting in England, maintaining the inverse movement in the two countries for a full century. After the 1650s, however, Dutch real wages rose rapidly once more to a new and substantially higher peak in the 1690s, after which they fell, uncertainly at first, but more quickly and without interruption from the 1740s until the end of the century. The trend of urban percentages moved broadly in sympathy with real wage movements, reaching a high point around 1700, when about 39 percent of the Dutch population was urban. It then declined slowly until, by 1800, it was not much higher than the English figure. Some Dutch towns experienced severe falls in population, and, since the population as a whole grew only modestly

---

22. On the growth of London, see Wrigley, 'A Simple Model of London's Importance in Changing English Society and Economy', *Past & Present*, 37 (1967), 44–70. The totals of towns with between 5000 and 10 000 inhabitants are taken from de Vries, 'Patterns of Urbanization', 93. For sources of data about English towns see source notes to Table 1.

in the eighteenth century, the total number of town dwellers fell slightly.[23]

Dutch rural population trends also warrant notice. During the long period of urban growth from 1550 to 1700 the rural population grew only modestly. It was 17 percent larger at the latter than the former date. In the eighteenth century, however, when there was urban decline and real wages languished, rural population numbers rose by 20 percent. In England in the eighteenth century the rural population grew by 49 percent overall, but the rural agricultural population by only 13 percent, even though the overall population growth in England during the century reached 71 percent compared with a Dutch figure of only 11 percent. If, therefore, it is safe to assume that the Dutch rural agricultural population was rising as fast as the rural population as a whole – a plausible supposition at a time of falling real wages – rural agricultural population totals in the two countries must have moved almost exactly in step in the eighteenth century, even though their overall rates of population growth diverged so markedly. Conversely, in the sixteenth century, while impoverishment increased in England and its rural agricultural population grew fast (by 58 percent between 1520 and 1600), in Holland there can have been little comparable increase, although the population of Holland was rising fairly rapidly. In columns 5 to 7 of Table 8 the rural population is subdivided between agricultural and other employment in conformity with arbitrary assumptions, the basis of which is explained in the notes to the table. To the degree that the figures mirror reality, they underline the points just made. The golden age of the Dutch rural economy was clearly one free from increasing pressure on the land, but it was succeeded by more trying times.[24]

A comparison of the urban sectors in England and Holland should not be pressed too far. It would make no sense, for example, to use estimates of urban percentages in Holland as an indirect measure of agricultural productivity, since Holland was a large importer of agricultural products, especially Baltic grain, and was not broadly self-sufficient as was England in the early modern period. Yet the beneficial effects of urban growth on Dutch agriculture in

23. For Dutch real wages, see de Vries, 'The Population and Economy of the Pre-industrial Netherlands', in *Journal of Interdisciplinary History*, 15, no. 4 (1985), Fig. 2. See Table 8 notes for sources for the estimates of Dutch urban populations. A. van der Woude provides much detail of urban fortunes in Holland between 1525 and 1795 in 'Demografische ontwikkeling van de Noordelijke Nederlanden 1500–1800', in *Algemene Geschiedenis der Nederlanden*, V (1980), 134–139.
24. De Vries, 'Population and Economy of Preindustrial Netherlands', Fig. 2, charts the fall in real wages from a late-seventeenth-century peak which, in a period of static or falling population, was eloquent testimony to Dutch difficulties.

TABLE 8 Dutch urban and rural population estimates (thousands)

	(1) Total population	(2) Proportion urban	(3) Population (1) × (2)	(4) Rural population (1) − (3)	(5) Rural agricultural proportion	(6) Rural agricultural population (4) × (5)	(7) Rural non-agricultural population (4) − (6)
1550	1250	0.21	260	990	0.75	745	245
1600	1500	0.29	435	1065	0.705	750	315
1650	1875	0.37	700	1175	0.66	775	400
1700	1900	0.39	740	1160	0.66	768	395
1750	1925	0.35	675	1250	0.66	825	425
1800	2100	0.33	700	1400	0.66	925	475

Notes: Urban is defined as relating to towns of 5000 inhabitants or more.

The population totals in columns (3) and (6) have been rounded to emphasize the approximate and arbitrary nature of the calculation.

The proportion urban in column (2) was estimated from data given by de Vries. His data refer to the percentages of the population living in towns containing 2500 inhabitants or more, and in towns containing 10 000 inhabitants or more. I assumed that half of those living in towns with 2500 to 9999 inhabitants were living in towns of 5000 to 9999 inhabitants. For some dates de Vries provides data only for the urban percentage in towns of 10 000 or more inhabitants, but sufficient paired estimates are given for other dates to make it feasible to provide plausible estimates at half-century intervals.

The rural agricultural proportions (column 5) stem from the following observations and assumptions. Mitchell provides data which show that 44.1% of the total labor force engaged in agriculture was 66% (0.441/0.67 = 0.66). I have assumed arbitrarily that in Holland in the mid-sixteenth century the comparable figure was 75%, a slightly lower figure than that used in the parallel calculation for England, because Holland was far more urbanized than England in the sixteenth century and non-agricultural rural employment was probably more common. I have assumed that it fell to 0.66 linearly over the next century but did not change thereafter as the great Dutch growth spurt ended.

Sources: Column 1: J. A. Faber, H. K. Roessingh, B. H. Slicher Van Bath, Van der Woude, and H. J. van Xanten, 'Population Changes and Economic Developments in the Netherlands: A Historical Survey', *A. A. G. Bijdragen*, XII (1965), 110.

Column 2: de Vries, 'Population and the Labor Market in the Netherlands, 1500–1850', paper given at the Conference on British Demographic History (1982), Table 1.

Column 5: Brian R. Mitchell, *European Historical Statistics, 1750–1975* (Cambridge, 1981; 2nd rev. ed.), 167 (see also notes above).

TABLE 9 French urban and rural population estimates (thousands)

	(1) Total population	(2) Urban population	(3) Percentage urban	(4) Rural population	(5) Rural agricultural population	(6) Rural agricultural population (4) × (5)	(7) Rural non-agricultural population (4) × (6)
1500	15 500	1410	9.1	14 090	0.80	11 270	2820
1600	19 000	1660	8.7	17 340	0.755	13 100	4240
1700	21 500	2350	10.9	19 150	0.71	13 600	5550
1750	24 500	2530	10.3	21 970	0.685	15 050	6920
1800	29 100	3220	11.1	25 880	0.66	17 080	8800

Notes: Urban is defined as relating to towns of 5000 inhabitants or more. France was treated as if it occupied its present territory; therefore towns such as Lille were included in urban population totals. The urban population in column (2) was estimated in several stages. Chandler and Fox provide estimates of urban populations of towns of 20 000 inhabitants or more for the dates shown. De Vries gives totals of towns in several size categories ('000s) 20–29, 30–39, 40–49, 50–99, and 100 and over. Where the total for a town given by Chandler and Fox falls into the size category given by de Vries, this total was used. Otherwise de Vries' calculations were preferred and a town population was assumed to be at the centerpoint of the size range (none fell into the open-ended top category). The discrepancies between the two sources, as might be expected, were much more marked at the earlier than the later dates. The number of towns of 20 000 or more inhabitants in the two sources were as follows at the five successive dates, Chandler and Fox in parentheses: 14 (20), 20 (15), 24 (26), 31 (32), 32 (36). De Vries' totals of towns between 10 000 and 20 000 were multiplied by 13 500 to give a population total for this size range of towns. These two operations provide a figure for all towns with populations of 10 000 or more, leaving the problem of estimating the number of French towns in the size range between 5000 and 10 000 inhabitants and above. It can be shown that the rank-size distribution of French towns was similar to that for Europe as measured by the ratio of the number of all towns above 10 000 in population to the number in the size range between 10 000 and 20 000. The ratio of the number of towns in the size range between 5000 and 10 000 to the number of towns larger than 10 000 derived from de Vries' data was used to estimate the total of smaller towns in France. (The ratios in question at the five successive dates are 2.15, 1.76, 1.60, 1.43, and 1.56; of these the third is interpolated from the second and fourth since de Vries provides no data for 1700.) The total of towns in the size range between 5000 and 10 000 estimated in this fashion was multiplied by 6500 to give a population total for each date. The breakdown of the individual totals was as follows ('000s):

Population totals by town size class

	20 and over	10–19	5–9	Total
1500	637	284	488	1409
1600	866	311	481	1658
1700	1389	405	559	2353
1750	1691	324	514	2529
1800	1810	621	793	3224

The proportion of the rural population engaged in agriculture is based on the following data and assumptions. In 1851 the proportion of the population living in towns of 5000 or more inhabitants was 17.9% (Pouthas, 22, 76). In 1856 the proportion of the total French labor force engaged in agriculture was 51.7%. In the mid-nineteenth century, therefore, about 63% of the rural labor force worked on the land (100 × (0.517/0.821) = 63). I have assumed that the comparable figure in 1800 was 66%. As in the case of England, I assumed that in France the comparable figure in the early sixteenth century was 80%. The proportions at intermediate dates were obtained by rough linear interpolation.

Sources: Column (1): Jacques Dupâquier, *La population française aux XVIIe et XVIIIe siècles* (Paris, 1979), 11, 34, 81; M. Reinhard, A. Armengaud, and Dupâquier, *Histoire générale de la population mondiale* (Paris, 1968; 3rd edn), 108, 119–120; C. McEvedy and Richard Jones, Atlas of World Population History (London, 1978), 55–60. Column (2): T. Chandler and G. Fox, 300 Years of Urban Growth (New York, 1974), 15–19, 21; de Vries, 'Patterns of Urbanization,' Tables 3.2, 3.4, 3.7. Column (5): C. H. Pouthas, *La population française pendant la première moitié du XIXe siècle* (Paris, 1965); Mitchell, *European Historical Statistics*, 163.

promoting specialization and making it easier to achieve higher production per man and per farm reflect the same processes at work in Holland as London's growth produced in England. Again, the Dutch passenger canal network was the transport wonder of its age, a response to urban growth and the closely associated rise in living standards, just as similar developments in eighteenth-century England promoted the investment of capital in turnpike roads and the construction of a new canal network.[25]

Both Holland and England, therefore, vividly illustrate the beneficial interactions among urban growth, rising living standards, and a surge in agricultural productivity which was possible within the context of an early modern economy. The food needs of towns were met through the operation of a commercial market in foodstuffs. Farming units benefited from specialization and avoided the subdivision and fragmentation of holdings which were commonly the bane of peasant societies when population increased. By the late eighteenth century yields per acre were substantially higher in England and the Netherlands than elsewhere in Europe, having roughly doubled over the previous two centuries. Yet in neither country was the agriculturally employed population much larger in 1800 than in 1600.[26]

The example of Holland also shows, however, that such progress was not necessarily a passport to further success. Smith, aware like so many of his contemporaries of the exceptional economic achievements of Holland, used it as an example of the limits to growth which must beset any country at some stage, making it difficult to sustain the gains of the past, much less secure further advances. The tide began to ebb in eighteenth-century Holland. Urban population fell slightly, even though numbers rose modestly overall. Real wages sagged. Far from forming part of the vanguard of the industrial revolution, Holland moved into the industrial era later than most of Western Europe, and even as late as 1850 was no more urbanized than it had been in the later seventeenth century.[27]

France provides a very different contrast to the case of England. Some relevant data are given in Table 9. The steps leading to the

25. Idem, 'Barges and Capitalism. Passenger Transportation in the Dutch Economy, 1632–1839', *A. A. G. Bijdragen*, XXI (1978), 33–398.
26. For yield data, see Slicher van Bath, *The Agrarian History of Western Europe, A. D. 500–1850* (London, 1963), 280–282.
27. Smith makes the general observation that, 'In a country which had acquired that full complement of riches which the nature of its soil and climate, and its situation with respect to other countries allowed it to acquire, which could, therefore, advance no further, and which was not going backwards, both the wages of labour and the profits of stock would, probably, be very low.' He subsequently suggested that Holland was approaching this state. Smith, *Wealth of Nations*, 43–44.

estimates given in the table are explained in the table notes. As with the English and Dutch estimates, they are subject to a margin of error which in some cases may be substantial because the empirical data base is insecure or inconsistent, because some of the assumptions are questionable, or because the chains of reasoning used to produce some of the estimates were long and there may have been a compounding of errors. Despite such uncertainties, the contrast between France and England stands out so strongly that no reasonable change in the assumptions used would significantly change the picture.

In 1500 France was not only a far more populous country than England, but it was also more urbanized. Within the present borders of France there were already fourteen towns with a population of more than 20 000 and twenty-one with populations between 10 000 and 20 000, while in England only London exceeded 20 000, and probably only two other towns, Norwich and Bristol, had 10 000 or more inhabitants. London was not only smaller than Paris but was also smaller than Lyon. Overall France was almost twice as urban as England, although much less urban than Holland, but, in the next three centuries, French towns grew hardly more quickly than the French population as a whole. France closely resembled de Vries' 'Europe' both in level of urbanization and in its change over time (Table 5). By 1800 the degree of urbanization reached in England was approaching three times the French level. Moreover, the proportion of the English rural population employed outside agriculture grew much faster than in France, and agricultural productivity, using the rough measure employed *faute de mieux* in this article, progressed far more rapidly in England than in France.[28]

Population always grew faster in England than in France, at times dramatically so (Tables 2 and 9), yet, because of the far faster urban growth in England and the swifter rise in the proportion of the rural population employed outside agriculture, the growth of rural agricultural employment was actually slower in England than in France, except in the sixteenth century. Between 1600 and 1800 the number of those dependent upon agriculture for a living in France grew by 30 percent, whereas in England the comparable figure was 9 percent. (Over the same period the national population growth rates were 53 and 111 percent respectively.) These apparently exact percentages should be viewed with reserve, but it is probably safe to assert that the rural agricultural population in England grew no

---

28. The French town population estimates are taken from de Vries, 'Patterns of Urbanization', 82–85. In some instances the effects of revolution and war caused a sharp drop in French city populations in the last decade of the eighteenth century. Jacques Dupâquier, *La population française aux XVII et XVII siècles* (Paris, 1979), 91–92.

faster than its counterpart in France. If the data used are taken on trust, inferences about comparative trends in agricultural productivity in the two countries are possible.

The upper panel of Table 10 sets out information for England and France in an indexed form to make it easier to appreciate the divergent course of development which characterized them. The value for 1600 has in each case been made equal to 100. In the sixteenth century, the differences between the two countries were chiefly related to the much higher rate of growth of the English population rather than to differences in the relative proportions of the populations falling into the urban, rural agricultural, and rural non-agricultural categories. After 1600, the contrasts between the two countries grew more pronounced. England continued to grow more quickly overall, but the rural agricultural element in its population grew little over the next two centuries. Indeed, it appears to have been falling for much of the time, whereas urban growth was meteoric; the rise in the rural non-agricultural component was also pronounced. Growth in France was much more balanced and, as a result, although the total population grew less than in England, the rural agricultural population grew appreciably faster.

If it were safe to assume that the level of food consumption per head was much the same in the two countries, that the estimates of rural agricultural population are accurate, and that each country may be regarded as having supplied its own food needs (except that in this table imports were assumed to meet 10 percent of English food requirements in 1800), then it is a simple matter to compare both levels of productivity in agriculture and their rates of change over time in the two countries. They are given in the lower panel of the table. The figures of columns 1 and 2 represent an absolute measure of productivity per head of the rural agricultural population whereas those in columns 3 and 4 index changes over time.

The extent of the contrast between England and France may well be understated by the table, both because it is reasonable to suppose that consumption of food per head was higher in England than in France since English real incomes appear to have been the higher of the two, and also because a higher proportion of the output of English agriculture may have been used as industrial raw material rather than food. Land and labor used for the raising of sheep for wool, for example, cannot also be used to grow corn. The effect, however, is difficult to quantify since output in such cases often consisted both of food and of industrial raw materials. Producing wool for cloth or hides for the leather industry also meant producing meat for human consumption. Pure industrial land usage, as with flax for linen, was a rarer phenomenon. The use of the land to provide 'fuel' for horses or oxen also suggests that the contrast between the two countries may be greater than appears in the table, since in England,

TABLE 10 English and French growth patterns compared

Populations relative to 1600 total (1600 = 100)

	England				France			
	Urban	*Rural agricultural*	*Rural non-agricultural*	*Total*		*Urban*	*Rural agricultural*	*Rural non-agricultural*	*Total*
1520	38	63	50	58	1500	85	86	67	82
1600	100	100	100	100	1600	100	100	100	100
1700	250	97	159	123	1700	142	104	131	113
1750	359	92	212	140	1750	152	· 115	163	129
1750	259	92	212	140	1800	194	130	208	153

Total population per 100 agricultural

	England (1)	*France (2)*	*England column (1) 1520 = 100 (3)*	*France column (2) 1500 = 100 (4)*
1520	132	1500 138	1520 100	1500 100
1600	143	1600 145	1600 108	1600 105
1700	182	1700 158	1700 138	1700 114
1750	219	1750 163	1750 166	1750 118
1801	248	1800 170	1801 188	1800 123

Note: See text for modification made at 1801 figure in bottom panel, column (1) and (3)

Sources: Tables 4 and 9

75

by the later eighteenth century, a substantial proportion of horses were employed outside agriculture on turnpike roads, on canal towpaths, and particularly for urban transportation of men and goods.[29]

In England, as in Holland at an earlier date, urban growth, rising productivity in agriculture, and improving real incomes were interwoven with one another, and were mutually reinforcing for long periods. The French economy did not follow the same pattern. On the assumptions used in constructing Table 9, there is evidence of increased pressure on the land in the eighteenth century. In a peasant economy this pressure may provoke serious economic difficulties and increase the proportion of excessively subdivided holdings, conforming to de Vries' peasant model of a rural economy. Both England and Holland accord better with his specialization model.[30]

Arguments couched in this manner are always too simplistic. It is misleading, for example, to treat pre-industrial countries as if they were homogeneous units. There were major differences among different areas, even within the smallest of the three countries considered. Sometimes even intraprovincial differences in Holland were marked: interprovincial contrasts could rival those among countries. The regional variety of a country as large as France was still more notable. It could scarcely be otherwise when it is recalled that France contained more than ten times as many people as Holland and had an area fifteen times greater. Furthermore, better knowledge would no doubt cause significant alterations to be made to many of the tables on which the arguments advanced in this article are based. Yet the contrasts and similarities between the three countries would probably remain even if perfect knowledge were available.[31]

29. Thirsk presents good reasons to suppose that the value of industrial crops rose rapidly in the later sixteenth and seventeenth centuries, and also provides abundant evidence of the enormous increase in rural employment outside agriculture. Thirsk, *Economic Policy and Projects. The Development of a Consumer Society in Early Modern England* (Oxford, 1978). There are some guarded attempts to quantify the scale of industrial crops and new food crops in ibid., 177–178.

   Thompson estimates that there were almost half a million (487 000) horses in use outside agriculture in 1811 (riding horses, carriage horses, post horses, trade horses, and those in the stage coach trade). At the level of consumption of oats and hay per animal which Thompson thinks appropriate, and on reasonable assumptions about yields of oats and hay per acre, sustaining such a large population must have meant devoting about 2 million acres to their fodder. Agriculture at that date is estimated to have required about 800 000 horses. F. M. L. Thompson, 'Nineteenth-Century Horse Sense', *Economic History Review*, XXIX (1976), 78, 80.

30. De Vries, *The Dutch Rural Economy in the Golden Age, 1500–1700* (New Haven, 1974), 1–21.

31. For national population totals see Tables 8 and 9. The area of France today is 212 209 square miles: that of Holland 13 967. Their areas varied somewhat over the early modern period.

It is not difficult to find convincing reasons why a major advance in agricultural productivity is a prerequisite of industrial growth. Only if resources can be spared from the task of ensuring an adequate supply of foodstuffs can a larger scale of industrial production be attempted. It may seem quaint that Smith should have associated the prosperity of, say, Sheffield's industry with the efficiency of agriculture in the vicinity of the town, but his remark is a parable of the circumstances needed for industrial success in a pre-industrial age.[32]

England was singularly fortunate in this regard. Output per head in agriculture appears to have risen by three quarters between the beginning of the seventeenth and the end of the eighteenth century. The annual gain in agricultural productivity per head was modest – about 0.3 percent – yet it permitted a more rapid overall rate of population growth than that found in either France or Holland, while simultaneously releasing into secondary and tertiary employment a far higher proportion of the active population than in any other European country. By 1800 little more than a third of the English labor force was engaged in agriculture at a time when it is improbable that the comparable figure elsewhere in Europe, apart from the Netherlands, was less than 55 to 60 percent. In many countries it was substantially higher.[33]

The pace of English population growth in the early modern period was exceptional. Between the mid-sixteenth and the early nineteenth century England's population grew by about 280 percent. The population of other major European countries rose much less rapidly. Germany, France, the Netherlands, Spain, and Italy all grew by between 50 and 80 percent over the same period. The demographic mechanisms by which the growth of England came about are now fairly well understood, but at one remove the problem of explaining the contrast remains. In this connection it is important to pay heed to the probability that there was nothing unusual in the rate of growth of English *rural agricultural* population, unless it was that it grew so slowly, especially after 1600. The great

---

32. See Smith, *Wealth of Nations*, 180–181.
33. In Finland in 1754, 79% of all economically active heads of families were engaged in agriculture, forestry, or fishing; in 1805, 82%. There are data for many European countries from about the middle of the nineteenth century. In the following list the percentages refer to the proportion of the total labor force (male and female) engaged in agriculture, forestry, or fishing, unless otherwise indicated: Belgium 1846, 51%; Denmark 1850, 49% (family heads); France 1856, 52%; Ireland 1851, 48%; Netherlands 1849, 44%; Spain 1860, 70% (males only); Sweden 1860, 64%; Great Britain 1851, 22%. Mitchell, *European Historical Statistics 1750–1975*, Table C1. Half a century earlier it is virtually certain that each of the comparable percentages would have been higher, sometimes substantially so.

bulk of the overall increase took place in that part of the population which made its living *outside* agriculture. This was what made England so distinctive.[34]

In one sense an explanation of English agricultural improvement may be sought in the relatively rapid and uninterrupted growth in the urban sector of the English economy, well able to afford food but producing none itself. The extraordinary stimulus to improvement afforded by the growth of London, which in 1500 was not even one of the dozen largest cities in Europe, but by 1700 was larger than any other, was probably the most important single factor in engendering agricultural improvement. The momentum first given by the growth of London was carried forward later by the more general urban growth in the later seventeenth and eighteenth centuries. It encouraged both change within agriculture itself and in a host of associated institutions and activities: transport improvement, credit facilities, capital markets, and commercial exchange. The joint effect of rising productivity and increasing urbanization also fostered a great expansion in rural employment outside agriculture. The combination of a steadily rising demand for goods and services other than food with a far more sophisticated market mechanism for exciting and satisfying such a demand was the basis of prosperity for the industries in the countryside.

Yet the reasons for the exceptional growth of London from the early sixteenth to the late seventeenth century remain imperfectly understood. Its rise both deserves and demands much more attention than it has received. Understanding of the phenomenon is likely to benefit especially from study of the connection between the development of the nation state under the Tudors and Stuarts and the growth of the capital city, and from considering London's fortunes within a wide framework of analysis of European commercial exchange.

Urban growth toward the end of the early modern period presents problems of interpretation no less difficult than those at its beginning. During the eighteenth century the urban hierarchy of England was turned upside down. The new industrial towns and port cities of the north and the midlands thrust their way past all rivals other than London. Only Bristol and Newcastle, among the traditional regional centers, matched the new challenge, and then only because they could benefit from the stimuli which had forced the pace of the growth in places like Liverpool and Sunderland. Many once-great

34. Wrigley, 'The Growth of Population in Eighteenth-Century England: a Conundrum Resolved', *Past & Present*, 98 (1983), 122–125. The secular changes in fertility and mortality which largely governed population growth rates in England are described in Wrigley and Schofield, *Population History*, 192–284.

centers were on the way to the pleasant obscurity of county rather than national fame – York, Exeter, Chester, Worcester, and Salisbury.

The upsetting of the old urban hierarchy in England was, at the time, an event without recent precedent in European history. Elsewhere the exact ranking of major cities in each country varied from time to time, but it was rare for tiny settlements to develop into major centers. The same lists of large urban centers may be found century after century only slightly rearranged. Occasionally one of the smaller centers made progress through the ranks. Atlantic and colonial trade brought Bordeaux and Nantes rapid advancement between 1500 and 1800, for example, but revolutionary changes were rare. The progress of the new centers in England was such, however, that not merely had Liverpool and Manchester outpaced all of their English rivals other than London in 1800, but by 1850 they were the seventh and ninth largest cities in Europe, and the largest anywhere in Europe other than those which were capital cities, an extraordinary tribute to their economic vitality unassisted by the employment in government, the professions, and the arts associated with capital cities.[35]

The history of urban growth in England was distinctive. The contrast with the course of events elsewhere in Europe was especially notable between 1600 and 1750, since the paralysis which affected all but the largest towns on the continent was absent in England. The expansion of secondary employment in the countryside was not a bar to urban growth in England in the manner hypothesized by de Vries for Europe as a whole. This fact may afford an important clue to the differences between England and her continental neighbors in real income levels or trends, in relative wage levels in town and country, in the terms of trade between the two, in urban institutions, or in still other factors.

In this article, however, I have concentrated on the narrower topic of the scale and speed of urban growth and the indirect measurement of the gain in agricultural productivity per head, which roughly doubled in England between 1600 and 1800. By the standards of the recent past, a doubling in agricultural productivity over a two-century span of time is not a startling achievement, but, in terms of the pre-industrial world, it is much more impressive and set England apart from the great bulk of continental Europe, conferring on the former advantages denied to economies unable to release

---

35. Chandler and Fox, *3,000 years of Urban Growth*, 20. The first nine in order of size were London, Paris, Constantinople, St. Petersburg, Berlin, Vienna, Liverpool, Naples, and Manchester.

more than a tiny fraction of the labor force from work with the flock or plow.[36]

Measuring agricultural advance through urban growth falls well short of *explaining* either phenomenon. It is easy to see how these developments might reinforce one another, but the fact that similar cases were so rare, and that when they did occur they tended to lose momentum after a while, suggests that noting the logical possibility of such a link is only a first step toward understanding what took place. The most fundamental and intriguing question may concern the circumstances in which Ricardo's law of declining, marginal returns to additional unit inputs of labor and capital may be circumvented in a land long fully settled. This law, if it had universal and invariable application, would prohibit a sustained development of the kind which took place in England.[37]

The population of England increased more than 3.5 times between the early sixteenth and the early nineteenth century without becoming dependent, other than marginally, on food imports. Some new land was taken into farming use, but the bulk of the increased output must have been obtained from land already under cultivation. Moreover, after 1600 there was little increase in the agricultural labor force.

What served to neutralize the operation of declining marginal returns? The usual answer given to this question is innovation. If other things were not equal – if new methods of farming had been introduced which significantly enhanced the productivity of labor and capital – then the operation of Ricardo's principle could have been postponed, indefinitely if the flow of suitable innovations were sufficiently sustained. In a sense this must be the right answer but, because it is inescapable, it may be unilluminating, for, although it may be logically necessary, it was historically contingent. Relief from such a source was not always or even commonly forthcoming. Can anything be found in the circumstances of early modern England which provides an answer to this conundrum?

To attempt a full examination of this issue is beyond the scope of this article, but one of its aspects may bear a slight elaboration. There was a remarkably strong and regular positive relationship between the long-term rate of growth of population and the

36. Grigg provides information about rates of growth in labor productivity in agriculture in Denmark, France, the United States, and the United Kingdom in the late nineteenth and early twentieth centuries, and for all major subdivisions of the world since 1960. David B. Grigg, *The Dynamics of Agricultural Change* (London, 1982), 171–172. Rates as high as 5% per annum have been commonplace in developed countries in recent years.

37. David Ricardo, *On the Principles of Political Economy and Taxation* (London, 1817).

comparable rate of change in food prices in England throughout the early modern period until 1800. At first sight this relationship suggests a uniform and inhibiting tension between population growth and the capacity to sustain rising numbers. But, although the tension was constant, it does not follow that all the demographic and economic variables involved stood in the same relationship to each other throughout. We have seen, for example, that there were major changes in national occupational structure and in agricultural productivity per head. The relationship between population growth and food prices may prove to have been common to England and other countries, but the changing structure of the component variables was not usually found elsewhere. The tension appears to have been beneficial and dynamic in England, when so often it was static and debilitating.[38]

Innovation may be the key to overcoming Ricardian constraints, but inasmuch as what happened in England was so rarely paralleled in other pre-industrial economies, it seems doubtful whether innovation could be counted upon to be forthcoming in response to need. When, as in England, events took a more favorable turn, the explanation may be found not in the urgency of human need, nor in the immediate price dynamics of the market place, nor in the accident of individual inventiveness, but in the unusual structural characteristics of the prevailing situation.

If, on the one hand, it were safe to assume that a community always exploited its knowledge of production methods to the full, it would follow that innovation meant the introduction of some element into the productive system which was previously unknown. If, on the other hand, there were a range of alternatives to existing practice capable of raising productivity, which were held in reserve because current circumstances did not encourage or even allow of their use, the nature of the case would be changed.[39]

---

38. On the relationship between the rates of change in population and food prices, see Wrigley and Schofield, *Population History*, Fig. 10.2. From the mid-sixteenth to the late eighteenth centuries the relationship was strikingly linear. This in itself may be suggestive. If there had been very tight constraints upon agricultural expansion, a curvilinear relationship might have been expected, with a steeper rise in price than in population as conditions worsened. Its absence may reflect the existence of an unusual capacity to rise to the challenge of increased demand on the part of English agriculture, especially when it is remembered that the absolute rate of population growth was at times quite high, approaching 1% per annum in the late sixteenth century and exceeding it in the late eighteenth. I owe this comment to Schofield's reflections on the point.

39. Some years ago Boserup made effective use of one form of this argument, but her model was one in which the changed methods of agriculture adopted to meet the challenge of rising population resulted in the broad maintenance of a given level of output per head per annum at the cost of a rise in the number of hours

It may not be sufficient to look exclusively at changes in technology to explain a rise in productivity – new crops, altered cultivation practices, improved breeding techniques, and so on; nor to turn to the gains in productivity per head arising from increasing specialization of function, the chief proximate cause of enhanced productivity in Smith's analysis of the question. Other developments need to be taken into account if they encourage the exploitation of previously untapped potential and thereby transform living standards and growth prospects. It is in this context that the exceptional scale and speed of urban growth and its particular nature were so important.[40]

worked per annum. I have in mind changes which substantially increase labor productivity whether measured by the hour or by the year, although a part of the latter may be achieved because the workload becomes less markedly seasonal and therefore there are fewer periods during the year when labor is intermittent. Ester Boserup, *The Conditions of Agricultural Growth* (London, 1965), 41–55.

40. Some further aspects of the gain in agricultural output per man and per acre are examined in Wrigley, 'Some Reflections on Corn Yields and Prices in Pre-industrial Economies', in John Walter and Schofield (eds.), *Death and the Social Order*, forthcoming.

Chapter 3

COUNTRY, COUNTY AND TOWN: PATTERNS OF REGIONAL EVOLUTION IN ENGLAND¹

Alan Everitt

[*Transactions of the Royal Historical Society*, 5th ser., 29 (1979)]

Alan Everitt's published work covers a dauntingly wide range of subjects from early to modern times, but he has always displayed a particular interest in urban and local history. These twin concerns come together in the article reprinted here. For readers of this volume the obvious focus of interest is the author's clear and elegant analysis of the English county town during its Georgian heyday. Six features are highlighted: the town's wide and increasingly varied occupational structure; its role as an inland entrepôt; its position as a centre of professional and entrepreneurial activity; leisured gentry life; culture; and craftsmanship. Everitt's exposition of these characteristics reveals the economic diversity that underlay the county town's Hanoverian prosperity, a well-being which contrasts with the difficulties many such centres had experienced at some point in the sixteenth and seventeenth centuries. In reading this piece it is tempting to treat the lengthy introduction only cursorily, and advance rapidly to the meat of the argument about the Georgian town. But this would be a mistake. In his preamble Everitt demonstrates how important he believes the concepts of region and locality are in understanding the basic features of preindustrial society. In this context he sees town and country as part of an organic regional unit, interacting closely in a way which shaped the identity of each. The notion of the county community, which Everitt was so influential in developing and which underpins the main argument of the article, has recently been subject to some criticism, raising doubts as to what extent a shire town drew upon a specific and rigorously defined county constituency.

1. A fuller version of pp. 97–111 was given as the Gregynog Lectures at the University College of Wales, Aberystwyth, in 1976.

I

It is a remarkable fact, and one that needs to be pondered, that almost all our current regional terms in this country are of very recent origin. Expressions like Tyneside and Merseyside, the West Midlands and the North-East, have no very lengthy lineage; such phrases as the Home Counties cannot be traced back beyond the early decades of the railway era;[2] the present usage even of a genuine historic name like Wessex is no more than an antiquarian revival; while the current reanimation of Mercia seems to be chiefly attributable to a contemporary police force. Perhaps the only regional name of this kind with a continuous history to the present day is East Anglia. In other words, behind most of our modern expressions, ideas and preconceptions lie implicit that were not necessarily of much significance to the people of earlier centuries. A phrase like the Home Counties, for example, implies a kind of regional unity between the shires surrounding London which until recent centuries – and in many respects until recent generations – is entirely fallacious. There was no connexion between the origins of settlement, for example, in Hertfordshire and in Sussex, and next to none between settlement in Essex and in Kent. Even in the Civil War period there was singularly little contact and no cohesion, as parliament quickly found to its cost, between the counties surrounding the capital.

These facts will bear thinking about. Most of us probably find it difficult to rid our minds of the unconscious preconceptions implicit in regional expressions like these. In studying the evolution of contemporary society, moreover, they obviously have a certain validity, and it would be cavalier to suggest that we should abandon them altogether. Yet there are dangers in reading them back into the past, and of attributing to them a kind of historic unity which in fact is of recent origin. It is not simply that the generalizations they give rise to are often likely to prove spurious, but that they usually impose the wrong kind of regional pattern upon the landscape of history. The tapestry of local and regional variation in England, as it appeared to our forebears, was more elaborately wrought, and more changing in its character, than such terms suggest.

As historians, what exactly do we mean, or ought we to mean, by a 'region'? In England this is a particularly difficult question to answer, and the purpose of this paper is to indicate something of

---

2. The *Oxford English Dictionary* gives no quotations to indicate the origin of this term. I have not been able to trace it before the 1870s, when it was used by Robert Furley in *A History of the Weald of Kent* (3 vols., Ashford, 1871–4). It probably derives from the Home Circuit of the assize judges.

the character of its complexity. To begin with, regions vary greatly in kind. There is a clear distinction between what one might call a 'conscious' region, on one hand, an area with a sense of its own identity, a sense of belonging together, and, on the other hand, a region which is rather a perception of historians or geographers, and which probably had no conscious significance for contemporaries. The geographers' distinction between the Highland Zone and the Lowland Zone is one example of this latter type of 'unconscious' region; what W. G. Hoskins once described in an illuminating phrase as the 'peripheral counties' of England is another; the vernacular architects' perception of a zone in which the longhouse was the characteristic form of traditional farm-building is yet another. In their own context these are useful expressions; they relate to real ideas; but one cannot say that they relate to a 'conscious' region, with its own sense of unity and identity.

Then, secondly, regional definitions may vary with the kind of social order, or class, that one is thinking of, particularly perhaps in recent centuries. In the early modern period, for example, the county came to have a meaning and a coherence for the gentry of the time which it can rarely have had for husbandmen, craftsmen, and labourers. Not that those of non-gentle status had no consciousness of the county unit; in some areas, such as Cornwall and Kent, they certainly had, at any rate in times of crisis, when the shire tended to act together as a united body. But they did not form part of a single interrelated community of families, as the county gentry themselves often did. A little later, we can trace the development of another kind of social region based in the leisured classes: the 'neighbourhood', or local visiting area of what came to be called 'carriage' families:[3] a peculiarly English kind of locality which figures prominently in our nineteenth-century literature – in the novels of Jane Austen, for example – but which can usually have had little meaning at other levels of society.

Thirdly, and most difficult of all to take account of, is the fact that regions are not necessarily constant or static units: there is a kaleidoscopic character about them. Whereas one can say that local communities, like Leicester, Norwich, or Tolpuddle, have always remained continuously identifiable, and in a sense the same place, one cannot say this of the regional pattern of this country. Some kinds of region, it is true, such as the country or *pays* of this paper – Dartmoor or the Cotswolds, for instance – have remained similar in extent for centuries. Such areas, moreover, often have a longer and more continuous influence on provincial development than we

---

3. See, for example, my 'Kentish Family Portrait' in *Rural Change and Urban Growth, 1500–1800*, ed. C. W. Chalklin and M. A. Havinden (London, 1974), pp. 193–4.

sometimes realize. The fact that at the present time the parliamentary constituencies of North Kent – Dartford, Gravesend, Rochester, Gillingham, and Faversham – all tend to be marginal Labour/Conservative seats arises partly from characteristics in their economy and society whose ultimate origins may be traced back for many centuries, in some sense even to the roots of Kentish settlement itself. To put it briefly, they belong to a tract of countryside that since Roman times has always formed the more workaday part of the county. Nevertheless, taken as a whole, the basic regional pattern in this country has in many ways not remained constant: it has been an evolutionary pattern. Not only have regional boundaries changed: at a more fundamental level, new kinds or types of region have from time to time come into existence and overlaid or transformed the old. Up to a point, after all, the reorganization of local government a few years ago, whatever we may think of its all too evident defects, was a recognition of that fact.

Of these diverse types of region, the two that will be discussed more particularly in this paper are the 'country' and the 'county'. The former term is not used here to denote 'country' as opposed to 'town', or 'country' as opposed to 'court', but 'country' in the old sense of a 'countryside' or a *pays*. This particular meaning of the word has largely died out in the common speech of English people today, though its disappearance is relatively recent, and it still survives in a few special phrases like the Black Country.[4] That particular expression is in fact an interesting and rather rare example of its application to a comparatively modern industrial district.

II

The influence of countrysides or *pays* upon the evolution of provincial society is probably something that most of us are now in some degree aware of. It first struck me forcibly when working with Joan Thirsk on the sixteenth-century volume of *The Agrarian History of England*. It struck me afresh, a few years later, in endeavouring to work out the distribution pattern of rural nonconformity in Kent and a group of Midland counties.[5] Since then it has impressed me yet again in working on the early settlement history of this country,

---

4. First recorded by the *Oxford English Dictionary* in 1834, when it was evidently not a new expression.
5. Alan Everitt, *The Pattern of Rural Dissent: the Nineteenth Century* (Leicester University: Dept. of English Local History, Occasional Papers, 2nd Ser., No. 4, 1972).

more particularly in Kent, though also in other areas.[6] What we see in all these periods is a landscape, a society, an economy, and in some respects a culture, that in every area was sharply divided into contrasting *pays*. Everything that we look at in past centuries is in some degree shaped by these contrasts. The fact that most of our historic regional names, apart from those of counties, are the names of countrysides is significant in this connexion: the Chilterns, the Mendips, the Cotswolds, and the Weald, for example; or Dartmoor, Charnwood, and Arden. It was their character as distinctive countrysides that impressed itself on the early peoples that named them, often in the Celtic period, and that character has in some sense remained apparent, though not of course unchanged, throughout their history.

There are still many areas where these differences of *pays* are plain to see in the English countryside of today. We can see them in Gloucestershire, for example, between the Severn valley on one hand and the Cotswolds on the other; in Yorkshire between the lush pasturelands of the valley-floors and the bare fellsides rising above them; or in Kent between the untrammelled sheep-country of Romney Marsh and the broken, wooded, upland overlooking it. In the days before parliamentary enclosure such contrasts were a good deal more obvious than they are at the present time, particularly in the old common-field areas, where nowadays it often requires an effort of imagination to re-create them. There were few counties, indeed, where they did not give rise to marked regional variations of some kind, and in some districts these variations were to be found within the borders of a single parish. In the Cambridgeshire parish of Carlton-cum-Willingham, for instance, there was a pronounced contrast between the western half of the area, with its vast common-field of some 800 acres, the only one in the parish, and the eastern half with its parcelled assart-and-coppice country along the Suffolk border.[7]

It is the exceptionally diverse physical structure of this island that lies behind this regional variation. That is why these contrasting types of countryside are rarely delimited by county boundaries, but regularly stretch across the borders of one shire into the next, and in their essential characteristics are often echoed on similar landforms elsewhere. There are obvious resemblances between the settlement of the Weald of Kent and the Weald of Sussex, for example, and the whole Wealden area is more like the Forest of Arden in Warwickshire, or even Sherwood Forest in Nottinghamshire, than

---

6. See my book on this subject, *Continuity and Colonization: English Settlement and the Kentish Evidence* (Leicester, 1986).
7. *V. C. H. Cambridgeshire*, vi, 152, 165.

the marshlands or the coastal plain of Sussex and Kent. There are also closer resemblances between the Gault Vale settlements of Kent on one hand, and of Oxfordshire and Buckinghamshire on the other, than there are between those of the Kentish Gault and of Romney Marsh. That does not mean that these areas are identical or that their history has been shaped by crude determinism; but it does mean that it has been influenced by complex human responses to particular kinds of environment. The fact that in Kent alone nearly a thousand years elapsed between the oldest English settlements of the coastal plain and the latest English settlements of the Weald bears testimony to the profound effect of these differences of *pays* upon the progress of colonization. The fact that that lengthy period elapsed also meant that very different types of economy and rural society developed in the various parts of the county. To a perceptive eye, these differences are still apparent within the social, economic, and political contrasts of the present day, though they are not of course the only factors to take account of in that connexion.

In approaching the problem of regional development, then, what we really need at the outset is a systematic map indicating the general framework or pattern of *pays* in the country as a whole. In some parts of England not enough is yet known regarding the origins of settlement or the subsequent evolution of local society to reconstruct such a map with any great confidence. But it seems clear that in general we must envisage a pattern of sharply-localized contrasts: an elaborate mosaic of interlocking rural economies more closely resembling the geological map than that of our modern regions or our ancient counties and kingdoms. Not that this pattern will exactly repeat the geological map, for geology is but one of many factors shaping a countryside or *pays*, but that it will bear the same kind of regional imprint, the same kind of localized diversity, the same intricacy and contrast.

In making these remarks one is clearly begging the difficult question of how far we may expect to find continuity of outline between the *pays* of the settlement period and the *pays* of more recent centuries. How closely do the agrarian countrysides of the late eighteenth century, say, really approximate to those of the pre-Conquest period? The answer to this question is obviously not at all simple, and may well differ widely from county to county. Nevertheless, although agrarian practice itself has varied greatly over the generations, in many *pays* it will be found to have varied only within the more or less distinct limits imposed upon it by the local environment. In many areas it was not until the period of parliamentary enclosure, the building of railways, the mechanization of agriculture, the invention of clay-pipe drainage, or some other technical advance, that fundamental change in regional outlines became possible. When it occurred at an earlier date, as in the development of orchards and hop-gardens in sixteenth-century Kent, it was usually restricted to certain types of countryside, and often fitted into the ancient pattern of farms, fields, woods, lanes, and boundaries.[8] In other words it did not as a rule create an entirely new countryside, or wholly redraw the outlines of the ancient *pays*. In many areas, therefore, though not in all, the historic framework of agrarian regions, before the changes of the last century took place, is of a broadly similar pattern to the framework of early settlement-zones. In some counties, such as Buckinghamshire and Kent, a marked correspondence has persisted to the present day, and there is really nothing surprising in this kind of continuity. The natural properties of districts like the Chilterns, the Weald, and Romney Marsh, after all, have necessarily entailed a certain basic, though not immutable, pattern upon their agrarian evolution.

It is not part of the present purpose to describe in detail how to set about reconstructing a systematic map of countrysides or *pays* in England. As a first step, however, it is useful to recognize that the English landscape is composed of a number of distinct types or species of country, so to speak, and on this subject something must be said. For although no two areas exactly repeat one another, it is possible to classify the multifarious local countrysides of England, and to perceive a tentative pattern both in the way settlement proceeded from one type to another, and in the varying kinds of society to which they tended to give rise. In the space available, attention will be devoted to their influence on the origins of settlement rather than their subsequent effect on local society.

Provisionally, and perhaps rashly, the present writer would suggest a broad classification into eight types or categories of countryside: the fielden or 'champion' areas, the forest areas, the fell or moorland areas, the fenlands, the marshlands, the heathlands, the downlands, and the wold or *wald* countrysides. These categories are only rough and ready ones; at many points they clearly overlap; and they must not be thought of as either rigid in their boundaries or unchanging in their character over the centuries. No classification can be altogether satisfactory, and a number of further subdivisions might obviously be suggested. There are marked differences, as well as resemblances, between the 'fell' or moorland countries of the Pennines, the Lake District, and Dartmoor, for example. There are also major differences between the 'fielden' countrysides of Warwickshire, Kent, and the Welsh Marches. In Sussex, Surrey, and Kent, the High Weald is in some ways very unlike the Low Weald, and in places little more than sandy heathland, though in general

8. As is still evident from the fact that most of the isolated farmsteads and many of the woodland names in the earliest fruit-growing area, around Faversham and Sittingbourne, are recorded in medieval or pre-Conquest documents.

both areas may be thought of as classic forest country. Nevertheless, for elementary purposes this broad classification of the English landscape into eight divisions will perhaps serve. At least it may help to fix in the mind a different kind of pattern from that of our contemporary regional terms.

Up to a point, it seems clear that these different types of country often tended to be settled in different periods.[9] In some areas we do not yet know enough to be positive on this point, and there must always have been wide variations of dating between similar types of landscape in different parts of the country. Nevertheless, a number of tentative generalizations can perhaps be advanced. In the fielden or 'old arable' countrysides many settlements are certainly very ancient – though of course not all – and it seems likely that most of the earliest English and pre-English places are to be found in these areas. They are particularly associated with river valleys – the Thames, the Ouse, the Nene, and the Medway, for example – and with major spring-lines, such as that of the Gault in Kent and Buckinghamshire, though not with all low-lying districts. The fell, forest, and heathland areas, by contrast, usually tend, by and large, to be settled relatively late. In the two latter types of country at least a good deal of colonization is of post-Conquest origin,[10] and in some areas new settlements were still being established in the sixteenth and seventeenth centuries. This seems to be the period of origin of many places called 'row', for instance, such as Keysoe Row in Bedfordshire and Whitley Row in Kent, and probably also of many settlements called 'common' and 'heath'.[11] In fenland areas a number of very early settlements may also be found, such as Ely in Cambridgeshire; but here there may have been wider diversities of date in different localities, since variations of a few feet above sea-

---

9. See my article, 'Place-Names and *Pays*', in *Nomina*, iii, 1979.
10. These views have recently been challenged by P. H. Sawyer in his 'Introduction: Early Medieval English Settlement', *Medieval Settlement: Continuity and Change*, ed. P. H. Sawyer (London, 1976), pp. 1–7. For a critique of Professor Sawyer's views, see my forthcoming book referred to in n.6 above, where the relationship of settlement origins and dating to types of countryside is explored in detail. I should not dispute that some forest settlements may be very early; but when topographical as well as documentary evidence is taken into account, it seems indisputable that permanent and continuous colonization (as distinct from summer pasturing) in areas like the Weald began late in the Old English period and was far from complete in the eleventh century. When closely examined, the evidence that Professor Sawyer cites does not in fact conflict with that view.
11. Such settlements usually arose through encroachment on common land, or on parish boundaries, during a period of rapid population growth, particularly *c.* 1570–1640. See, for example, *The Agrarian History of England and Wales, IV, 1500–1640*, ed. Joan Thirsk (London, 1967), pp. 409–12. Keysoe Row developed on the boundary of Keysoe and Bolnhurst; Whitley Row on that of Sundridge and Chevening.

level dictate essentially dissimilar topographical conditions in this type of country. In marshland areas it is also occasionally possible to find very early places, such as Lydd in Kent. But if the Kentish evidence in general is any guide – it may well not be – much marshland settlement did not originate until the tenth or eleventh century, or even later, owing to problems of drainage and reclamation. In these areas early settlements often' seem to have developed from very localized circumstances: at Lydd itself from the existence of a shingle island at the tip of a tidal lagoon in the Romano-British period.[12]

It is the *wald* and the downland areas of England that are in some ways the most enigmatic and perhaps the most diverse in their settlement origins. In these terms one must probably include most of the upland or watershed countrysides of the Lowland Zone, apart from the late-settled forests and heaths, whether they are known as 'wolds' and 'downs' or not. Amongst them we must thus think of regions like the Chilterns, the Kesteven uplands, the West Cambridgeshire uplands, and perhaps much of the higher country of the eastern counties, as well as classic downland areas like the Berkshire Downs and the Yorkshire Wolds. In some of these regions settlement as we know it began relatively early in the Saxon period, and in many cases it seems to have been more or less complete by the tenth or eleventh century.[13] Unlike the fielden areas, however, these were generally *pays* of colonization, or in some cases re-colonization of secondary woodland, rather than of primary settlement. Except in river valleys, as at Lambourne in Berkshire or Chilham in Kent, it does not seem to be usual to find very early primary settlements in downland countryside, though in some areas there was substantial prehistoric and Roman settlement. Further examination may well modify this view, however, in some parts of the country.

Nowadays, the typical wold and downland areas of England – in Lincolnshire, Wiltshire, Berkshire, or East Sussex, for example – are notably bare of trees, and many people think of them as always having been woodless. There are grounds for thinking, however, that some of them were at one time extensively wooded, and in

12. Lydd is recorded in a charter of 774, much earlier than any other marshland settlement. Its Roman remains include an earthwork, a track, and second-century pottery. There is Saxon work in the church. (J. K. Wallenberg, *Kentish Place-Names* (Uppsala, 1931), p. 55; G. J. Copley, *An Archaeology of South-East England: a Study in Continuity* (London, 1958), p. 277.)
13. Cf. Alan Everitt, 'River and Wold: Reflections on the Historical Origin of Regions and *Pays*', *Journal of Historical Geography*, III, i (1977), 1–19. Nearly all the parishes in a typical 'wold' area, such as the West Cambridgeshire uplands, are recorded in Domesday Book.

regions like the Kentish Downs and the Chilterns substantial wooded stretches still remain. At present we cannot be sure that the Yorkshire and Lincolnshire Wolds, or the Berkshire and Wiltshire Downs, were ever so afforested, and the archaeological evidence suggests that parts of the latter at least have been bare since prehistoric times. In a recent article in the *Journal of Historical Geography*, however, the present writer was able to show from place-names and topographical evidence that the bare downland areas of East Kent were at one time thickly forested, and the word *wald* still survives in many local names, such as Womenswold and Waldershare. A further article, by Della Hooke, shows that the Cotswolds also were once well-wooded; and so too were areas like the West Cambridgeshire uplands, the Kesteven uplands, the Bromswold of Bedfordshire, Huntingdonshire, and Northamptonshire, the upland country bordering Essex, Cambridgeshire, and Suffolk, and the south Leicestershire uplands overlooking the Welland valley.[14] If areas like the Lincolnshire and Yorkshire Wolds were in fact once wooded, they nevertheless gave rise to very different types of settlement and society from those of the Kentish Downs or the Chilterns, so that it is convenient to think of them as a distinct kind of country, although their period of colonization was often probably similar. It is for this reason that the word *wald* is used here to distinguish the early-colonized but wooded upland countries from the barer wolds and downlands. Like the classic forest countries, much of the *wald* and downland countryside of England thus originated from the clearance of woodland, or *wald*, from which the word 'wold' is itself derived. It differs from the true forests, as the term is used here, in that its clearance began at a much earlier period, and in many cases was probably approaching completion when that of the true forests began. As a rule, moreover, the social and ecclesiastical structure of the *wald* areas was very different from that of the classic forests. By and large the *wald* and downland countrysides thus seem to have been areas of intermediate colonization, predominantly settled between the invasion period and the Norman Conquest.

This broad classification of English countrysides into eight types, it must be stressed, is no more than a provisional one. It seems useful, however, to keep a general outline or framework of regional evolution of this type in mind. It is important to recognize that, within wide limits, the settlement of these various kinds of countryside tended to originate in different phases of colonization,

---

14. Ibid.; Della Hooke, 'Early Cotswold Woodland', *Journal of Historical Geography*, IV, iv (1978), 333-41; Alan Everitt, 'The Wolds once More,' ibid, V, i (1979), 67-71.

and to give rise to different kinds of society, however diverse the dating of those phases may have been in different parts of the country. There can also be no doubt that these differences of origin ultimately lie at the root of many of the regional contrasts that we still see in the Tudor, Stuart, and Hanoverian countryside. The work of Joan Thirsk and others, after all, has shown how basic was the division between fielden and forest countrysides in the early modern period, and how continuously that division has shaped our history. More recently this kind of regional analysis has been further exploited in varying ways by scholars like Margaret Spufford in Cambridgeshire and W. J. Ford in Warwickshire.[15] In the writer's view it may now be pressed further in studying and comparing the settlement, the economy, and the society of the heathland, fenland, downland, marshland, moorland, and wold or *wald* types of countryside, both with one another and with their counterparts in different parts of the kingdom. It may well shed a good deal of light on such vexed questions as the origins of the common fields,[16] for example, or the distribution of deserted medieval settlements.[17]

III

Important though this kind of regional division is, it is obviously not the only one that needs to be taken account of in studying provincial society. A country or *pays* is basically a natural region; the county or shire, to which we now turn, is basically an artificial one, an essentially human creation, often with no significant natural boundaries. In other words the map of our 'coloured counties' has no

15. See, for example, *Agrarian History*, ed. Thirsk, ch. I; Joan Thirsk, 'Industries in the Countryside', *Essays in the Economic and Social History of Tudor and Stuart England*, ed. F. J. Fisher (Cambridge, 1961); Margaret Spufford, *Contrasting Communities: English Villagers in the Sixteenth and Seventeenth Centuries* (Cambridge, 1974); W. J. Ford, 'Some Settlement Patterns in the Central Region of the Warwickshire Avon', *Medieval Settlement*, ed. Sawyer, pp. 274–94.
16. The fields of Carlton-cum-Willingham in Cambridgeshire, referred to earlier, provide a good example of the way field-systems tend to become eccentric towards the outer edge of a common-field countryside. Those in the Granta valley to the south-west of Carlton, by contrast, broadly conform to the classic common-field system.
17. To some extent the sites of deserted medieval villages have been related to different types of terrain; but a more rigorous examination is desirable. In particular the word 'village' itself needs to be more carefully defined. In areas of scattered settlement, such as Kent, the idea is often inappropriate, and Deserted Medieval Village status has been claimed for many isolated church sites where in all probability no true village ever existed.

obvious relation with that of our countrysides: the regional pattern is of a quite different kind.

All our historic counties go back in some form for centuries. Several of them, like Sussex, have developed from Old English kingdoms, or, like Kent, from territories whose ultimate origins lie beyond our present knowledge. It is the later phases in their history that concern us in this paper, the period when these ancient units of local government seem to have entered on a new phase in their life-span with what has been described as the 'advent of the county community' in the post-medieval period.[18] Although this development was obviously an evolutionary process that cannot be dated with any precision, and in some areas may have begun earlier than is generally supposed, we can probably look to the Elizabethan, Stuart, and Hanoverian periods as the time when the county as a self-conscious society achieved its *floruit*. It is not part of the present purpose to trace this process, or to explore the complex reasons behind it: political, social, administrative, economic, cultural, familial, religious, and so on. I have nothing new to add to what I have said elsewhere on this head, or to what others have said better than I can: Professor Hassell Smith in Norfolk, for example, Professor Fletcher in Sussex, and Dr Morrill in Cheshire.[19] Although these and other studies have naturally brought to light much diversity between the different shires, and a good deal of variation in the sense of identity and degree of cohesion within them, the 'county commonwealths', as Namier called them, now seem to have found an established place in our historical thinking. During the period under discussion, they surely ceased to be simply administrative units and in many cases became genuine self-conscious regions, with a life of their own, and an obviously growing authority in provincial society.

There is one aspect of this subject, however, to which one wishes to draw particular attention, and that is the rise of the county town as the focus or heart of the county community, or in other words as a kind of regional capital. There are two reasons why it seems desirable to discuss this point. First, it is doubtful if one can really understand a regional society in the full sense without some appreciation, some sympathetic recreation, of the life of its capital: and as yet there are remarkably few such places for which this has

---

18. By Peter Clark in *English Provincial Society from the Reformation to the Revolution: Religion, Politics, and Society in Kent, 1500–1640* (Hassocks, 1977).
19. Alan Everitt, *The Community of Kent and the Great Rebellion, 1640–60* (Leicester, 1966); A. Hassell Smith, *County and Court* (Oxford, 1974); Anthony Fletcher, *A County Community in Peace and War: Sussex, 1600–1660* (London, 1975); J. S. Morrill, *Cheshire, 1630–1660: County Government and Society during the English Revolution* (Oxford, 1974).

been adequately undertaken.[20] Quite a good case might indeed be made out for the view that without an urban focus of some kind a truly regional culture can hardly come into existence. Our modern regions, after all, are essentially based on industrial and commercial capitals like Birmingham and Newcastle. The rise of 'occupational regions' in the early modern period was likewise associated with the development of 'entrepreneurial' towns like Sheffield in the metal trades and Northampton in the shoe industry. The great regional cultures of the medieval world were no less obviously centred on European cities like Florence and Venice. Some theorists might go further and suggest that the relative insignificance of regional cultures of this kind in medieval England is in some way linked with the relative insignificance of our medieval towns. It seems doubtful if such abstract arguments are very convincing, and certainly many of the countrysides spoken of earlier existed for centuries with a culture of their own, yet without any major urban focus. Nevertheless, over the last three or four centuries there can be no doubt that the English town has fulfilled a crucial function in the development of regional self-consciousness. The county capital, the 'entrepreneurial' town, and the industrial city have all exerted a decisive influence in this respect.

The second reason why one wishes to draw attention to the county town is that it was there that both 'county' and 'country' met. These regional capitals, in other words, were not only the natural focus of the county community; they were also the natural focus of the countrysides or *pays* surrounding them; and it was the influence of both county and country that shaped their distinctive economy and society. In this sense, although there was no obvious relationship between the pattern of shires and the pattern of *pays*, there was a close connexion between them, and a constant interplay, within the county capital. What one really means by that statement is this. During the period of emergence of the county community, we also see the development of increasing specialization in agriculture in the contrasting English countrysides. Like the county itself, this specialization was not an altogether new development, and to some extent it was implicit in the basic diversities of these countries themselves. Nevertheless, there was a massive intensification of regional specialization in farming in the early modern period, and in consequence a massive increase in internal trade between one kind of countryside and another, an increase which was necessarily

20. The best-known study is Sir Francis Hill's four-volume work on Lincoln. Some of the more recent *V. C. H.* volumes, such as those covering York and Warwick, are also valuable in this connexion. In another category is Alan Armstrong's quantitative and sociological study, *Stability and Change in an English County Town: a Social Study of York, 1801–51* (Cambridge, 1974).

channelled through the market towns of the kingdom. Yet when we turn to look at the pattern of these market towns, and compare it with that of the high medieval period, what we find is that there has been a drastic decline in the number of markets, a reduction, in fact, of at least fifty per cent, from more than 1500 in the late thirteenth century to a mere 750 in the seventeenth. This is now a well-known theme and needs no labouring; but the consequence to note was the evolution of a widespread network of 'regional' or 'cardinal' markets through which the market trade of this country came to be increasingly channelled. This network of regional markets, it is true, was not at all points identical with that of the county towns; the former were in fact more numerous than the latter, and in a few counties, such as Buckinghamshire and Somerset, the old capitals never became important commercial centres. Nevertheless, by and large, it was the county towns of England, in most areas, that also became the dominant regional markets.[21] One thinks of places like Norwich and Exeter, for example, of Chester and York, of Leicester and Nottingham, of Worcester and Shrewsbury, of Canterbury, Salisbury, and Oxford, of lpswich, Colchester, Maidstone, and so on. These were the places, in other words, that focussed not only the life of the county community, but also the life of the countries or *pays* around them.

How was it that this double influence, of county and country, was actually articulated in the economy of the county town? What exactly were its urban consequences? In what way did these places develop over this period in response to it? What. kind of regional culture, if any, did they give rise to? The answers to these questions are obviously far from simple and vary widely from place to place. At the risk of considerable oversimplification, however, they can mostly be grouped under six interrelated headings. The following pages are based on an examination of five towns in particular – Exeter, Shrewsbury, Canterbury, Maidstone, and Northampton – together with a more superficial analysis, for comparative purposes, of several other county capitals and a group of smaller market towns. In most cases the period under review is George III's reign; but for Northampton the study has been extended back into the late sixteenth century. Altogether, the occupations of more than 50 000 townsmen have been traced and tabulated. What are the main conclusions, very briefly summarized, to which the evidence points?[22]

21. Cf. Alan Everitt, 'The Marketing of Agricultural Produce', *Agrarian History*, ed. Thirsk; Alan Everitt, 'The Primary Towns of England', *The Local Historian*, xi, 1975. I owe the phrase 'cardinal' markets to J. D. Goodacre, 'Lutterworth in the Sixteenth and Seventeenth Centuries,' Leicester Ph.D. thesis, 1977, chapter I.
22. For the sources employed, see Appendix at end of this article.

First, the county towns of Hanoverian England were not generally centres of staple trades, nor were they usually industrial towns in the sense in which we use that term of the Industrial Revolution. Some of them had once been centres of this kind, as Exeter was of the serge industry; a few, like Norwich, still remained so; and a few were developing into major centres of new industries. Maidstone, for instance, was gradually becoming the dominant focus of the paper industry; Worcester of the glove industry; Northampton of the shoe industry; and Leicester and Nottingham of the hosiery trades. But in the period under review we must not exaggerate this tendency. In none of the five towns in question did any single trade occupy more than 15 per cent of the recorded population, and the emphasis everywhere was on occupational variety.[23] Altogether some 400 distinct occupations have been traced in the five towns under review: 142 in Northampton, 150 in Canterbury, 174 in Shrewsbury, and 246 in Exeter.[24] The real total was no doubt substantially larger than that, since it is not possible to compile a fully exhaustive census, and it had certainly increased greatly over the period since Queen Elizabeth's reign. Amongst the thousands of apprentices recorded in the Northampton Registers, for example, the number of separate trades to which they were articled rose from forty-five under Queen Elizabeth to eighty-three in the latter half of the seventeenth century, and 114 between 1716 and 1776. This was a real increase, moreover; it does not simply represent old trades masquerading under new guises; and it was an increase that was far more strikingly apparent in county towns than in most other urban centres. The fundamental development that it points to is the expanding role of these places first as centres of organization, and secondly as nurseries of skill.

One of the aspects of their role as centres of organization was their remarkable development over this period as inland entrepôts,

23. Shoemakers formed the most numerous occupational group in four of the five towns: in Northampton (1768), fifteen per cent of the population; in Shrewsbury (1796), twelve per cent; in Canterbury (1818), eleven per cent; in Exeter (1803), six per cent. In Maidstone (1802) papermakers formed the largest recorded group (thirteen per cent), closely followed by the Medway hoymen and watermen (eleven per cent); but the Maidstone poll-book is much less full in its coverage. By 1831, significantly, the Northampton shoemakers had increased nearly five-fold, and accounted for thirty-six per cent of the recorded population.
24. Compare these figures with 283 separate occupations in Bristol (1812); sixty seven in Wellingborough (1777), the largest Northamptonshire town after Northampton itself; thirty in Thrapston, a typical small market-centre; and fourteen in Clipston, a large Northamptonshire village.

as exchanges or meeting-places of traders, factors, drovers, middle-men, wholesalers, and wayfaring merchants of all kinds. This is the second point to note in the evolution of the county town. In part it arose from the position of these places as regional markets; but it also went a good deal further than that. It gave rise to a whole range of new business facilities based on urban inns, for example, whose numbers in Northampton increased, not untypically, by 300 per cent between 1570 and 1770.[25] It also gave rise to a rapidly expanding network of stage-coach routes and, perhaps more important, to a vast nexus of local and long-distance carriers' services.[26] It gave rise, moreover, to a fascinating development of these towns as regional shopping-centres, a subject on which the evidence is massive and yet in most places is still virtually unexplored.[27] Finally, and in one sense perhaps most important of all, it both encouraged and was itself encouraged by the development of the provincial newspaper, particularly after 1720. Not all early papers, it is true, were centred in county towns. Some were established in ports like Bristol; some in rising industrial centres like Birmingham; some in social capitals like Bath; and a few in minor market towns like St Ives. But the overwhelming majority were produced in the old county capitals: in Canterbury, Exeter, Northampton, Salisbury, Derby, Norwich, Nottingham, York, Worcester, Gloucester, Leicester, and so on. It might well be argued that no single development has been more important in the rise of regional self-consciousness in this country than the establishment of provincial newspapers. Though to begin with their local news was scanty, their advertisement pages from the outset focussed the life of their hinterland, week by week, as nothing else had done hitherto.[28]

Closely connected with the entrepôt character of the county town was its third characteristic: its development as the professional and entrepreneurial centre of its region. During the eighteenth century old professions like those of the doctors and attorneys continuously expanded in numbers, while a wide range of new professions arose in response to the new requirements of the age: land-surveyors, appraisers, printers, publishers, accountants, architects, engineers, bankers, insurance offices, and so on – often appearing roughly in

25. Everitt, 'Marketing of Agricultural Produce'; Alan Everitt, 'The English Urban Inn, 1560–1760', *Perspectives in English Urban History*, ed. Alan Everitt (London, 1973), pp. 91–137.
26. J. A. Chartres, 'Road Carrying in England in the Seventeenth Century: Myth and Reality', *Econ. H. R.*, 2nd Ser., xxx (1977); Alan Everitt, 'Country Carriers in the Nineteenth Century', *Journal of Transport History*, New Ser., iii (1976).
27. Particularly informative is the evidence of probate inventories, wills, and newspaper advertisements.
28. As G. A. Cranfield has shewn in his fine study, *The Development of the Provincial Newspaper, 1700-1760* (Oxford, 1962).

that order. In addition to these general professional occupations, moreover, which by 1800 were to be found in virtually every county town, and in addition to the facilities for business education developing alongside them, a number of towns also developed a more specialized entrepreneurial role, as centres of organization of some particular regional craft or industry. One of the salient themes in occupational development in this country over the past three centuries or so has been the tendency for certain staple crafts, once practised widely, to become concentrated in a gradually narrowing circuit of countryside, or occasionally in two or three separate areas, until a distinct *craft-region* emerges, with its own character, its own traditions, its own sense of identity, and its own distinctive culture. Such developments did not occur in all staple trades;[29] they did not always take place during the same period; they were often more gradual than is generally realized;[30] and they were highly complex processes about which, in many cases, little is yet known. Nevertheless, the evolution of distinct occupational regions of this kind can clearly be observed in such industries as glove-making, shoemaking, lacemaking, nail-making, scythe-making, needle-making, stocking-knitting, and plush-making: and in every case an 'entrepreneurial' town of some kind played a crucial role in this development. By no means all these towns, it is true, were county capitals: many of them had originated as lesser market centres, and either eventually developed into industrial cities like Birmingham and Sheffield, or else remained local market towns like Banbury and Newport Pagnell. In a substantial number of cases, however, it was the county town that became the predominant centre of organization in the development of 'occupational regions', and where this occurred it added a further dimension to their role as nurseries of business expertise. In the hosiery industry, for example, it was chiefly Leicester and Nottingham that fulfilled this function; in the glove industry it

29. They did not occur in the wood-crafts, for example, although some towns acquired a notable reputation in certain specialized fields: e.g. Wymondham for spoon-making, King's Cliffe for turnery ware, and High Wycombe for chairmaking.
30. As in the case of the shoe industry, for example, which despite increasing concentration in Northamptonshire (and to a lesser extent in Norwich, Leicester, Somerset, and Westmorland), still remained widely dispersed in the late nineteenth century. See P. R. Mounfield's three studies: 'The Place of Time in Economic Geography,' *Geography*, lxii (1977), 272 ff; 'Early Technological Innovation in the British Footwear Industry', *Industrial Archaeology Review*, ii (1978), 137; 'The Footwear Industry of the East Midlands (IV): Leicestershire to 1911', *East Midland Geographer*, iv, No. 25 (1966), 8–23. See also V. A. Hatley and J. Rajczonek, *Shoemakers in Northamptonshire, 1762–1911: a Statistical Survey*, Northampton Historical Series, No. 6, 1971.

was Worcester; in the paper industry it was Maidstone; and in the shoe industry it was Northampton.[31]

The fourth characteristic of the county town to note was its development as a centre of leisured life – the life of the gentry. For county families this often involved an annual migration into town, usually at the time of the assizes and horse-races, when they came to spend part of the winter in their town houses, or in one of the great inns. Both races and assizes, as a consequence, often became the occasion for county meetings of every description: administrative, economic, political, charitable, scientific, cultural, social, horticultural, and so on. According to Edward Hasted in the 1790s, the Canterbury races, for example, were 'attended by most of the Kentish gentry and a great number of people from the neighbouring parts; and this city being their usual rendezvous, it brings a vast concourse of them to it for the time, when there are assemblies, plays, and other entertainments, during the whole time of the race week.'[32] When Hasted wrote, places like Canterbury were still at the zenith of their influence as social capitals of the county aristocracy. Within a generation, by the 1820s, this particular role of theirs had begun to decline, as transport improved, as wealth increased, and as the superior charms of the London season were opened up to a widening circle of landed families.

As residential centres for the minor gentry, by contrast, and for the ever-growing numbers of landless or pseudo-gentry of the time, such places continued to expand. What Hasted said of Canterbury in this respect may be paralleled in many such towns between Charles II's reign and Queen Victoria's: 'many gentlemen of fortune and genteel families reside in it, especially within the precincts of the cathedral, where there are many of the clergy of superior rank and fortune belonging to it; and throughout the whole place there is a great deal of courtesy and hospitality.'[33] The precise numbers of these landless or 'town' gentry, as they were sometimes called,

---

31. Other 'entrepreneurial' towns, both large and small, included such places as Birmingham and Wolverhampton (metal trades); Sheffield (cutlery, scythe-making, etc.); Olney, Newport Pagnell, Towcester, and Stony Stratford (Bucks lace industry); Honiton and Ottery St Mary (Honiton lace industry); Charlbury (glovemaking); Hinckley and Mansfield (framework-knitting); Kettering and Wellingborough (shoemaking); Redditch (needle-making); Gloucester (pin-making); Luton and Hitchin (straw-plait industry).
32. Edward Hasted, *History and Topographical Survey of the County of Kent*, 2nd edn., Canterbury, xi, 101–2.
33. Ibid., p. 101. The Hasteds themselves were typical of this social class, and the historian lived for some time in Canterbury. I have traced their history in 'Kentish Family Portrait', *Rural Change*, ed. Chalklin and Havinden, pp. 169–99.

are usually not at all easy to establish and no doubt fluctuated.[34] In the second half of the eighteenth century there may have been about 600 of them, including dependants, in Shrewsbury, a town of some 15000 people, and about 220 in Northampton, a town of some 6000.[35] If these figures are at all typical, the urban gentry may have comprised about four per cent of the population in the county town, and thus formed an important element in its society. In a sense, indeed, because they were permanent rather than seasonal residents, their influence was ultimately more significant than that of the aristocracy.

Two things in particular seem to have attracted them. First, there was the charm of a more urbane way of life, the polite social intercourse hinted at by Hasted, or what *The Northampton Mercury* nicely called 'the soul of conversation',[36] in an expanding circle of like-minded people. So we find contemporaries like Defoe commending Exeter, for example, as a city that was 'full of gentry and good company,' and Maidstone, a little surprisingly, as a town 'where a man of letters, and of manners, will always find suitable society, both to divert and improve himself . . .'[37] But although these families were leisured folk, we must not think of them as necessarily very wealthy; and as well as the soul of conversation it was often the charm of economical living that attracted them. '. . Its a pleasant town to live in', said Celia Fiennes of Shrewsbury,

---

34. The phrase 'our town gentry' first appears in Northampton shortly after the great fire of 1675 and subsequent rebuilding. Not all such families were landless. John Toke of Canterbury, for example, came of old Kentish landed stock and moved to the county town only after his wife's death in 1770, leaving his family-seat and estates at Godinton to his eldest son. Probably many town-gentry, moreover, like the Hasteds themselves, invested in landed property, though they did not build up an estate as such or reside on their scattered farmlands.

35. Parliamentary poll-books form the most obvious source. In many cases they probably under-record local gentry; but at Shrewsbury in 1796 and Northampton in 1768 the figures they give, of 129 and forty-seven respectively, may be near the mark. Assuming an average household of between four and five, these would suggest a total of about 600 gentlefolk in Shrewsbury and 220 in Northampton. The households of widows and spinsters are not included in these figures; but it should be remembered that some of the gentlemen who voted were no doubt unmarried.

36. In the first number of *The Northampton Mercury* (hereafter cited as *NM*), 2 May 1720: 'It is surprising to think that this famous, this beautiful, this polite corporation, has not long ago been the object of those many printers who have established printing offices in towns of less note. And certainly it argues their want of thought: for the soul of conversation must be absolutely necessary to a body of people that excel therein.'

37. Daniel Defoe, *A Tour through England and Wales*, Everyman edn. (1959), I, pp. 222, 115 (first published 1724–6). At Maidstone Defoe attributed this character partly to the numerous gentlemen's houses in the surrounding countryside.

'and great plenty, which makes it *cheap living* . . .'. '. . . Abundance of good families live here,' Defoe said of York, 'for the sake of the good company and *cheap living*'.[38] Cheap living, of course, was one of the advantages which a town that was a good regional market could offer: just as today a city like Leicester offers more economical living than a small market town like Lutterworth, because it affords greater variety and commercial competition.

It was from such roots as these, predominantly though not exclusively, that the county town also developed in this period as a cultural centre. This is its fifth characteristic to note, and one that has recently been the subject of scholarly study by Peter Borsay and others.[39] We must not exaggerate its importance, of course. The places one refers to obviously cannot be compared with London or Vienna in these respects. Though they gave birth to a fair number of celebrated figures, such as Garrick and Johnson at Lichfield,[40] the magnetic influence of the metropolis ultimately attracted much of the brightest talent away from them. Yet if they were rarely peopled by many men of genius, the scale and variety of cultural life in towns that rarely numbered more than 15000 inhabitants was often remarkable. It surely indicates a very substantial cultural public.

If they produced little of truly international genius, moreover, it is worth noting how many of them, while imitating all the cultural modes of their neighbours – literary, scientific, antiquarian, artistic, dramatic, musical, educational, and so on – also managed to shine out in some particular speciality of their own. One thinks, for example, of the important school of water-colourists at Norwich; of the highly original group of early industrial artists headed by Joseph Wright at Derby; of the Three Choirs Festival founded in connexion with Worcester, Gloucester, and Hereford; of the similar Southern Choirs Festival of Salisbury, Winchester, and Chichester; of the literary, antiquarian, and publishing circle around Canterbury in East Kent;[41] of the architectural and building connexions of War-

---

38. *The Journeys of Celia Fiennes*, ed. Christopher Morris (London, 1947), p. 227; Defoe, *Tour*, II, p. 230. The italics are mine.
39. Peter Borsay, 'The English Urban Renaissance: the Development of Provincial Urban Culture, *c.* 1680–1760', *Social History*, v (1977); Everitt, 'English Urban Inn', pp. 113–20.
40. In Staffordshire the characteristics of a county town were in a sense divided between Stafford, the assize-town, and Lichfield, the ecclesiastical centre. Neither place was altogether comparable with such shire-towns as Leicester or Exeter.
41. An interesting insight into this circle is given in the list of 338 subscribers to Hasted, *History . . . of Kent*, first edition (1778–99). Both editions were published in Canterbury (by different firms), where there were then several printing and publishing houses, and where an interesting range of antiquarian and

wick and York; or of the musical life of Hanoverian Leicester, where Haydn's chamber music was played at picnics in Bradgate Park, and where the music of Beethoven was first introduced to the British public by a master-hosier, of all people, William Gardiner (1770–1853). It is to Gardiner's autobiography that we owe much of our knowledge of this musical life, and surely no autobiography ever had a more felicitous title – *Music and Friends* (1838).[42] Amongst those friends, one whom he visited on the continent, was Beethoven himself.

Such matters as these by no means exhaust the range of broadly cultural, intellectual, and humanitarian activities arising in the county town at this time. Typical of another aspect of Hanoverian enterprise was the movement to found county infirmaries, for example, beginning with Winchester in 1736, York in 1740, Exeter and Northampton in 1743, Gloucester and Shrewsbury in 1745, and Worcester in 1746.[43] No less interesting was the widespread development of private and business schooling at this time,[44] and an apparently massive expansion of the reading public indicated by some thousands of book advertisements, covering virtually every subject, in newspapers like *The Salisbury Journal* and *The Northampton Mercury*. Quite different again, yet equally important in its own sphere, was the remarkable revival of the *devotio moderna* under Philip Doddridge and his followers at Northampton: an unexpected and far-reaching movement of human feeling and religious enterprise which stemmed from purely local and provincial roots, and yet ultimately became crucial to the Evangelical Revival, to the development of English hymnody, and to the foundation of missionary

topographical works was produced. In addition to Hasted himself, these antiquarian and literary figures included, *inter alia*: Andrew Ducarel, John Duncombe, William Gostling, John Burnby, Henry Todd, Osmund Beauvoir, and John Monins, all of Canterbury itself; together with William Boys of Walmer, Edward Jacob of Faversham, Egerton Brydges of Denton, William Boteler of Eastry, Bryan Faussett of Heppington, and (at an earlier date, d. 1747) John Lewis of Minster-in-Thanet.

42. Gardiner's own musical compositions are now forgotten; but the account of him in the *D. N. B.* seems unduly scornful. Paganini and Weber were also among his many friends and cultural acquaintances.

43. Courtney Dainton, *The Story of England's Hospitals* (London, 1961), pp. 85–8; *Imperial Gazetteer*, 1870, *sub* York; *NM*, 5 December 1743. Other early hospitals included Bristol in 1737 and Liverpool in 1745; but the great majority were in the county towns. Dainton's list is not complete.

44. Between 1723 and 1760, for example, more than 100 schools in the Northampton area, many of them newly established, though not all private, advertised in *NM* (Cranfield, *Provincial Newspaper*, pp. 195–6, 215). The most popular subjects advertised were the three Rs, 'followed by Latin and Greek, and, significantly, book-keeping and accounts'.

activity overseas.[45] This was a movement, by the way, which touches on yet another kind of English region: the region of religious influence.

V

The last characteristic of the county town to note, and one that in a sense was fundamental to the others, was its development as a centre of craftsmanship, as a nursery of skill. In many ways this was its most important characteristic, as it is also the least understood, so that it is worthwhile commenting on it in some detail. To begin with, the sentimental belief that the craftsman was essentially a pre-industrial and a rural figure, a picturesque survival if not an anachronism by the time of the Industrial Revolution, must be firmly dismissed from our minds. The reality is more complex, and much more interesting. In the fullest occupational census we have for any county in the eighteenth century, the Northamptonshire Militia Lists of 1777, the names and callings of nearly 12 000 people are recorded. Amongst these occupations, there are about eighty that must be classified as crafts, and of these eighty about half-a-dozen basic skills were widely represented in Northamptonshire villages: blacksmiths, shoemakers, tailors, carpenters, weavers, and wheelwrights, who between them accounted for ninety per cent of all rural craftsmen. The remaining seventy or so crafts, by contrast, were almost entirely confined to a few towns, and in many cases largely confined to Northampton. Even blacksmiths, tailors, shoemakers, and carpenters were more numerous in towns than in villages, and there is really nothing surprising in this fact. Craftsmanship, after all, depended on a lengthy apprenticeship, and apprenticeship was in essence an urban idea. Although the Northamptonshire pattern was not repeated in all areas, it was not an untypical one. Outside the new industrial districts, the concentration

---

45. As minister of the Independent congregation at Northampton, and principal of the Dissenting Academy there from 1729 until his death in 1751, Doddridge was a seminal figure in eighteenth-century religious development. I hope to publish elsewhere my work exploring his influence, based partly on the subscribers' lists to his *Family Expositor* (1739–56) and his voluminous correspondence. Dr G. F. Nuttall's work on Doddridge is invaluable, particularly *Philip Doddridge, 1702–51* (London, 1951), and *Richard Baxter and Philip Doddridge: a Study in a Tradition* (Oxford, 1951). Characteristically Doddridge was the moving spirit behind the Northampton Infirmary, and one of the founders of the Northampton Philosophical Society.

of the more highly skilled and recondite crafts in county towns was a general phenomenon.

Secondly, craftsmen everywhere seem to have formed an expanding section of the urban population: expanding that is in numbers, though not necessarily in wealth or status.[46] Whereas in Northampton the population just about doubled between Queen Elizabeth's reign and George III's, the number of boys apprenticed in each decade more than trebled. In the none too easy employment conditions of the time, moreover, masters were often able to pick and choose their apprentices, so that up to a point intelligence and enterprise were channelled into the craft-structure, and these towns came to be widely recognized as centres of training. By the late eighteenth century, as a consequence, craftsmen usually formed about half their recorded population, a substantially higher proportion than in smaller urban centres.[47] In most places they were apparently three or four times as numerous as the unskilled labourers and domestic servants put together,[48] and nearly four times as numerous as the retail shopkeepers, despite a massive increase amongst retailers themselves. Everywhere, in short, they formed by far the most numerous occupational category, and in a very real sense the craftsman's shop was the hallmark of the Hanoverian county town. One wonders, indeed, if the phrase 'a nation of shopkeepers', which is often attributed to Napoleon but in fact antedates the French Revolution, did not originally refer to workshops as much as retail businesses.[49] Certainly in the eighteenth century it might have borne either meaning.

46. In Northampton, which was probably not untypical in this respect, their inventories usually indicate only a modest level of prosperity, never comparable with that of the major innkeepers, drapers, tanners, etc. Very few of them ever became mayors or aldermen. The pattern in York seems to have been similar. P. A. Berryman, 'The Manufacturing Crafts in York, 1740–1784', Leicester M. A. dissertation, 1978.

47. The proportion varied from forty-three per cent at Canterbury to fifty-three per cent at Northampton; but the Canterbury poll-book is less complete in its coverage and no doubt under-represents craftsmen. In the non-county towns studied, the proportion rarely exceeded about a third, except in an important city like Bristol.

48. These figures are based on the Militia Lists for Exeter in 1803 and Northamptonshire in 1777. The latter covers all the towns in the county. No reliable figures of servants and labourers can be based on poll-books. Militia lists should not under-record these groups proportionately speaking; but one gets the impression that they in fact under-record domestic servants.

49. It was used on both sides of the Atlantic in 1776: by Adam Smith in *The Wealth of Nations*, and by Samuel Adams in a speech reputedly at Philadelphia (*Oxford Dictionary of Quotations* (1948), p. 1,403). Presumably it was not then a novel expression.

Thirdly, we must not think of the traditional skills of the craftsmen as having survived unchanged from a timeless past, as the Arts and Crafts Movement sometimes seemed to suppose.[50] On the contrary, they were in process of gradual but continuous evolution, and in the period under discussion their most remarkable feature was certainly their adaptability and inventiveness. For the craftsman, we must remember, was first and foremost a man who was skilled with his hands, often extremely skilled at the end of his seven-year apprenticeship: twice as long a training, after all, as that of a modern undergraduate. It is not surprising, therefore, that in the eighteenth century the English craftsman came to be associated with all those qualities of deftness and individual ingenuity that we now associate with the Japanese.

When one turns to examine the craft-economy of any particular place in depth, as a consequence, what one finds is certainly not a static or hidebound structure. On the contrary, new branches of established crafts were developing all the time, new skills were arising in response to new needs as if by spontaneous generation, and old skills were continually splitting up and splaying out into new specialisms. By 1700 the old trade of the wheelwrights, for example, had given rise to the separate skill of the coachbuilder, that of the joiner to the cabinetmaker, and that of the brazier to the clockmaker; while the millwright was branching out into a wide range of mechanical contrivances. By the time of the Industrial Revolution, as a consequence, the number of separate crafts that had arisen in this way, each with its own distinct training, was remarkable. In the five towns under review there were at least 160 different types of craft workshop, and if it were possible to reconstruct an exhaustive occupational census, the real total might well exceed 200. There were sixty-two separate kinds of craft shop in Northampton, for instance, a town of only 6000 people, and almost 100 in Exeter, where there may have been nearly 1000 craft workshops in a city of 17 000 inhabitants.[51]

Mere figures, however, do not convey an adequate impression of this vivid diversity. Take the metal trades, for example, although

---

50. This is perhaps the one misconception in parts of George Sturt's great work, *The Wheelwright's Shop* (Cambridge, 1923).
51. The figure of 1000 is a tentative guess. Thirteen hundred craftsmen are recorded in the Exeter Militia List. This includes journeymen as well as masters; but masters are under-represented since men over fifty-five were excluded. We know very little of the average size of craftsmen's shops at this time; but such indications as there are suggest that in county towns they were normally small family affairs, with perhaps one or two journeymen and one or two apprentices apiece on average. With an average of one master and two journeymen a population of perhaps 5000–6000 adult males, of whom half were engaged in crafts (49.7 per cent in the Militia List), would suggest *c*. 850–1000 workshops.

any other group, such as the wood-crafts, would serve equally well. None of the five towns under review was particularly notable as a metal-working centre; they were not miniature Sheffields or Birminghams, yet they contained at least 350 master metal-craftsmen, and the real total was probably nearer 500. Of these 350, 150 were engaged in a single trade, that of blacksmith; but the remaining 200 followed a great variety of crafts, at least thirty-five in all. In Shrewsbury, for instance, they included braziers, cutlers, whitesmiths, pewterers, pump-makers, scythe-makers, gunsmiths, gun-finishers, locksmiths, pin-makers, nailers, chape-makers, and so on. Elsewhere they included many of these occupations, and often a number of others as well, such as scalemakers, stilliers, warming-pan makers, clockmakers, mathematical instrument-makers, and makers of surveyors' equipment. None of these trades was on a large scale; there were rarely as many as a dozen of any of them in most county towns; as a rule they were clearly not producing for an over-seas or a national market, but essentially for a regional one, for an extensive rural hinterland. That is why crafts of this kind came to be centred predominantly in the county towns of England: in those old centres of skill, in other words, that you naturally went to for all your more unusual requirements: just as in Leicestershire today you still visit the capital of the shire for these purposes.

What sort of goods, then, did these craftsmen make? A typical cutler, such as one of the Tuckwell family of Northampton, made not only knives and forks, but all sorts of scissors, razors, pen-knives, lancets, flems, butchers' steels, shoemakers' knives, heelmakers' knives, shop-knives, sheep-shears, swords, and scab-bards.[52] A typical brazier or whitesmith, such as one of the Tyers or Revell families, made not only all kinds of saucepans and other cooking-ware, but tea-kettles, coffee-pots, plate-warmers, barrel-cocks, tea-canisters, fenders, coal-scoops, chimney-cowls, coffin-furniture, and so on.[53] Everywhere, moreover, such men were branching out into new directions in response to the new demands of the age. One of the Tuckwells, for example, specialized as a maker of instruments, probably for surveyors.[54] One of the Revells became a well-known maker of warming-pans and 'salamanders', that is a pan 'which does its office without leaving any sulphurous smell' in the bed.[55] One of the whitesmiths became a surgical beltmaker,

---

52. *NM*, 24 and 31 May 1725.
53. *NM*, 5 and 12 April 1756.
54. Thomas Tuckwell was described as a cutler and instrument-maker when made free, 18 September 1671 (Northampton Borough Records, Assembly Book, 1627–1744, p. 222). His son, Samuel, seems to have taken over his late father's business in 1725 (*NM*, 24 May 1725).
55. *NM*, 1 October 1759.

and was highly commended by the medical profession.[56] One of the scalemakers, Richard Butlin, became a notable land-surveyor; and it was he who made the exceptionally fine survey of Northampton in 1746, on which every street, lane, yard, garden, and ground-plot is accurately delineated.[57] Perhaps most interesting of all was the ebullient Thomas Yeoman, a Northampton millwright whose occupation extended into both the metal and the wood-working fields. As well as designing and building many mills in the area, including a cotton-mill which for a time he managed himself, he erected weighbridges and invented a new machine for cleaning corn which was described in the *Gentleman's Magazine* in December 1746. Amongst a whole range of goods that were made in his shop were air-pumps, bucket-engines for raising water, ventilators for hospitals and granaries, backheavers for winnowing corn, hollow-sticks for ventilating corn, refracting and reflecting telescopes, mathematical instruments, philosophical instruments and 'electrical machines for the studies of the curious'. As if this were not enough, he was also a skilled land-surveyor, a leading member of the early Northampton Philosophical Society in the 1740s, the author of a *Treatise on Mechanics*, principally for the use of other millwrights, a Fellow of the Royal Society, and one of the founders of the Royal Society of Arts.[58]

Individually, developments like these may seem perhaps trivial, and even in some cases a little comic, in the light of the great inventions of the Industrial Revolution. But we need to see them as part of a whole, as symptoms of an attitude of mind, as signs of a climate of ingenuity. Even relatively small and slowly-expanding county capitals, like Northampton, need to be visualized as vital nur-

---

56. *NM*, 27 September 1756.
57. See Northampton Borough Records, Assembly Book, 1627–1744, pp. 390, 528; *Gentleman's Magazine*, XVII (1747), p. 446; *NM*, 20 April and 6 July 1752, where Butlin's shop is said to be continued as a scalemaker's and stillier's after his death. A 'stillier' was a maker of distilling equipment.
58. *NM*, 1 December 1746, 23 March and 27 April 1747; *Gentleman's Magazine*, XV (1745), p. 355; *V. C. H. Northants.*, ii, 334–5; Eric Robinson, 'The Profession of Civil Engineer in the Eighteenth Century: a Portrait of Thomas Yeoman, F. R. S., 1704 (?)–1781', *Annals of Science*, xviii, 4 (1962), 195–215. The latter article, on the development of the engineering profession from the ranks of millwrights and instrument-makers in the eighteenth century – Yeoman in fact described himself as a millwright, not an engineer – is of more than local interest. It justly points out that 'the vitality of market-town society was a sound basis on which to construct a community of scientific interest among engineers and gentlemen' (p. 215). The Northampton Philosophical Society, founded in 1743, was one of the earliest provincial scientific societies. Other leading members included Doddridge and such prominent local gentry as Sir Thomas Samwell. It met from an early date at Yeoman's house in Gold Street ('Portrait of Thomas Yeoman', 202–3).

series of skill, as centres of an inventive temperament, as fertile seedbeds of discovery. The career of a man like Thomas Yeoman, though in a sense unique, was also in a sense intensely typical, both of his town and of his time, and it clearly illustrates how occupations once relatively simple in their nature[59] were now developing into complex and recondite skills. Although the old peasant-world of the English countryside was everywhere disintegrating in this period, under the impact of population-pressure, capitalist farming, landed aggrandizement, parliamentary enclosure, and other forces, the infrastructure of craft-occupations that had grown up alongside it was thus by no means disintegrating. On the contrary, it was still going from strength to strength alongside the new industrial world, which had developed out of it and which at many points still remained a part of it. The craft-economy of these county towns or regional markets, in short, found a new role for itself in adapting its skill to the needs of an increasing population, a changing countryside, and an expanding leisured class. Of the impact of the demands of the leisured class on the craft-structure little has been said; but it was certainly very apparent in the fine work of the wood-carvers and stucco-artists, for example; of the cabinet-makers and coach-builders; or of the watchmakers, clockmakers, statuaries, goldsmiths, and other fine-craftsmen.

The evolution of this craft-structure in seventeenth and eighteenth century England would well repay more thorough and systematic investigation, both locally and nationally, than it has yet received. In considering the origins of the Industrial Revolution, we need to take more serious account perhaps of the remarkable efflorescence of craftsmanship that heralded it, and of the evolution of the older craft-centres of this country. Most of these places, it is true, were not destined to advance very far into the next phase of industrialization and become fully developed manufacturing cities during the Victorian period. It is chiefly for that reason, perhaps, that their economy has rarely been studied in detail and has perhaps been visualized as hidebound and reactionary. Yet to read back the conditions and preconceptions of the nineteenth century into the eighteenth and seventeenth is surely unhistorical, and can only distort our understanding of the origins of manufacture itself. The Industrial Revolution did not develop on the basis of hidebound custom, and it certainly could not have arisen out of a static world. In many ways the revolution of industry really arose out of the evolution of crafts.

---

59. But only relatively simple: a mill, after all, is itself a complicated piece of machinery, so that it is not surprising that millwrights became key-figures in the early mechanization of industry in this country.

When we turn to examine the nineteenth century itself, moreover, we find that this craft-structure not only survived until a remarkably late period, but in many trades continued to expand alongside the industrial world of the Victorian era. Judged by its contribution to overseas trade, perhaps, or by the yardstick of productivity, that structure may seem relatively unimportant. Judged by its contribution to the basic needs of the home market, however, and by the substantial numbers of people employed in it, it was far from negligible. In the Census of 1861 about a quarter of the occupied population of the so-called 'agricultural' counties of the Lowland Zone was reckoned as 'industrial', in comparison with forty-three to forty-six per cent in the four most industrialized counties – Lancashire, the West Riding, Warwickshire, and Nottinghamshire.[60] Amongst that quarter there was in fact a good deal of small-scale industry, such as brewing and malting;[61] but there can be no doubt that craftsmen also formed a substantial element in it. In Kent alone, for example, Kelly's *Directory* of 1870 lists nearly 6000 master-craftsmen engaged in some 140 separate trades, and that list is evidently not an exhaustive one. At that date there were still some 1300 shoemakers' workshops in the county, 600 smithies, 350 wheelwrights' shops, 200 saddlers' and harness-makers' shops, and a whole range of other craft-activities: 110 cabinet-makers' shops, for instance, eighty stonemasons', eighty shipwrights' and barge-builders', seventy-five coopers', seventy-five coachbuilders', seventy basket-makers,' fifty-five braziers' and tinmen's, and so on.[62] To a greater degree than is sometimes realized, the domestic

---

60. See the summary tables in *The National Gazetteer of Great Britain and Ireland*, [1868], XII, Appendix, p. 5. In seventeen of the thirty counties generally thought of as 'agricultural', including all those south of the Thames except Berks and Wilts, the 'industrial' population actually outnumbered the 'agricultural'. It was chiefly in the eastern counties that the 'industrial' population was lowest.

61. Kelly's *Directory of Kent* for 1870 lists 115 breweries and sixty-five maltings in the county.

62. The figures are rounded to the nearest five or ten. Victorian trade directories of this kind were concerned with recording business units, and hence normally list masters only, not employees. In general I have therefore assumed that each individual represents a separate shop, unless two or more men occupy the same premises. Those described as 'manufacturers' have generally been excluded, though many 'manufactories' were probably little more than workshops. All who appear to be retailers only (e.g. 'curriers and leather-sellers') have also been excluded, and all engaged in processing and wholesale trades, such as brickmaking and malting. Where crafts are concerned, it is impossible to say how complete the directory is. About 4600 farmers are listed, which may represent something like two-thirds of the total, since there were then about 7000 farms in Kent. A few craft-occupations are obviously under-represented, such as sawyers, of whom only two are listed; but these seem to be exceptional. One might hazard the guess that perhaps two-thirds of the master-craftsmen in the county as a whole

world of mid-Victorian England was still the hand-made world of the craftsman.[63]

VI

Behind all these multifarious characteristics of the county town we can see one simple, inescapable human tendency at work, a tendency that explains much in the evolution of early modern society: birds of a feather flock together. None of these features, it is true, was entirely peculiar to places of this kind. The capitals of our shires were not the only inland entrepôts of the seventeenth and eighteenth centuries, or the only cardinal markets and regional shopping-centres. They were not all significant entrepreneurial towns, and the urban life of the leisured classes was by no means wholly confined to them. They did not form the only focal points of cultural and religious activity, or of medical enterprise and educational opportunity. Neither were they the sole centres of specialist craft-training, or the sole nurseries of ingenuity and skill. Some of these activities were certainly to be found in secondary towns like Stamford and Banbury, or in many smaller market centres, while others were more prominently developed in rising industrial towns like Birmingham, in social capitals like Bath and Brighton, and above all in the metropolis. Yet what was remarkable about the English county town of the Hanoverian period was the concentration of so many varied functions within it, and the range, the scale, the scope, and the quality of the facilities it afforded.

For that reason these places came increasingly to focus the economic and social activity of the countryside around them in the early modern period. Within a pattern of great diversity from one county to another, there was clearly a certain common mode to which most of them tended to approximate, and in most counties

are recorded. This would give a hypothetical total of some 9000 masters, and if these employed an average of two men and two apprentices apiece, the craft-occupations would account for roughly half the total 'industrial' population of the county (93 000). No doubt large numbers of the remaining half were employed as 'craftsmen' of a kind in the dockyard towns.

63. A recent study of the furniture industry in 1800–51 has found no evidence of mass production even at the end of the period. English furniture was still made overwhelmingly in cabinetmakers' workshops, and in the 1851 Census the average shop still employed only five craftsmen, including the master; ninety per cent of all shops, in fact, still employed fewer than ten men. (*Times Lit. Supp.*, 24 March 1978, reviewing E. T. Joy, *English Furniture, 1800–1851*.)

their influence on the new currents of the time was evidently magnetic. It was not only the life of the county community itself that they attracted, but the life of its constituent *pays* as well, in all their absorbing contrasts. As they expanded in scale, as a consequence, and as the scope of their facilities increased, they also began to give rise to a new kind of region, the modern urban hinterland, and to impart to that region a growing sense of solidarity, a deepening consciousness of belonging together. Within their ambit, moreover, the people of the area were gradually brought into increasing touch with the trade and industry of the country at large: with the agriculture, the commerce, and the manufacture of other regions; with the drovers, the factors, and the carriers of distant counties; with the wayfaring traders of Scotland, Ireland and London; and with the products of the Mediterranean, the Caribbean, and the Orient. Silks and velvets from Italy, wine and brandy from France, sugar and spices from the Indies, tea and porcelain from China, timber from Honduras and the Baltic: by 1750 these and many other overseas commodities had become commonplace amongst the merchandise of the English county capital: chiefly imported to meet the demands of the local gentry, no doubt, yet also opening up a world of wonder and novelty to townsman and countryman as well.

It has been the argument of this paper that the historic pattern of English regional development is a good deal more subtle and complex than at first sight appears. Although in contemporary matters it is often convenient to employ such terms as Merseyside, the West Midlands, and the Home Counties, historically speaking these phrases conceal at least as much as they illuminate. Behind them we must envisage a whole spectrum of local and regional diversity of which they fail to take cognizance. England, after all, is one of the most varied countries in the world in its physical structure, and this variety has inevitably given rise to very diverse landscapes within a relatively small compass: often within the borders of a single county, and certainly within the borders of our contemporary regions. Moreover, these contrasts are not confined to physical characteristics alone; they are also marked by different periods of settlement, and they have given birth to very varied forms of local life. In tracing the social and economic development of this country as a whole, in consequence, we must not expect to find a homogeneous or coherent pattern of evolution, but a piecemeal, localized, and fragmented one: a pattern of regional paradoxes and survivals, in short, where landscapes of poverty and plenty exist for centuries side by side, and where in almost every county the advanced and the primitive, the familiar and the remote, remained strangely intermingled until the eve of the railway era. Gradually, moreover, and particularly over the last three or four centuries, this basic small-network of contrasting *pays* has been further complicated, and in places transformed, by the rise of a succession of human regions, if so they may be called, such as the county community, the urban hinterland, the occupational region, the industrial region, the social neighbourhood, the region of religious influence, and so on. It is from such origins as these that the modern manufacturing areas of South Yorkshire and the Black Country have arisen, for example, no less than the old lacemaking districts of East Devon and the South Midlands, or county communities like Norfolk, Sussex, and Kent. And yet within these new 'human' regions, the old English *pays* still survived until well into the nineteenth century, still embedded in their local environment, still vivid with their own historic idiosyncracies, as readers of Hardy or George Eliot will realize.

Such are the circumstances that have given rise to that elusive and kaleidoscopic character of regional development in this country which was remarked on at the beginning of this paper. The coexistence of contrasting landscapes and economies, each with its own history and its own individual life-span, surely forms one of the most pronounced, the most persistent, and the most far-reaching themes in the evolution of English provincial society. If the pattern outlined in this paper seems to complicate unduly the task of recreating that society, it should perhaps be remembered that it is from the perpetual interplay between these diverse economies, from their impact upon one another over the centuries, and from their occasional conflicts and collisions, that the vital spark of progress and originality in this country has often arisen.

APPENDIX

The principal sources on which the study of county towns is based include the following.

(1). *Exeter Militia List, 1803* ed. W. G. Hoskins for Devon and Cornwall Record Society, 1972 (lists occupations of 2642 men); *Northamptonshire Militia Lists, 1777*, ed. V. A. Hatley for Northants. Record Society, 1973 (11 955 men, of whom 8188 were rural); parliamentary poll-books for Northampton in 1768 (1299 men), Shrewsbury in 1796 (1967 men), Canterbury in 1818 (1125 men), and Maidstone in 1802 (433 men); Northampton Apprenticeship Registers 1562–1776, formerly in Town Hall, now in Northants. Record Office (*c.* 7000 boys). These are the sources on which most of the figures for occupations cited in the text are based. They give the occupations of a total of some 18 250 townsfolk, but in the case of Northampton there is some overlap between the sources, and apprenticeship figures obviously cannot be amalgamated with others in the same table. For Northampton, a wide range of borough records has also been examined; together with all the surviving wills and inventories for the town, from *c.* 1560 to 1770, in the County Record Office (the inventories survive only from *c.* 1660); the complete run of *The Northampton Mercury*, 1720–70; and a very varied collection of printed material in the Local History Collection in the Borough Library.

(2). In addition to the above, the following poll-books have also been systematically analysed: Northampton, 1774, 1784, 1796, 1818, 1826, 1831, 1837; Canterbury, 1790, 1796, 1826, 1830; York, 1807; Norwich, 1812; Great Yarmouth, 1754 and 1831; Nottingham, 1754; and Bristol, 1812. These give the occupations of a further 23 450 townsmen; but in the cases of Northampton and Canterbury there is again some overlap between the sources. They also vary widely in their coverage from place to place and for different years in the same town, so that a combined tabulation is not practicable. For Northampton and Canterbury, however, they afford a useful indication of the changing occupational pattern in the urban economy. In the former town, for example, they show that numbers engaged in the shoe-trades gradually increased from 192 in 1768 to 910 in 1831, or from fifteen per cent to thirty-six per cent of the recorded population. Amongst other towns for which poll-books have been analysed are Newark, Dover, Rochester, and Newcastle-upon-Tyne.

(3). A full critique of these sources would be out of place in this article. It should be pointed out, however, that militia lists tend to under-record the gentry and professional classes. Since they exclude men over about the age of forty-five (fifty-five at Exeter in 1803), they also under-record the older master-craftsmen and other senior groups. On the other hand, one would expect them to provide a useful check on the number of servants and labourers, who must often be under-recorded in poll-books. In the cases of Shrewsbury in 1796 and Canterbury in 1818, however, labourers actually formed a larger percentage of the recorded population (*c.* ten per cent) than in the Exeter Militia list (7.5 per cent). Is it possible that the very large percentage of unskilled labourers found in sixteenth and early seventeenth-century towns, sometimes as much as a third of the male working population, had dwindled so substantially, by the late eighteenth century? If so, there may be a connexion here with the increasing number of trained craftsmen.

(4). Poll-books obviously vary widely in usefulness according to the local franchise. The most useful relate to towns where the vote was vested in the householders, as at Northampton. Where the vote was limited to freemen, as was often the case, poll-books may nevertheless sometimes afford quite substantial coverage of master-craftsmen and master-tradesmen. Of the poll-books used in the main tabulation (see (1) above), those for Northampton in 1768 and

Shrewsbury in 1796 were chosen because, for various local reasons, they happen to be particularly full for the years in question; that for Canterbury in 1818 is the best available for that town, though it is not as good as the two former. In Northampton many non-householders as well as householders voted (illegally) in 1768, so that the poll-book lists almost 1300 adult males (i.e. of voting age) out of a total male population (including children) of *c.* 3000. The least full of the poll-books is that for Maidstone in 1802; but it has been included because of its unusual evidence of family trade-groupings and of the migration of men trained in the town (particularly in paper-making) to other centres. In all towns, out-voters have been excluded from the figures. In most cases, these were purely political and are of little or no interest from the point of view of the local economy. At Maidstone, however, they included many of the locally-trained men who migrated to other towns, and in that respect are of great interest, though necessarily excluded from the tabulation of townsmen. In addition to under-representing servants and labourers, many poll-books also appear to under-record gentry, professional men, and a few other groups, such as inn-keepers. For most towns few, if any, exist before 1750 (or indeed 1780), though there are earlier ones for such cities as Norwich and York. Poll-books of county elections, it should be stressed, are of relatively little use for occupational analysis owing to the limitation of the franchise.

Chapter 4

URBAN IMPROVEMENT AND THE ENGLISH ECONOMY IN THE SEVENTEENTH AND EIGHTEENTH CENTURIES*

E. L. Jones and M. E. Falkus

[from P. J. Uselding (ed.), *Research in Economic History*, vol. 4 (Greenwich, Conn., 1979)]

Both Eric Jones and Malcom Falkus have written elsewhere on the subject of the eighteenth-century town: Jones on the impact of fire and Falkus on street lighting (see the references at the end of the piece reprinted here, and also E. L. Jones, S. Porter, and M. Turner, A Gazetteer of English Urban Fire Disasters 1500–1900, Historical Geography Research Series, no. 13 (Norwich, 1984)). Their substantial and fertile essay places these subjects in the context of the much wider theme of urban improvement. The authors emphasize that advances were underway long before the classic period of the Industrial Revolution, and that their effects were felt not so much in the 'industrial' towns of the North as in the smallish agricultural centres of the South. Two main themes are developed: the mounting investment in the public and private urban fabric, and the subtle but significant changes in the structure of local government, particularly as demonstrated by the rise of improvement commissions. Underpinning much of the detailed argument is the notion of what may be called qualitative, as opposed to quantitative urbanization. Jones and Falkus argue that although between 1660 and 1750 provincial urban centres experienced only limited population growth, a process of urbanization was clearly underway: towns were becoming more environmentally commodious, economically efficient and culturally sophisticated. The authors may underestimate the degree of growth occurring, but the general point, that urbanization is not exclusively or even necessarily a demographic process, is one well worth considering in the context of eighteenth-century towns.

Town growth before the Industrial Revolution has been generally neglected by economic historians, at least until very recent years and

116

with the outstanding exception of London. The reasons for this neglect are not difficult to fathom. The very dominance of London and the host of ways in which the metropolis influenced economic and social life throughout the country has, naturally, deflected attention from provincial urban centers. England was, indeed, even by contemporary standards, a relatively nonurbanized society in 1700 or 1750 (although obviously the vast capital city and constellation of lesser centers sprinkled over the countryside was a mechanism for diffusing urban ideas widely). In 1700 London was Europe's largest city, and by 1750 had become even larger, relatively. Yet nearly every major European country had a cluster of medium-sized provincial towns far bigger than those in England, and notwithstanding variations in total populations, comparisons show striking differences. Of the top thirty European cities in 1700, England had only London represented, whereas France had five, 'Italy' seven, and Spain four (Chandler and Fox, 1974). At that date no English provicial town exceeded 30,000 and only three Bristol, Norwich, and Newcastle – were above 20,000. By contrast, France had no fewer than fourteen cities, excluding Paris, greater than 30,000, and twelve between 20,000 and 30,000. The German states had fourteen cities above 20,000; in Spain there were twelve above 25,000: and in the various Italian states and provinces there were twenty-two cities above 25,000, including nine above 50,000. In the Dutch provinces and 'Belgium' there were thirteen cities greater than 20,000. Even in 1750 England had only four provincial towns larger than 20,000, with Bristol the chief one at 45,000. At this date France had seven cities, excluding Paris, with greater populations than Bristol.

By contrast with the considerable developments in eighteenth-century English agriculture, transport, and of course industry, the role of provincial towns in the economy may seem to have been only a modest one. Moreover, until the very end of the century the great industrial changes were not associated directly with urban change; rural location based on waterpower or underemployed agricultural labor was more often the characteristic of newly developing industries. Urban improvement in the old corporate boroughs and market towns, many situated far away from the expanding northern industrial regions, appears somewhat anachronistic and remote from the new currents of the age. Yet, we suggest in this paper that it was precisely this widespread improvement, which occurred so often

* This is a report of work in progress on the topic of the title. For simplicity, references to individual towns have been kept to a minimum. The authors acknowledge a grant from La Trobe University Schools of Social Science and Economics joint research fund.

117

in small southern market towns and which was less represented in the new manufacturing areas, that most needs emphasis. Improvement can be seen well before the classic period of industrial expansion, and in many of the nonmanufacturing towns continued well into the Industrial Revolution. Such urban improvement immediately suggests three points. First, it represents a theme of continuity in urban economic history across the gulf of the Industrial Revolution and to this extent suggests the need for a model of economic change that focuses on gradual and widely diffused elements.

Second, and more generally, is the point that wealth and prosperity were widely dispersed in early eighteenth-century England, and were to be found in numerous urban centers. A recent study has suggested that until well after the Industrial Revolution, the major English fortunes originated from agriculture and from London-based commercial and professional occupations, with the new manufacturing regions by no means dominant (Rubinstein, 1977, pp. 602–23). Similarly, our study of towns before the 1780s suggests also the roots of an *urban* prosperity originating in other than manufacturing industry or the traditional commerce of the major port towns.

A third point worth emphasis is the social implication of urban improvement before 1780. Urban amenities connected with better building and street improvement developed to a significant extent before the Industrial Revolution. Without wishing to exaggerate either the extent of such improvement or the numbers of the urban populations they affected, although in sum they were substantial, it may be suggested that such changes marked a significant rise in urban living standards. Since such a suggestion is so much at variance with traditional descriptions of the horrors of industrial towns, it seems worth stressing two of its aspects. Improvement outside the industrial regions should not be ignored in any general account of economic change, although the dramatic rise of the northern towns makes this easy to do. Also, the new institutional arrangements and other forces making for improvement were probably for a time successful, even in some of the industrial districts. If the massive growth of urban populations set the seal of inadequacy on such endeavors, this became evident only in the largest northern cities of the nineteenth century.

The lack of data on town growth in early modern England has been somewhat improved upon by several recent studies (Clark and Slack, 1972; Daunton, 1978, pp. 85–114; Borsay, 1977, pp. 581–603; Chalklin, 1974). Yet it is probably fair to say that no coherent model of urban change has emerged, due in large measure to the difficulties of integrating provincial development with existing studies of national development. This paper attempts to move toward such a model. In the first place, urban change was linked integrally with other advances in the early modern economy, above all agricultural improvement, transport development, and the growth of internal trade. Indeed, market towns were a critical element in the expansion of internal trade and distribution, and wealth from this source, supplemented by the far-better understood generation of wealth in foreign commerce and manufacturing production, had a major function in the generation of urban improvement. A second aspect relates to the apparently slow growth of so many provincial towns, other than a small category of fast-developing manufacturing, port, and resort towns. As we have seen, the prolonged unremarkable numerical impact of urbanization has made it difficult to fit the function of towns into the overall framework of the economy. This paper suggests that the relatively slow expansion of market towns before the second half of the eighteenth century, in the context of an already expanding economy, signals an increase in their efficiency. Greater efficiency was promoted, in part, by such developments as better market facilities, wider roads to cater to a greater volume and weight of traffic, new and enlarged bridges, and a host of other achievements. To some extent, therefore, capital was substituted for labor. Investment in towns also involved improvement in social amenities. Indeed, throughout the eighteenth century it is possible to trace a wide variety of specifically urban developments, such as paving, lighting, and the erection of various public buildings, even in towns with virtually static populations. To this extent, the conception of a process of 'urbanization' which necessarily involves the absolute increase of town populations is misleading. In 1660 most provincial towns were very much adjuncts, in physical appearance, function, and administrative authority, of the age-old agrarian structure. By 1760 a great many such towns were either transformed, or on the threshold of transformation, into urban centers with markedly different administrative structures, with a variety and profusion of town amenities unknown to earlier generations, and no doubt with a novel degree of impact on their rural neighborhoods.

A final general point, which continues a theme emphasized by F. J. Fisher for an earlier period, is the striking dominance of London as a motive force for economic change, both through the demands of her vast population in generating trade and through the direct example of metropolitan improvements which were followed in the provinces (Fisher, 1948, pp. 37–50: 1971, pp. 3–16). Most of the urban problems that arose after the Restoration were felt first, and most acutely, in London, and it was not surprisingly in the metropolis that most of the principal responses were first evident.

The detailed purpose of this paper is to present evidence and analysis of urban improvement during the period between, roughly, the Restoration in 1660 and the close of the eighteenth century. In particular, we draw attention to the generation of improvement from two principal sources, which may be labeled *private* and *public*. Private improvement involved above all the new development and reconstruction of residential areas and market centers in towns throughout the country with nonflammable materials, that is to say, brick and tile. New developments associated with rapid population growth in such regions as Bath and a number of London suburbs were sometimes undertaken on a large scale. Numerous building contractors, employing the services of leading architects, transformed many hitherto rural surrounds of urban areas with imposing and elegant squares, walks, and residences. C. W. Chalklin has examined in some detail the origins and finance of such developments in several towns, this activity being characteristic of the years primarily from the middle of the eighteenth century (Chalklin, 1974). In this paper we emphasize a different, less imposing, but more widespread form of improvement: the substitution of brick for timber buildings in numerous town centers throughout the period. Such substitution was well in evidence before the turn of the eighteenth century and can be traced in a growing number of towns from the time of the Restoration. In effect, the brick rebuilding involved the reshaping of the urban landscape throughout the country, and by about 1750 there were few towns of any size that had not experienced considerable reconstruction in this manner. There can be no doubt that the frequent fires that occurred in the closely clustered timber and thatch dwellings in so many medieval and Tudor and Stuart towns provided a major opportunity for such reconstruction, and their reduction a major incentive for it, and it is a thesis of this paper that the 'last major fire' in the various towns provides a rough guide to the period of major brick reconstruction.

The transformation of the urban landscape in this period – for such it was – involved not only widespread and substantial private construction, but also a variety of public improvements that resulted from the activities of town authorities. This paper concentrates primarily on those measures that had a perceptible environmental impact. As we will show, the measures undertaken by various town authorities covered an impressive range of activities, from the laying out of gardens and public walks to the erection of new public buildings and the removal of noxious trades, such as slaughtering, from town centers, but above all the improvement of streets by paving, lighting, cleansing, and widening. The main concerted burst of such activity occurred during the second half of the eighteenth century, although there were many earlier instances, especially in the larger towns.

The chronology of the changes discussed here thus demonstrates two clear phases, though with considerable overlap, as might be expected. The first phase, the reconstruction of town centers with brick and tile, was largely completed by about 1750. By contrast, the local-authority street improvements were most marked after this date. Together, the various improvements amounted to a significant modification of the urban environment, taking place before, as well as during, the classic Industrial Revolution; and in towns both proximate to and remote from the centers of industrial change. For the purpose of this paper, a terminal date of the close of the eighteenth century has been chosen, but it should be stressed that the major trends of street improvement discussed here continued throughout the country until the general reforms of urban administration in the 1830s.

I

An immediate consequence of the widespread diffusion of brick and tile from the later seventeenth century was a reduction in the very high incidence of fire below its medieval and early modern levels. Some towns were admittedly already rather fireproof, those on the stone belts for instance, such as the fifteenth-century woollen towns of the Cotswolds. However, most towns had not by the Restoration experienced the same facelift, being too distant from natural deposits of building stone and slate. Buildings remained constructions of timber framing, infilled by wattle hurdling plastered with earth or mud; dried, hardened and lime-washed; and roofed with straw thatch, or in some regions with reeds. The houses were close together along narrow, twisting streets, often still within town walls, and behind the houses were clusters of thatched outhouses, barns, and workshops.

Towns so built and laid out were potential firebombs. A concentration by historians on a few of the later very extensive fires, notably the Great Fire of London, has obscured the frequency and seriousness of urban fire damage that in reality lasted until the eighteenth century. Typical of the perpetual hazard posed by fire was the case of Stratford-on-Avon, which experienced two great fires in the 1590s. Queen Elizabeth was petitioned to grant relief on the grounds that 200 houses with effects worth in total £12 000 had been burned down. Another major fire in 1614 burned 54 houses, together with barns, stables, and stores of grain, hay, and timber, all valued at £8000, whereupon the council ordered more buckets and firehooks (to pull off burning thatch) and ladders, but more to the purpose, petitioned the Lord Chief Justice to forbid thatched roofs. As was well known, 'the wynde taketh the Thatch and carryeth it very far of and there fireth other Thatched howses' with the result that 'very many fayer tyled howses have byn burned to the grounds'. A Royal Patent was issued authorizing five individuals to make collections of alms on behalf of the sufferers; Shakespeare may have struck the name of one of them out of his will because of improper dealings over the collection (Eccles, 1963 ed., pp. 97, 135–136). Other than a possible connection with William Shakespeare, there is, however, nothing abnormal about Stratford's fire history, not in the dates or extent of its losses – there was another fire in 1641 which caused losses of nearly £9000 – and therefore in the dates of rebuilding, not in the licensed collection of charity or complaints about its abuse, not in the petition to enforce the use of nonflammable roofing materials, only slowly made effective, and not in efforts to have combustible materials stored outside the town (Porter, 1976, pp. 98–100). What the petition indicates is that extensive reconstruction was vital if the first few tiled houses were not to remain at risk of being set alight by burning thatch blown from the other houses. The suppression of thatch was the biggest single step in the right direction, but brick construction was important too, since exterior woodwork (especially the overhangs) even of tiled houses readily caught fire. Change to brick-and-tile construction on the required scale came only after the Restoration.

In London 13 200 houses were destroyed by the Great Fire of 1666, a large proportion having been wholly or mainly of wood. In their stead over 9000 standardized brick houses were erected (Buer, 1926, p. 78: Reddaway, 1951, p. 129). The Great Fire was not, however, the end of destruction in London by fires. There were serious outbreaks in eighteenth-century London, one at Change Alley in 1748, which burned 118 houses (Ash, 1964, p. 93). Much of eastern, unfashionable, workaday London escaped regulation even after 1666 and remained crowded with timber houses, of which still more were actually put up. Only from the mid-1780s were these substantially replaced by brick, and often then only when fire had made the opportunity, the biggest single chance coming in 1794 when over 600 houses in the East End were destroyed by a fire (George, 1966, p. 346). But the City and western districts of London were never again so devastated after the time of the Great Fire. Many smaller towns were less fortunate: East Dereham (Norfolk), 1679; Newmarket (Suffolk), 1683; New Alresford (Hampshire), 1689; Warwick, 1694; Woburn (Bedfordshire) and Buckingham, 1725; Blandford Forum (Dorset), 1731; and Tiverton (Devon), as late as 1794 were among those severely burned, some almost totally leveled. There were several towns that suffered two or three or even up to ten or twelve major conflagrations between the Restoration and the beginning of the nineteenth century, including Tiverton as an extreme case. Such towns were, however, exceptional in continuing to suffer the high fire incidence of earlier centuries.

So frequent had fires been in the Middle Ages that some leases contained the phrase 'usque ad primam combustionem' since landlords wished to be able to recover the building plot from any tenant who might not be able to afford to rebuild after a fire or keep up the rent (Stacpoole, 1972, p. 257). Thatched roofs mixed unhappily with the naked flames used for lighting and heating and the open fires for manufacturing or processing tasks carried on in the middle of towns. Medieval corporations tried, and their successors tried, to banish crafts that used open fires, such as smithery, pottery making, dyeing, tanning, tallow chandling, and malting. The workshops of these trades were all too often the origin of serious fires. At Andover, Hampshire, in 1668, the tanners were ordered to shift their kilns to the riverside 'and sufficiently tile them' because it had been found 'by sad experience' that they had several times nearly set the whole town on fire (Child, 1972, p. 23). Regulations of this kind lapsed as often as they were promulgated, for business premises and dwellings remained one and the same and new businesses were constantly starting up inside the towns. Further, it was impossible to cut the fire risk drastically when open fires were needed for domestic heating and cooking and when stacks of hay and straw and firewood continued to be stored close to every house. Given that the materials of the buildings themselves remained highly combustible, no mere administrative or legislative action could be wholly effective in preventing the outbreak and spread of fires.

The technology of firefighting was weak. Hooks to pull off burning thatch or to pull thatch out of the way of the flames, ladders, and leather buckets were widely provided at public expense and kept by many households, but were often stolen or let fall into disrepair. There were repeated borough orders to repair or renew this equipment and many presentments to local courts for carrying naked flames about after dark or failing to observe the curfew. Some extensions of conduits and water pipes in the lesser towns during the seventeenth century must have been a help, but not a decisive one. Neither were the new squirts and manual pumps decisive. Manually operated tanks with squirts were introduced from Nuremburg about 1625 and some 60 were manufactured in England between 1625 and 1660. A Dutch improvement in the form of a delivery hose was incorporated in English engines of the 1676-1689 period. Larger, side-operated manual pumps were made by Richard Newsham of Cloth Fair, London, by 1729, and these remained the chief type until the nineteenth century. Engines of this sort had been bought by many small market towns by the mid-eighteenth century, but they were not particularly forceful and had only a small tank, and some of the engines in use were so small that they could be carried indoors and upstairs on poles. Once a blaze had taken hold, they were impotent, and therefore they could have played only a contributory role in suppressing fires (Jones, 1968, pp. 143–144).

The critical change was indeed the spread of brick and tile, generalizing a trend towards nonflammable materials begun in the Middle Ages with attempts by many towns to insist on stone party walls and stone chimneys. Tile roofs were, on paper, a requirement in London as early as 1212, Coventry from 1474, Nottingham from 1503, and Norwich from 1509. In medieval Reading the legal opening hours for shops were supposedly enforced by levying a given number of tiles from offenders (Salzman, 1923, p. 174; Hinton, 1954, p. 54). Certainly a few better townhouses used tile from at least the thirteenth century. In the sixteenth and seventeenth centuries it becomes commoner to find borough authorities passing ordinances forbidding the roofing of dwellings with thatch. Enforcement was another matter. At Oxford, for example, thatching continued despite injunctions and bylaws and was implicated in the spread of a fire in 1671, following which the Mayor and Vice-Chancellor both signed a notice prohibiting its use, which was displayed 'on every corner and every inn dore' (Fasnacht, 1954, p. 134).

Seventeenth-century municipal leases came to have clauses enjoining the use of tiles (or slates, meaning stone slate rather than Welsh slate) for roofing and implicitly or explicitly banning thatch. Private house leases began to follow suit. In the eighteenth century the new insurance companies discriminated in their schedules of premiums against thatch in favor of tile or slate. Building in brick and tile, or at any rate without thatch, was increasingly required – usually with the impetus of fright from a fire in the neighborhood – by public agreements, bylaws, and in a significant shift of institutional form, by local Act of Parliament. An early case of the stipulation comes from Winchester, where the Corporation in 1656 made regulations 'for y^{e}avoyding of the greate inconveniences we^{ch} are found by experience to grow by thatcht Houses within that city, both in respect of the danger it occasions by Fire and the unseemliness thereof in so ancient and famous a city . . .' No house was to be thatched, and 'all such Houses that are already thatched, [are] to be covered with Tyle or Slatt within One year next ensuing . . .' Anyone making a mud wall within the city or setting a hedge in the High Street was to be fined (Bailey, 1856, pp. 129–30). This is a nice example of the twin roles of fire precaution and municipal ambition in urban improvement.

Brick-and-tile towns in Georgian, and slightly earlier, styles were rather uniform in appearance, often the result of postfire construction. The absence on central streets of houses earlier in date than the eighteenth century often represents the effect of some great conflagration. Any timbered buildings that chance to survive tend to be around the edges of these core areas, while the near exemption of a solid expanse of brick-and-tile from fire and subsequent decay accounts for the still-recognizable Georgian centers of so many smaller towns. In detail, the architectural history of most individual buildings, let alone streets or towns, proves to be full of complexity and even irony, such as that of the Tudor House Hotel at Tewkesbury, where a timber-framed building of the sixteenth century was refronted in brick in 1701 but now bears a false timber-framed front that was superimposed in the late nineteenth century (Victoria County History, 1968, pp. 130–31). The success of tiling and brick infilling and refronting on older buildings accounts for much of the stylistic and chronological variety in urban housing. Nevertheless, the archaeology of fire has been a prime influence on the architecture and layout of towns. As Defoe wrote of two remarkable instances, Northampton, burned down in 1675, was 'finely rebuilt with brick and stone, and the streets made spacious and wide,' so that, 'as at Warwick, the beauty of it is owing to its own disasters' (1928, Vol. II, p. 86).

Brick was initially dear and rather experimental in the hands of small builders. It was first used in southeast England during the early seventeenth century for refronting; only gradually were whole houses for all but the very rich constructed of brick. Over most of the country brick building occurred after the 1660s, and even then some parts of the north and west were behind other regions. After the Great Fire of London information about the use of brick, as well as about other means to reduce fire damage (such as abolishing overhanging gables and recessing the windows), became more freely available. Building craftsmen who had been drawn to London by high wages, and let in by the seven-year relaxation of prohibitions on non-freemen labor (Reddaway, 1951, p. 115), spread their training through other towns. With the publication of builders' pattern books following the London 'Building Acts' of 1707–1709, these ideas were taken up in the smallest places. Fire danger had prompted these acts. That of 1707 was in reality entitled 'An Act for the better preventing mischiefs that may happen by fire' (Knowles and Pitt, 1972, p. 37).

The wider availability of coal in the seventeenth century probably started the large-scale use of brick since the baking of bricks on any scale required cheap fuel. Coal was used for that purpose from at least 1610 and became more freely available with the fast growth of the Newcastle coal trade between 1634 and 1674. According to Sir William Petty, it was this trade that was responsible for the expansion of baking brick (Nef, 1966, Vol. I, *passim*). A single brickyard tenant in one of the three London producing areas supplied 5 506 000 bricks in three years from 1667 to 1670. Prices of the enormous supplies of bricks needed to rebuild London after the Great Fire appear to have risen steeply only once, when the Dutch temporarily stopped the voyage of the collier fleet from the northeast (Reddaway, 1951, pp. 114, 128). The inland distribution of coal was facilitated by the canalizing of rivers, notably during the generation after the Restoration; the substitution of cheaper brick followed as we have seen. Cheapness is however relative to income, and poorer northern regions were slow to adopt brick despite privileged access to coal.

There is no adequate direct measure of the temporal spread of brick-and-tile construction. The literary references are too few and too vague. We therefore suggest that the inverse of the list of last serious fires offers an acceptable proxy measure. Obviously, there are drawbacks to the method: a town built of flammable materials does not necessarily burn down, nor is one built of comparatively nonflammable materials necessarily exempt. Also, the data on fires depend substantially on collections of alms licensed by royal letters patent (Briefs) and while, to judge from independent evidence, most major fires were included, it is not certain that large numbers of buildings were destroyed by each reported fire. Further, strategically placed tile roofs sometimes reduced fire losses without much use of brick.[1] The systems of Briefs declined in the late eighteenth century as private insurance increased and may exaggerate the earliness of the fires so recorded. Despite these reservations, the use of the series drawn from Briefs appears to be justified. The *relative* increase of Briefs for nonfire disaster losses, such as those caused by floods and hailstorms, despite the absolute decline of Briefs, implies that their use does really pick up the decrease of fires. In addition, local histories fully confirm the picture given by the Briefs for the counties we have examined in greatest detail. Accordingly, evidence from Briefs and other sources has been used to compile Graph 1. The sample is of 154 town fires and is geographically wide. Evidence before 1650 is not cited since it is unlikely that there was extensive building in brick and tile; the first half of the seventeenth century represents the 'early adopter' phase for brick construction. The period 1650-1730, when over 80 percent of the sample of town fires occurred, was apparently the 'majority adopter phase' for brick, and the period after 1730 that of 'laggard adopters'.

---

1. As at Dorchester in 1775, where the fire 'raged with great fury for several hours, taking very irregular directions, making great havock amongst the thatched houses, and passing those which were roofed with tiles or slates.' Quoted in E. L. Jones (1968), p. 145; see also p. 144 on Blandford.

·The advantages of brick construction for purposes other than fire protection are obvious. Boxlike houses of brick were comparatively easy to keep clean and were unattractive to uninvited organisms such as rats. As a result, the urban habitat became healthier, as eighteenth-century observers remarked (Buer, 1926, pp. 87–88). In 1652, long before brick building was widespread, London authorities already had noted that brick was efficient 'for avoiding the infection of plague' (Mullet, 1956, p. 186). When other depressants of population growth were also removed, the reduction of dirt diseases resulting from better housing, street cleaning, and other improvements may have been able to add its influence to the growth of population.[2]

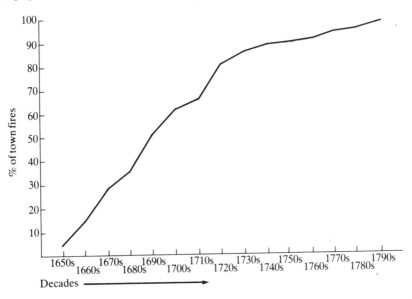

Graph 1 Inferred spread of brick and tile (inverse of last major town fires), 1650–1800 by decades. (N.B. the total does not sum to 100 percent because of rounding.) *Sources*: A. T. Hart (1962); Jones (1968); Money (1892); Snell (1892); Walford (1882), p. 74. A list of the fires included is available from the authors.

2. Referring to measures to clean the streets of Nottingham regularly from 1748, J. D. Chambers noted that, 'in accounting for the remarkable improvement in public health which took place in the middle of the century, the crude measures taken by obscure town officials cannot be ignored' (1960), p. 105.

II

In this section we turn to various aspects of 'public' improvement, especially those connected with town streets, which, together with the private building and rebuilding already described, brought about unprecedented changes in the environment and urban landscape of the great majority of towns between the Restoration and 1750, and even greater changes during the second half of the eighteenth century.[3]

Street improvements and maintenance by town authorities had, of course, an ancient history. For centuries civic authorities had been involved with the basic activities of paving, lighting, watching, cleansing, and otherwise maintaining the town streets and footpaths. Similarly, from time to time the local authorities had concerned themselves with suppressing a host of 'nuisances', such as removing obstructions from the streets, preventing encroachments into the streets by piecemeal building and the extension of shop fronts, ordering the collection of rainwater through gutters and drainpipes rather than spouts onto the streets, regulating the traffic through towns, and removing such trades as animal slaughtering from the main thoroughfares and residential areas. From Tudor times and before, many town authorities provided public water supplies, regulated the local markets, and in a variety of other ways governed the day-to-day functioning of urban affairs. Such early endeavors are beyond the scope of this paper, although it should be stressed that some improvements, notably the provision of better water supplies which occurred in many towns, especially from the last two decades of the seventeenth century, were an integral part of the gradual transformation of English town life.[4]

There can be no doubt, however, that from roughly the last two decades of the seventeenth century, and especially after about 1750, the pace of public urban improvement increased substantially in a great number of English towns. To some extent, progress consisted

3. For reasons of space, we do not discuss in detail the aspect of the medieval or early modern town, nor the constant and inconclusive battle to maintain its public facilities which is evidenced in recurrent municipal ordinances and endless presentments for failing to comply with them. It will be evident that we consider a favorable view of improvement in towns of those periods, indeed the whole concept of an amelioration rather than attempted stabilization of their condition, such as that of Platt (1976, pp. 146, 190), to be overdrawn.
4. We have compiled a long list of towns where pumping rather than gravity-fed systems of water supply were introduced in the 1680s and 1690s and after, often the work of the celebrated engineer Sorocold. See, for example, Williamson (1936, pp. 43–94). We hope to return to this aspect of improvement on a later occasion.

of an extension of customary activity. At the same time, however, a number of town authorities undertook new kinds of improvement. The most notable new activity was the widening of existing streets and the construction of new ones. In this way, the new spacious enterprises of the private developers in cities such as Bath found their counterparts in the reconstruction of older centers. Very often, wider streets were connected with rebuilding, and rebuilding after fires was, as we have seen, a powerful force for change. The opportunity lost for publicly directed rebuilding in this manner in London was lamented by Massie in 1754. '*Porticos* and *Piazzas* are not now to be expected in the City: where indeed, two proper Opportunities for such kind of Ornaments have been supinely neglected', the opportunities arising from the Great Fire of 1666 and the more recent conflagration in Cornhill in 1748 (Massie, 1754, p. 28). In many towns opportunities were taken, however, and stringent building regulations attempted to provide wider and more efficient thoroughfares. Improvements connected with growing inland trade – new bridges and turnpike roads, for example – also gave impetus to the widening of streets to cater to the extra traffic generated. At the same time, the period saw the construction of various public buildings in many towns. Such building and rebuilding often involved the purchase and demolition of existing buildings and ancient town walls and gates, and the consequent opportunity to widen streets. Such removal was connected almost invariably with measures to cater for a growing volume of town traffic, and to provide more appropriate street entrances and exits.

Generalizations about the activities of English town authorities present many hazards. In their monumental study of English local government, Webb and Webb showed how varied and complex were the municipal regimes prior to the Municipal Corporations Act of 1835 (Webb and Webb, 1963, 2 vols). Incorporated boroughs might be governed by a close-knit and powerful municipal corporation, able to undertake most or all of the normal urban improvements that are dealt with in this paper. Many such corporations levied a borough rate, whereas others, with substantial income from corporate property and other sources, needed no such levy. Elsewhere, authority might well be diffuse to the point of absence. In some places, even at the close of the eighteenth century, manorial courts still attempted to enforce lighting and paving regulations, while the Lord of the Manor (who might be a town corporation) sometimes retained privileges such as market tolls in return for certain obligations such as paving or repairing bridges. Towns, parishes, and counties all had their different authorities and sources of income. In some places one might find a combination of overlapping authorities, as at Sheffield, where throughout the eighteenth century the streets and markets were under the divided jurisdiction of the

'Common Burgery of Freeholders', the Capital Burgesses, and the Lord of the Manor (Webb and Webb, 1963, Vol. I, p. 201). To unravel in even a handful of towns the actual details of town improvement, where passiveness by one authority might have been counteracted by diligence in another, is clearly a complex task.

Despite this reservation, it is nevertheless possible to establish a number of general points about the course of eighteenth-century improvement undertaken by town authorities. First, there was a significant expansion in both the extent and scope of improvement in the period. Second, improvement was accompanied by a number of fundamental administrative changes which provided a more flexible framework within which improvement could be undertaken. One change was the gradual move from individual responsibility placed on householders for the repair, lighting, and other maintenance of the streets adjoining their houses to a system whereby the local authorities themselves assumed responsibility. In the process the individual obligations of householders were replaced by the levying of local paving and lighting rates. The new system ensured steady and predictable revenues from rates while at the same time allowing rates to be mortgaged to raise capital for costly improvements.

Local authority rather than individual activity meant a greater uniformity in the carrying out of work than was possible hitherto. As one writer lamented in 1754: 'Now, one housekeeper mends or paves with small Pebbles, another with great, a third with Ragstones, a fourth with broken Flints, a fifth is poor, a sixth is able, but backward and unwilling' (*Public Nuisance Considered . . .*, 1754, pp. 4–5). Indeed, it was the difficulty of enforcing individual responsibility, the absence of proper machinery for inspection and for ordering the method of construction to be used, and the vagueness as to when exactly the obligations should be met that resulted so often in broken and dangerous town pavements. A further problem was the constant breaking of streets by water companies, especially in the larger towns where local authorities often tried fruitlessly to force the companies to repair their damage. Once responsibility for paving and other improvements was in the hands of a single public body, it was far easier to maintain a reasonable standard of street repair and to oblige water companies to make good their breakages.

The change from individual householder responsibility to this form of collective action gave, above all, tangible prospects for *improvement,* that is, not simply the more effective compliance with traditional standards but also the raising of those standards through new technologies and areas of application. The basis of householder obligation was rooted in custom and tradition, and it had been difficult for local authorities to impose upon citizens obligations that surpassed those of earlier generations. The adoption of a system of 'improvement rates', levied on the value of property, marked a considerable advance in the prospects for better urban environments.

A further administrative change which became increasingly evident during the course of the eighteenth century was the decline in the principle of universal voluntary service among citizens holding such posts as constables, watchmen, surveyors, and scavengers, and their replacement by paid officials (Webb and Webb, 1963, Vol. I, p. 125). Specialization of functions, which in the case of town streets would be such matters as cleansing, policing, and paving, was clearly more efficient and opened the way to better standards of street laying and maintenance. One more important step should be noted. During the second half of the eighteenth century a great many towns vested their improvement activities and rate-levying powers not in the existing corporate and parish authorities, but in bodies of trustees. Thus, in town after town, bodies of 'street commissioners', 'paving commissioners', 'lamp commissioners', and other variously named boards were set up by Act of Parliament as new local authorities. It is an argument of this paper that the establishment of these bodies marks a significant advance in urban improvement, and that the Acts of Parliament setting them up give a guide, albeit a rough one, to the timing and geographic extent of improvement in the period.

The advent of less-congested town streets and better paving and lighting was accompanied by a significant, though gradual, change of attitudes towards social and economic progress. Before the eighteenth century the prevailing attitude had been very much to contain change, and to confine developments within the established and known framework and organization. Thus, when London's vigorous expansion began to perturb authorities early in the seventeenth century, the King and Parliament sought to check London's growth by prohibiting new buildings. When ironbound wheels on carts, big wagons, and large teams of horses threatened to break up the flimsy pavements, numerous local bylaws and parliamentary legislation endeavored to protect streets by checking and regulating the types of carts, width of wheels, numbers of horses, and so on. Traffic restrictions remained, but slowly the notion of adapting roads to vehicles rather than the other way around began to prevail. As Hanway wrote of London's streets in 1754: 'Pavements should be adapted to the carriages they bear; and as ours, from an unavoidable necessity, must bear great weights, the materials made use of, and the manner of disposing of them, should be proportioned' (Hanway, 1754, p. 15). With street lighting, a different, though also significant, change in social attitudes became evident during the course of the late seventeenth and early eighteenth centuries. Before the Restoration lighting regulations (almost always the responsibility of individual householders) had been very much an adjunct to the enforcement of law and order – a police measure to light town streets on dark evenings before the curfew restrictions took over and 'nightwalking' was prohibited. By 1700 there were many signs of change (Falkus, 1976; de Beer, 1941, pp. 311–24). In some towns lighting hours were extended and restrictions on nightwalking no longer enforced. In larger centers a flourishing night life was evident, and adequate lighting became as much a social amenity as an aid to civil order. By the middle of the eighteenth century better lighting, it was claimed, was able to 'afford pleasure, and convenience, to every passenger on foot or in carriages' (Hanway, 1754, p. 34).

The widespread adoption of the various public improvements in the course of the eighteenth century, undertaken in the main by specially created bodies of trustees levying rates, marked an important step towards what might be termed *urban collectivism*. The new bodies, and the statutory powers acquired by existing corporations, were more appropriate to meet the needs of heavier traffic and to initiate better amenities at a time when expectations were rising. Moreover, the old system of individual obligation, both in service to corporations and in performance of statutory duties such as paving, tended to break down with the appearance of shifting, anonymous populations, and with changes in the residential structure of towns which led to large areas where the poor clustered, such areas being impossible to improve by householder duty.

Interestingly, the functions of urban corporations that dealt with agriculture tended to move in the opposite direction during the course of the eighteenth century. Many boroughs owned considerable land, while the complicated array of urban and manorial courts had very often been primarily concerned with matters such as common pasturage and otherwise regulating the use of the corporate property. With enclosure came a decline in many traditional functions of the borough authorities and a rise of their 'urban' functions instead. At one level, therefore, it is possible to view the administrative changes taking place in many English towns from the end of the seventeenth century as a rise in individualism in agriculture (enclosure) away from the former corporate responsibility, and a reverse process with regard to those functions related directly to urban improvement. And both processes permitted the achievements of new standards which the traditional framework had tended to check. At the same time, it must be stressed that the form in which urban improvement such as paving and lighting was carried out also provided an important role for the private contractor. Nearly everywhere the new improvements were put out to contract, and paving and lighting contractors were paid by the various local authorities out of local rates.

The administrative framework of town improvement that emerged by, say, 1780 was a varied pattern of different authorities, powers, and functions, sometimes overlapping, rarely uniform, and each governed by local variations in enthusiasm and endeavor. Not everywhere by any means did towns obtain the special statutory bodies of trustees referred to earlier. When they did, the new bodies were frequently the middle of a chain of improvements rather than the beginning. Thus, in many towns individual obligations for paving and lighting were supplemented increasingly from the late seventeenth century by direct intervention from town corporations. When the need for greater revenues and powers arose, Parliament was entreated to establish bodies of improvement commissioners, especially after 1750. Town corporations themselves frequently obtained Acts of Parliament to enable them to undertake various improvements, to raise rates, and to borrow money. And in some small towns – even in 1835 – the obligations on inhabitants to hang lanterns outside their windows and to pave and cleanse before their doors still stood.

III

The pattern of urban improvement undertaken by town authorities seems nevertheless to be fairly clear in outline. The progress of urban street lighting may illustrate a number of aspects of general improvement: the growth of local authority activity, the establishment of special commissioners, and the influence of the metropolis on provincial centers. Under the ancient 'candle and lanthorn' regulations both the enforcement of by-laws and the raising of standards of lighting were difficult. Only the wealthier parts of towns were lit as a rule, since inhabitants in poorer quarters could not afford the cost of lighting, and it was in the poorer areas that the enforcement by town and parish officials would be most feeble. Moreover, customary lighting hours were limited both as regards the actual hours of evening lighting (normally until nine o'clock) and the season of lighting (only in winter months, when there was no moon shining).

Major improvements in street lighting took place in London in the 1680s with the formation of companies to exploit patents for newly developed oil-burning street lamps (Falkus, 1976, pp. 255–57; de Beer, 1941, pp. 311–24). The companies contracted with householders to provide lighting in place of the customary obligations. Since one street lamp gave more than sufficient light to illuminate the street in front of one house, and since the lamps were relatively costly to erect and maintain, agreement was generally necessary among occupiers in a particular street to contract with a lighting company. The local authorities were involved since they were responsible for enforcing lighting requirements; and because the new street lights gave better lighting, and could be lit longer than had hitherto been possible, the City and Westminster authorities encouraged their use. Monopolies were granted to lighting companies while both City and Westminster authorities extended the requirements of householders for lighting the streets by lengthening the hours of lighting, but exempted those who 'agree to make use of lamps of any sort to be placed at such distances in the street as shall be approved by two or more Justices of the Peace' (2 W & M Sess. 2. c. 8). In 1735 the City of London authorities decided to take lighting powers into their own hands. Accordingly, the following year an Act was obtained that allowed the City to raise a special lighting rate, and stipulated that lighting contracts should be for no more than one year at a time. As a result of this measure, and a further extension of powers in 1744, there was a significant improvement in London's lighting. In 1694 the number of nights each year when lighting was obligatory had been no more than 117, whereas in 1736 lights were to be lit each night of the year. In 1694 lamps were lit from six o'clock until midnight; from 1736 they were lit from sunset until sunrise. And the numbers of lamps increased considerably. Elsewhere in London, too, various rate-levying authorities had begun to set up street lamps. In 1738, for example, the Vestry of the 'great and populous' parish of Christ Church was allowed by Act to levy a rate of up to 8d. in the pound towards street lamps, and a number of other parishes were lit and watched in this manner (11 GII c.35). Trustees were appointed to improve several London squares from 1725 by levying rates and borrowing on the security of such rates; in 1762 an Act of Parliament established improvement commissioners in Westminster, and this body at once initiated considerably better lighting and other improvement measures (2 GIII c.21; Webb and Webb, 1922).

Following the developments in London, a number of other towns began to adopt the new street lighting. In 1700 Bristol and Norwich both obtained Acts that established special lighting rates (11 & 12 WIII c.23; 11 & 12 WIII c.15). As in London, the Bristol Act strengthened householder obligations and increased fines for non-compliance, unless the householders in any parish 'shal agree to make use of Lamps of such sort and soe to be placed as shall be approved by Justices of the Peace'. The lighting rate was to be collected by the parish authorities. In Norwich, similarly, the 1700 Act extended lighting hours and penalties, but allowed householders to contract for oil lamps instead, by paying a rate to the parish authority. At the same time Norwich householders were obliged to pay toward the cost of lights hung out by the corporation, thus making probably the earliest compulsory lighting rate levies by a town authority. Other early examples of special lighting rates were Bath (1707), Great Yarmouth (1721), Canterbury (1727), and Salisbury (1737). Until the second half of the eighteenth century, however, the great majority of publicly undertaken lighting improvements were the result of action by corporations within the existing administrative framework and paid for out of customary revenues.

The early spread of street lighting in the wake of London's initiatives normally involved simply the setting up of a few glass lamps in the market square or other main centers, paid for and maintained by the Corporation. Thus, in Canterbury in 1687 the town was presented with 'a great light or lucidiary' on the model of one in Cheapside; the Exeter corporation in 1689 bought a lamp from London to be hung at the Guildhall, and in 1692 London lamps were brought to Norwich (Gardiner, 1933, pp. 108–9; Webb papers, *Devon*, p. 110; Norfolk, p. 205). By the end of the 1730s most large towns (though with notable exceptions such as Nottingham and Newcastle) and many small towns had adopted some form of public oil lighting in the streets.

Paving improvements, the laying down of pebbles or stones to form a hard carriageway, were undertaken in a broadly similar fashion to lighting; that is, obligations on individual householders to pave and repair the street fronting their houses were gradually discarded in favour of collective action, either by corporations or bodies of trustees. Even more than in the case of lighting, the multiplicity of urban authorities and the complex jurisdictions governing the paving of streets even within a single town makes the history of improvement perforce the history of administrative organization as well. From medieval times the City of London and a number of the leading provincial towns had levied 'pavage' tolls. At the end of the seventeenth century corporations frequently paid for paving and repairing in the market places and major high streets. In small towns such paving was still sometimes carried out by the Lord of the Manor, but principally the costs of paving, and particularly repair and maintenance, fell on individual householders. Only in the eighteenth century, and especially after 1750, did towns adopt the same solution as they had done for lighting, levying special rates and substituting corporate for individual action.

In London, where growing traffic had brought increasing complaints about the state of the streets, a major step forward was taken by the establishment of the Westminster paving commissioners in 1762. These commissioners were entitled to borrow money and to raise a local rate, and as a result were able to lay down a surface of smooth granite stones imported from Aberdeen. By the early

1770s it was estimated that the commissioners had spent some £400 000; not only was the surface of the carriageway improved, but a footway was also formed and paved with smooth stones (Webb and Webb, 1963, pp. 282–89). The standard of paving introduced in Westminster was not matched in the City of London, although in 1766 the commissioners of sewers were empowered to light, pave, and cleanse by levying a rate (6 GIII c.26). Nor was the standard upheld in Westminster, because during the 1780s various parish vestries obtained special Acts enabling them to make their own paving rates and so step outside the jurisdiction of the Westminster commissioners.

Outside London there are increasing references to paving by town authorities as a supplement to householder obligations from the end of the seventeenth century. Wisbech, a small town with a population of about 2000 in 1700, was paved by the corporation from the 1680s, and by this time the corporation was also laying down sewers to carry away waste water and providing street-cleansing service. Penzance, with a similar population, also paved its streets at the end of the seventeenth century, and in 1718 the Corporation paid two guineas for 'advice in London about paving the streets' (Webb Papers,ʼ *Cambridgeshire,* p. 100; Webb and Webb, 1963, Vol. II, p. 408). At Nottingham in 1723 new paving was undertaken partly by public subscription and partly by grants from the corporation, and in the seventeenth century there were several instances of Bristol corporations undertaking paving and charging the occupants of the adjoining houses (Latimer, 1893, p. 38; Bailey, 1852–1855, p. 1138). In 1700 Bristol Corporation obtained an Act permitting the raising of a rate for paving, and in Hull in 1750 a master builder was appointed 'to pave and repair the Streets, Lanes and Alleys of this Town' (11 & 12 WIII c.23; Jackson, 1972, p. 201). Even more general was the provision of some form of street cleansing in the chief streets and marketplaces. By 1700 most towns seem to have spent money on scavenging, carting refuse from the streets, and similar activities. Under an Act of Parliament in 1715, English city authorities were generally permitted to levy a local rate not exceeding 6d. in the pound toward the cost of scavenging, and in 1736 this provision was extended to all market towns (1 GI c. 52; 9 GII c. 18).

By the 1750s and 1760s, that is, before the general introduction of improvement Acts, there were numerous other signs of urban improvement. In the years after 1680, and especially after about 1735, there is evidence of much public building to supplement the private building that has been detailed already. In town after town new shirehalls, guildhalls, exchanges, market centers, assembly rooms, and other public buildings, including churches and gaols, were erected. And partly as a consequence of these improvements, streets were widened, and old buildings and ancient town gates and walls demolished. It is possible to compile a lengthy list of improvements in numerous towns before the middle of the eighteenth century. An inhabitant of Chichester writing in his old age in 1784, detailing each and every jot of amelioration – a replacement conduit, a wooden fish shambles renewed in stone, the footpaths fenced and paved, a new assembly room, a town gate taken down, a new and wider bridge built, and so forth – could observe 'I have seen almost the whole city and town new built or new faced, a spirit of emulation in this way having run through the whole' (Steer, 1962, pp. 18ff). In Nottingham the first decades of the eighteenth century had seen 'the Improvement of the Town, by mending Roads and raising and paving streets as well as by beautifying it with Sightly Buildings' (Chambers, 1960, p. 106). In Wotton-under-Edge a new market house was begun in the 1690s, and loans of £370 had been taken up by 1700 for the purpose; in York an Assembly Room started in 1730, and in 1744 the Nottingham guildhall was rebuilt; in Leicester between 1748 and 1750 a new market hall and Assembly Rooms were built. And such examples could be multiplied (Rodgers, 1951, p. 67; Skillington, 1923, p. 133; Hinton, 1954, p. 133; Lindley, 1962, p. 74; Borsay, 1977, p. 582). Yet the extent of such improvements was necessarily limited as long as traditional methods of administration and sources of finance were relied upon. Few corporations were prepared to spend large sums out of their customary revenues for street improvements, although some with considerable revenues, like Liverpool, undertook many major improvements without resort to a rate. There is no doubt that the costs of paving and street widening in particular could involve substantial sums; such activity frequently involved the raising of loans, and while some corporations could do this without explicit parliamentary authority, the uncertainty of the legal position and the nature of the security on which loans could be raised meant that the towns usually sought an Act of Parliament to sanction substantial borrowing.

The numbers of parliamentary Acts obtained for street improvement indicate an increased momentum of change in the second half of the eighteenth century. From the late 1740s rarely a year passed without a cluster of town acts, some of them setting up bodies of rate-levying improvement commissioners to operate alongside the established town corporations. In all, over 100 separate bodies of commissioners were established in towns in England and Wales by 1800.

The historical strands leading to the formation of such bodies were varied. There was, for example, a lengthy history of the creation of special rate-levying bodies authorized by Parliament. Analogous to improvement commissioners were the various harbor trustees established from the 1690s, and in 1710 the first body of separate trustees of turnpike roads was set up with powers to levy tolls. Earlier turnpike acts had vested powers in existing county authorities, so that the transition to distinct bodies was a very similar process. Other bodies of trustees had long been instituted by Act for specific purposes, for workhouses, bridges, charitable institutions of various kinds, and so forth. Rate levying by established town corporations and county authorities for specific purposes also had a long history. There was the county poor rate, while county highway authorities obtained rating powers as statute labor was commuted into money payments. Tolls on bridges, levied by a variety of parish and municipal authorities, had existed since at least the thirteenth century. Rates also were sometimes levied for specific urban improvements. One of the earliest paving rates occurred in 1605 when the Middlesex justices were allowed to raise a rate for paving Drury Lane and St. Giles (3 Jac c. 22). Later, in 1662, the street commissioners established under the important London and Westminster Act (the first time the two cities were linked for administrative purposes) were empowered to raise a rate for scavenging (3 & 4 Car c. 2).

The first body of separate improvement trustees was established for St James's Square, Westminster, in 1725. In this case there was no established local authority, and the inhabitants were allowed 'to make a rate of themselves' and to borrow up to £6000 for this purpose. The first body of improvement commissioners to be set up alongside an existing municipal corporation was at Salisbury in 1737, and the functions of this body were 'repairing, paving, watching, and enlightening the streets' (10 GII c. 6). The commissioners consisted of the local mayor, the town recorder, and the justices and four inhabitants from each of the three town parishes, to be elected annually. Nearly all subsequent bodies of trustees likewise included the principal civic officials and a group of citizens usually drawn from the wealthy and influential inhabitants. The particular Act did not include any borrowing provisions, and the scope of improvement was very limited by comparison with what became common by the 1770s.

Table 1 gives the total number of these new administrative bodies, including those in London, established during the eighteenth century, and the total indicates clearly the sustained nature of activity during the second half of the century.

The work of improvement commissioners has been largely neglected since the pioneering studies of the Webbs. Certainly, there are major difficulties in any assessment of their activities. Like so many British local government institutions, the bodies of improvement commissioners evolved gradually, never operating to a coherent plan, and varying in powers and functions from town to town. There are many instances, as in Bristol and Hull, where existing corporations obtained Acts of Parliament to establish or confirm rating and borrowing powers. As might be expected, the concrete achievements of local bodies in the improvement of town streets varied considerably from place to place, and in any particular town from time to time. Zeal vied with indolence, civic pride with parsimony and corruption. Certainly, contemporary local pamphlets and topographical guides abounded with criticisms of corporations and commissioners. Clearly in many instances, even after the passage of an improvement Act, little or nothing resulted. Paving carried out in Lincoln under the 1791 Act, for example, was very tardy, and the Southampton commissioners did little to extend the town's lighting for more than a decade after the Act of 1770 (Hill, 1966, p. 185; Patterson, 1966, Vol. 1, pp. 47–49). Preambles often make clear that the powers granted under earlier Acts were either insufficient, or for some other reason a number of the clauses were inoperative. Although the effective carrying out of improvement was of course less likely to attract attention than was tardiness, there are numerous examples of considerable improvement activity by commissioners (Hart, 1965, pp. 262ff).

For purposes of this paper, two important features of the bodies of improvement commissioners need to be noted. First, they were generally given the power by Act of Parliament to raise local rates, or occasionally tolls from bridges or markets or other revenue-raising concessions. Second, especially after 1760, it became common for improvement commissioners to be empowered to borrow money, usually for a specified maximum sum, on the security of their revenues. It was the need for rate-levying and borrowing powers that normally necessitated Acts of Parliament because such a power could be granted only by Parliament. Work undertaken as a result of an improvement Act did not normally involve a one-time expenditure. On the contrary, much improvement work was necessarily continuous, and individual towns returned to Parliament on several occasions for new Acts with greater rating and borrowing powers, and with wider areas of application. Some early Acts do indicate

TABLE 1   New bodies of improvement commissioners, 1725–1799.

Years	Number	Total
1725–1749	4	4
1750–1759	17	21
1760–1769	31	52
1770–1779	36	88
1780–1789	39	127
1790–1799	33	160

Sources: Statutes at Large; House of Commons Journals.

that improvement costs were sometimes thought of as once-and-for-all expenditure. At Salisbury in 1737, rates were levied at 2 shillings for the first five years, and at 1 shilling thereafter (10 GII c. 6). At New Windsor in 1769, the commissioners were allowed to borrow up to £2500 on security of the rates for paving and other purposes, but the rates could be up to 1 shilling in the £1 for the first three years only, and thereafter there was a maximum of 9d. (9 GIII c. 10).

Within their evident limitations, the improvement Acts do show wide-spread urban improvement, especially after 1762, when the flow of measures became continuous. The new rating and borrowing powers gave to the authorities greater flexibility in undertaking new improvement measures than had hitherto been possible. This is seen particularly in the greatly expanded range of activities that commissioners were able to undertake in the last third of the eighteenth century.

The specific powers granted to improvement commissioners varied considerably, but the great majority were concerned with various aspects of street improvement and safety. Most common were provisions for paving, cleansing, watching, and lighting of town streets. On occasions, commissioners were established to deal with individual functions, like the Exeter lighting trustees in 1760, but from the 1760s the majority of Acts included all the major elements of street improvements, and also from this time their scope became generally wider. Thus, the 1770 Southampton Act, in addition to the normal paving, lighting, and scavenging regulations, allowed the commissioners to regulate building encroachments onto the streets, and ordered also that new buildings were not to have projections. As the Rochester Act of 1769 expressed it, new buildings should 'for the effectual and absolute Prevention of all Manner of Projections, Annoyances, and Inconveniences thereby, rise perpendicularly from the Foundation' (9 GIII c. 32). In regulations such as this, it is easy to understand the emergence of the classic Georgian frontage so characteristic of towns of this period.

From the 1760s it also became common to vest in the various bodies of commissioners power to limit and prevent the host of 'nuisances' that had plagued the different urban, parish, and manorial authorities for centuries. At the same time, the list of such offences became more extensive and detailed. As early as 1608 bylaws in Manchester forbade the playing of football in streets and also forbade wagons to stand in the thoroughfares (Webb and Webb, 1963, Vol. 1, p. 105). At Bristol in 1615, in order to protect the narrow streets and rough paving, no cart with iron-bound wheels was permitted to enter the city; a regulation in 1705 forbade the use of iron in the sledges which were commonly drawn about the streets by dogs (Webb and Webb, 1963, Vol. II, p. 446). Enactments like these were common, as were restrictions on a variety of noxious trades carried out in town centers, such as animal slaughtering. But to judge by the frequency of regulations and the complaints of contemporaries, it would appear that in many instances the power of established authorities was insufficient, or the authorities were unwilling, to enforce the bylaws sufficiently. It is probable, therefore, that the transfer of such powers to the bodies of street commissioners from the 1760s marked an improvement in their application.

One element in the improvement Acts that deserves special attention is the frequency of provisions for widening streets, demolishing existing buildings, and erecting new ones. Again and again the Acts empowered trustees or corporations to widen streets and make new roads, and often such powers were granted as part of other improvements, for example, the construction of bridges or new markets. In 1769 the Gainsborough commissioners were empowered to borrow money to widen streets by buying and demolishing any 'Messuage, House, Shop or Tenement' and 'lay the Ground . . . into any of the said Streets, Lanes, Alleys or Passages' (9 GIII c. 21). At Southampton in 1770 the Commissioners could buy and take down buildings 'for enlarging, widening, or rendering more commodious' the streets, and for this purpose they were to take down the East Gate (10 GIII c. 25).

The impetus to improve came from a number of quarters. Pressure came from a growing volume of inland trade which stretched the existing resources and amenities of towns. Town streets suffered from the ravages of coaches and wagons, from the encroachments of buildings in central areas, and from the expansion of local markets which outgrew the areas customarily reserved for them. The prosperity and rebuilding of Stamford in the late seventeenth century was directly connected with the river Welland being made navigable and with the growth of stagecoach traffic on the Great North Road (Thirsk, 1965, pp. 68–73). An Act obtained by the City of London in 1737 drew attention to the necessity for improved paving and the establishment of 'footpassages' because of 'the great Increase of Coaches, Carts, and other Carriages, etc . . .' (10 GII c. 22). Salisbury's 1737 Act noted that the existing laws were entirely inadequate to maintain the streets in reasonable repair because it was a town 'through which the main Western Road from the City of London to Exeter, Cornwall, and the Towns and Places adjacent, directly leads, which together with the pleasant Situation of the Place and Country thereabout, occasions great Numbers of Gentry and other Persons to resort to, and reside in the said City . . .' (10 GII c. 6). An Act obtained by Doncaster Corporation in 1764 noted that, 'the Borough of Doncaster . . . . has a navigable River, and is a great Thoroughfare between the South and Northern Parts of the Kingdom, by Means whereof a considerable Trade is carried on in the said Borough' (4 GIII c. 40).

The passage of improvement Acts frequently coincided with local transport and navigation development. Table 2 shows the dates of some early improvement Acts and the corresponding road turnpike Acts. Parliamentary measures are, as stressed earlier, only a rough guide to actual improvement; nevertheless, the passage of road Acts does indicate a period of pressure on existing transport resources, and in the case of 'town-centred' Acts, where turnpikes were established on roads leading into particular towns, the resulting effects on local streets and markets were considerable. As well as road Acts, better bridges and river improvements also attracted traffic, and in the case of bridge construction sometimes led directly to street widening and opening.

A further stimulus to improvement came from the development of 'civic consciousness' which seems to have occurred quite generally in eighteenth-century provincial towns. New wealth brought new standards and expectations of comfort. Many corporations tried to make the urban environment more pleasant in addition to the normal concern with streets. A writer in 1754 claimed that many towns and cities 'are diligently embellishing and adorning, justly perceiving the substantial Benefits arising therefrom' (Massie, 1754, p. v). At Plymouth and Southampton in the 1730s and 1740s, the corporations began to plant trees, and in Liverpool in 1767 public walks and gardens were laid out (Webb papers, *Devon*, p. 110; Patterson, 1966, Vol. I, p. 43; Webb and Webb, 1963, Vol. II, p. 484; Borsay, 1977, p. 583). In some towns, such as York, Newcastle, Nottingham, and Bristol, the local gentry bought townhouses, and a pale reflection of the London 'season' became evident. In these centers the marks of leisure and elegance could be seen in the new residences and squares. The effort of towns great and small to mimic the metropolis was the subject of contemporary comment by the mid-eighteenth century, and provincial life found expression through a variety of outlets, through the local press, theaters, public buildings, and enhanced social activity generally. As Hanway expressed it in 1762: 'And *Reason* and *Experience* teach, that in proportion as improvements are made in the Seat of Empire, will either trading Cities and Towns emulate the Glory of the Metropolis, though on a smaller scale' (Hanway, 1762, p. 80).

All such factors stimulated improvement, and the geographical clustering of improvement Acts at certain times also provides evidence of civic consciousness and the existence of a 'demonstration effect'. Coventry's Act of 1763, for example, was modeled on the one just obtained by Nottingham (Webb and Webb, 1963, Vol. II, p. 443). Similarly, Southampton's Act of 1770 was explicitly copied from one obtained by Portsmouth in 1768: the paving contract was

TABLE 2   Improvement and Road Acts, selected towns, 1706–1764.

Improvement Acts (year)		Road Acts (year)	
1706	Bath	1707	Town centred
1727	Canterbury	1725	Chatham-Canterbury
		1725	Rochester-Canterbury
1744	Beverley	1744	Hull-Beverley
1750	Gloucester	1747	Gloucester-Cirencester
1755	Leeds	1752	Leeds-Harrogate
		1755	Leeds-Preston
		1758	Leeds-Stratfield
1756	Poole	1756	Town centred
1756	Shrewsbury	1752	Shrewsbury-Wrexham
		1752	Shrewsbury-Bridgnorth
		1756	Shrewsbury-Shawbury
1757	Bath	1757	Corsham-Bath-Easton Bridge
1759	Guildford	1757	Stoke-Guildford-Arundel
		1758	Leatherhead-Stoke
		1758	Guildford-Farnham
1760	Exeter	1753	Town centred
		1759	Exeter-Bideford
1762	Chester	1760	Chester-Whitchurch-Newport
1762	Nottingham	1759	Grantham-Nottingham-Derby
		1759	Nottingham-New Haven
		1764	Trowell-Nottingham
1763	York	1764	York-Kexby Bridge
1764	Whitby	1764	Whitby-Middleton
1764	Doncaster	1764	Tinsley-Doncaster

Sources: Statutes at Large; House of Commons Journals.

given to Portsmouth undertakers, and Portsmouth surveyors were also appointed (Patterson, 1966, Vol. I, p. 47). There are many examples of 'clusters'. In London several parishes in Whitechapel, Southwark, Wapping, and Aldgate, as well as the parishes of St. Luke, Christchurch, St. Pancras, St. Sepulchre, and also Hydon Square, got improvement Acts in 1771 and 1772. Henley, Devizes, and Oxford obtained Acts in 1781; Dorchester and Weymouth in 1776; Maidstone, Deal, Ramsgate, Folkestone, and Hythe in Kent in the mid-1790s; Wells and Bridgewater in Somerset in 1779; Stourbridge and Dudley in 1791.

The geographical distribution of improvement Acts is revealing. Table 3 shows the breakdown of Improvement Commissioners, established by Act of Parliament outside London in the eighteenth century.

TABLE 3   Regional spread of Improvement Acts (excluding London), 1736–1799.

Year	Industrial Areas[a]	Total	Market Towns and Non-industrial Ports	Total
1736–1749	1	1	7	7
1750–1759	1	2	8	15
1760–1769	5	7	14	29
1770–1779	3	10	25	54
1780–1789	1	11	27	81
1790–1799	4	15	29	110

[a]Industrial areas include the West Riding of Yorkshire, South Lancashire, the North-East, and the Midlands.

Particularly noticeable from this table is the absence of many towns in the northern industrial regions and the relatively late adoption of improvement commissioners in such towns there as did obtain Acts; it is clear that in general they were far tardier in improvement than the southern market towns. The differences cannot be accounted for by relative population sizes. By 1801 Warrington, Wigan, Oldham, Blackburn, and many other Lancashire and Yorkshire towns had populations of over 9000, but no body of improvement commissioners and little evidence of widespread activity by local authorities. By contrast, most towns in the south of this size had undertaken substantial improvement by the end of the eighteenth century, and many small towns of fewer than 3000 or 4000 were active also.

A number of reasons suggest themselves for the divergent experiences of south and north. One was the social composition of the towns. Many southern towns contained residences of prosperous merchants and agricultural gentry which implanted standards of comfort and resources of finance. The market functions of so many of the improving southern towns also seem to have been significant. The new northern towns were mostly production oriented rather than trade oriented. The social composition of many northern industrial towns was different, and only the largest, such as Leeds, Liverpool, and Manchester, had substantial areas of high-class residences. Large masses of urban poor were hardly conducive to the development of civic pride, nor could they provide much in the way of rate revenues. In the northern towns, too, there was sometimes, though not always, no established corporate authority. Another factor that possibly delayed the spread of improvement in the north was the very rapidity of population growth which set in during the second half of the eighteenth century, presenting problems of a size and nature which were beyond the scope of these new institutional arrangements. There was also the existence of alternative local investment opportunities in manufacturing in northern districts. Loans to local authorities at fixed interest may well have been an attractive investment for the wealthier inhabitants of southern market towns, and it is striking how little difficulty there seems to have been in raising such loans in the eighteenth century. A writer in 1762 spoke of loans on the security of local rates as 'being a better security than any I know of' (Massie, 1762, p. 1). There was never any fear voiced in contemporary discussions about local improvement Acts that capital might not be forthcoming. At the same time, the merchants and gentry, who provided the bulk of loans for improvement (and also bore the brunt of the rates), stood to gain the most from improved channels of commerce and better civic amenities.

IV

The transformation of the provincial towns was so extensive that with only slight exaggeration, it might be termed their exit from medievalism (Reddaway, 1951, p. 286). Since provincial towns were numerous, though small by European standards, and because they were so widely scattered about the countryside, they transmitted near-metropolitan models of a way of life and standards of consumption to almost the whole rural population. To that extent, at least once its towns began to undergo improvement, England became an essentially urbanized nation. Further, investment in improvement Acts did not fluctuate downward with passing downturns in economic activity (Falkus, 1976, p. 268). The demand for urban improvement was to prove inelastic. Better 'middle-class' housing became widespread and was no longer quite beyond the bounds of ordinary ambition, as the dwellings of the rich had clearly been in previous times, and thus it could exert a demonstration effect.

What explains urban improvement in preindustrial and non-industrial England? For the second half of the eighteenth century, we have discussed some of the factors, above all the growth of inland trade, which brought both greater wealth and new pressures. Rising expectations and 'civic consciousness' set against a background of increasing population led to widespread attempts to improve urban environments. For the earlier period, however, the causes of change are not so evident. Two predominant sources of growth in the late preindustrial economy – agricultural change and trade expansion – suggest themselves. These forces acted above all through London, which was the major market for farm products and the main center from which trade goods were distributed. Brick building and fire-resistant styles of architecture, street improvements, fashions for social amenities, and the new institutional form of the improvement Act all tended to start out in London. The postfire rebuilding of London was said in 1801 to have 'produced in the country a spirit of improvement which had till then been unknown, but which has never since ceased to exert itself' (Heberden, 1973, p. 77). Mere size gave London bigger problems than other towns, but many more chances of being first to solve them. London legislation was most likely to take national form, that is, the Act of Parliament. London's easy and extending communications with other centers speedily transmitted metropolitan ideas. There are examples of independent provincial improvement, but the notion of London as the chief center and mart of new ideas rings true.

What enabled relatively small provincial towns to copy such a gargantuan model? The core of the answer, it is suggested, is that they became more efficient at handling a growing inland trade, and that although their facilities – such as narrow, unpaved streets – were choked and tattered by the increase in traffic, they acquired enough wealth to improve them. Income from the same source enabled them to extend their range of social amenities and allowed the individual inhabitants to rebuild their houses in the new styles, in brick. Greater efficiency is suggested by three factors: first, an increase in traffic; second, the rather slight growth of population, which, coupled with the greater volume of business done, is the most persuasive indirect indication of an increase in urban efficiency; third, the nature of business activity, demonstrating directly that distributive functions were becoming more specialized and efficient. In the closing years of the eighteenth century the environment of change was modified significantly by the burgeoning population and expansion of the industrial north. But the phase of improvement belonging to this period was built securely on the foundations laid already.

TRAFFIC

Traffic problems became quite serious after the introduction of coaches in the sixteenth century. Long-distance coach services between London and the north of England were running by 1658. By 1700 the system of changing horses had increased the speed of coach travel from 10–15 miles per day to 50 miles per day (Parkes, 1965, p. 72). The practice of binding wagon wheels with iron was resulting in damage to the streets in provincial towns in the early seventeenth century (Weinstock, 1953, p. 19). After the Restoration there came a big upturn in the volume of heavy traffic, notably with the acquisition of wagons by farmers: samples of probate inventories from Oxfordshire show that only 2 percent of farmers owned wagons in the 1660s, 20 percent by the 1690s, and 34 percent by the 1720s (Havinden, 1967, p. 78). At Farnham, Surrey, which was the largest market for wheat outside London, Defoe found an informant who told him that, 'he once counted on a market-day eleven hundred teams of horses, all drawing waggons, or carts, loaden with wheat at this market' (1928, Vol. I, p. 142). According to Chartres, the number of wagons apparently continued to rise over the 1681–1775 period (1977, p. 77, Table 1; Pawson, 1975, p. 10, Tables 1 and 2).

As a measure of the increasing road carriage between London and the provinces, Chartres gives data on service quotients – the frequency per week multiplied by the number of carrier services. Between 1637 and 1681 these service quotients rose in total 36.5 percent, and between 1681 and 1715 they rose a further 64.3 percent. The main regions of growth were the northern Home Counties, the South-East, the East Midlands, and the South and West. Chartres associates the rise with a growth of domestic trade that came about partly because of a diversion from coastal shipping, which was threatened by privateers between 1688 and 1713, raising insurance costs and thereby putting the total cost of coastwise freight above that of the roads. Privateering, according to Chartres, 'caused' a number of home-investment booms and led to an increase in inland traffic. This artificial, 'hothouse' climate helped to induce a permanent shift to road transportation, the real costs of which were presumably lowered by investment in routes and facilities. Certainly, there are abundant signs that the increase in traffic, which was part of a general expansion of domestic trade, exerted pressures on the layout and fabric of the towns and on facilities such as market halls. For instance, congestion in the street markets at Bristol became so great that the various produce markets were moved during the early eighteenth century and new corn markets and covered markets were erected, and the overcrowding of the market house at Hereford by 1706 meant the intrusion of grain sacks into the doorways of shops and houses all around (Minchinton, 1954, p. 79; Chartres, 1973, p. 68). Streets were churned up, pedestrians endangered, and marketplaces and gateways through the walls jammed. Individual householders continually obtruded their stalls, signs on poles, mounting blocks, sheds, projecting windows, and steps onto the pavements and into the streets; ironically, more trade was likely to multiply these obstructions. Urban improvers set about putting right all these matters, if only to prevent trade passing to neighboring towns.

POPULATION

Data that purport to represent population figures for provincial and even market towns over the period 1660–1750 are numerous. However, on inspection there are rarely enough hard figures for that precise period to assess the trend of urban populations; there are census figures or contemporary estimates for a number of towns, but rarely more than a single datum within those years. The misleading impression of concreteness (and growth) in urban population data for 1660–1750 largely arises from extrapolating back the growth which undoubtedly did occur during the second half of the eighteenth century.

Two approaches suggest themselves if we wish to ascertain whether or not provincial and market-town populations did grow at that time. One approach is to cite what hard figures exist, the other is to try to arrive at a figure for provincial town population growth as a whole by treating it as a residual (national population less London and the countryside). Table 4 supplies such few data as are available.

The second approach, using national population estimates, supports the conclusion suggested by the table that provincial towns experienced only limited growth. Indeed, this method implies that the average growth of small market towns must have been very slight. According to Chalklin, the percentage of all dwellers in towns

TABLE 4   Population data for provincial towns, *c*. 1660–1750.

Town	Growth	Period
Bury St Edmunds	0.3%	*c*.1675[a] –1757
York	5.3	1670–*c*.1730
Faversham	7.25	1676–1753
Northampton	14.1	1676–1746
Hertford	28.4	1676–1753
Guildford	39.1	1676–1740
Chichester	54.7	1676[a]–1739

Source: Extracted from C. W. Chalklin (1974), p. 18, Table 1. His note 41 refers to the dearth of reliable evidence of this sort and adds that he has excluded market towns because he has traced evidence for only two or three of them; however, the towns listed, which he calls *regional centers*, had marketing and servicing functions.
Note: We have accepted only those estimates where the former figure dates from 1650 to 1679 and the latter from 1730 to 1759, where the resultant span is sixty years or more, and where both estimates are contemporary productions, not modern calculations.
[a]Average of estimates.

rose by only 5 or 6 percent from 1650 to 1750, or from one-fifth to one-quarter of the national population, which went up from 5 to 6 million (1974, pp. 3, 17). Half of this increase was attributable to the growth of London, which leaves a growth of only 2.5–3 percent for the rural areas together with *all* other towns including those major ports and northern industrial cities that were growing quite fast from at least the beginning of the eighteenth century. Conceivably, rural population on balance actually fell, but not by much or this would have drawn attention, and the category of provincial towns, including market towns, can overall have experienced very slender growth between 1660 and 1750. One must therefore seek for the explanation of the ability of these towns to handle the observed increase of traffic and trade in their more efficient use of such resources of labor as they already had.[5]

BUSINESS ACTIVITY

The numbers of merchants increased considerably in the period 1650–1750 and there is no evidence that this led to a fall in their per capita commercial activity. However, there seems to have been a sharp decline in the rate of growth of the trade of London during the first half of the eighteenth century. Whereas after the Restoration London became the hub of trade and wealth, after about 1700 the capital became more a financial than a mercantile center. Westerfield's explanation of this is that diseconomies of scale began to affect London's trade, with rapid increases in the cost of carriage within and to and from the metropolis, and in the charges for factorage, hallage, porterage, packing, lighterage, and wharfage (1968, pp. 412–14, 419–28). Port charges were higher than in the outports, and the cost of living for workers was higher. The port became crowded and inconvenient. Customs dues were more vigorously collected than in other ports, to which, indeed, merchants and traders migrated. Provincial retailers began to buy more extensively (and more cheaply) from the out-ports, some of which necessarily proved better situated for particular overseas trades than London. The monopoly trading companies of London were not competitive with the merchants who traded as individuals in the outports. Population began to shift to the outports after 1720, accompanied by a decentralization of metropolitan commerce. A greater dispersal of ports dispatching sizeable quantities of imports and receiving goods for themselves and for export was the result, and in this there were

---

5. It is improbable that they had significant resources of underemployed labor in 1660. Compare with Chalklin (1974), note 41.

pickings for the merchants and retailers of the inland towns around the country.

London of course remained much the largest single market, exerting a profound influence over trading patterns. Lesser towns in southern England in a great ring around London, were switching out of textile production and expanding their agricultural processing, servicing, and marketing functions with an eye to the metropolitan market (Jones, 1974, pp. 423–30: Fisher, 1971, pp. 3–16). London itself had no malt works and few flour mills. There was a comparable shift of specialization among the northern towns: Wakefield switched in the seventeenth and eighteenth centuries from making cloth (which Leeds expanded) to acting as a mart for grain, cattle, leather, and wool from eastern England for the whole of south Lancashire and the West Riding. Wakefield's chief new eighteenth-century buildings were grain warehouses and a Corn Exchange. Associated with this, Wakefield came to own more corn merchants and insurance offices than Leeds, and at least twice as many attorneys and banks per head of population by the early nineteenth century (Rimmer, 1967, pp. 127–28).

The efficiency gains made by the provincial towns were unlikely to have lain much in processing. Corn milling saw some technical advances made by John Smeaton and Andrew Meikle, but not before the 1750s. In malting and tanning there were few changes. Although malting expanded – for instance, Essex supplied much more malt to London after 1700 (Brown, 1969, p. 60) – extra malting floors were seldom added to existing works. Instead, new maltings were built, using the old methods, and economies of scale were not reaped. Much the same may be said of tanning. Swan (1821) stated that tanners remained content to follow 'their great grandfather's steps, in which they had trod 100 years ago', and Burridge (1824) expostulated that tanners were 'miserable, illiberal, sluggish, illiterate bigots'. Changes, technological or organizational, had conceivably emerged in these and other processing trades rather earlier, in the late seventeenth or early eighteenth century, but it is more likely that the main advances had come in marketing and servicing activities relating to the distribution of goods and the supply of inputs to agriculture. There was probably a host of little, almost unremarked, changes in small-business organization and administration and a tendency to substitute capital for labor in small ways in a wide spectrum of trades.

There are two or three studies that indicate developments in commodity-specialized trading practices and growing competition among market centers and between kinds of market such as fairs and shops. Grain marketing and cheese marketing became increasingly specialized, that is, subject to the division of labour (Baker, 1970, pp. 126–50; Henstock, 1969, pp. 32–46; Chartres, 1977, pp. 73–94;

Everitt, 1965, pp. 57–71; Borsay, 1977, p. 585). The period was the one which saw the establishment of a range of retail shops in the smallest town. There was vastly better reporting of commercial news and London prices, particularly as provincial newspapers were beginning to be founded in the first half of the eighteenth century (Cranfield, 1962, pp. 95–96). It is likely that the level, or even slightly downward, trend of prices during this period made farmers closer bargainers and that their search for more efficient, lower-cost methods communicated itself to the marketing sector. Transaction costs would have been reduced, with wide consequences for the economy.

As to the physical consequences for the towns, because of the relative indestructibility of brick and the technological advances in water pumping and oil lighting, and for institutional reasons connected with defined, continuous, and enforceable rating powers vested in improvement trusts and applicable to new and extended purposes, the changes of the period made a permanent mark. There was a rachet effect to improvement. Most of its individual forms were old civic goals, but after the Restoration they became sustained developments. Savings became more productive, consumption went up, and urban improvement fed back impulses to the economy at large. In addition, provincial towns gave rise to a creative social, educational, and intellectual life, perhaps undergoing a transition in culture such as that observed very shortly in preindustrial Massachusetts (Brown, 1974, pp. 29–51). At a time when London was dominant in English cultural life and when the provincial towns were far smaller in population than they are now, their status as producers of culture and science, not as mere consumers, was worthy of remark.

If the increase of trade and traffic put pressure on the physical fabric and layout of the provincial towns, it simultaneously brought more money into the hands of their populations. With town populations mostly growing slowly, so that there were few more innkeepers, liverymen, carters, warehousemen, ironmongers, drapers, grocers, or lawyers to handle the greater volume of business, their per capita incomes were likely to rise. Trade certainly put money into the pockets of the shopkeeper class, enabling them to rebuild their premises in brick and tile, to pay the rates that financed 'improvement', and to become rather fine ladies and gentlemen. As such, they were demonstrably conscious of their dignity, position, and interest, keen for law and order, for the watch and paid constables, for fire precautions, good potable water, and broad, clean, paved, and lighted streets and pavements where they might go about their daily business and evening pleasures in a comfort and convenience never before known. Their towns acquired the sedate fripperies of, say, Lichfield only a little later in time (1771) when a walk was laid out along the Minster Pool, followed (in 1773) by the giving of a serpentine form to the pool in imitation of Queen Caroline's Metropolitan Serpentine (Thorpe, 1950–1951, p. 194). Already in the first half of the eighteenth century luxury services had become available in quite small towns; as Cranfield shows in his study of their newspapers, 'the picture that [emerged] from the trade notices in the advertisement pages is one of a steady migration of skilled craftsmen from the capital into the provinces' (Cranfield, 1962, p. 212).

V

The evidence assembled here indicates that the habitat of English provincial towns underwent a very substantial improvement between about 1660 and 1780. Improvement consisted of private and public activity as well as changes in social aspirations and administrative machinery. The most visible and noteworthy form of private improvement was the spread of brick, far faster than before, together with the extensive spread of tile. This produced a whole range of effects. Much the most important consequence was the reduction of the formerly numerous and wholesale fires in towns. As a consequence of the reduced danger of fire, capital was released from the expensive treadmill of reconstruction that existed when one rebuilding with flammable timber and thatch succeeded another. The cycle was broken. Since the provinces soon tended to conform to the rather boxlike style required for purposes of fire precaution by the London Building Acts of Queen Anne's reign, many English town centers came to acquire their unmistakeable Georgian aspect. Brick building also contributed to the cleanliness, comfort, and convenience of living.

Public or corporate improvement similarly brought about major alterations in urban appearance, salubrity, and convenience as well as administration. The economic and social consequences of such improvement were far-reaching. A healthier urban environment may well have been a factor in the overall fall in urban death rates in mid-eighteenth century England, noted by Chambers (1972, pp. 103, 123). At the same time, the impact of improvement investment was certainly widespread, and in aggregate substantial. The growth of a market for local authority debt was one channel whereby savings could be translated into local improvements. Moreover, the changes in local administration that accompanied improvement, especially after the 1740s, laid the basis for developments in the nineteenth century. The modern forms of rating and rating authorities set up under the 1835 Municipal Corporations Act owed much to these earlier developments. Taking all the various changes together, the amelioration of the urban environment was marked, unprecedented, and, above all, sustained. The massive population growth in north- ern industrial centers in later years may have caused a new environmental deterioration there, but the advances were never set back in the southern towns. This paper has concentrated on describing the improvements and relating them to one another. They do not fall altogether neatly into periods, but we can see that there was a burst of improvement activity during the last quarter of the seventeenth century, another perhaps after about 1735, and certainly one from the third quarter of the eighteenth century: this is not to say that activity fell away to nothing between these peaks.

Our explanation of the process of improvement has been largely in terms of the efficiency of towns in handling the growth of the inland trade, the profits made, and the attractiveness of investing in public works with the return secured on the rates. Broader implications for the understanding of the workings of the English economy in late preindustrial times lie behind this explanation, above all for the pre-1750 period. C. M. Law has referred to a common impression that urbanization is not a result of economic growth but is instead itself a cause of growth (1972, p. 13). We have not, however, concentrated on urban growth in this usual meaning of greater population in towns and cities, but on essentially qualitative refinements of the habitat of quite small towns which mostly grew, demographically, rather little. Assembling these changes into a view of the economy before the vigorous growth spurt of industrial output and industrial cities which took place from the last years of the eighteenth century reveals an unfamiliar perspective. There has perhaps been an excess of abstract, deductive reasoning of the 'take-off' variety about the onset of industrialization which has tended to denude views of the previous economy of much sense of variety and vitality. The improvement of provincial towns in the seventeenth and eighteenth centuries leads to a strong, not a weak, view of late preindustrial prosperity and social improvement and focuses attention on the emergence of a pattern of well-ordered, physically pleasing towns set in a prosperous countryside in the Lowland Zone of England.

Certain processes and features of the late preindustrial economy accordingly need to be stressed. They include the expansion of trade, notably the inland trade: the increase of farm output, contributory to the growth of trade: and London as a 'role model' for other towns and cities. Connected with the growth of London and as part of the expansion of domestic trade was the greater use of coal, particularly for the baking of brick, and connected with this were better communications, such as the canalization of rivers in the seventeenth century, which made it easier to move coal and all the other commodities traded. Indeed, it may be correct to see the greater availability of coal in southern England as an externality that resulted from the rise of London and the elaboration of the communications network centering on it.

The remodeling of the provincial towns was one element in an economy that when presented with powerful, though diffuse, stimuli proved widely responsive. The process of remodeling apparently began about 1670 or 1680 as a slightly lagged (and regionally staggered) effect of the activity in agriculture and commerce which was released by the Restoration settlement. The lag was short, indicating, it may be, that impulses for growth were latent in the system, with its given levels of income, economic organization, distribution of towns, and so forth inherited from the early seventeenth century and before, but suppressed by the uncertainties of the Commonwealth. The economy of Restoration times was already resilient enough to take in its stride the entire rebuilding of towns destroyed by fire. This was true even of London after the Great Fire. What the opportunity costs may have been of the investment in reconstruction can only be surmised, but there was no obvious faltering of the economy's pace. Brick and tile did not rise in price enough to cause complaint, despite the vast quantities used, because coal and brick-earth were in elastic supply. Timber was readily shipped from Norway, and even stone was not impossibly difficult to come by. Labor was obtainable at rates which did not soar because, by the Rebuilding Act of 1667, Parliament overrode the London craft companies and allowed in building artisans from elsewhere, workers who were attracted by wages nevertheless higher than in the countryside. A similar removal of restrictions on non-freemen occurred after the Warwick fire of 1694. The overall responsiveness of the economy in terms of new communications, shipping capacity, supplies of labor and capital, and enterprises and administrative flexibility must reflect prior change.

The pre-Restoration economy had, of course, been vital and had seen important changes in many ways, but perhaps falling short of bringing about sustained growth in incomes *per capita*. The elements of the later achievement were all present early in the seventeenth century, whether we look to the use of brick or coal, agricultural techniques, the swelling of London, or the canalization of rivers. Mercantile elements were straining to have England's share – or London's share – of world trade expanded, if need be by the use of nonmarket (governmental) violence against competitors like the Dutch. It was a secure domestic political climate for investment that was lacking. In this respect, for all its endeavors on behalf of the London merchants, the Protectorate marked a hiatus. Up to this period there was definitely no widescale *improvement* of the towns.

With the comparative certainties of the Restoration, and *a fortiori* of the Glorious Revolution of 1688, the urban economy picked up. Less pressure of population than the economy had been obliged to contend with in late Tudor or early Stuart times may have prompted a relatively rapid rise of real income per head in a context of competition and rearrangement in the market. The provincial towns shared in the burgeoning of the inland trade, they proved efficient in their function as markets and servicing centers, and they were physically remolded as a consequence. Georgian provincial towns afforded a progressively more attractive environment for living and working. To this development, northern industrialization bore little relation. The detailed processes of habitat improvement with which this paper has been concerned bore their own logical relationships to the wider political and economic context. The connections between urban improvement and subsequent industrialization we leave to another occasion.

REFERENCES

Ash, Bernard, (1964), *The Golden City: London Between the Fires, 1666–1941*, London: Phoenix House.

Bailey, Charles, (1856), *The Municipal Archives of Winchester*, Winchester, England: Hugh Barclay.

Bailey, T., (1852–1855), *Annals of Nottinghamshire*, II, Nottingham, England: W. F. Gibson.

Baker, Dennis, (1970), 'The Marketing of Corn in the First Half of the Eighteenth Century', *Agricultural History Review*, 18: 126–50.

Bewes, W. A., (1896), *Church Briefs or Royal Warrants for Collections for Charitable Objects*, London: A & C. Black.

Borsay, P., (1977), 'The English Urban Renaissance: The Development of Provincial Urban Culture, *c.* 1680–*c.* 1760', *Social History*, 5: 581–603.

Brown, A. F. J., (1969), *Essex at Work 1700–1815*, Chelmsford, England: Essex County Council.

Brown, Richard D., (1974), 'The Emergence of Urban Society in Rural Massachusetts, 1760–1820', *Journal of American History*, 34: 29–51.

Buer, M. C., (1926), *Health, Wealth, and Population in the Early Days of the Industrial Revolution*, London: Routledge & Kegan Paul.

Burridge, J., (1824), *The Tanner's Key*, London: C. F. Cock.

Chalklin, C. W., (1974), *The Provincial Towns of Georgian England*, London: Edward Arnold.

Chambers, J. D., (1960), 'Population Changes in a Provincial Town', in L. S. Pressnell (ed.), *Studies in the Industrial Revolution*, London: Athlone Press.

——. (1972), *Population, Economy, and Society in Pre-Industrial England*, London: Oxford University Press.

Chandler, T. and Fox, G., (1974), *3000 Years of Urban Growth*, New York: Academic Press.

Chartres, J. A., (1973), 'The Marketing of Agricultural Products in Metropolitan Western England in the Late Seventeenth and Eighteenth Centuries', *Exeter Papers in Economic History*, 8: 63–74.

——. (1977), 'Road Carrying in England in the Seventeenth Century: Myth and Reality', *Economic History Review*, 2nd ser., 30: 73–94.

Child, M. T. H. (ed.), (1972), *The Community of Andover Before 1825*, Andover, England: Local Archives Committee.

Clark, P. A. and Slack, P. A. (eds.), (1972), *Crisis and Order in English Towns, 1500–1700*, London: Routledge & Kegan Paul.

Cranfield, G. A., (1962), *The Development of the Provincial Newspaper 1700–1760*, Oxford, England: Clarendon Press.

Daunton, M. J., (1978), 'Towns and Economic Growth in Eighteenth Century England', in P. Abrams and E. A. Wrigley (eds.), *Towns in Societies*, Cambridge: Cambridge University Press.

de Beer, E. S., (1941), 'The Early History of London Street Lighting', *History*, 25: 311–24.

Defoe, Daniel, (1928), *A Tour Through England and Wales*, vols. I and II, London: Everyman Press.

Eccles, Mark, (1963), *Shakespeare in Warwickshire*, Madison, Wisc.: University of Wisconsin Press.

Everitt, Alan, (1968), 'The Food Market of the English Town 1660–1760', *Contributions* 3rd International Conference of Economic History, Munich, 1965, Paris: Mouton., I, pp. 57–71.

Falkus, M. E., (1976), 'Lighting in the Dark Ages of English Economic History: Town Streets Before the Industrial Revolution', in D. C. Coleman and A. H. John (eds.), *Trade, Government, and Economy in Pre-Industrial England*, London: Weidenfeld & Nicolson.

Fasnacht, Ruth, (1954), *A History of the City of Oxford*, Oxford, England: Basil Blackwell.

Fisher, F. J., (1948), 'The Development of London as a Centre of Conspicuous Consumption in the Sixteenth and Seventeenth Centuries', *Transactions* of the Royal Historical Society, 30: 37–50.

——. (1971), 'London as an "Engine of Economic Growth"', pages 3–16 in J. S. Bromley and E. H. Kossman (eds.), *Britain and Netherlands, IV: Metropolis, Dominion, and Province*, The Hague: Martinus Nijhoff.

Gardiner, Dorothy, (1966), *Canterbury*, London: Sheldon Press.

George, M. D., (1966), *London Life in the Eighteenth Century*, Harmondsworth, England: Peregrine Books.

Hanway, J., (1754), *A Letter to Mr. John Spranger, on His Excellent Proposal for Paving . . .* , London.

——. (1762), *Serious Considerations on the Salutory Design of the Act of Parliament . . .* , London.

Hart, A. T., (1962), *Country Counting House: The Story of Two Eighteenth Century Clerical Account Books*, London: Phoenix House.

Hart, G., (1965), *A History of Cheltenham*, Leicester, England: Leicester University Press.

Havinden, M. A., (1967), 'Agrarian Progress in Open-Field Oxfordshire', in E. L. Jones (ed.), *Agriculture and Economic Growth in England, 1650–1815*, London: Methuen.

Heberden Jun. William, (1973), in B. Benjamin (introd.), *Population and Disease in Early Industrial England*, Gregg International Publishers Ltd.

Henstock. Adrian, (1969), 'Cheese Manufacture and Marketing in Derbyshire and North Staffordshire', *Derbyshire Archaeological Journal*, 89: 32–46.

Hill, J. W. F., (1966), *Georgian Lincoln*, Cambridge, England: Cambridge University Press.

Hinton, M., (1954), *A History of the Town of Reading*, London: Geo. Harrap & Co.

Jackson. G., (1972), *Hull in the Eighteenth Century*, London: Oxford University Press.

Jones, E. L., (1968), 'The Reduction of Fire Damage in Southern England, 1650–1850', *Post-Medieval Archaeology*, 2: 140–49.

——. (1974), 'The Constraints on Economic Growth in Southern England, 1650–1850', *Contributions* to 3rd International Conference of Economic History, Munich, 1965, Paris: Mouton, pp. 423–30.

Knowles, C. C. and Pitt, P. H., (1972), *The History of Building Regulation in London, 1189–1972*, London: Architectural Press.

Latimer, J., (1893), *Annals of Bristol in the Eighteenth Century*, II, Bristol, England: privately printed.

Law, C. M., (1972), 'Some Notes on the Urban Population of England and Wales in the Eighteenth Century', *The Local Historian*, 10: 13–26.

Lindley, E. S., (1962), *Wotton Under Edge*, London: Museum Press.

Massie, J., (1754), *An Essay on the Many Advantages Accruing to the Community . . .* , London.

Minchinton, W. E., (1954), 'Bristol–Metropolis of the West in the ·Eighteenth Century', *Transactions of the Royal Historical Society*, 5th ser., 4: 69–89.

Money, Walter, (1892), *Collections for the History of the Parish of Speen*, Newbury, England: W. J. Blacket.

Mullett, Charles L., (1956), *The Bubonic Plague and England*, Lexington, Ky.: University of Kentucky Press.

Nef, J. U., (1966), *The Rise of the British Coal Industry*, 2 volumes, London: F. Cass.

Parkes, Joan, (1965), *Travel in England in the Seventeenth Century*, cited by J. Thirsk in A. Rogers (ed.), *The Making of Stamford*, Leicester, England: Leicester University Press.

Patterson, A. Temple, (1966), *A History of Southampton 1700–1914*, Southampton, England: Southampton University Press.

Pawson, Eric, (1975), 'The Turnpike Trusts of the Eighteenth Century: A Study of Innovation and Diffusion', University of Oxford, School of Geography Research Paper 14.

Platt, Colin, (1976), *The English Medieval Town*, London: Secker & Warburg.

Porter S., (1976), 'Fires in Stratford-upon-Avon in the Sixteenth and Seventeenth Centuries', *Warwickshire History*, 3: 97–105.

Public Nusance Considered . . . (1754), London.

Reddaway, T. F., (1951), *The Rebuilding of London After the Great Fire*, London: Edward Arnold.

Rimmer, W. G., (1967), 'The Evolution of Leeds to 1700', *Thoresby Society Publications*, 50: 91–120.

Rodgers, J. C., (1951), *York*, London: Batsford.

Rubinstein, W. D., (1977), 'The Victorian Middle Class', *Economic History Review*, 30: 602–23.

Salzman, L. F., (1923), *English Industries of the Middle Ages*, Oxford, England: Clarendon Press.

Skillington, S. H., (1923), *A History of Leicester*, Leicester, England: Edgar Backus.

Snell, F. J., (1892), *The Chronicles of the Twyford*, Tiverton, England: Gregory & Co.

Stacpoole, Alberic, (1972), *The Noble City of York*, York, England: Cerialis Press.

Steer, Francis W. (ed.), (1962), *The Memoirs of James Spershott*, Chichester, England: City Council.

Swan, J., (1821), *Explanation of a New Mode of Tanning*, London.

Thirsk, Joan, (1965), 'Tudor and Stuart Stamford', in A. Rogers (ed.), *The Making of Stamford*, Leicester, England: Leicester University Press.

Thorpe, H., (1950–1951), 'The City of Lichfield: A Study of Its Growth and Function', Staffordshire Record Society, *Collection for a History of Staffordshire* (1950/51).

Victoria County History, (1968), *Gloucestershire*, 8.

Walford C., (1882), *King's Briefs: Their Purpose and History*, London: privately printed, 1882, reprinted from *Transactions of the Royal Historical Society*, 10: 1–74.

Webb, S. and Webb, B., (1963), *The Manor and the Borough*, 2 vols., London: 1908; reprinted F. Cass, 1963.

——. *Statutory Authorities for Special Purposes*, London: 1922; reprinted F. Cass. 1963.

Webb papers (unpublished), British Library of Political and Economic Science, Local Government Collection, *Devon*, 110; *Norfolk*, 205; *Cambridgeshire*, 100.

Weinstock, Maureen, (1953), *Studies in Dorset History*, Dorchester, England: Longmans.

Westerfield, Ray B., (1968), *Middlemen in English Business*, New York: Augustus M. Kelley.

Williamson, F. G., (1936), 'George Sorocold, of Derby: A Pioneer of Water Supply', *Derbyshire Archaeological & Natural History Journal*, pp. 43–94.

Chapter 5

THE ENGLISH URBAN RENAISSANCE: THE DEVELOPMENT OF PROVINCIAL URBAN CULTURE c.1680 – c.1760[1]

Peter Borsay

[Social History, 2, no.2 (1977)]

Research on the early modern town made great strides forward in the late 1960s and early 1970s, but work was concentrated heavily on the years before the Civil War. The present article was written as an attempt to redress that imbalance by identifying the special characteristics of the late seventeenth- and eighteenth-century town, and rescuing it from the rather crisis-orientated interpretation which emerged as the orthodox view of the post-medieval urban scene. The article has now been followed by a full-length study, The English Urban Renaissance: Culture and Society in the Provincial Town 1660–1770 *(Oxford, 1989). This investigates in greater detail the upgrading of the town's landscape and the growing provision of cultural facilities, and extends the social analysis of the urban renaissance to include not only the pursuit of status, but also the more idealistic quest for civility and sociability, and the impact of change in terms of growing cultural differentiation. Doubts about how widespread was the urban renaissance are voiced in Angus McInnes, 'The emergence of a leisure town: Shrewsbury 1660–1760',* Past and Present, *120 (1988), which argues that the post-Restoration growth in leisure and luxury was sharply focused on a specific category of 'leisure towns'.*

The English provincial town in the century or so immediately preceding the Industrial Revolution has remained remarkably unexplored territory. Was it still in the grip of the economic and cultural

---

1. This essay is a revised version of a paper given to the Urban History Group Meeting at the Economic History Society Conference of Spring 1975. It has benefited considerably from the criticism and comment of Professor G. S. Holmes of Lancaster University, who has encouraged and guided my research. I also owe to him the reference to the Tory victory celebrations at Chester, in note 7.

malaise which many towns are believed to have suffered during the sixteenth and seventeenth centuries?[2] Or was it undergoing some sort of change and revival that may have helped to lay the foundations for the transformation of England into an industrial urban society? Given the present paucity of research, any approach to answering these questions must be made with caution. However, allowing for this proviso, my essay presents a tentative thesis which I hope will help to disturb certain entrenched assumptions about post-Restoration urban society, as well as promote further investigation into the history of the town during this period.

The pioneering work of Professor Everitt on the pre-industrial town, and Professor Plumb on the commercialization of leisure, has suggested a fruitful angle from which the problem of the post-Restoration town may be approached: that of the growth and changing nature of its cultural life.[3] With this in mind, I have concentrated on the way in which two elements, leisure and luxury, influenced the development of provincial urban culture between the late seventeenth and mid-eighteenth centuries. In the first half of this essay I sketch in four areas of urban life where these influences were felt: leisure facilities, the economy, public amenities and architecture. This examination suggests that a transformation was occurring in the nature of provincial urban culture, which with some justice could be called an urban renaissance. In the second half of this essay some explanations are offered of why this renaissance took place, of what towns were most likely to benefit from it, and of what social function it fulfilled. I conclude by speculating on a number of ideas raised by this thesis.

I

In his recent study of sixteenth-century Worcester, Dr Dyer has argued that in the intellectual and cultural life of the town '. . . it is difficult to abstract any element and label it distinctly "urban" . . .'.[4] Such a conclusion would be unthinkable for an important provincial town in 1760. By then contemporaries had little doubt that England was a country of two different, but not necessarily exclusive, cultures: one based on the countryside, the other on the

2. Such is the thesis of P. Clark and P. Slack (eds.), *Crisis and Order in English Towns* (1972), introduction.
3. See the works of Everitt and Plumb referred to below.
4. A. D. Dyer, *The City of Worcester in the Sixteenth Century* (Leicester, 1973), 253.

town. Although the development of the alternative urban culture was deeply linked with the growth of London, it owed much, especially from the late seventeenth century onwards, to the important provincial town.

One of the key elements in shaping this culture was the appearance in such towns of leisure facilities designed to cater for the upper and middling groups in society. Foremost among these were the town assemblies. They began to appear in a wide variety of English towns from the very end of the seventeenth century. As early as 1696 it was being reported from Bath that 'our city is very full and balls every night in the town hall . . .'. In York the weekly assemblies probably began around 1710. As two of the most important social centres in the provinces, it was natural these towns should soon acquire purpose-built assembly rooms. In 1708 Thomas Harrison opened an assembly house on the Terrace Walk at Bath; a large ballroom was added in 1720. Such was the growth in demand that a rival establishment – Lindsey's – was introduced to the opposite side of the Walk in 1730. This year also saw the foundation stone laid for Burlington's magnificent rooms at York.[5] Not that permanent assembly rooms were confined to the haunts of the county gentry. Birmingham and Manchester, two of the growing industrial centres of the early eighteenth century, had acquired sets of them by 1750.[6] In smaller towns the assemblies grew up in 'public' buildings. The Tory celebrations at Chester, following their victory in the 1710 county election, 'concluded with a ball for the ladies in the town hall'. The new town halls built at Warwick and Preston in the late 1720s were used to house the towns' assemblies. At Warwick a special ballroom, complete with a minstrels' gallery, was constructed. Perhaps even more frequently inns were used for large social gatherings of this kind.[7]

One of the primary functions of the new leisure facilities was that of personal display. In none of these facilities was this motive more

---

5. Hist. MSS. Comm. *Hastings MSS.*, 2, 279; *Victoria County History (VCH), Yorkshire: the City of York* (1961), 245; W. Ison, *The Georgian Buildings of Bath* (1948, reprinted Bath, 1969), 49–50; *Leeds Mercury*, 9–16 March 1730. I owe this last reference to John Quinn of Lancaster University.

6. W. Hutton, *A History of Birmingham to the End of the Year 1780* (Birmingham, 1781), 731; J. Aikin, *A Description of the Country within Forty Miles of Manchester* (1795), 187.

7. *The Post-Boy*, no. 2415, 2–4 November 1710; Preston Corporation Manuscripts (P. C. MSS.), White Book, 4 August 1727; P. C. MSS., Council Minutes, 10 May and 20 September 1728; *VCH Warwickshire*, VIII (1969), 431–2. For the use of inns to accommodate the town assemblies, see J. W. F. Hill, *Tudor and Stuart Lincoln* (Cambridge, 1956), 202; A. F. J. Brown, 'Colchester in the eighteenth century', in L. M. Munby (ed.), *East Anglian Studies* (Cambridge, 1968), 163; A. Everitt, 'The English urban inn 1560–1760', in A. Everitt (ed.), *Perspectives in English Urban History* (1973), 114–15.

apparent than in the walks being laid in many towns. The case of Preston is a good example. The main walk was situated on a spur of land that jutted out of the southern slopes of the town. It probably received its first formal treatment when in 1698 the Corporation ordered it to be paved. It is clear from Buck's prospect of Preston that by 1728 it had acquired the form it still survives in today, a land-based pier lined with trees. In 1710 and 1736 the seats provided on the walk were repaired, while in the early months of 1737 plans were laid for 'enlarging, repairing and beautifying' the walk with a combination of Corporation money and a public subscription.[8] The directing of Borough capital into such projects seems a common practice during the period. The 'New Walk' at York, whose construction began at the same time as Burlington's assembly rooms, was funded by the Corporation. Like the assembly rooms, some thought had been given to its aesthetic appeal. A contemporary visitor wrote that the completed walk 'runs parallel with the navigable river one mile, and is protected on the other side by a row of full grown trees. Near the middle is a small plantation which the walk winds through. An arm of the river is passed over by means of a handsome bridge with one arch built of stone.'[9]

Much of the new urban social life revolved round sporting activities. Bowling greens were quite common in towns of any size, often one suspects attached to an inn, as at Preston.[10] Several places supported town hunts in the first half of the eighteenth century; not just county towns like York, Lewes and Preston, but also growing commercial and industrial centres such as Liverpool and Leeds.[11] But without question one of the most important urban social institutions to be established in this period, and in considerable numbers, were the town races. The Warwick meeting, for example, was founded in about 1707. By 1714 the vicar of nearby Wellesbourne could write: '. . . there is great expectation of good diversion at the

8. P. C. MSS., Small Order Book (1697–1703), 7 November 1698; P. C. MSS., Council Minutes, 20 March 1709/10, 3 April 1733, 6 April 1736, 28 January and 18 February 1736/7.

9. *VCH York*, 207; Hist. MSS. Comm. *Verulam MSS.*, anonymous, 'A northern tour from St Albans 1768', 236. In 1703 the Northampton Corporation voted £30 towards planting trees, making walks, etc., *VCH Northamptonshire*, III (1930), 23.

10. P. C. MSS., Small Order Book, 5 February 1699/1700. For a fine bowling green at Newcastle-upon-Tyne, see C. Morris (ed.), *The Journeys of Celia Fiennes* (1947), 211.

11. *VCH York*, 246; John Macky, *A Journey through England*, vol. 1 (1714), 62–4; P. C. MSS., Council Minutes, 18 April 1748; J. A. Picton, *City of Liverpool Municipal Archives and Records* (Liverpool, 1886), 129; R. G. Wilson, *Gentlemen Merchants: The Merchant Community in Leeds 1700–1830* (Manchester, 1971), 230–2.

horse race at Warwick . . . this must be our public entry and coronation too . . . '. The meeting was not a particularly extended affair; that for 1754 was only scheduled to last two days, with a race on each day. None the less it attracted a high-class clientele: in 1754 there were seven peers among the subscribers, together with eight baronets or knights. By the mid-eighteenth century there was often a considerable variety of meetings open to the gentry, even without straying very far from their country seats. Sir Roger Newdigate lived at Arbury Hall near Coventry. Between 1751 and 1754 he attended meetings at nearby Rugby, Nuneaton, Warwick and Lichfield.[12]

Like sporting activities, the arts provided another major focal point for the growth of leisured urban life. By 1760 the provincial theatre had firmly established itself, despite legislative attempts to restrain its growth. Permanent theatre companies were set up in more important towns such as York, Norwich, Bristol and Bath. These companies serviced not only the needs of the base town itself, but also those of a circuit of smaller urban centres. Probably on a lesser scale, the public concert was beginning to take root during this period. The cathedral towns, with their reservoir of musical tradition and performers, established a series of festivals; for example, that running in Salisbury in the 1740s and 1750s, or the Three Choirs Festival – centred on Worcester, Gloucester and Hereford – which began about 1713 and is still an annual event. Other towns turned to their growing reservoir of wealth to promote public music. Newcastle began regular subscription concerts in 1736, Manchester in 1744, while at Birmingham public concerts flourished from at least the 1740s, housed in the local assembly rooms, theatres and inns. In other smaller towns musicians could be hired to give a single concert. In a county town this might have formed part of the programme for the gentry season, as at Northampton in 1737.[13]

The new leisure facilities being developed in many English towns were an important element behind the growing sophistication of provincial urban life. However, just as significant in this process was the contribution made by the changing shape of the urban economy. The evidence suggests that this involved a shift from an economy

12. *VCH Warwickshire*, VIII, 512; Warwickshire County Record Office (Warws. CRO.), CR 1368 (Mordaunt MS), 2/100; Warws. CRO., CR 229 (Shirley MS), 2/2; Warws. CRO., CR 136 (Newdigate MS), 582–5.
13. S. Rosenfeld, *Strolling Players and Drama in the Provinces 1660–1760* (Cambridge, 1939); J. H. Plumb, *The Commercialisation of Leisure in Eighteenth-Century England* (Reading, 1973), 11–16; 12 George II, ch. 28, 1737, 'An act to explain and amend so much of an act made in the twelfth year of the reign of Queen Anne . . . as relates to common players of interludes.'; P. M. Young, *A History of British Music* (1967), 312–14; J. Sutcliffe Smith, *The Story of Music in Birmingham* (Birmingham, 1945), 10–22; Everitt, 'The English urban inn', 119.

almost wholly concentrated on the manufacture and marketing of basic necessities, to one far more concerned with what may be called luxury elements in personal expenditure. This trend is probably detectable from the mid-Tudor period onwards, but it is rapidly accelerating from the end of the seventeenth century.[14] At Hereford a surprisingly large number of the forty-five men whose trade and admission to the town's freedom are recorded in the Corporation minute book for the years 1694-1707 practised 'luxury' trades; they include two clockmakers, a bookseller, an upholsterer, two innholders, a writing master, two barbers, a musician, and a registrar, as well as three gentlemen and two esquires.[15]

In tracing the development of this new element in the urban economy, it seems two areas should be highlighted: services and professions, and luxury craftsmen. The first of these shows perhaps the most remarkable growth of the two. A comparison of late sixteenth- and late seventeenth-century sources for the town of Warwick suggests services and professions constituted an almost wholly new sector in the town's economy.[16] In Preston an examination of the Guild Rolls for the years 1702, 1722, 1742 and 1762 points to a similar trend.[17] During this period the major structural change in the town's economy was the growth of the service sector. In the 1702 Roll this appears to encompass only 6 per cent of the town's labour force; by the three later Rolls it has doubled to 13 per cent. A major contribution to this growth came from those trades associated with health and personal grooming, especially barbers. The 1702 Roll points to only one barber working in the town, that for 1742 no less than thirty-three. Though this is misleading in that almost twice the proportion of Preston freemen in the later Roll (25 per cent) are assigned a trade than those in the former (14 per cent), it still constitutes a spectacular increase. Another area of growth in the service sector was leisure and sport. The 1702 Roll

14. See J. F. Pound, 'The social and trade structure of Norwich 1525–1575', *Past and Present*, XXXIV (1966), 57–64; V. Parker, *The Making of King's Lynn* (Chichester, 1971) 14–16; A. Everitt, *Ways and Means in Local History* (1971), 35–9, for Northampton; *VCH York*, 166–7. I am at present engaged in a computer project, with Mr Alan Rogers of the computer unit of Lampeter, to analyse wills and inventories for the town of Preston (1660–1760). One of the aims of this study is to examine the role of leisure and luxury in the town's economy, and in patterns of personal consumption. We would be delighted to hear from anybody engaged in a similar project, so we can compare both our use of the computer and our results.
15. Hereford Corporation Manuscripts, Common Council Minutes (1693–1736).
16. P. N. Borsay, 'A County Town Renaissance: Warwick 1660–1760', MS copy deposited in Warws. CRO., 51–8.
17. See the Appendix of this paper for a detailed occupational analysis of the Guild Rolls, and my qualifications about using them as a source.

contains five Preston gardeners; that for 1742, twenty. By this time the town also supported a musician, a jockey and a huntsman. The trend displayed in the growth of the service sector was reflected in the changing nature of the food distributive trades. We find growing numbers of shopkeepers, such as confectioners, tobacconists and grocers, selling relatively sophisticated products. At Preston these last two trades rose from a mere one and three representatives respectively in the 1702 Roll to nine and twenty-six in that for 1742.[18] Underpinning the expansion in services, and indeed the growth in the economy as a whole, was the development of the inn. The 1702 Roll boasts only five innkeepers who appear to be working in Preston; by 1722 this has increased to twenty-eight, and by 1742, thirty-two. One change in the economy led to another. The 1702 Roll names only one Preston man in the drink and allied trades, a maltster; by 1742 there were three maltsters, a maltman, four brewers and a wine merchant. Finally, Preston also nurtured a growing legal profession to service the demands of the local hinterland. Whereas the 1702 and 1722 Rolls fail to list any attorneys or counsellors at law working in Preston, the 1742 Roll contains seventeen.

The second area of growth in the new urban economy was that of luxury craftsmen. The most important element here was the construction industry (building, furnishing, etc.), whose significance will be dealt with when we turn to the development of urban architecture later in this article. The trend towards highly skilled — often luxury — craftsmanship was also visible in other traditional areas of the

---

18. A grocer could sell a rich variety of foodstuffs. Those in the shop of William Blackledge when an inventory was taken in 1685 (the only detailed grocer's inventory I have yet discovered for Preston, 1660–1760) amply display this. His stock contained fruit and nuts (prunes, citron and lemon chips, preserved quinces, raisins, currants, Barbary and Valencia almonds), spices (coriander seeds, cloves, mace, fennel seeds, long pepper, smooth pepper, white pepper, jemers pepper, turmeric, bayberries, cinnamon, capers, ginger, saffron and nutmeg), sweet products (sugar, loaf sugar, double refined, white and brown candy), drink and tobacco (brandy, Spanish white, malt, hops, cut and dried tobacco), as well as French barley, rice, grains, wafers, best sweet oil, vinegar and anchovies. He also sold a bewildering array of other products, from spectacles to linseed oil. See Lancashire Record Office, wills proved within the archdeaconry of Richmond, inventory of William Blackledge, 15 May 1685. The increasing number of grocers indicated in the Guild Rolls suggests a trend towards the sale of more sophisticated food products; an argument supported by the growing importance of groceries in the import trade (though of course much of this went into reexports: see W. E. Minchinton (ed.), *The Growth of English Overseas Trade in the Seventeenth and Eighteenth Centuries* (1969), introduction, 23–4). It would be interesting to examine in detail the ways in which the food distributive trades were adapting to and stimulating (perhaps through advertising) the new demands being placed on them. However, this is clearly beyond the scope of this article.

urban economy. The metallurgical sector saw the growth of gunsmiths, jewellers, pumpmakers, wrought-iron smiths, watch- and clockmakers. The case of Nicholas Paris of Warwick will help to illustrate the nature of this trend. He probably began working in Warwick shortly after the Restoration, establishing a business which was in the family for almost a century, despite his death in 1716. When Nicholas's house and shop were destroyed in the great fire of Warwick in 1694, he was described as a gunsmith, and his inventory of losses included £20 worth of 'timber for stocking guns'. Surviving examples of the handsome pistols, breechloaders and blunderbusses he produced show the quality and variety of his workmanship. But this only scratches the surface of his talents. From the 1680s he was working on the restoration of the Beauchamp Chapel in St Mary's Warwick, 'enameling, gilding and varnishing the Escocheons &c. of the Earl of Beauchamp's Mont' and 'gilding the statue and other parts of the said tomb'. To this skill he added that of a clockmaker. For the same church he constructed a clock after the fire, maintaining it and another at St Nicholas's in the town, for several years after. His talents in producing domestic instruments can be seen in the elegant long case clock in the local museum at Warwick. Nicholas also turned his hand to engineering on a larger scale to meet the growing demand for water engines. In 1685 he built a fire-engine for Stratford Corporation and later repaired the one at Warwick, while in 1705 he constructed 'a new engine to serve the castle with water'. It is clear he also did a variety of odd jobs for the corporation and Castle at Warwick; for example, in the 1690s he fitted a street lamp in the centre of the town opposite the Court House, and when William III visited Warwick in 1695 provided 'the pitch and tar used for the illuminations on Guy's tower'. But all these activities seem to be secondary to his main trade, that of a blacksmith. Much of his work probably involved plain, functional iron work; such must have been the bulk of the large contract he won, with William Marshall, for the rebuilding of St Mary's after the fire of 1694. Yet it is also clear his business produced a great deal of intricate wrought-iron work displaying considerable skill in design and execution. For this he had a widespread county clientele among the local churches and gentry, forging elaborate brackets, screens and gates for them. It also appears he had an even wider reputation that stretched deep into the South-West; Frome, Salisbury and Taunton are all claimed to have contained examples of his church work. Paris was clearly a remarkable craftsman, even in what Professor Everitt has called 'the golden age of English craftsmanship'. But his versatility – as gunsmith, gilder, clockmaker, engineer and blacksmith – shows the pressures being placed on craftsmen for an increasing variety of consumer goods. The skill demanded and displayed in his work also points to that underlying shift in consumer demand towards quality products.[19]

Some of the new luxury trades cannot be classified in terms of the traditional economy. Perhaps the most important of these are the ones associated with literature and the press. At the Restoration the provinces could probably only boast a handful of booksellers, yet by 1705 John Dunton could claim there were as many as 300. An important instrument in increasing the availability of books was the growth of the circulating library, which by 1760 could be found in a considerable number of provincial towns. In 1742 Preston, as well as having a bookseller and a bookbinder, also had two printers. One of these was responsible for publishing the *Preston Weekly Journal,* which originally appeared in 1740 and was probably the town's first newspaper. It placed Preston among a group of over fifty towns that between 1700 and 1760 were responsible for issuing the first provincial newspapers. Although the contents of these were not necessarily very adventurous, they were an important element, along with the bookshops and libraries, in turning the town into an agent for disseminating news and culture across provincial England.[20]

The emergence in the town of sophisticated leisure facilities, trades and services, was doing much to raise the standard of urban living. Less obvious, but also of importance in this process, were

19. For printed accounts of Paris's work see P. B. Chatwin, 'The rebuilding of St Mary's Church Warwick', *Transactions of the Birmingham Archaeological Society,* LXV (1943/4), 22–6; *VCH Warwickshire,* VIII, 444, 474, 507; W. Dugdale (ed.), *The Restoration of the Beauchamp Chapel* (Oxford, 1956), 14; and R. Lister, *Decorative Wrought-Iron in Great Britain* (2nd ed., Newton Abbot, 1970), 122–4, which places Paris in a national context. For manuscript sources, see Warws. CRO., Warwick Borough Records (Warw. BR.), W. 28 (Inrollment of Freeman 1684); Warw. BR., WA. 4 (Fire Records), box 2, 'An Estimate of the Losses Sustained In and By the Late Fire . . . 1694', and box 1 which contains the personal inventories that form the basis of the Estimate; much of Paris's work on the rebuilt St Mary's can be traced in 'A Book of Receipts and Payments Collected for the Use of the Sufferers by the Late Fire in Warwick', in box 2 of the above records; Warw. BR., W. 13/15 (Corporation Accounts 1693–1728), 1695/6, 1706/7, 1707/8, 1712/13, 1713/14, 1714/15, 1726/7; Warw. BR., W. 10 (Petitions of Householders for Restitution etc.), bundle 1, petition from Nicholas Paris dated 31 May 1697; Warwick Castle, Warwick Castle MSS. Accounts, 1695–97. These accounts show payments to Paris not only for the illuminations, but also for repairing guns, watches and clocks, and for servicing what is probably a fire-engine.

20. D. Davis, *A History of Shopping* (1966), 171; Plumb, *Commercialisation of Leisure,* 7; *Preston Weekly Journal,* no. 16, 9–16 January 1740/1; G. A. Cranfield, 'A handlist of English provincial newspapers and periodicals, 1700–1760', *Cambridge Bibliographical Society,* monograph 2 (1956). See also G. A. Cranfield, *The Development of the Provincial Newspaper, 1700–1760* (1962).

developments in the field of public amenities. There is little doubt that towns, at least for the better-off inhabitants, were becoming safer, pleasanter and more convenient places to live in. The risk of large-scale fire, a fear that must have haunted the minds of pre-industrial town dwellers, was declining. Safer building materials (brick, stone and tile) were increasingly being used in towns, fire insurance schemes were becoming available, and local authorities had begun to provide rudimentary fire-fighting appliances.[21] Along with greater safety came a cleaner, more pleasant living environment. Streets were built wider and more open to the air. Growing attention was paid to providing or improving paving, scavenging facilities, and street lighting. One suspects that much of this attention affected only selected areas of the town. When Warwick was rebuilt after its fire in 1694, obnoxious and dangerous trades were expelled from the principal streets and banished to the less socially important areas of the town.[22]

Certainly it was the more wealthy inhabitants who would benefit most from one of the more striking developments in public amenities, the improvement in urban water supplies. Though various simple systems had been used to bring water into the town before the late seventeenth century, most provincial town dwellers obtained their supplies simply by carrying it from the nearest well, spring or river. The demands of a growing population, and the desire for greater convenience, led to a rash of schemes to introduce a sophisticated piped water supply into the town. After a short-lived scheme earlier in the century, York acquired a permanent system in the late 1670s. The 1690s was the real 'take-off ' decade. Bills were introduced for supplying Bristol, Norwich and Deal, while schemes went ahead in Warwick, Hereford, Stamford, Newcastle and probably Bath. No doubt many other towns – Sheffield and Liverpool, for instance – also tried to introduce schemes in this decade that were to prove abortive. Not that set-backs meant anything amidst the growing craze for water technology. Sheffield eventually acquired a system around 1712, at the third attempt, and Liverpool in 1720, at the fifth. It is likely that most supplies were similar to that introduced into Warwick in 1693. Water there was pumped up from a series of pools that lay in the Priory grounds at the foot of the town, into a water house at the end of the present-day Northgate Street. From there it was distributed in pipes along various streets into the houses of those who could afford it. When the parish clerk, James Fish, lost his house in the fire of 1694, he appended a note to his inventory of losses to the effect that 'his house was newly supplied

---

21. For the development of the fire-engine see the entry under Thomas Newsham in the *D.N.B.*; above p. 166.
22. Borsay, 'A County Town Renaissance: . . .', 28–30.

with water having two cocks at his kitchen and brew house, the leaden pipes being about 30 yards long'.[23]

If provincial towns were becoming safer and more comfortable places to live in, they were also becoming pleasanter places to look at. It is clear that from the late seventeenth century many towns experienced a transformation in the way their buildings were designed which suggests an architectural renaissance was under way.[24] Prior to this period provincial urban architecture had paid little attention to questions of aesthetics and planning. The tall unit house that had characterized the principal streets of larger towns was a response to the problem of space rather than aesthetic considerations. Where there was decoration, with patterned half-timber work or carved gables and figures, it was often idiosyncratic and did little to relate one house to another. Streets were narrow, on occasions closed in by jettied storeys, and often far from straight. Buildings in the suburbs were probably little different from those in the surrounding countryside. What was new about the late seventeenth-century approach was that it introduced an urban aesthetic into urban architecture. At the core of this aesthetic lay an attempt to exploit the specific potential of the town (against the village) as a social and physical unit. Towns allowed opportunity for wide social intercourse and large-scale planning. It came to be realized that urban architecture could promote and take advantage of this, by stressing the similarity between individual buildings, and linking them together where possible into whole architectural units.

This new aesthetic was a major step forward in the development of urban consciousness. It showed itself in the urban landscape in three main ways.[25] First, individual buildings began to look more

23. W. G. Hoskins, *Local History in England* (2nd ed., 1972), 80–3; V. Parker, *King's Lynn*, 133; *VCH York*, 162, 460; E. Hughes, ' The "New River" water supply for Newcastle upon Tyne, 1698–1723', *Archaeologia Aeliana*, XXV (1947), 115–24; *VCH Warwickshire*, VIII, 440–1; Warws. CRO., Warw. BR., WA. 4/2, Inventories of loss, Church Street; Hereford Corporation Manuscripts, Common Council Minutes, January 1695/6; J. Thirsk, 'Tudor and Stuart Stamford', in A. Rogers (ed.), *The Making of Stamford* (Leicester, 1965), 72–3; Bath Corporation Manuscripts, Council Minutes, 30 March 1696; M. Walton, *Sheffield: its Story and its Achievement* (3rd ed., 1952, reprinted, Wakefield and Sheffield, 1968), 99; Picton, *Liverpool*, 24–8.
24. See J. Harris, 'The architecture of Stamford', in Rogers (ed.), *The Making of Stamford;* I. and E. Hall, *Historic Beverley* (York, 1973); V. Parker, *King's Lynn*, chs. 4–6; J. H. Plumb, *The Growth of Political Stability in England* (Penguin ed., 1969), 19–20; E. Johns, *British Townscapes* (1965), 59; T. Sharp, *The English Panorama* (2nd ed., 1950), chs. 2 and 3; J. Summerson, *Architecture in Britain 1530–1830* (5th ed., 1969), ch. 23.
25. The English model for the new urban classicism was of course post-fire London. See J. Summerson, *Georgian London* (1945), chs. 2–7; and D. Cruikshank and P. Wyld's splendid book, *London, the Art of Georgian Building* (1975).

like each other. This was due to a growing acceptance of a common language of architecture; what may be called urban classicism. It stressed the use of more solid building materials, and in design of flush façades, cornices and regularly spaced windows and doors decorated with suitably restrained ornamentation. In some cases the style was introduced through legislation, or by manipulating the covenants attached to a lease. The act for rebuilding Warwick after its fire laid down strict controls over the design of houses and the building materials to be used. Two leases drafted by Preston Corporation in the 1720s and '30s stipulated building materials, height of house, and in one case the use of sash windows.[26] More important than legal enforcement were the dictates of fashion, since new houses built in the old style would run the risk of being stigmatized. So strong were the pressures that many old buildings had their façades reconstructed or plastered over to give the impression of stonework. The Corporation accounts at Warwick for the year 1713/14 include a payment of over £16 to a local craftsman 'for plastering the outside of the college in imitation of stonework'.[27] An important factor in promoting and servicing the new fashion was the growth of the urban building industry, and its education, not least through the pattern books which appeared from the 1720s, in the language of classicism. In 1750 Robert Morris published a pattern book of designs for rural buildings. He had originally intended to include a section on urban architecture, but omitted this because 'there are already published, and executed, such a variety of town houses, and so many persons who are daily concerned in the practical part of that branch, that I was doubtful how it might be received . . .'.[28]

A second way that the new urban aesthetic impinged itself on the town was in the growth of specific units of urban architecture. The pressures towards conformity among individual houses inevitably increased the presence of the street *as a street,* and opened the way for terracing. In the late seventeenth century, Sir Edward Moore and Sir John Lowther went to considerable trouble to ensure that streets built on their respective estates at the growing ports of Liverpool and Whitehaven were treated as units, with houses that closely

---

26. 6 William and Mary, 1694, 'An act for rebuilding the town of Warwick . . .'; P. C. MSS., Council Minutes, 10 February 1726/7, 6 April 1736.
27. Warws. CRO., Warw. BR., W. 13/5 (Corporation Accounts 1693–1728), 1713/14. See also *VCH Gloucestershire*, VIII (1968), 130–1, for Tewkesbury. This is a good example of a town where, during our period, wide-scale reconstruction and refacing of established buildings was apparently occurring.
28. R. Morris, *Rural Architecture* (1st ed. 1750, reprinted, Farnborough, 1971), preface.

conformed to each other.[29] The most striking of the new urban units to appear in the English town was the fashionable square, which made its first appearance in the provinces in the early decades of the eighteenth century.[30] It was social architecture *par excellence:* not only did it house people in similar houses, but it also provided an arena (i.e. the square) in which they could socialize. Some architects attempted to link the street and square into a more ambitious scheme. Hawksmoor drew up plans for reconstructing substantial parts of Oxford and Cambridge, but they failed to be realized.[31] More successful was John Wood at Bath. As has recently been shown, the town he played such a crucial part in constructing was not pragmatically 'thrown together'; it was the product of a mind profoundly influenced by Renaissance ideas of beauty and the social function of architecture.[32] It was a measure of how much the importance of the town had been raised in people's perceptions that it deserved such attention, and that this could be translated into economic reality. Finally, we might like to see as a further sign of the growing importance of the urban aesthetic, and of urban consciousness, the expansion in the construction of public buildings: not only commercial buildings, but charity schools and hospitals, town halls, and for the first time since the Reformation, churches.[33]

II

At the outset I suggested that these four areas of development in town life that I have sketched in (leisure facilities, the economy, public amenities and architecture) could be said to constitute an urban renaissance. Why was this renaissance occurring, and which towns were benefiting most from it? It is clear that the sort of items that constituted these four areas have one feature in common; they arise from that part of personal expenditure that is surplus to the basic necessities of life. Assemblies, books and newspapers are not

29. C. Chalklin, 'The making of some new towns c.1600–1720', in C. W. Chalklin and M. A. Havinden (eds.), *Rural Change and Urban Growth 1500–1800* (1974), 240–1; W. F. Irvine (ed.), *Liverpool in King Charles the Second's Time* (Liverpool, 1899), see especially Fenwicke Street, 133–50.
30. See below, note 42.
31. K. Downes, *Hawksmoor* (1969), 90–4.
32. R. Neale, 'Society, belief and the building of Bath, 1700–1780', in Chalklin and Havinden (eds.), *Rural Change,* 268–77.
33. Some of these can be traced in Summerson, *Architecture in Britain,* parts 3 and 4.

essential to keep alive; palladian façades and piped water supplies might provide shelter and water, but they are not necessary in obtaining them. This suggests that the urban renaissance was built upon the 'surplus wealth' content of personal expenditure. Pre-industrial societies are notoriously deficient in the number of people possessing surplus wealth to any marked degree; hence leisure and luxury are confined to a very small élite. However, in the case of England the evidence points to these numbers increasing considerably in the centuries immediately preceding the 'classic' period of the Industrial Revolution. First, the size and personal wealth of the traditional ruling class, the gentry, seems to have grown significantly in the sixteenth and early seventeenth centuries. Stone suggests that in the century before the Civil War their numbers trebled and that the level of their real incomes also showed a striking increase.[34] Second – and the really dynamic element in post-Restoration England – there appears to have been a rapid expansion in the 'middling' groups in society. Endless litigation and a growing demand for monetary and trained medical services had increased the number of lawyers, attorneys, doctors, surgeons and apothecaries. The unique scale of the French wars begun under William III was crucial in the rise of the military and naval professions: the need to administer and raise money for these wars was also responsible for the remarkable growth in the civil service. In the business sector war finance created a new wealthy élite, the London 'monied interest', while the demand for munitions stimulated the growth of prosperous manufacturers. These new groups built on to the established bulwark of the business sector, the merchants, who themselves had expanded greatly during the post-Restoration boom in English trade. Finally, and more easily overlooked, there were increasing numbers of prosperous tradesmen and craftsmen, whose wealth was often derived from the growing demand for leisure and luxury.[35]

Given this expansion in the numbers of people enjoying surplus wealth, it is clear that certain towns benefited from their patronage rather than others, and it was these towns that were most influenced

34. L. Stone, *The Causes of the English Revolution* (1974), 72–4.
35. See for the growth of the 'middling' groups in society P. G. M. Dickson, *The Financial Revolution in England* (1967), ch. 11; A. Everitt, *Change in the Provinces: the Seventeenth Century* (Leicester, 1969), 43–4; G. S. Holmes, *British Politics in the Age of Anne* (1967), ch. 5, esp. 151; W. E. Minchinton (ed.), *English Overseas Trade*, esp. introduction, 47–8; L. Stone, ' Social mobility in England 1500–1700', *Past and Present*, XXXIII (1966), 52–4; W. A. Speck, ' Social status in late Stuart England', *Past and Present*, XXXIV (1966), 127–9; P. Styles, 'The social structure of Kineton Hundred in the Reign of Charles II', *Transactions of the Birmingham Archaeological Society*, LXXVIII (1962), esp. 103, 113–17.

by the urban renaissance. Two different types of centres can be distinguished here: those that attracted surplus wealth, and those that created it. Among those towns attracting wealth, the most dramatic example of growth was to be found in the rise of the health resorts.[36] Their primary founding characteristic was that they offered medical treatment through the use of their local waters, whether by bathing in or drinking them. While their role as health resorts remained of great importance, several also became 'holiday resorts'. As such, the quality of their social facilities and clientele was crucial in attracting visitors. Most of the important resorts had a wide catchment area. Bath and Tunbridge had an almost national market, while others – such as Scarborough, Buxton and Harrogate in the north, or Cheltenham, Bristol and the London spas (Epsom, Islington, etc.) in the south – were more regionally orientated.

Much of the attraction of the health resort as a social centre was that it was cosmopolitan and had no specific extra-urban roots. There was a second sort of town able to attract large quantities of surplus wealth for quite the opposite reason. This was the urban centre which *because* of its affinity with a specific rural area could depend upon the patronage of a substantial number of the local gentry. The best example of this was the county town. Its wide area of influence depended on the fact that it was not only an important market town, but also, normally, the focus of the county community. This was a social and political unit into which the growing cohorts of the gentry had tended loosely to coalesce, especially during the political conflicts of the seventeenth century. As the normal home of the community's legal, administrative and political business – the seat of the assizes, the quarter sessions and of shire elections – it was natural that the county town should also be its social forum.[37] One of the great events in the county year was the period of the assizes. The austere legal function of the occasion was not allowed to undermine its social possibilities. In 1763 a correspondent wrote of the Salisbury assizes 'we had the greatest appearance of gentlemen I ever saw at the assizes; we dined fifty with the Sheriff and above fifty with the Grand Jury . . . we had two exceeding good balls and I can find no fault but that the Sheriff, in high spirits at being so well attended . . . he made us drink much more higher than I approved of . . . the Sheriff could not get to his lodgings without

---

36. The best modern works on spas are R. Lennard, 'The watering places', in R. Lennard (ed.), *Englishmen at Rest and Play: Some Phases of English Leisure 1558–1714* (Oxford, 1931), 1–78; S. McIntyre, 'Towns as health and pleasure resorts; Bath, Scarborough, and Weymouth, 1770–1815', unpublished Ph.D. thesis, University of Oxford, 1973. I am indebted to Sylvia McIntyre for allowing me to use her thesis, and for discussions we have had on health resorts.
37. See Everitt, *Change in the Provinces*, 25–6.

some supporters, and Lord Seymour Webb on the way home walked into the dirtiest ditch . . .'.[38]

One of the advantages of the county town was that as a legal and often diocesan centre, it had a resident professional élite whose wealth could help to develop the facilities the town offered. However, this could lead to problems if these administrative functions were geographically divided. In Staffordshire the county town (Stafford) was the home of the assizes, but Lichfield was the centre of the diocese. It has recently been argued that Stafford declined in the seventeenth century.[39] One of the reasons may have been that it faced, on its home patch, a competitor in the market for gentry patronage. In Lancashire the problem was rather different. The county had two legal centres, Lancaster for the county assizes and Preston for the Duchy courts. Though Lancaster was the official county town, Preston because of its southerly position was to prove a far more important centre for the county gentry. Even if a town suffered little from competition, it was still at the mercy of the socio-economic structure of its rural hinterland. Dr Thirsk argues that Stamford was unable to benefit from gentry patronage because the town was surrounded by fen and forest land; this produced villages inhabited by many small peasants but few rich gentry. However, as can be seen by its fine surviving architecture, the urban renaissance did not bypass Stamford. It represents a third sort of town able to attract wealth. Situated on the road north, it was one of a growing number of 'travel towns' benefiting from the rapid expansion in road transport.[40]

Some towns have greatness thrust upon them, and some gain it by their own endeavours. Unlike the health resorts, county towns and 'travel towns', there was a second category of urban centre that created *its own* surplus wealth. From the late seventeenth century many industrial towns and ports entered a phase of considerable economic and demographic growth. In some cases this was on a dramatic scale. In 1700 both Birmingham and Liverpool had populations of under 7000; by 1750 each had trebled – perhaps quad-

38. Wiltshire County Record Office, 947 (Long MS), unsorted letters, 29 July 1763, unidentified writer to Dorothy (Long). For the 'assize week' see also R. W. Ketton-Cremer, 'Assize week in Norwich in 1688', *Norfolk Archaeology*, XXIV (1932), 13–17; W. A. J. Prevost (ed.), 'A journie to Carlyle and Penrith in 1731', *Transactions of the Cumberland and Westmorland Antiquarian and Archaeological Society*, New Series, LXI (1961), 223–7.
39. K. R. Adey, 'Seventeenth-century Stafford: a county town in decline', *Midland History*, vol. 2, no. 3 (1974), 152–67.
40. Thirsk, 'Tudor and Stuart Stamford', 68–9; Harris, 'The architecture of Stamford'.

rupled – their size to over 22 000.[41] Several of these rapidly expanding centres produced a substantial and wealthy bourgeoisie that placed their towns in the van of the urban renaissance. The fashionable square made its first provincial appearance not in the county centres or spas, but in the industrial towns of Manchester and Birmingham, and ports of Bristol and Liverpool.[42] The smoke and grime that later settled over some of these cities should not obscure the fact that they were among the pioneers of Georgian elegance. Finally, it must be added that many towns both attracted and created surplus wealth. For example, Nottingham, Norwich and Exeter were county towns as well as important industrial centres or ports.

III

We have examined the economic foundations of the urban renaissance and suggested the sort of towns in which it was most evident. But what of its social function? One aspect of this function may be highlighted which stands in sharp contrast with the tranquil light some historians have shed over the first half of the eighteenth century. The possession of surplus wealth is not simply an opportunity to buy more of the basic necessities of life; it is rather the key to a different style of living. Above all, surplus wealth allows entry to what may be called the world of social competition. Therefore, given an increase in the numbers of people holding surplus wealth, one would also expect a growth in that part of society engaged in 'the pursuit of status'. Such a growth unquestionably took place during the period with which this essay is concerned. The town was to play a crucial role in servicing the increasing demand for status, and absorbing the pressures being laid upon the social structure.[43]

---

41. C. W. Chalklin, *The Provincial Towns of Georgian England: a Study of the Building Process 1740–1820* (1974), 17–25.
42. Bath Municipal Reference Library Manuscripts, access no. 38/43, MS 'Diary of a tour undertaken by three students . . .' (1725), 51, 121; B. Little, *Birmingham Buildings* (Newton Abbot, 1971), 11; G. Burke, *Towns in the Making* (1971), 108; Picton, *Liverpool*, 60–1.
43. This paper does not seek to argue that the pursuit of status was a new phenomenon, merely that it encompassed far more people in the post-Restoration period. For the trend towards growing social mobility in the century before the Civil War, see C. Wilson, *England's Apprenticeship 1603–1763* (1965), ch. 1; the works of Stone referred to in notes 34 and 35 above; J. Thirsk, 'Younger Sons in the Seventeenth Century', *History*, LIV (1969), 358–77; and A. Everitt, 'Social

It did this firstly by providing the instruments of battle. In the 1699 edition of his *New State Of England*, Guy Miège tackled the problem of how a man acquires gentility. He writes 'gentlemen are properly such as are descended of a good family bearing a coat of arms . . .', which would seem to shut the door to any *arriviste*, but then adds: '. . . on the other side, anyone that without a coat of arms, has either a liberal or genteel education, that looks gentleman like (whether he be so or not) and has the wherewithal to live freely, is by the courtesy of England usually called a gentleman'.[44] In other words, physical and mental possessions can be used as a way of transforming wealth into status. In this sense the new sophisticated urban economy can be seen as a munitions factory in the pursuit of status. When the milliners, drapers, mercers, jewellers, and so forth, dispensed their luxury products, it is hard to imagine their customers were unaware of the uses to which they could put their purchases. As Mandeville wrote in 1714, 'fine feathers make fine birds, and people where they are not known are generally honoured according to their clothes and other accoutrements they have about them . . .'.[45] Equally, the town dispensed, partly through its new book-shops, libraries and press, partly through its theatre, concerts, coffee-houses and inns, the knowledge and culture that went with an educated and genteel mind. Ruling all these elements were the dictates of fashion. They provided guidelines to the status value of any particular object. They also allowed, because of fashion's essentially fluid nature, these guidelines to be changed at a frequency commensurate with the level of demand for status at any given time or place.

If the town equipped potential combatants with the instruments of war, it also provided the arena in which battle took place. However fine a man's mind and clothes, they are of little use in the pursuit of status unless displayed amongst those people willing and able to compete with him. The village could hardly provide this competition; the town could. Hence we can see the new urban leisure facilities – the assemblies, walks, theatres and race meetings – as

Mobility in Early Modern England', *Past and Present*, XXXIII (1966), 56–73, who, while agreeing with this trend, warns us not to over-emphasize the growth in social mobility. Professor Fisher has shown how before the Civil War London was already being transformed into 'a centre of conspicuous consumption', one suspects to service the growing demand for status. See his article, 'The development of London as a centre of conspicuous consumption in the sixteenth and seventeenth centuries', *Transactions of the Royal Historical Society*, 4th ser., XXX (1948), 37–50.
44. G. Miège, *The New State of England* (3rd ed., 1699), part 2, ch. 20.
45. P. Harth (ed.), *The Fable of the Bees* (first published 1714; Penguin ed., 1970), 152.

arenas for personal display. Defoe tells us of Tunbridge, 'After the appearance is over at the Wells (where the ladies are all undress'd) and at the chapel, the company go home; and as if it were another species of people, or a collection from another place, you are surpriz'd to see the walks covered by ladies completely dress'd and gay to profusion; where rich clothes, jewels, and beauty not to be set out by (but infinitely above) ornament, dazzles the eyes from one end of the range to another.'[46]

Given this underlying competitive function, it is natural the town should accentuate its role as an 'open society'. It would only restrict competition if artificial barriers existed to a man transferring his wealth into status. Here the town clearly offered its supreme advantage as an alternative culture to the 'closed society' of the rural world. Contemporaries emphasized the cosmopolitan nature of the health resorts. We are told of Bath in 1721 '. . . the town is as full as possible, but such a mixture as was never got together at the building of Babel . . .', while in 1748 a poet wrote of the spa: 'Now from all parts the company resort, Sailing, like Vessels, to this neutral Port . . .'. A year later Mrs Montagu could claim 'Tunbridge seems the parliament of the world, where every country and every rank has its representatives . . .'.[47] There were also pressures to prevent social distinctions from interfering with competition. At Bath Nash took measures to ensure this, while at Newmarket Macky tells us '. . . all mankind are here upon equal level . . .'.[48] Likewise there were conscious efforts to keep people in the public gaze as long as possible. Public breakfasts were encouraged and arranged at Bath, Tunbridge and Bristol Hot Wells, while at Matlock we hear 'the company . . . live, as in most other public places, in a very sociable manner, always meeting at meals in a common room . . .'.[49] It may be argued that the new urban architecture helped to encourage an open society. To take the square. All houses in it would be similar, reducing distinctions, while the physical structure of the square ensured it would be impossible

46. G. D. H. Cole and D. C. Browning (eds.), *A Tour through the Whole Island of Great Britain* (first published 1724–6; Everyman ed., 1962), vol. 1, 126.
47. 13 May 1723, Lady Bristol to Lord Bristol, a letter quoted in R. Peach, *The Life and Times of Ralph Allen of Prior Park* (1895), 216–17; anonymous, *Bath: a Poem* (1748), 5; a letter from Mrs Montagu dated 1749, quoted in M. Barton, *Tunbridge Wells* (1937), 234.
48. L. Melville, *Bath under Beau Nash* (1907), 52–3; Macky, *Journey through England*, vol. 1, 91.
49. Warws. CRO., L6 (Lucy MS)/1467, 18 April 1762, George Lucy to Mrs Hayes; M. Barton, *Tunbridge Wells*, 202; V. Waite, 'The Bristol Hotwell', in P. McGrath (ed.), *Bristol in the Eighteenth Century* (1972), 121; Hist. MSS. Comm. *Verulam MSS.*, 'A Northern Tour 1768', 233.

to leave the front door without being subject to the full gaze of the surrounding arena. But I do not want to exaggerate the 'openness' of the new provincial urban society. It was only open to those with money to enter. Moreover, social distinctions continued to be of immense importance; after all, the acquisition of distinction was precisely what the pursuit of status was about.

The competition for status was not confined to posturing or to 'psychological warfare'. There is one sense in which it took a very concrete form. Recently historians have stressed the crucial role of marriage in early eighteenth-century society as a means of acquiring wealth or status.[50] In this context it seems clear that many of the urban social centres I have been discussing served as marriage markets.[51] In 1714 Macky called Bury St Edmunds fair 'more a market for ladies than merchandises', while in 1754 Pococke argued of Bath that 'there is no place in the world so fit for the necessary and honourable business of making alliances . . . '.[52] George Lucy, a Warwickshire gentleman, echoed these sentiments when six years later he wrote from Bath 'Sir Charles Hardy took a wife with him from hence on Saturday last and I hear many more are upon the same plan . . .'. He went on to add, 'they tell me, I have a twenty thousand pounder my next neighbour, and only parted by one thin partition . . . '.[53] His later remark points to the goods being offered for sale in the marriage market. To simplify matters considerably, the woman brought wealth and the man status; a woman was as beautiful as she was wealthy, a man as handsome as he was superior. As a contributor to *The Tunbridge and Bath Miscellany* of 1714 wrote, 'With scorn Clodalia's haughty face we view, /The Deaden'd aspect, and the sordid hue, /Her wealth discover'd gives her features lies, /And we find charms to reconcile our eyes . . . '.[54] This mechanism could allow a gentleman fallen upon hard times to renew his wealth and thereby maintain his status. We hear from Buxton in

50. See C. Clay, 'Marriage, inheritance, and the rise of the large estates in England, 1660–1815', *Economic History Review*, 2nd Series, XXI (1968), 503–18; W. A. Speck, 'Conflict in society', in G. S. Holmes (ed.), *Britain after the Glorious Revolution* (1969), 145–7.

51. On the town as a marriage market see R. Williams, *The Country and the City* (1973), 51–4. Professor Laslett has recently suggested that the eighteenth-century assemblies were marriage markets, he argues for the purpose of patrilineal repair. He proposed this in a paper, 'Social promotion, social descent and the demography of an élite in traditional society', read to the Social History Society Conference held at Lancaster University in January 1976.

52. Macky, *Journey through England*, vol. 1, 3–5; R. Pococke, 'The travels through England', *Camden Society*, 2nd series, XLIV, 32.

53. Warws. CRO., L6/1451, 10 January 1759/60, George Lucy to Mrs Hayes.

54. Anonymous, 'An epistle to a friend', in *The Tunbridge and Bath Miscellany for the Year 1714* (1714), 12.

1744 that Sir Archibald Grant, whose estate had been sequestered for his mismanagement of a charitable organization, had 'made love to Mrs Jessop to mend his private affairs . . . '.[55] Equally the mechanism allowed a rich merchant to acquire status by marrying his daughter to a gentleman. In the open society of the town the market could be intensely competitive. The walks and assemblies would be packed with over-dressed men and women seeking to appear more than they were worth, thereby hoping to drive the best possible bargain. As the Duchess of Marlborough wrote of the York races in 1732, 'all the young women lay out more than they can spare to get good husbands . . . '.[56] Yet this open-market situation was all important if the town was to act as an instrument for absorbing the tensions inherent in a society carrying a rapidly expanding surplus income group. Wealth could be freely transferred into status while at the same time cushioning those whose status was imperilled by economic decline.

IV

The tentative thesis of this paper has been that from the late seventeenth-century English provincial towns underwent a cultural change – in the broadest sense – of such a magnitude that it amounts to an urban renaissance. I have suggested that the economic basis of this renaissance was the widening distribution of surplus wealth in society. This raised the level of demand for a range of personal aspirations, crucial among which was status. The development in the town of sophisticated leisure facilities, manufactures and services, public amenities, and architecture, was an attempt to satisfy these new demands. The towns in which these changes were most evident were those best able to attract or create surplus wealth.

I should like to conclude by speculating on a number of ideas that are inevitably raised by this thesis. Whatever the malaise of English urban society in the sixteenth and early seventeenth centuries, the gloom had decisively lifted by the end of the seventeenth century. As part of this transformation there emerged a far more acute urban culture and consciousness, sharply defined from that of rural society. The town/country conflict, so much a part of Restoration and eighteenth-century literature, reflects this change. Addison's 'Foxhunting Gentleman', Fielding's Squire Weston, or

55. Hist. MSS. Comm. *Egmont MSS.*, 3, 'Diary of Viscount Percival afterwards 1st Earl of Egmont', 1730–47, 297–8.
56. G. Scott Thomson (ed.), *Letters of a Grandmother 1732–1735* (1943), 58.

Smollett's Matthew Bramble, all perplexed and upset by their contact with metropolitan culture, inhabit a world in which urbanization was creating real tensions in society.[57] But these are archetypal characters. It would be wrong to assume that the British split into either country or town lovers. For many (perhaps most) people, the new urban consciousness was not an alternative, but an additional strand in their cultural make-up. The letters of George Lucy the Warwickshire squire, written from Bath in the mid-eighteenth century, are full of nostalgic enquiries about his estate, and criticisms of town life. None the less, he regularly visited Bath for at least twenty years, often staying for several months at a time.[58] In this sense we are seeing the development of a personality built on a dual cultural response, the elements of which could be in contradiction with each other. Though my paper has been based on evidence almost exclusively drawn from the upper and middling groups in society, I feel it would be wrong to assume that this duality of response was confined to a narrow social stratum. The considerable urban migration that appears to have been responsible for the rapid expansion of English towns in this period suggests urban life exerted an attraction that permeated deep into society.[59]

But it is one thing to discuss the growth of urban culture and consciousness, another to show in what way this affected people's style of living. This can only be assessed by examining and defining urban culture itself. Difficult as this is, my feeling is that the central characteristic of this culture was the concept of space, for it was to the town that people turned to escape from the closed consciousness in which they were imprisoned by rural society. Because the town was a meeting place and transit point, it provided contact with

57. See the group of essays on 'Country humours' in J. R. Green (ed.), *Essays of Joseph Addison* (1898), 245–78; H. Fielding, *The History of Tom Jones* (1749); T. Smollett, *The Expedition of Humphrey Clinker* (first pub. 1771; Penguin ed., London, 1967), esp. 146–55. Addison's essays represent a concerted attempt to 'urbanize' his readers by satirizing rural culture. One of the key symbols of this culture was foxhunting since it epitomized the irrational, barbarous nature of rural society. Addison's attack on it is paralleled by other writers. Squire Weston is obsessed by hunting. *The Preston Journal* of 1750 carried in its August issues (nos. 287, 289) two poems – perhaps echoing Addison's 'he (the Tory foxhunter) fell into a long panegyric upon his spaniel' – one eulogizing the intelligence of a spaniel, the other bitterly satirizing this. It is in the same spirit that Nash sought to ban riding dress in the assembly rooms at Bath, again using the medium of satire. See O. Goldsmith, 'The life of Richard Nash', in A. Friedman (ed.), *Collected Works of Oliver Goldsmith* (1966), vol. 3, 306.
58. Warws. CRO., L6 (Lucy MS), see the letters, accounts and bills of George Lucy.
59. See E. A. Wrigley, 'A simple model of London's importance in changing English society and economy 1650–1750', *Past and Present*, XXXVII (1967), 44–9, 67; and the same author's, 'London and the Great Leap Forwards', *The Listener*, 6 July 1967, 7–8.

'geographical space'; because it published and sold books, and housed institutions like the theatre, it offered access to 'intellectual space'. But, above all, the town was increasingly the focus of 'social space', the space that separates individuals by status. By providing an armoury and arena in the pursuit of status, the town offered the vehicles by which individuals could traverse social space.[60] It is as a purveyor of social mobility that the town did most to change people's style of life, because it helped to generate a competitive, aspiring society.

Finally, it may be suggested that the town, by aiding the development of a competitive society, also contributed to future economic change. Increasingly historians have stressed the importance of social factors in the origins of the Industrial Revolution. Specifically, social emulation has been selected as a key force in stimulating new patterns of work and consumer demand.[61] The urban renaissance began almost a century before the 'classic' period of the Industrial Revolution. By implanting the idea of social space in people's minds, and servicing their demand for this space, it encouraged the pursuit of status. May we then see the town as the engine of social emulation, and to some extent of the Industrial Revolution?

60. I think it is about the growth in social space that Lionel Trilling is writing when he argues in *Sincerity and Authenticity* (1972), 20, that it was in the early modern period that 'the idea of society, much as we now conceive it, had come into being'. One might also suggest that the rise of the idea of sincerity, which he connects with the rise of the idea of society, is a product of the conflict between the dual cultural strands developing in the individual. The search for sincerity was an attempt to protect the integral nature of personality.
61. See E. W. Gilboy, 'Demand as a factor in the Industrial Revolution', reprinted in R. M. Hartwell (ed.), *The Causes of the Industrial Revolution in England* (1967), 121–38; H. J. Perkin, *The Origins of Modern English Society 1780–1880* (1969), 89–95; N. McKendrick, 'Home demand and economic growth', in N. McKendrick (ed.), *Historical Perspectives* (1974), 191–202. Specifically on the role of the town in developing social emulation see Wrigley, 'A simple model of London's importance . . .', 67; M. J. Daunton 'Towns and economic growth in eighteenth-century England', *Past and Present*, Annual Conference (1975),106–7.

Appendix

Trades and professions of Preston In-Burgesses 1702–1762 (A = 1702, B = 1722, C = 1742, D = 1762.)

	A	B	C	D
Textiles				
Weaver	—	4	45	28
Linen weaver	1	—	1	—
Lace weaver	—	—	1	—
Stuff weaver	—	—	—	1
Stocking weaver	—	—	1	3
Webster	8	4	—	—
Woollen webster	2	—	—	—
Linen webster	6	—	—	—
Feltmaker	2	3	—	—
Thrower	—	—	—	1
Throwster	—	—	1	—
Thread maker	2	1	1	1
Whitener	2	—	—	—
Dyer	2	4	7	3
Thread Dyer	1	—	—	—
Dryster	2	—	—	—
Flax Dresser	1	3	3	9
Tousor	2	—	—	—
Woolcomber	—	1	—	—
Silkcomber	—	1	—	—
Rag man	—	—	1	—
Fustian man	—	—	4	1
Flax man	2	—	2	—
Chapman	—	2	6	6
Silkman	—	—	1	1
Linen tradesman	—	—	—	1
Mercer	—	4	—	—
Draper	1	—	—	1
Woollen draper	—	—	7	7
Linen draper	1	1	7	5
Haberdasher	1	—	3	—
Taylor	29	28	45	27
Breeches maker	—	—	3	1
Hosier	3	2	1	1
Hatter	—	—	2	2
Total	68	58	142	99
Percentages	25	16	19	19
Leather Trades				
Skinner	5	5	5	4
Currier	3	2	5	8
Leather miller	—	—	—	1
Tanner	5	1	2	3
Shoemaker	15	25	62	38

Appendix (*cont.*)

	A	B	C	D
Cordwainer	—	—	—	1
Glover	4	5	6	4
Sadler	3	5	8	4
Total	35	43	88	63
Percentages	13	12	11.5	12
Metalwork				
Blacksmith	7	9	9	8
Whitesmith	—	2	7	3
Pewterer	1	1	—	—
Goldsmith	2	1	—	1
Silversmith	4	1	2	2
Tinman	—	1	3	3
Brazier	—	1	—	3
Nailor	1	2	4	4
Buttonmaker	1	—	1	1
Anchor smith	—	—	—	1
Sword cutler	—	1	—	—
Gunsmith	3	1	2	1
Pisteller	1	—	—	—
Pumpmaker	—	—	2	—
Clockmaker	2	1	5	4
Watchmaker	3	2	3	1
Ironmonger	1	1	4	—
Hardwareman	—	—	2	3
Total	26	24	44	35
Percentages	10	7	6	6.5
Miscellaneous				
Printer	—	—	2	1
Bookbinder	—	—	1	1
Bookseller	—	1	1	2
Stationer	1	2	—	—
Limner	—	—	1	—
Tobacconist	1	5	9	2
Tobacco Spinner	—	1	—	—
Pipemaker	—	1	—	—
Peruke maker	—	—	1	—
Staymaker	—	—	6	4
Collar maker	2	—	3	1
Chandler	2	—	3	2
Candler	—	—	—	2
Ropemaker	1	—	—	—
Brush maker	—	—	—	2
Fur Cutter	—	—	2	3
Labourers	8	11	22	15
Total	15	21	51	35
Percentages	5.5	6	7	6.5

Appendix (*cont.*)

	A	B	C	D
Construction trades				
Mason	1	—	—	—
Brickman	3	2	1	—
Brickmaker	—	—	3	4
Bricklayer	4	4	7	5
Slater	1	3	8	3
Pavier	1	1	5	3
Plasterer	4	—	5	—
Whitelimer	—	4	10	5
Thatcher	1	2	2	—
Glazier	6	4	8	8
Painter	—	1	5	2
Plumber	—	1	—	—
Sawyer	—	—	4	4
Carpenter	13	12	15	15
Joiner	6	12	35	23
Cabinetmaker	2	2	—	3
Turner	—	—	1	1
Woodthrowster	—	—	1	—
Canyer	1	—	—	—
Reedmaker	1	1	—	2
Upholsterer	—	2	4	3
Upholder	—	—	—	2
Cooper	2	9	15	7
Wine Cooper	—	—	1	—
Wheelwright	2	2	1	3
Coachmaker	—	1	—	—
Organmaker	—	—	1	1
Saddle-tree maker	1	—	—	—
Shuttlemaker	—	—	1	—
Total	49	63	133	94
Percentages	18	18	18	18
Food and drink				
Miller	5	4	5	3
Baker	—	—	2	2
Bread baker	—	2	1	3
Pastry cook	—	—	1	—
Ginger-bread maker	—	—	1	—
Butcher	21	21	36	30
Grocer	3	10	25	21
Cheesemonger	—	—	2	—
Malster	1	2	3	3
Maltman	—	—	1	—
Maltmaker	—	1	—	—
Brewer	—	—	4	2
Wine merchant	—	—	1	2

Appendix (*cont.*)

	A	B	C	D
Total	30	40	82	66
Percentages	11	11	11	13
Carrying and transport				
Navigator	—	1	—	—
Mariner	1	—	7	9
Sailor	—	1	6	4
Porter	—	—	1	—
Carrier	—	—	2	—
Coal carrier	—	—	1	1
Carter	1	1	4	2
Messenger	—	—	1	1
Coachman	—	—	1	1
Total	2	3	23	18
Percentages	1	1	3	3
Services				
Innkeeper	5	28	32	10
Drawer	—	—	—	1
Druggist	—	—	1	1
Apothecary	2	3	5	5
Farrier	1	—	2	2
Barber	1	7	33	23
Musician	—	—	1	—
Dancing master	—	1	—	—
Jockey	—	—	1	—
Groom	—	—	1	—
Huntsman	—	—	1	1
Gardener	5	8	20	18
Cook	—	—	1	—
Servant	2	—	4	8
Total	16	47	102	69
Percentages	6	13	13.5	13
Agriculture				
Husbandman	15	33	38	17
Yeoman	—	1	3	3
Total	15	34	41	20
Percentages	5.5	10	5	4
Professions				
Attorney at Law	—	—	15	13
Counsellor at Law	—	—	2	2
Dr of Physik	—	—	2	1
Dr of Medicine	2	1	—	—
Surgeon	1	3	2	—
Schoolmaster	4	1	6	4
Merchant	2	2	3	—
Sea captain	—	—	2	1

Appendix (*cont.*)

	A	B	C	D
Scrivener	—	1	—	1
Clerk	5	11	6	—
Dissenting minister	—	—	1	—
Customs, excise and				
tax men	—	1	6	3
Postmaster	—	1	—	—
Total	14	21	45	25
Percentages	5	6	6	5

Source: P.C. MSS Guild Rolls, 1702, 1722, 1742, 1762.

Note:

The Preston Guild was held every twenty years, and a list of freemen of the town produced on each occasion. These Rolls are divided into two main parts, In-Burgesses and Out-Burgesses; only the former of these is used to construct the above table. The In-Burgess Roll can only give an impression of the structure of the town's economy, albeit a useful one, since it suffers from two serious problems as a source. First, not all those on the Roll are ascribed a trade or profession, especially in the earlier Rolls.

	1702	*1722*	*1742*	*1762*
Total number of In-Burgesses	1896	2650	2997	2720
Those ascribed a trade or profession	385 (20%)	488 (18%)	1579 (53%)	1149 (42%)

Second, the place of habitation of those In-Burgesses ascribed a trade or profession is not always stated. Again, the earlier Rolls are worst here.

	1702	*1722*	*1742*	*1762*
Outside Preston	115	134	828	625
Preston	35	70	657	474
Not specified	235	284	94	50

It seems probable that most of those whose habitation is unspecified in fact worked in Preston. Using the 1741 Preston Poll Book (Lancashire CRO. DDKe 'An Alphabetical List of the Freemen-inhabitants of the Town of Preston . . . Who Polled for Members of Parliament . . . 1741') many of those unspecified in the 1742 Guild Roll can be identified as Preston inhabitants. I have therefore added together the Preston and the unspecified entries, and it is these that appear in the table. A final reservation about the use of the Guild Rolls is that I feel the declining numbers in the 1762 Roll compared with that for 1742 suggest the Rolls are beginning to be less comprehensive by this date, since it is unlikely the town's population declined during this period. Perhaps it reflects a trend towards the declining importance of freeman registration in being permitted to practise a trade in the town.

N.B. Please note Peter Borsay's request in footnote 14 for others working on patterns of personal consumption and the role of leisure and luxury in the development of a town's economy to get in touch with him in order to compare methodology, use of a computer and their results.

Chapter 6

THE LONDON 'MOB' IN THE EARLY EIGHTEENTH CENTURY

Robert B. Shoemaker

[*Journal of British Studies*, 26, no. 3 (1987)]

The study of popular disturbances has attracted a good deal of attention from modern historians of the eighteenth century, perhaps because such events seem to offer an obvious interface between social and political history. Towns, due to their role as economic, administrative, and political centres, were more subject to the effects of demonstrations and riots than rural settlements. London was particularly prone to 'mob' activity, which according to Robert Shoemaker was probably increasing in frequency during the late seventeenth and early eighteenth centuries. His wide-ranging examination of the metropolitan crowd addresses vital questions about its social composition, contemporary attitudes to the legitimacy of its actions, the links between old and new forms of protest, the extent to which participants expressed a popular consensus, and the similarities and differences between urban and rural forms of protest. One of Shoemaker's most important conclusions in the context of the development of popular politics, is that the early eighteenth century was 'a crucial period in the long process in which the political élite lost control of popular disturbances in London'. This appears to echo the findings of Nicholas Rogers, 'Popular protest in early Hanoverian London', Past and Present, 79 (1978) , which emphasizes 'the self-generating aspects of plebeian political culture' (p. 100), but runs contrary to the evidence of mob manipulation from above revealed in Geoffrey Holmes, 'The Sacheverell riots: the crowd and the Church in early eighteenth-century London', Past and Present, 72 (1976).

Shortened from the Latin phrase *mobile vulgus* (the movable or excitable crowd), 'the mob' was first used to denote rioters in London

TABLE 1 Number of riots prosecuted at selected August/September meetings of the Middlesex Quarter Sessions, 1663–1721

	Total number of riots in sample						
	1663–70	1672–80	1682–90	1693–1701	1703–11	1713–21	Total
Recognizances:							
Urban parishes:							
About person	2	1	2	8	13	17	43
About house	0	3	3	7	6	18	37
Against officer	0	4	5	5	7	10	31
Disturb or defame	7	4	11	8	27	27	84
Property	0	0	0	2	0	7	9
Rescue	2	2	0	8	3	7	22
Violent	1	2	4	3	4	0	14
Assault (no detail)	5	8	11	15	18	24	81
Miscellaneous	8	6	6	20	40	20	100
Total	25	30	42	76	118	130	421
Rural parishes	3	2	0	6	5	3	19
Total recognizances	28	32	42	82	123	133	440
Indictments	31	44	58	92	104	83	412

Source: – Greater London Record Office (RO), Middlesex Quarter Sessions rolls.
Note.– Five meetings of the August or September Middlesex Quarter Sessions were sampled in each column. For col. 1 (1663–70), the years sampled were 1663, 1664, and the other even years; for cols. 2 and 3 (1672–80, 1682–90), even years; for cols. 4–6 (1693–1701, 1703–11, 1713–21), odd years.

during the Exclusion Crisis (1678–81).[1] The term gradually entered
the language Londoners used to describe disorder over the next few
decades; justices of the peace did not commonly use it to refer to
riots in the Quarter Sessions court records until the first decade of
the eighteenth century. By 1721, 44 percent of the rioters who were
bound over by recognizance to appear at the Middlesex Quarter
Sessions were accused of raising, or participating in, a mob. Concurrently, the total number of recognizances for riot in urban
Middlesex increased 520 percent between the 1660s and the early
1720s (Table 1). These changes in the frequency and the language
of London rioting recorded in the Middlesex court records around
the turn of the eighteenth century raise several questions. Did the
fundamental character of rioting in London also change? How (and
when) did rioting become such a common occurrence on London's
streets? What was the relation between riots prosecuted at Quarter
Sessions and the larger, primarily political disturbances of the period
that were first studied by George Rudé?[2] How does urban rioting
as a social phenomenon compare with rural riots such as food riots,
riots against enclosures, and ridings, which have also been the subject of considerable recent research? What are the implications of
the existence of widespread collective disorder for our understanding
of social relations in London during a time of rapid population
growth and socioeconomic change?

Rioting encompasses a wide variety of disorderly behavior in
preindustrial London, from small groups of people shouting insults
to major insurrections in which several houses were destroyed.
Legally, any gathering of three or more people could be construed
as a riot if their behavior intentionally disrupted (or threatened to
disrupt) the peace.[3] Group disorder was occasioned by disputes concerning a wide variety of issues, including sexual and marital
immorality, business practices,and politics, as well as more private

1. William Sachse, 'The Mob and the Revolution of 1688,' *Journal of British Studies* 4 (November 1964): 23 and n. 2. *The Oxford English Dictionary* (OED) lists the first use of *mobile vulgus* in English in 1600 and of the shortened *mobile* in 1676.
2. George Rudé, 'The London "Mob" in the Eighteenth Century', *Historical Journal* 2 (1959): 1–18. See also George Rudé's *Paris and London in the Eighteenth Century* (London, 1970); and the following more recent works: T. J. G. Harris, 'The Politics of the London Crowd in the Reign of Charles II' (Ph.D. diss., Cambridge University, 1984), and 'The Bawdy House Riots of 1668', *Historical Journal* 29 (1986): 537–56; Nicholas Rogers, 'Popular Protest in Early Hanoverian London', *Past and Present*, no. 79 (1978), pp. 70–100; G. S. De-Krey, *A Fractured Society: The Politics of London in the First Age of Party, 1688–1715* (Oxford, 1985); G. S. Holmes, 'The Sacheverell Riots: The Crowd and the Church in Early Eighteenth-Century London', *Past and Present*, no. 72 (1976), pp. 55–85.
3. Michael Dalton, *The Countrey Justice* (London, 1618), pp. 191–96.

grievances. Although recent research has documented the importance of crowds in popular politics, little attention has been paid to protests concerning other issues that occurred more frequently on London's streets. An analysis of these riots, which were often prosecuted at Quarter Sessions, suggests that rioting was a significant facet of London life in the early eighteenth century and that, whatever the subject of protest, rioters followed commonly accepted codes of behavior.

I   THE GROWTH OF DISORDER

No source systematically records the number of riots that occurred in preindustrial London. Evidence of riots can be found in private papers, the State Papers, and newspapers, but none of these sources comprehensively lists disturbances over a significant period of time.[4] The best available source is the records of criminal prosecutions at Quarter Sessions.[5] It is likely that even this source seriously underestimates the number of riots that actually occurred since the court system depended on private citizens to initiate most prosecutions. Many types of riots were unlikely to result in prosecutions, especially political disturbances and incidents in which crowds apprehended and punished suspected criminals. Nevertheless, the massive increase in the number of riots prosecuted during this period could be indicative of a significant change in the actual level of disorder in London. The Quarter Sessions evidence used in this study is primarily from Middlesex, which included almost 80 percent of the population of the metropolis north of the Thames by 1700.[6] In a sample of prosecutions by recognizance and indictment at the Middlesex Quarter Sessions for the period from 1663 to 1721, the number of riots prosecuted by indictment more than doubled, while the number of riots prosecuted by recognizance increased more than five times (Table 1). These increases occurred most dramatically in

4. For a brief survey of the evidential problems associated with the study of rioting, see the introduction to Anthony Fletcher and John Stevenson, eds., *Order and Disorder in Early Modern England* (Cambridge, 1985), pp. 26–31.
5. Although prosecutions for riot were also filed at King's Bench and occasionally at Gaol Delivery Sessions, the vast majority of prosecutions were initiated at Quarter Sessions. In 1720, there were no prosecutions for riot at the Gaol Delivery Sessions for the City of London and Middlesex.
6. Roger Finlay and Beatrice Shearer, 'Population Growth and Suburban Expansion' in *London, 1500–1700: The Making of the Metropolis*, ed. A. L. Beier and Roger Finlay (London, 1986), p. 42.

the 1690s and the first decade of the eighteenth century. In 1720, there were 152 riots prosecuted by recognizance and fifty riots prosecuted by indictment in Middlesex; since some riots were prosecuted by both procedures, the total number of riots prosecuted that year was approximately 167.[7] To this total should be added the twenty-one indictments for riot prosecuted as cases of first instance at King's Bench and the twelve recognizances and four indictments for riot filed in the City of London.[8] In 1720 a riot that resulted in a criminal prosecution occurred, on the average, once every other day in London. In comparison, prosecutions for rioting in Middlesex between 1614 and 1617 averaged only eight per year.[9] While the population of Middlesex quadrupled in the seventeenth century, the number of prosecutions for riot increased over twenty times between 1614 and 1720.[10]

It is of course possible that this increase was due to an increased propensity to prosecute riots rather than to an increase in the number of riots actually committed. Contemporary fears about crime in the metropolis, combined with the political instability of the 1710s, may have resulted in an increased awareness of disorder and a growing tendency to prosecute rioters.[11] Yet against this hypothesis must be weighed the evidence that the proportional increase in the num-

---

7. Greater London Record Office (RO), sessions rolls 2339–56, January-December 1720. This total does not include recognizances for riot from the February sessions roll, which is currently 'unfit' for consultation. Recognizance numbers are hereafter abbreviated as 'R', indictments as 'Ind.', and jail (gaol) delivery recognizances as 'GDR'. Since recognizances were normally issued for only one defendant, more than one recognizance was often issued for the same riot. In such cases, the recognizances have been counted as a single riot, although it was not possible to identify all such multiple recognizances. Consequently, the number of separate riots actually prosecuted by recognizance is somewhat inflated in these figures. Approximately 25 percent of the defendants bound over by recognizance at Quarter Sessions were also indicted, and 62 percent of indicted defendants were also bound over by recognizance (Robert B. Shoemaker, 'Crime, Courts and Community: The Prosecution of Misdemeanors in Middlesex County, 1663–1723' [Ph.D. diss., Stanford University, 1986], pp. 126, 185).

8. Corporation of London RO, sessions rolls, January–December 1720; Public Record Office (PRO), King's Bench (KB) 10/17. Perhaps because of the superior efficiency of its ward system of local government, there was far less disorder in the City of London (Valerie Pearl, 'Change and Stability in Seventeenth-Century London', *London Journal* 5 [1979]; 15–27).

9. T. C. Curtis, 'Some Aspects of the History of Crime in Seventeenth–Century England, with Special Reference to Cheshire and Middlesex' (Ph. D. diss., University of Manchester, 1973), table 7, p. 86. Curtis appears to have added recognizances and indictments together in this table.

10. For estimates of the population of Middlesex, see Finlay and Shearer, p. 42.

11. Leon Radzinowicz, *A History of English Law* (London, 1948), 2 : 1; John Beattie, *Crime and the Courts in England, 1660–1800* (Princeton, N. J., 1986), pp. 216–18, 488, 496–97, 500, 516–17.

ber of prosecutions for riot far exceeded the increase in the total number of prosecutions for all crimes.[12] Moreover, rioters were treated leniently by both prosecutors and the courts.[13] If contemporaries were so concerned about disorder, why did they treat rioters so leniently? Moreover, the character of disorder, in terms of the grievances of the rioters, the sex of the participants, and the language used to describe disorder, did change significantly during this period. Although the evidence is somewhat thin, it seems likely that the frequency of rioting may also have changed.

II TYPES OF DISORDER

The Quarter Sessions records document more riots than any other source during this period; however, they often do not provide much evidence concerning the causes of the riots or the behavior of the rioters. Nevertheless, many recognizances are descriptive, and when they are studied in conjunction with other evidence, such as newspapers, accounts of trials at the Old Bailey, and the State Papers, it is possible to draw some conclusions about the issues that prompted people to riot. Riots were sparked by a wide range of both private and public grievances. Many of the riots that cannot be identified no doubt fall into the first category, which includes disorder occasioned by arguments in taverns, brothels, and gaming houses and by property disputes. [14] Riots of more public import, on the other hand, sought to enforce popular norms, especially norms concerning marital, sexual, and economic behavior; and it is these riots that are the focus of this study. Although a significant number of riots were politically motivated, these have been the subject of considerable recent research and are largely excluded from this study.

The declining power of the ecclesiastical courts in the late seventeenth century left Londoners without an effective means of

---

12. Peter Linebaugh, 'Tyburn: A Study of Crime and the Laboring Poor in London during the First Half of the Eighteenth-Century' (Ph. D. diss., University of Warwick, 1975), graph 2, p. 46.

13. See Sec. VII below.

14. For riots at taverns, etc., see, e.g. Greater London RO, sessions rolls 1294, R 69, October 1663; 1291, R 20, 22, August 1663; and 1895, R 66, September 1697; Peter Clark, *The English Alehouse: A Social History, 1200–1830* (London, 1983), p. 147. For property riots, see, e.g. PRO, KB 1/1, deposition dated February 3, 1720/1; Greater London RO, sessions rolls 2361, R 1–12, Ind. 28, February 1721; and 2373, R 66, Westminster Sessions, October 1721.

enforcing sexual morality.[15] In response, Londoners took matters into their own hands with two strikingly different approaches. More prosperous Londoners participated in the Societies for the Reformation of Manners, which prosecuted over 90 000 cases of 'lewd and disorderly' conduct, brothels, Sabbath breaking, and profanity and swearing between 1694 and 1725.[16] Others took to the streets: the number of riots expressing disapproval of sexual misconduct appears to have increased dramatically during this period. Many of the riots in the 'disturb or defame', 'about person', and 'about house' categories in Table I concerned the victim's sexual behavior, and the number of such riots prosecuted at Quarter Sessions increased dramatically in the 1690s and early 1700s. Crowds gathered around persons in the street or in front of victims' houses, shouted insulting words (such as calling women 'whore', 'bitch', or 'bastard bearer' or men 'cuckold', 'rogue', or 'dog'), and committed defamatory acts (such as spitting, throwing excrement or mud, breaking windows, or, in one case, pinching the stomach of a pregnant woman). Because the alleged misdeeds of the victims of the riots were rarely specified, it is impossible to determine precisely how many of these disturbances were protests against sexual deviance. Almost two-thirds of the riots raised 'about' individuals or involving defamation or disturbing were directed, however, against women; this suggests that the crowds objected to the victims' sexual behavior since female sexual promiscuity, especially among servants, was a topic of considerable contemporary concern.[17]

Two types of economic disputes were particularly likely to result in riots during this period: disputes with shopkeepers and labor conflicts. Several riots took place at markets or outside shops, where transactions were unregulated and unstandardized and customers had to be wary of deceit.[18] Two women were accused in 1719 of 'making a riot' about a woman's market stall 'and driving away her

15. Shoemaker, pp. 36–38.
16. T. B. Isaacs, 'Moral Crime, Moral Reform, and the State in Eighteenth-Century England: A Study of Piety and Politics' (Ph. D. diss., University of Rochester, 1979), p. 259. See also T. C. Curtis and W. A. Speck, 'The Societies for the Reformation of Manners: A Case Study in the Theory and Practice of Moral Reform', *Literature and History* 3 (1976): 45–64; Shoemaker, pp. 325–46.
17. Keith Thomas, 'The Double Standard', *Journal of the History of Ideas* 20 (1959): 195–99; Shoemaker, pp. 295–97.
18. Dorothy Davis, *Fairs, Shops and Supermarkets: A History of English Shopping* (Toronto, 1966), p. 99; Avril D. Leadley, 'Some Villains of the Eighteenth-Century Market Place', *Outside the Law: Studies in Crime and Order, 1650–1850*, ed. J. Rule, University of Exeter Papers in Economic History, no. 15 (Exeter, 1982), pp. 21–34.

customers to the great detriment of her trade'.[19] The rioters appear to have intended to discredit the keeper of the stall in the eyes of her customers. In 1720, John Murphy was bound over for raising a riot about a shop, 'pretending he had a note [a bill of debt] upon him swearing if he [the shopkeeper] did not pay him, he would expose him to all his neighbors'.[20] While these incidents suggest that the rioters were motivated by certain standards of economic behavior that might be labeled a 'moral economy', the evidence does not reveal the nature of these standards; nor did the rioters explicitly claim to enforce 'traditional' rights or practices.

The late seventeenth century was a crucial period in the history of labor organization in London. As many guilds became dominated by industrial merchant-capitalists, they disregarded traditional regulations and hired foreigners or large numbers of apprentices, who for the most part could look forward only to careers as journeymen because few had the capital to set up businesses for themselves. In order to defend their interests, journeymen and small masters formed organizations that were important forerunners of trade unions.[21] Because these organizations had no legal basis from which to negotiate, street protest was one of several methods members used to press their cause. For example, apprentices, journeymen, and small master weavers destroyed labor-saving 'engine looms' in 1675; a 'scab' journeyman was the victim of a charivari-like protest during the felt makers' strike in 1696; journeymen weavers destroyed knitting frames belonging to masters who took too many apprentices in 1710; and a mob of journeymen tailors attempted to pull down a master's 'house of call' during a strike in 1720.[22]

19. Greater London RO, sessions roll 2325, R 20, Westminster Sessions, April 1719. See also Greater London RO, sessions rolls 2369, R 201, July 1721; 2343, R 99, Westminster Sessions, April 1720: and 2396, R 34, 35, 78, Westminster Sessions, January 1723.
20. In fact, Murphy was unable to produce the note (Greater London RO, sessions roll 2353, calendar of prisoners no. 23, Westminster Sessions, October 1720).
21. J. R. Kellett, 'The Breakdown of Gild and Corporation Control over the Handicraft and Retail Trades in London', *Economic History Review*, 2d ser., 10 (1958): 388; George Unwin, *Industrial Organization in the Sixteenth and Seventeenth Centuries* (Oxford, 1904), pp. 198–201, 225–26; C. R. Dobson, *Masters and Journeymen: A Pre-history of Industrial Relations, 1717–1800* (London, 1980), pp. 38–40, 47–49, 60–63; James Rule, *The Experience of Labor in Eighteenth-Century Industry* (London, 1981), p. 33.
22. Richard Dunn, 'The London Weavers' Riot of 1675', *Guildhall Studies in London History* 1 (1973): 13–23; Unwin, pp. 221, 250–51; Gravener Henson, *A History of the Framework Knitters* (1831; reprint, New York, 1970), pp. 95–96; Greater London RO, sessions roll 2353, R 51, Ind. 18, and House of Correction calendar, Westminster Sessions, October 1720; Dobson, pp. 38–39, 62.

Not all industrial disorder during this period involved disputes between masters and their employees. On several occasions employers and employees banded together to try to coerce Parliament into protecting their trade. Parliament was besieged by large groups of protesting silk weavers in 1689, weavers in 1697, and shoemakers in 1714.[23] The weavers, however, who had a history of direct action dating from the destruction of engine looms in 1675, did not confine their protests to petitions and marches. During the 1697 campaign they attacked the East India house and the houses of two prominent merchants.[24] Despite the passage of a bill in 1700 limiting the importation of calico, this problem worsened in the early eighteenth century; and in 1719 and 1720 the weavers mounted another campaign against calico with new tactics: both in Parliament and in direct action on the streets they attacked the vendors and consumers of calico. Calico goods found in shops were destroyed, and women wearing calico gowns were attacked by groups of weavers who slit their dresses with knives or spoiled them with ink or nitric acid.[25]

III SCALE

How large were the 'mobs and tumults of people' described in newspaper accounts and the Quarter Sessions records? Since a small proportion of rioters were apprehended or prosecuted, the judicial records, with one exception, provide little evidence of the number of participants in riots. Indictments for routs, however, typically include an estimate of the number of participants. Like many of the riots described on recognizances, routs typically involved persons who stood outside the victim's home and shouted scandalous words.[26] Although the shouts allegedly caused as many as fifty people

---

23. E. M. Thompson, ed., *Correspondence of the Family Hatton*, Camden Society, 2d ser., vol. 23 (Westminster, 1878), 2: 138–39; Greater London RO, sessions roll 1746, calendar of prisoners, Westminster Sessions, August 1689; Alfred Plummer, *The London Weavers' Company* (Boston, 1972), pp. 293–94; Historical Manuscripts Commission, *Portland*, 5: 452, 454.

24. Max Beloff, *Public Order and Popular Disturbances, 1660–1714* (Oxford, 1938), pp. 85–86.

25. The best secondary account of these riots is Plummer, pp. 292–314.

26. In contrast to the legal definition of a riot, which occurred when three or more persons gathered together with the intent of committing an unlawful act and then set out and committed it, a rout occurred when the said group 'moved forward to the execution of any such act' but did not actually commit the crime (Dalton [n. 3 above], p. 191).

to gather around the house, the eight routs indicted in 1721 caused an average of twenty-seven people to congregate per incident. It is unlikely that the mobs and tumults described on recognizances were much bigger since they generally did not attract much attention from newspapers and other contemporary commentators.

On the other hand, riots during this period could be much larger: 100 rioters buried the foundation of a brick wall that was under construction in Hampstead in 1720; more than 200 people attacked a group of constables who were trying to arrest a gambler in December 1721; and thousands of weavers (and accomplices) destroyed engine looms in 1675, marched to Parliament in 1689, attacked the houses of prominent East India merchants in 1697, and participated in the first attacks on women wearing calico gowns on June 16 and 17, 1719.[27] The weavers' riots in 1675 and 1719, however, primarily involved small, roving groups of weavers. As the *Original Weekly Journal* reported on June 27, 1719, more than ten days after the riots against calico began, 'the weavers continue to be mischievous in small bodies, chiefly towards evenings'.[28] Despite the occasional larger disturbances, the average London riot probably rarely involved more than a few dozen people.

IV SPONTANEITY

Most of the defendants who were bound over by recognizance for rioting were accused of 'raising a mob and a tumult of people', which implies that the defendants had incited a crowd of people to gather in order to express a specific grievance. Like most riots, these mobs were composed of several different types of participants: instigators, participants who had planned to join the action in advance, those who participated at the spur of the moment, and spectators, who may well have outnumbered the participants. It is the spontaneous participation of passersby and spectators that is remarkable about early eighteenth-century rioting in London. On

27. These estimates, which were made by contemporary observers, must be treated skeptically. Greater London RO, sessions roll 2361, R 1–11, February 1721; February 3, Greater London RO, sessions roll indictment of Maccave and seven others, dated December 21, 1721. Gaol Delivery Sessions, February 1722; Dunn, p. 18; Narcissus Luttrell, *A Brief Historical Relation of State Affairs* (1857; reprint, Farnborough, 1969), 4: 199–200; *Original Weekly Journal* (June 13, 1719).

28. *Original Weekly Journal* (June 27, 1719). See also Dunn, p. 17; PRO, State Papers (SP) 35/16/116.

learning of a disturbance, men and women immediately investigated it, and, if they sympathized with the grievances being expressed, they occasionally joined the protest. When Richard Woodley went to Tom's Coffee House in Southwark in 1720 to demand repayment of a debt from Francis Craddock, a crowd surrounded them. According to Woodley, 'Hot words . . . given to this deponent by the said Craddock . . . occasioned some people to come together about the coffee house door'.[29] Although there is conflicting testimony as to whether a riot actually took place, this example illustrates how a crowd could gather spontaneously at the scene of a potential conflict. Crowds could gather so easily because of the large number of people on the streets in London, traveling on foot, shopping, hawking, and begging.[30] During a visit by Will Stankes, a yeoman from the country, Samuel Pepys complained that Stankes made 'a stir . . . with his being crowded in the streets and wearied in walking in London'.[31]

Thus mobs often began when a significant number of passersby were incited to gather. Spectators were transformed into rioters if they shared the grievances expressed by the instigators and began to shout, march through the streets, damage some property, or otherwise physically join the protest. The fine line between spectators and participants in London riots during this period was embodied in the different meanings contemporaries attached to the term 'mob'. Although it was frequently used to denote rioting, 'the mob' was also used more generally to refer to the people present on London's streets. A pamphleteer writing in defense of street sellers in 1700 argued, 'There are vast quantities of damaged goods that would never be sold, if 'twere not for carrying *to the mob* in this manner' (emphasis added).[32] Since they outnumbered their social superiors and did not travel in coaches or chairs, the majority of pedestrians must have been from the middle and lower classes, and 'the mob', correspondingly, was often used to refer specifically to people with low social status. According to Roger North, it was during the Exclusion Crisis that 'the rabble first changed their title, and were called

29. PRO, KB 1/2, Hillary & Geo. 1, deposition no. 27, and Easter 8 Geo. 1, deposition no. 42.
30. Davis (n. 18 above), p. 110; John Ashton, *Social Life in the Reign of Queen Anne* (London, 1882), 2: 158–60.
31. Robert Latham and William Matthews, eds., *The Diary of Samuel Pepys* (London, 1971), 4: 118, April 29/30, 1663.
32. John Houghton, *A Collection for the Improvement of Husbandry and Trade* (March 15, 1700), in *Seventeenth-Century Economic Documents,* ed. J. Thirsk and J. P. Cooper (Oxford, 1972), pp. 428–29.

the mob' [33] When 'mob' served to describe disorder, it was used both with and without the implication that the participants were from the lower class. Edward Chamberlayne explained to foreigners that tumults committed by 'the common sort' in England were 'called the mobile'.[34] Yet, because it was often used to refer to persons with low social status, 'mob' was also used in a derogatory sense to describe a crowd as unmannerly regardless of the social class of the participants. For example, the participants on both sides of a riot in 1721, in which constables met resistance while attempting to search gaming houses in Drury Lane, described their opponents as a 'mob'.[35]

'Mob' could thus be used both to describe a class of people and to describe rioters. Moreover, it could be used specifically to describe the lower class or to insult people regardless of their social status. These ambiguities suggest that people could be easily mobilized to riot and that rioting was not restricted to a specific social class. The line between passivity and activity in a crowd gathered on the street could be (and often was) crossed very easily. Rudé, who stressed 'the element of spontaneity in these affairs', noted that most of the participants in London riots had not traveled far from their homes.[36]

V PARTICIPANTS

As suggested by contemporary usage, the London 'mob' was composed of a cross section of the London population who were likely to be in the streets; most, but not all, of its members were from the middle and lower classes. Most rioters had sufficient social connections to find sureties to guarantee their appearance at Quarter

33. Roger North, *Examen: or an Enquiry into the Credit and Veracity of an Intended Complete History* (London, 1740), 3: 574, quoted by the OED, 6: 559. See also William Smith, *The Charge Given by Sir William Smith, Baronet, At the Quarter Sessions of the Peace held for the County of Middlesex* (London, 1682), p. 4.
34. Edward Chamberlayne, *Angliae Notitia*, 18th ed. (London, 1694), p. 458.
35. *The Proceedings on the King's commission of the Peace and Oyer and Terminer, and Gaol Delivery . . . in the Old Bailey* (London, 1722), January, pp. 7–8, and February and March, p. 6 (hereafter cited as *Old Bailey Proceedings*); *An Account of the Endeavours that have been used to Suppress Gaming Houses* (London, 1722), pp. 22–26.
36. Rudé, 'The London "Mob" in the Eighteenth Century' (n. 2 above), pp. 4–5. Though there is not much evidence on this issue, it appears that Rudé's assertion that rioters acted near their homes also applies to the riots under discussion.

TABLE 2 Social status of defendants Bound over by Recognizance for riot

	Unknown (% of total)	Total female (% of total)	Total male (% of total)	Gentleman (% of total male)	High-social-status trade/craft (% of total male)	Low-social-status trade/craft (% of total male)	Other trade/craft (% of total male)	No bail risked (% of total male)	Total number
1663–1721 sample:									
About person	5	67	28	14	33	10	19	24	76
About house	5	56	39	5	5	32	27	32	57
Against officer	2	30	68	9	6	6	12	68	50
Disturb or defame	4	49	47	18	7	20	25	30	152
Property	..	..	100	9	32	21	6	33	34
Rescue	3	24	73	4	12.5	33	25	25	33
Violent	3	13	84	16	16	19	22	28	38
Assault (no detail)	2	31	66	9	15	16	36	24	163
Miscellaneous	1	39	59	7	10	17	30	36	150
Total percent	3	39	58	10	14	18	26	33	
(Total number)	(22)	(296)	(435)	(45)	(59)	(78)	(113)	(140)	753
1663 (entire year):[a]									
Percent	2	20	78	12	12	24	22	31	
(Number)	(1)	(13)	(51)	(6)	(6)	(12)	(11)	(16)	65
1721 (entire year):									
Percent	..	43	56	11	9	24	27	29	
(Number)	(1)	(129)	(169)	(18)	(15)	(41)	(46)	(49)	299

Source.– Greater London RO, Middlesex Quarter Sessions rolls. The 1663–1721 sample is described in the note to Table 1 above.

Note.– Indictments have been excluded from this table because a high proportion of defendants were labeled on their indictments as yeomen, an agrarian category of social status whose meaning is unclear when applied to urban residents. The levels of social status assigned to occupations in this study are based on findings from Y. B. Elliott's study of apprenticeship indentures and marriage licenses in late seventeenth-century London, in which she was able to rank many tradesmen and craftsmen according to the marital and apprenticeship choices of their children ('Single Women in the London Marriage Market: Age, Status and Mobility', in *Marriage and Society: Studies in the Social History of Marriage*, ed. R. B. Outhwaite [New York, 1982], pp. 81, 132). The category of 'other' tradesmen and craftsmen includes occupations that could not be placed in a status category because of insufficient information.

[a] Defendants who were indicted (fifty-four) are excluded from this sample. A significant proportion of these defendants (twenty-three) did not risk bail on their recognizances (and thus were not identified by their occupation or social status), apparently because they had been indicted and not because they could not afford to risk bail. Adding them to the 'no bail risked' column would have distorted the findings by adding many defendants who probably could risk bail to those who could not. For more on 'risking bail', see n. 38 below.

Sessions; few ended up in a prison or a house of correction.[37] Never-theless, many were no doubt quite poor: a third of the men who were bound over did not incur any financial risk on their recogniz-ances (Table 2).[38] On the other hand, 10 percent of all male rioters bound over by recognizance were gentlemen, and up to 14 percent were yeomen or relatively respectable craftsmen, including black-smiths, bricklayers, and joiners. Rioting was not an exclusively lower-class occupation.

In contrast to their minimal role in London political riots, women constituted over a third of the rioters bound over by recognizance in the Quarter Sessions sample.[39] Moreover, the proportion of women in the recognizance sample more than doubled during this period, from 20 percent in 1663 to 44 percent in 1721. Since women tended to participate in different types of disorder than men, this dramatic increase contributed significantly to the expansion and changing character of London rioting during this period. In the Quarter Sessions records, women were infrequently accused of par-ticipating in riots occasioned by conflicts over property rights and legal authority (as indicated by riots against officers and rescues of prisoners), issues that were outside their traditional sphere of in-fluence. Instead, female rioting was focused primarily on disputes concerning sexual morality and economic issues. As Table 2 demonstrates, women were proportionally most frequently accused of participating in riots 'about' people in the streets or in front of their houses and in riots that involved 'disturbing' or defaming the victim, riots that often protested deviant sexual behavior. Just as women played a significant role in riots concerning economic issues in rural areas (food and enclosure riots), in London they participated

---

37. Shoemaker (n. 7 above), table 24, p. 263.
38. Sureties provided a financial guarantee that defendants bound over by recog-nizance would appear in court – if the defendant failed to appear, the surety would be obliged to pay the sum pledged on the recognizance (typically from £10 to £40, depending on the severity of the crime). Although defendants nor-mally pledged twice the sum pledged by their sureties, 17 percent of the male defendants at the Middlesex Quarter Sessions (33 percent of the defendants accused of riot) did not pledge any money. Presumably, these male defendants did not have sufficient wealth to pledge (Shoemaker, pp. 151–52). Some of these defendants may have been youths, especially apprentices, who played a prominent role in disorder during this period (Keith Thomas, 'Age and Authority in Early Modern England', *Proceedings of the British Academy* 62 [1976]: 219).
39. For women in political riots, see Harris, 'The Politics of the London Crowd in the Reign of Charles II' (n. 2 above), p. 301. On the other hand, women played a major role in petitioning Parliament in the 1640s (Patricia Higgens, 'The Reactions of Women, with Special Reference to Women Petitioners', in *Politics, Religion, and the English Civil War*, ed. Brian Manning [London, 1973]).

in riots directed against shopkeepers and in the weavers' riots in 1675, 1689, and 1697.[40]

Why did so many women riot in London? In part, as in food and enclosure riots, women may have made 'deliberate use . . . of their ambiguous socio-legal status to articulate the community's sense of grievance'.[41] As a consequence of the 'double standard', women were expected to preserve their own sexual purity and, by implication, the purity of other members of their sex.[42] Yet women did not consistently uphold such norms in rural areas: few women took part in ridings, ritual protests against the violators of community standards concerning marital behavior.[43] The greater role played by women in riots protesting sexual and marital misbehavior in London is thus exceptional and is no doubt related to the greater social and economic independence of urban women.[44] Paradoxically, female rioters in London protested against violations of community norms in an environment in which they themselves were becoming less constrained by traditional social expectations.

VI   THE ROOTS OF DISORDER

In order for a gathering of spectators to be transformed into a riot, spectators had to cross the fine line that separates observers in a

40. For riots at shops, see Sec. II above. For women in rural food and enclosure riots, see E. P. Thompson, 'The Moral Economy of the English Crowd in the Eighteenth Century', *Past and Present*, no. 50 (1971), pp. 115–17; Peter Clark, 'Popular Protest and Disturbance in Kent, 1558–1640', *Economic History Review*, 2d ser., 29 (1976): 376–77. For women in the seventeenth-century weavers' riots, see Harris, 'The Politics of the London Crowd in the Reign of Charles II', pp. 232–33; *Journals of the House of Commons (CJ)*, 11: 683, January 29, 1696/7 (I am indebted to Tim Keirn for this reference). Perhaps because women were the principal victims of the 1719–20 weavers' riots against persons wearing calico clothing, few women participated in the riots.
41. John Walter, 'Grain Riots and Popular Attitudes towards the Law', in *An Ungovernable People*, ed. J. Brewer and J. Styles (New Brunswick, N. J., 1980), p. 64.
42. Thomas, 'The Double Standard' (n. 17 above), pp. 195–203.
43. M. J. Ingram, 'Ridings, Rough Music and the "Reform of Popular Culture" in Early Modern England', *Past and Present*, no. 105 (1984), pp. 79–113, esp. p. 102; David Underdown, 'The Taming of the Scold: The Enforcement of Patriarchal Authority in Early Modern England', in Fletcher and Stevenson eds. (n. 4 above), p. 133.
44. John Beattie, 'The Criminality of Women in Eighteenth-Century England', *Journal of Social History* 8 (1975): 97–102. It is not possible to analyze the social composition of female rioters because their social status or occupation was very rarely identified on the Quarter Sessions rolls.

crowd from participants in a riot. Those who chose to get involved did so both because they shared the grievance voiced by the instigator(s) of the riot and because they believed that disorderly behavior, whether it involved verbal attacks or more violent actions, was legitimate in that situation. Although there was certainly no shortage of widely held grievances in preindustrial London, it remains to be explained why Londoners believed that the best way of addressing those grievances was by voicing them in riotous street protest.

Unfortunately, the sources for studying popular disorder rarely include statements by rioters justifying their actions. An examination of the behavior of London rioters, however, suggests that their beliefs in the appropriateness of street protest were derived from at least three traditions of licensed disorder that occurred in the metropolis. First, the legal system relied heavily on private citizens, often acting in groups, for the detection and arrest of suspected criminals and occasionally for their punishment. Second, traditional holidays, festivals, and processions provided a precedent for popular participation in what were often disorderly expressions of communal solidarity. Finally, the growing intensity of party politics during the late seventeenth and early eighteenth centuries resulted in a growing number of demonstrations in London and Westminster in which ordinary citizens were invited to take part. By manipulating these patterns of legitimate disorder, Londoners were able to express a wide variety of grievances in the streets, often without incurring popular or official disapproval of their actions.

Seventeenth-century Englishmen were expected to play a far greater role in apprehending criminals than they are today. Private citizens were required to assist any officer of the peace who raised a hue and cry in the pursuit and arrest of suspected felons and breakers of the peace. At their own initiative, moreover, individuals could arrest anyone whom they suspected of having committed a felony or having dangerously hurt a man and bring the suspect before a constable or a justice of the peace.[45] In practice, these powers were frequently exercised by groups of ordinary citizens. In a densely populated urban area, victims of crimes were able to obtain the assistance of nearby pedestrians or residents simply by yelling for help. When a young gentlewoman was kidnapped coming out of a playhouse in 1722, she 'cried so loud for help, that in a minute there were fifty butchers, and a great rabble after the coach, crying stop the coach': whereupon the kidnapper jumped out of the

45. John Bond, *A Complete Guide for Justices of the Peace*, 3d ed. (London, 1707), pp. 44–45, 153; Dalton (n. 3 above), pp. 56–57, 256–57.

coach, and the woman was saved.[46] When William Smith awoke one morning in 1690 to discover his shed door was open and people running away from it, 'he called out thieves', and the culprits were 'stopped by the neighborhood'.[47]

The public was also occasionally asked to participate in punishments meted out by the courts. When convicted criminals were sentenced to stand in the pillory or to be whipped through the street at the cart's tail, the court intended to expose the criminal to the abuse and vilification of passersby and spectators. Although such punishments were rare during this period, punishments administered by crowds continued without the sanction of the courts.[48] From apprehending criminals it was but a short step for crowds to determine their guilt and punish them by dunking them in a pond, attacking them with stones and dirt, or serenading them with 'rough music'. Such punishments were especially likely when it was believed that the culprit would not be convicted in court. In 1720, the *London Journal* noted that three pickpockets were apprehended and, because they were detected before they had actually stolen anything, 'were only seized and delivered up to the mob, who, according to the justice of their usual proceeding, doomed them to a drench or two in the Horse Pond behind the Post Office'.[49] Even where there was sufficient evidence to convict a thief in the courts, the crowd (because of its desire for immediate revenge) and even the criminal (in order to avoid more serious punishments) often preferred popular justice to the courts.[50]

While pickpockets appear to have been a favorite target, crowd punishments were not restricted to persons accused of theft and other felonies. Although private citizens did not even have the legal right to arrest them, persons who committed misdemeanors were also punished in the streets. Crowds punished a woman who tore another woman's dress (by dunking her in the Thames), a man who dressed in a costume ridiculing King William (by dunking him in a horse pond), the authors of false accusations of theft (by causing a riot about their doors), and keepers of brothels (by breaking win-

---

46. *London Journal* (February 10, 1722).
47. Greater London RO, sessions papers, April 1690, no. 25.
48. For court-ordered punishments, see Shoemaker (n. 7 above), pp. 225–27.
49. *London Journal* (July 16, 1720). See also Alexander Drawcansir [Henry Fielding], *Covent Garden Journal* 47 (June 13, 1752).
50. Daniel Defoe, *Moll Flanders* (1722) (Harmondsworth, 1980), p. 206. A man accused by a crowd of picking pockets in an incident described in *The Nightwalker*, however, desired the rioters to bring him before a magistrate, and they did ([John Dunton], *The Night Walker: or, Evening Rambles in Search After Lewd Women* [September 1696], p. 21). This was a prudent course of action since at least one pickpocket was killed by a mob (*London Journal* [February 24, 1722]).

dows, pulling the houses down, or slandering the keeper).[51] Groups of Londoners thus convicted and punished a wide variety of criminals in the streets. As the weavers' attacks on women wearing calico suggest, crowds also punished some misdeeds that were not illegal but that violated popular norms of behavior. Nevertheless, crowds were selective in the types of criminal behavior they punished. The Middlesex Quarter Sessions complained in 1663 that inhabitants often failed to apprehend persons guilty of murders committed in duels and murders resulting from 'sudden quarrels in the streets', perhaps because neighbors believed that these offenses were not culpable.[52] Popular definitions of illegal behavior often did not coincide with those of the courts.

As a means of legitimating crowd punishments that had no legal justification, rioters occasionally explicitly imitated the legal forms by which ordinary people were expected to participate in apprehending and punishing criminals. During the anticalico riots in 1720, for example, a printed broadsheet in the form and style of an official proclamation was distributed. After outlining the weavers' grievances against clothing made out of calico, the proclamation concludes: 'Now, this is to give notice to Madam Callicoe, that if she will pass quietly out of this kingdom, she shall have free passage without molestation; but if she be seen once again in the streets, this is to command all Hang-men, Bailiffs, Yeomen and all other such officers, to secure her, and bring her to Spitalfields, where she shall undergo the punishment our law in such cases provides. Given at our Court at the Three Sterv'd Lyons eating Shuttles in Spitalfields, this 13th day of May 1720.'[53]

By 'commanding' 'officers' to arrest women wearing calico dresses, this proclamation extended a sense of legitimacy to the weavers' attacks, although in fact the suspects were not brought before the 'court'. As in the case of pickpockets, rioters usually punished offenders on the spot by destroying their calico clothing.

Paradoxically, the procedures and institutions that were meant to enforce the law could thus provide the precedents and justifications for disorder. Most dramatically, the procedures of the militia (the 'trained bands'), which were often called out to prevent or suppress

---

51. Greater London RO, sessions papers, May 1720, no. 10; *London Newsletter*, no. 7 (May 11–13, 1696); Greater London RO, sessions rolls 1276 , R 59, October 1663; 1286, R 40a, 118, April 1664; and 1820, R 20, September 1693. See also Defoe, pp. 235–37.

52. Greater London RO, gaol delivery sessions papers, 1663, no. 2. Donna Andrew, 'The Code of Honour and Its Critics: The Opposition to Duelling in England, 1700–1850', *Social History* 5 (1980): 412–13; Beattie, *Crime and the Courts in England* (n. 11 above), pp. 81–98.

53. PRO, SP 35/21/57.

rioting, were replicated in London disorder, including the weavers' riots of 1675 and 1719.[54] Rioters mustered to the beat of drums, organized themselves into regiments led by 'captains', and marched behind colors.[55] The procedures of the trained bands thus provided Londoners with both methods for organizing and disciplining crowds and symbols for claiming legitimacy for their actions.

Popular beliefs in the legitimacy of disorder were also derived from the ritualized inversionary disorder embedded in traditional holiday celebrations, when grievances could be expressed and tensions released in the form of processions, plays, and other events.[56] Several holidays, including Shrove Tuesday, Ascension Day, May Day, Midsummer, and St Bartholomew's Day, were celebrated in early modern London with disorderly activities, including the destruction of brothels and playhouses and attacks on foreign ambassadors.[57] Between 1603 and 1642, Shrove Tuesday riots (mostly involving attacks by apprentices on brothels and playhouses ostensibly to remove sources of temptation during Lent) occurred at least twenty-four times, and there were eight May Day disturbances.[58]

The evidence suggests, however, that the character of these celebrations shifted in late seventeenth-century London. While holidays continued to be celebrated, they appear to have lost many of their traditional rituals, and the disorder associated with them was transformed. No evidence survives of any attacks on bawdy houses on Shrove Tuesday after 1660, though an alehouse was attacked for unknown reasons by 500 rioters on May Day in 1672, and apprentices destroyed bawdy houses in several parts of London in 1668.[59]

54. For the 'trained bands', see K. J. Lindley, 'Riot Prevention and Control in Early-Stuart London', *Transactions of the Royal Historical Society*, 5th ser., 33 (1983): 122–23; D. F. Allen, 'The Political Role of the London Trained Bands in the Exclusion Crisis, 1678–81', *English Historical Review* 87 (1972): 293–95, 301–2.

55. Harris, 'The Politics of the London Crowd in the Reign of Charles II' (n. 2 above), pp. 34, 236, 266; Greater London RO, sessions rolls 2321, GDR 21, January 1719; and 2331, R 98, 110, July 1719; Abel Boyer, *The Political State of Great Britain* (1719), 17: 627.

56. Peter Burke, *Popular Culture in Early Modern Europe* (San Francisco, 1978), pp. 187–190, 199–204; Natalie Davis, 'The Reasons of Misrule', in *Society and Culture in Early Modern France* (Stanford, Calif., 1975), p. 100; Robert W. Bushaway, 'Ceremony, Custom and Ritual: Some Observations on Social Conflict in the Rural Community, 1750–1850', in *Reactions to Social and Economic Change, 1750–1939*, ed. W. Minchinton, University of Exeter Papers in Economic History, no. 12 (Exeter, 1979), pp. 9–29.

57. Peter Burke, 'Popular Culture in Seventeenth-Century London', in *Popular Culture in Seventeenth-Century England*, ed. Barry Reay (London, 1985), pp. 35–38.

58. Lindley, pp. 109–11.

59. Greater London RO, sessions roll 1428, Ind. 6, R 2, 52, 105, May 1672 (reprinted in J. C. Jeaffreson, ed., *Middlesex County Records* [London, 1882],

The latter riots, which began on Easter Monday, were in fact largely directed against Charles II's proclamation, issued on March 10, to reimpose the laws against Protestant nonconformists.[60] In 1680, a riot was planned for Whit Sunday (May 29) involving the destruction of bawdy houses and nonconformist conventicles by apprentices.[61] Although the 1680 riot never took place, these examples demonstrate that after 1660 the tradition of destroying bawdy houses was interpreted in new ways; it was thought that the attacks could take place on several different holidays and that they could be used to express religious grievances on both sides of the spectrum.

A more spontaneous type of traditional festive disturbance was the riding (also called shivaree, charivari, or skimmington), in which violators of marital and sexual mores were the subject of a clamorous procession ridiculing their actions. As Martin Ingram has shown, ridings had 'close affinities' with other traditions of licensed disorder such as popular involvement in official punishments and celebrations of holidays.[62] Like holidays, however, the evidence suggests that ridings in their traditional ritualized form rarely occurred in early eighteenth-century London. The few recorded instances of ridings in London were described by contemporaries in language that suggests that the reenactments of the offending behavior typically found in rural ridings were considered unusual and eccentric in the metropolis.[63]

Although full-fledged ridings appear to have been infrequent in London, both the social function of a riding, which was to express community disapproval of violations of norms governing marital or sexual behavior, and symbolic and behavioral elements of ridings persisted during this period in many of the incidents described in the Middlesex Quarter Sessions records in which mobs and tumults

4: 34–35). In a similar incident, four apprentices attacked a disorderly alehouse on the day before Trinity in 1664 (Greater London RO, sessions roll 1289, R 115–18, July 1664).

60. Harris, 'The Bawdy House Riots of 1668' (n. 2 above), p. 547.
61. *Calendar of State Papers, Domestic (CSPD), 1679–80*, pp. 422–23; K. H. D. Haley, *The First Earl of Shaftesbury* (Oxford, 1968), p. 572; Harris, 'The Politics of the London Crowd in the Reign of Charles II', p. 210.
62. Ingram (n. 43 above), p. 94. See also Joan R. Kent, 'Folk Justice and Royal Justice in Early Seventeenth-Century England', *Midland History* 8 (1983): 78–81; Underdown (n. 43 above), p. 133.
63. Greater London RO, sessions rolls 2175, R 108, 113, 114, September 1711; and 2368, R 72, Westminster Sessions, July 1721; *The Country Journal: or, The Craftsman*, no. 563 (April 16, 1737); Shoemaker (n. 7 above), pp. 481–82. In contrast, David Underdown has recently suggested that ridings were more 'elaborate and theatrical in urban areas' (*Revel, Riot and Rebellion: Popular Politics and Culture in England, 1603–1660* [Oxford, 1985], pp. 100–103). See also N. Davis (n. 56 above), pp. 109–10.

were raised 'about' persons in the street or around their houses. The 'rough music', which in a traditional riding was generated by beating pots and pans, can be found in urban riots in the form of clamorous shouting and clapping hands. In June 1664, a laborer's wife was bound over by recognizance for following a woman 'in the streets clapping her hands and crying out whore whore whore thereby raising a great tumult of rude people to the endangering of her life'.[64] Like 'rough music', these actions attracted public attention to the victim's misdeeds, and the discordant sounds symbolized her antisocial behavior. Like rural ridings, moreover, the victims of London riots were sometimes covered with spit, dirt, or the contents of chamber pots, with obvious symbolic significance.

Although riotous protests that borrowed from the symbols and function of ridings were frequent in London, the types of misbehavior that occasioned such protests differed from rural ridings. Most frequently, ridings in early modern England protested against husbands who had been beaten by their wives.[65] Except for the rare ritualized demonstrations, London protests that resembled ridings, on the other hand, were directed against sexually promiscuous individuals: prostitutes (or keepers of brothels), adulterers, and mothers of illegitimate children. Ridings, which were used for many different purposes even in rural areas, were thus adapted to address the social problems of the metropolis.[66] They even occurred during economic and political disputes. Ridings were especially appropriate for men who refused to take part in strikes. When a journeyman hatter failed to abide by a strike resolution in 1696, his peers encouraged some apprentices to tie him to a wheelbarrow and 'in a tumultuous and riotous manner to drive him therein through all the considerable places in London and Southwark'.[67] The weavers' riots in 1719 and 1720 also involved the public shaming of their victims. Women's calico dresses were ruined in the streets, and their misbehavior was portrayed as a form of sexual immorality. Evoking the more common types of misbehavior against which urban riding-like protests were directed, the weavers called the women 'calico madams', a sexual innuendo that was more explicitly stated in a ballad as 'pocky damned calico madam'.[68]

64. Greater London RO, sessions roll 1289, R 43, July 1664.
65. Ingram, p. 86; E. P. Thompson, 'Rough Music: Le Charivari Anglais', *Annales: Economies, Sociétés, Civilisations* 27 (1972): 294–96.
66. Thompson, 'Rough Music', pp. 289, 294, 305; Ingram, pp. 90–92, 108.
67. Unwin (n. 21 above), pp. 220–21.
68. Plummer (n. 23 above), p. 297; Old *Bailey Proceedings* (n. 35 above), July 1719, p. 7.

Political riots, which could also borrow from traditional ridings, primarily developed from official processions and celebrations.[69] Although royal entries and the Lord Mayor's Show were designed to legitimate the existing political order, they occasionally provided a context for disorder.[70] Several persons were apprehended in 1693 'for throwing of squibs and making a riot in the streets on the Lord Mayor's Day'.[71] Although the disorder on these occasions often amounted to nothing more than a little rowdiness, the Lord Mayor's Shows provided a model for other politically sponsored demonstrations such as the calendar of celebrations of political anniversaries that developed over the course of the seventeenth century.[72] By the 1710s, Londoners had frequent opportunities in parades and at bonfires to express their support of or discontent with both political parties.[73]

Although it is unclear whether ordinary Londoners played a significant role in organizing these demonstrations, the fact that they were frequently invited to participate in them is in itself significant. By the 1710s, the calendar of anniversaries began to involve 'increasingly vehement initiative from below'.[74] Participation in these licensed demonstrations acquainted Londoners with a sense of the legitimacy, the mechanics, and the possible uses of street protest. It is not a coincidence that the anticalico riots commenced in 1719 on a political anniversary, the Pretender's birthday. Although the rioters took the precaution of shouting 'King George forever' to show that they were not seditious, they took advantage of the tradition of popular demonstrations on June 10 to attract support for

69 For political riots incorporating behavior found in ridings, see Rogers (n. 2 above), p. 87; O. W. Furley, 'The Pope-burning Processions of the Late Seventeenth Century', *History* 44 (1959): 20; Sheila Williams, 'The Pope-burning Processions of 1679, 1680 and 1681', *Journal of the Warburg and Courtauld Institutes* 21 (1958): 109, 113.

70. For their legitimating function, see Burke, 'Popular Culture in Seventeenth-Century London' (n. 57 above), p. 45; D. M. Bergeron, *English Civic Pageantry, 1558–1642* (London, 1971), pp. 299–305; Lois G. Schwoerer, 'The Glorious Revolution as Spectacle: A New Perspective', in *England's Rise to Greatness,* ed. S. B. Baxter (Berkeley and Los Angeles, 1983), pp. 109–49.

71. Corporation of London RO, sessions roll, December 4, 1693, R 111, 112, 115, 118.

72. On disorder at Lord Mayor's Shows, see Smith (n. 33 above), p. 4; N. Ward, *London Spy Compleat,* 5th ed. (London, 1718), pp. 293–98; S. Williams, 'The Lord Mayor's Show in Tudor and Stuart Times', *Guildhall Miscellany* 10 (1959): 13–18.

73. J. E. Neale, 'November 17th', *Essays in Elizabethan History* (London, 1958), pp. 10–15; DeKrey (n. 2 above), pp. 248–58. For a calendar of these anniversaries, see John Stevenson, *Popular Disturbances in England, 1700–1870* (London, 1979), p. 19.

74. DeKrey, p. 253.

their protests.[75] Like organized political demonstrations, the weavers' riots led to the composition of several ballads (such as 'The Weavers' Delight' and 'The Weavers' Complaint Against the Calico Madams') as well as numerous pamphlets and broadsides.[76]

In sum, Londoners in the early eighteenth century became acquainted with the possibilities of street protest through the survival and transformation of several traditional forms of licensed disorder: crowds apprehending and punishing criminals, ridings, and celebrations of religious holidays and political anniversaries. Elements of these traditions can frequently be found in London riots in the early eighteenth century, especially the anticalico riots of 1719 and 1720. Although direct evidence of rioters' motivations does not exist, it appears that the weavers and other rioters manipulated these traditions of licensed disorder in order to assert the legitimacy of their protests.

VII THE TOLERATION OF DISORDER

By adopting patterns of behavior derived from traditionally accepted forms of disorder, eighteenth-century London rioters appear to have sought legitimacy for their actions. Did they succeed? To a remarkable degree, small-scale riots were tolerated, and even on occasion encouraged, by both ordinary Londoners and the judicial authorities. Only a small proportion of rioters was ever prosecuted for the crime.[77] Far fewer were actually convicted and punished.

Two types of rioters were rarely prosecuted at all. Riots in which suspected criminals were punished by crowds, which were technically crimes when (as was usually the case) the punishments had no legal justification, rarely appear in the court records, no doubt because the victims of such punishments did not wish to call atten-

---

75. P. J. Thomas, *Mercantilism and the East India Trade* (London, 1926), p. 145 (citing the *Flying Post* [August 8, 1719]).
76. Greater London RO, sessions roll 2331, R 98, 99, July 1719; Corporation of London RO, sessions roll, July 1719, R 107; Plummer, pp. 296–97; P. J. Thomas, pp. 143–47; *Weekly Journal; or, British Gazeteer* (June 20, 1719); Guildhall Library, London collection of pamphlet literature related to the riots, shelfmark A.1.3, no. 64.
77. Any gathering of three or more people who intentionally disturbed the peace could be defined as a riot (Dalton [n. 3 above], pp. 191–96). Although the incidents under discussion were largely nonviolent, the participants usually disturbed the peace by shouting threatening words, jostling the victim, or damaging some property.

tion to their own illegal activities. Defoe commented that, although 'the rage of the street . . . is a cruelty I need not describe', thieves preferred it to being sent to prison.[78] Political riots also rarely resulted in prosecutions, especially when the riots supported the ascendant political party.[79] Though political riots and demonstrations rarely occurred during the summer months, it is nevertheless remarkable that only two of the 440 riots sampled from the Middlesex Quarter Sessions recognizances for the August or September sessions between 1663 and 1721 can be identified as politically motivated.[80]

Most major riots, however, resulted in at least a few arrests and prosecutions, though of course only a small proportion of rioters was ever arrested, fewer prosecuted, and still fewer convicted. The weavers' attacks on women wearing calico gowns, which occurred sporadically between June 1719 and July 1720, led to a total of only thirty-five prosecutions.[81] Only seven people were indicted for the riot in Brown's Lane in Spitalfields on June 12, 1719, for example, when between 200 and 400 weavers tore calico dresses and attempted to pull down a house in which there were several more women wearing calico.[82] Similarly, only one person was indicted out of the 'multitude of weavers' who assaulted Dorothy Orwell and 'tore, cut, pulled off her gown and petticoat by violence, threatened her with vile language, and left her naked in the fields'.[83] Even riots directed against public officials, such as the violent attack by 200 men on a group of constables who were trying to search gaming houses in 1721, resulted in few prosecutions.[84]

78. Defoe (n. 50 above), p. 206.
79. James L. Fitts, 'Newcastle's Mob', *Albion* 5 (1973): 44–47; Harris, 'The Politics of the London Crowd in the Reign of Charles II' (n. 2 above), p. 283.
80. It is not certain that even these riots were politically motivated. Both involved abusive attacks on 'the king's soldiers' (Greater London RO, sessions rolls 1291, R 127, August 1664; and 1651, R 17, September 1684).
81. Twenty-eight of the rioters were prosecuted at the Middlesex Quarter Sessions or a Gaol Delivery Sessions at the Old Bailey; two were prosecuted at the City of London Sessions; two were committed to the house of correction in the City (Bethlem Hospital, minutes of the Court of Governors of Bridewell and Bethlem, July 24, 1719); and three were tried at the Surrey Assizes. In addition, many weavers were apparently apprehended by press gangs (*Original Weekly Journal* [June 20, 1719]).
82. *Old Bailey Proceedings* (n. 35 above), July 1719, p. 7; Greater London RO, sessions roll 2327, Ind. dated 12, 1719, Gaol Delivery Sessions, April and July, 1719.
83 *Old Bailey Proceedings*, July 1720, p. 6; Greater London RO, sessions roll 2350, Ind. 20, Gaol Delivery Sessions, July 1720.
84. Eight of the rioters were indicted; one was only bound over by recognizance; and two more were arrested but not prosecuted (Greater London RO, sessions rolls 2378–83, January – March 1722). These figures do not include the two

Indicted rioters, moreover, were treated leniently. Because of prosecutors who abandoned their cases and sympathetic juries, only 20 percent of the 220 defendants indicted for riot in 1720 and 1721 were actually convicted and punished. In comparison, the conviction rate for other indicted offenders against the peace was 35 percent.[85] Although defendants who were indicted for more serious disturbances, such as the calico riots or the gaming house riot, were more likely to be found guilty, about half the defendants indicted from even these riots were dismissed without punishment.[86] Furthermore, except for a handful of the participants in the most serious riots, convicted rioters were typically fined a small sum. Of the forty-three rioters convicted at Quarter Sessions in 1720 and 1721, 72 percent were required to pay a fine of 3*s*. 4*d*. or less, 19 percent more paid fines up to and including 13*s*. 4*d*., and only 7 percent paid more than 13*s*. 4*d*.

Although participants in the most serious riots continued to be prosecuted primarily by indictment, starting in the 1700s more riots resulted in prosecutions by recognizance than by indictment (Table 1).[87] Defendants who were bound over by recognizance were treated quite leniently; most faced only the inconvenience of finding sureties and appearing at Quarter Sessions. They could not be convicted or punished without being indicted, and only 24 percent of the rioters bound over by recognizance were ever indicted.[88]

There are two fundamental reasons why rioters were so rarely arrested and punished in preindustrial London: the weakness of officers of the peace and the widespread belief that certain types of riotous protest were legitimate or at least did not merit criminal prosecution. Officers of the peace, who were often vastly outnumbered and overpowered by the rioters, were frequently unable to arrest them. Edward Chamberlayne noted that magistrates needed 'great courage and virtue to oppose' rioters and recommended that the best way of responding to rioters was 'by kind words, pitiable harangues, condescensions or some such resigning method [to]

---

constabls and a soldier who were indicted for murdering one of the rioters (Greater London RO, sessions roll 2380, Ind. of Edward Vaughan and two others for the murder of Henry Bowes, Gaol Delivery Sessions, January 1722).

85. The conviction rate for other offenders against the peace is based on a 20 per cent sample of the Middlesex indictments between April 1720 and March 1722.

86. Greater London RO, sessions rolls 2327, Ind. dated June 12, 1719, Gaol Delivery Sessions, April and July 1719; and 2382, Ind. dated December 21, 1721, Gaol Delivery Sessions, February 1722; *Old Bailey Proceedings*, July 1719, p. 7, January 1722, p. 7, and February and March 1722, p. 6.

87. On the other hand, according to a sample of indictments from 1720 to 1722 assaults were more likely to be prosecuted by indictment than by recognizance (Shoemaker [n. 7 above], table 24, p. 263).

88. Ibid., table 6, p. 131.

get free from 'em and leave them to themselves'.[89] Any attempt by a magistrate to arrest rioters was sure to meet with resistance from the crowd and rioters often attempted to rescue anyone who was arrested.[90] The Riot Act of 1715 did not increase the powers of magistrates to apprehend rioters. The act, which elevated riots involving twelve or more people to a felony if the rioters did not leave the scene within an hour after a proclamation was read, had the primary effect of encouraging rioters to disperse, not of facilitating their arrest.[91] In order to prosecute rioters it was therefore necessary to apprehend them after the fact, when they were of course much more difficult to locate. Because of the inefficiency of the unpaid, part-time officers of the peace, the task was largely left to the victims of riots. Even when victims were able to identify and locate rioters, the trouble and expense involved in initiating prosecutions may explain why few victims prosecuted more than one or two rioters (often the instigators or 'ringleaders' of the riot).[92]

In addition to practical obstacles, both officers and victims appear to have been reluctant to apprehend and prosecute rioters because most types of riotous protest were commonly regarded as acceptable behavior. Disorder was largely tolerated for three reasons: rioters borrowed from traditions of licensed disorder, their grievances were widely (though not always universally) held, and their protests were mostly nonviolent. When groups of apprentices destroyed bawdy houses in 1668, some of their masters failed to discourage them, allegedly saying 'that if they meddle with nothing but bawdy houses, they do but the magistrates' drudgery'.[93]

Because the weaver's riots against calico in 1719–20 involved physical attacks on women and the destruction of property, even the supporters of the weavers' cause (the passage of a bill to prohibit the importing of calico) were forced to condemn the rioting. Nevertheless, many pamphleteers implicitly justified the weavers' attacks by stating that the weavers were forced to riot by their poverty.[94]

---

89. Chamberlayne (n. 34 above), p. 458.
90. PRO, SP 35/16/114; *Original Weekly Journal* (June 20, 1719); Harris, 'The Bawdy House Riots of 1668' (n. 2 above), p. 539.
91. See, e.g. PRO, SP 35/16/115, 122, June 13, 1719. Prosecutions under the Riot Act were extremely rare. Henry Fielding remarked in 1749 that he knew of only two riots that had led to prosecutions under the act since it had become law in 1715 (*A True State of the Case of Bosavern Penlez* [London, 1749], p. 27).
92. For the cost of prosecuting, see Shoemaker, pp. 137–38, 198–202.
93. *CSPD, 1667–68*, p. 310.
94. *Weekly Journal; or, Saturday's Post* (August 8, 1719); *Manufacturer*, no. 1 (October 30, 1719); Claudius Rey, *The Weavers' True Case*, 2d ed. (London, 1719), pp. 41–42; [Daniel Defoe], *The Just Complaint of the Poor Weavers Truly Represented* (London, 1719), p. 6.

Further encouragement for the rioters came from the Weavers' Company, which did not condemn the riots until three weeks after they began.[95] Although they were soundly condemned by some, the rioters were treated so leniently by the public, the press, and the master weavers that this leniency was abused by opportunists.[96] In September 1719, 'three fellows under pretence of being weavers, when they were downright thieves', robbed a woman while pretending to tear her calico gown.[97]

The fact that officials often did not act against rioters cannot be entirely due to fear since they typically did act once it became clear that the riot was out of control. In 1675, when groups of weavers destroyed engine looms because they believed that they caused unemployment, the weavers appear to have won widespread support, and local constables, the trained bands, and even the lieutenant of the Tower, Sir John Robinson, initially refused to act against them.[98] One magistrate even played a major role in a riot: in 1721, Justice John Ellis was at the head of a mob of over 100 people in Drury Lane that threatened two informers associated with the Reformation of Manners campaign and forced them to leave the parish.[99] Arguably, it is this general tolerance of disorder that allowed the few large-scale riots of the period to get out of hand so easily.

There were of course limits to the types of riotous behavior that were tolerated. Riots were expected to be nonviolent and not threaten to undermine the rule of law. The English are unique among nations, Roger North wrote in 1740, because 'they will bawl

---

95. The 'Advice of the Master Weavers to the Journeymen of their Trade', dated July 1, 1719, was published in the *Daily Courant* on July 19 and in Rey, pp. 45–47. Two days after the riots began, the company issued an order, which I have been unable to locate, that apparently did not address the riots or the calico issue directly but instead, in order to increase the employment prospects for legitimate journeymen, condemned masters who employed unlawful journeymen (those who had not performed a proper apprenticeship) (*Weekly Journal; or, Saturday's Post* [June 20, 1719]; see also *A Further Examination of the Weavers' Pretences* [London, 1719], pp. 28, 39).
96. See, e.g. the condemnations of the riots in *A Further Examination of the Weavers' Pretences*; and letters to the editor in the *Weekly Journal; or, Saturday's Post* (June 27, August 15, and September 5, 1719).
97. *Orphan Revived, or Powell's Weekly Journal* (September 5–12, 1719). See also the *Daily Post* (May 14, 1720). In a different context, Defoe complained that the legitimacy accorded to the practice of crowds punishing prostitutes led to abuses: 'Under this pretence many honest women are mobb'd, and oftentimes robb'd in the very face of the world' (Andrew Moreton [Daniel Defoe], *Parochial Tyranny* [London, 1727], p. 21).
98. Harris, 'The Politics of the London Crowd in the Reign of Charles II' (n. 2 above), pp. 233, 238; Dunn (n. 22 above), p. 18. See also Lindley (n. 54 above), p. 126.
99. Greater London RO, sessions papers, August 1721, no. 5.

and crowd terribly, but do not love the cry of murder'.[100] Where violence was used, it was typically directed against property rather than persons. In 1675, when groups of weavers destroyed engine looms, the only interpersonal violence was committed by the owners, who attacked the rioters while attempting to protect their property.[101] Because the property damaged in the calico riots was clothing, the potential for violence against persons was greater than usual. The *London Journal* reported the more egregious cases of violence in a manner that suggests that it condoned the weavers' less violent attacks. An attack in August 1720 prompted the following comment: 'It is notorious how they tore [the victim's] clothes, and would not spare so much as her under petticoat, tho' her husband offered them ten shillings for that small favor; and, at the same time, a stranger offered them five more, and for reproving them had his brains beat out.'[102] Ultimately, rioters were expected to submit to the rule of law. Weavers who continued to attack women wearing calico after the act banning the importing and wearing of calico was passed in June 1720 were attacked by Defoe, who called them 'desperate jades'.[103] With the new law the public acquired legal means of punishing people who wore the offending fabric. Rioting was no longer justified as the weavers' only course of action.

Not surprisingly, participants in the largest riots were treated less leniently by the government; the threat posed by any significant riot that involved violent attacks on individuals, widespread destruction of property, or opposition to government policies had to be answered firmly. Defendants were tried at a Gaol Delivery Sessions (or by a special commission of Oyer and Terminer) at the Old Bailey and were given harsher punishments. The three convicted defendants from the gaming house riot, in which several constables and soldiers were attacked by over 200 people with swords, brickbats, and chamber pots, were given fines of between £50 and £100 together with prison sentences of between one and three years.[104] Both in 1675 and in 1719, a few convicted weavers were sentenced

---

100. North (n. 33 above), 1: 571. See also Daniel Defoe, *More Reformation. A Satyr upon Himself* (London, 1703), preface. But Beattie (*Crime and the Courts in England* [n. 11 above], pp. 133–35) suggests that crowd violence was common and widely tolerated during this period.
101. Harris, 'The Politics of the London Crowd in the Reign of Charles II', p. 232.
102. *London Journal* (August 13, 1720). See also *London Journal* (August 20. 1720).
103. *Weekly Journal; or, Saturday's Post* (June 18, 1720). See also *Original Weekly Journal* (January 12 and 19, 1723).
104. Greater London RO, sessions roll 2382, Ind. dated December 21, 1721, Gaol Delivery Sessions, February 1722.

to stand in the pillory and either pay a large fine or spend three months in prison.[105]

VIII   A POPULAR CONSENSUS?

Descriptions of London rioters as 'the mob' imply that rioters acted as a single body and that all rioters shared the same motivations. Indeed, the traditional forms of licensed disorder imitated in London riots presupposed the existence of shared values. While celebrations of holidays and political anniversaries were meant to strengthen religious, civic, and patriotic values, for example, ridings punished the violators of norms governing marital or sexual behavior. Yet a popular consensus on the values upheld by riotous protest did not in fact always exist in London. Despite their common tolerance of nonviolent rioting, Londoners could not agree on a single code of sexual or economic behavior, and riots expressing opposing points of view frequently occurred.

Attitudes toward sexual license, especially prostitution, had always been ambiguous, but in the late seventeenth century, partly as a consequence of the zeal exhibited by the supporters of the Reformation of Manners campaign, popular opinion became so divided that riots occurred both attacking and defending prostitutes and brothels.[106] On the one hand, following the tradition of ridings, Londoners frequently rioted at their neighbors' doors, calling their victims 'whores' or 'bastard bearers', to protest their sexual indiscretions. Although apprentices apparently no longer pulled down brothels (except for the politically motivated attacks in 1668), other Londoners continued to attack brothels and their proprietors. In 1719, Faith Jervice was accused of 'raising a great tumult and mob' about the house of Anne Walton in Shorts Gardens, 'swearing she would blow up her bawdy house'.[107] When two bawdy-house keepers stood in the pillory at Charing Cross in 1719, 'they were treated with the highest resentment of the mob on those occasions,

---

105. Dunn, pp. 21–22 (some of the 1675 rioters were subsequently pardoned); Greater London RO, sessions roll 2327, Ind. dated June 12, 1719, Gaol Delivery Sessions, April and July 1719; *Old Bailey Proceedings* (n. 35 above), July 1719, p. 7.
106. For attitudes toward prostitution, see Thomas, 'The Double Standard' (n. 17 above); Keith Wrightson, *English Society, 1580–1680* (London, 1982), pp. 99–100; Dunton (n. 50 above). pp. 10–11.
107. Greater London RO, sessions roll 2016, R 123, September 1703.

in showers of rotten eggs, dirt, etc.'.[108] On the other hand, mobs attacked constables and members of the Societies for the Reformation of Manners who were trying to apprehend prostitutes and search bawdy houses, and crowds rescued relatives or friends who had been arrested for prostitution.[109] Within a decade, two constables were murdered by rioters shortly after they had apprehended suspected prostitutes.[110] By the early eighteenth century crowds could easily be raised both to protest prostitution and adultery and to prevent the arrest of suspected prostitutes.

Popular opinion concerning the weavers' riots in 1697 and 1719–20 was also divided. In 1697, some of the protesters complained that the linen drapers in Cornhill and Cheapside had taunted the weavers during their march to Westminster by 'pulling out their East-India silks and calicoes, and showing of it [sic] to them, as they passed along'.[111] Not everyone objected to the wearing of clothing made out of calico. Although there is no evidence of any riots that opposed the weavers in 1719–20 (unless the woman who was dunked in the Thames by a mob for having torn a dress [of unknown fabric] in 1720 was a participant in the weavers' campaign), rioting weavers did encounter scattered opposition.[112] In August 1719, when a woman dressed in calico was attacked by a group of weavers in Spitalfields (where support for their cause should have been greatest), she was able to escape to an alehouse whose inhabitants protected her.[113] A major reason why many of the poor did not support the weavers was that they could not afford to wear anything other than calico in the summer, when it was too hot to wear wool.[114] Like riotous attacks on brothels, riots against calico reflected the sentiments of only one segment of the population.[115]

108. *Weekly Journal*; or *British Gazeteer* (June 27, 1719).
109. See, e.g., Corporation of London RO, sessions rolls, October 1693, Ind. dated August 26 for a riotous assault on James Jenkins; and January 1720, R 34.
110. *A Looking Glass for Informing Constables; Represented in the Tryals . . . for the Murder of Mr. John Dent*, 3d. (London, 1733); Josiah Woodward, *A Sermon Preached at the Parish Church of St James Westminster . . . At the Funeral of Mr John Cooper* (London, 1702); Greater London RO, sessions paper, July 1702, nos. 50–54, and sessions book no. 595, May 1702, p. 35.
111. *CJ*, 11: 683.
112. Greater London RO, sessions papers, May 1720, no. 10.
113. *Weekly Journal; or, Saturday's Post* (August 15, 1719; see also June 27, 1719).
114. *Weekly Journal; or, Saturday's Post* (June 27, 1719).
115. Similarly, historians have recently noted that political riots in the late seventeenth and early eighteenth century supported opposing views (Harris, 'The Politics of the London Crowd in the Reign of Charles II' [n. 2 above], pp. 258, 298–99; DeKrey [n. 2 above], p. 258).

IX CONCLUSION

By evoking traditions of licensed disorder, London rioters expressed a sense of the legitimacy of their protests, and the wider public and the authorities responded with toleration. In these respects, London riots shared many characteristics with the rural disorders studied by E. P. Thompson and others. In his influential study of English food riots, Thompson provided a model for understanding rural disorder: 'It is possible to detect in almost every eighteenth-century crowd action some legitimizing notion. By the notion of legitimation I mean that the men and women in the crowd were informed by the belief that they were defending traditional rights and customs; and, in general, that they were supported by the wider consensus of the community'.[116]

Recent research has generally upheld Thompson's argument that rioters generally defended traditional rights and values, had a sense of the legitimacy of their actions, and acted with the support of the wider community. These qualities have been found in most types of preindustrial rural disorder, especially ridings and riots against enclosures, turnpikes, changes in the administration of forests, and the drainage of the fens.[117] Nevertheless, some historians have questioned whether the values defended by rioters, such as the food rioters' 'moral economy', were in fact commonly held. Just as the beliefs advanced by London rioters did not always reflect a popular consensus, there is evidence of conflicting values among rioters, the general public, and the authorities in the communities in which food riots occurred.[118]

These similarities between patterns of urban and rural disorder have implications for our understanding of the differences between urban and rural society in preindustrial England. Social relations in

---

116. Thompson, 'The Moral Economy of the English Crowd in the Eighteenth Century' (n. 40 above), p. 78.
117. Stevenson (n. 73 above), pp. 309–16; J. A. Sharpe, *Crime in Early Modern England 1550–1750* (New York, 1984), p. 139; Philip D. Jones, 'The Bristol Bridge Riot and Its Antecedents: Eighteenth-Century Perceptions of the Crowd', *Journal of British Studies* 19 (Spring 1980): 79–81; Ingram (n. 43 above), pp. 109–13; Buchanan Sharp 'Popular Protest in Seventeenth-Century England', in Fletcher and Stevenson, eds. (n. 4 above), pp. 294, 303.
118. Buchanan Sharp, *In Contempt of All Authority* (Berkeley and Los Angeles, 1980), pp. 33–36; Elizabeth Fox Genovese, 'The Many Faces of the Moral Economy: A Contribution to a Debate', *Past and Present*, no. 58 (1973), p. 167; John Stevenson, 'The Moral Economy of the English Crowd: Myth and Reality', in Fletcher and Stevenson, eds., pp. 236–38.

rural and urban areas may have shared more characteristics than is generally believed; the theoretical presupposition that rural villages were significantly more socially stable and cohesive than towns and cities needs to be reexamined. There is evidence that the communities in which rural rioters lived were socially and culturally divided.[119] In both urban and rural areas, riots were perhaps less an expression of existing community solidarity than an attempt to generate such solidarity where it was weak.[120] Nevertheless, urban and rural disorder differed in a few important respects: many of the traditional rituals are absent in London riots; riots in London not only did not express a popular consensus but often actually supported contradictory points of view; and women, though not excluded from rural riots, played a much more significant role in urban rioting. These differences suggest some of the ways in which urban life did contrast with rural life in preindustrial England: fewer traditional pastimes; the existence of potentially destabilizing 'subcultures' with contrasting values (based perhaps on occupations or the geographic origins of immigrants); and the greater independence experienced by women.[121]

London riots differ from their rural counterparts in one other important respect – their frequency. Any explanation of the origins of rioting as practically a daily phenomenon will no doubt have to take into account the social, economic, and demographic changes that London experienced during this period, but it must also account for the influence of the less frequent but much larger political disturbances of the period. It is between the Exclusion Crisis, when large-scale political disorder emerged for the first time since the Restoration (and the term 'mob' was first used), and the early eighteenth century that party conflict first led to widespread disorder, and it is no doubt not a coincidence that it is these same years that witnessed a rapid increase in the number of riots prosecuted at Quarter Sessions.[122] Indeed, by training Londoners in the vocabulary and mechanics of street protest, major political riots may have facilitated day-to-day street protests, and vice versa. Thus the history of specific types of rioting needs to be studied in the context of a broader history of crowds and popular disorder.

119. Underdown, *Revel, Riot and Rebellion* (n. 63 above), pp. 72, 104–5, 226; Wrightson (n. 106 above), pp. 55–56.
120. R. J. Holton, 'The Crowd in History: Some Problems of Theory and Method', *Social History* 3 (1978): 231–32.
121. On subcultures, see Burke, 'Popular Culture in Seventeenth-Century London' (n. 57 above), pp. 33–34.
122. For disorder occasioned by party conflict, see Stevenson, *Popular Disturbances in England*, pp. 19–23; DeKrey, pp. 39–42 and *passim*.

Viewed from this angle, the question of whether political riots were 'organized from above' can be interpreted in a new light. While riots such as the Sacheverell riots and the mug-house riots were undoubtedly organized by the political elite, the fact that many of the participants in these riots may have been schooled in more spontaneous street protests expressing other types of grievances explains why these political riots were so easy to instigate.[123] Regardless of elite leadership, political riots depended on considerable initiative 'from below'.[124] Lower-class rioters, moreover, were not necessarily motivated by the same grievances as the politicians. As Nicholas Rogers has demonstrated, political disorder could provide plebeians with 'a cultural base for noising their grievances', grievances that were not narrowly 'political' but included economic and religious issues.[125] Just as ridings could be adapted to voice political grievances, political riots provided opportunities for other grievances to be expressed. As E. P. Thompson has argued, a significant feature of English social relations in the eighteenth century was the tendency for the lower classes to manipulate traditions of acceptable behavior in order to express their grievances, often against their social superiors.[126] Riots including elements of traditional forms of licensed disorder were frequent in London, but they protested such irrelevant and untraditional grievances as the importing of calico and the arrest of prostitutes.

In this respect, the early eighteenth century appears as a crucial period in the long process in which the political elite lost control of popular disturbances in London. Whereas the London riots that helped precipitate the Civil War involved 'a strong element of political direction and discipline', in 1780 the Gordon riots, the most violent and destructive riots in London history, had the quality of 'an assault on symbols of authority'.[127] Concurrently, the early eighteenth century witnessed not only an apparent increase in the frequency of small-scale rioting in the metropolis but also a weakening of the role of traditional rituals in disorder and an expansion of the range of grievances expressed. Although rioting was not yet seen

123. Holmes (n. 2 above), pp. 78–82: Fitts (n. 79 above).
124. DeKrey, pp. 119–20, 248–58; Rogers (n. 2 above), p. 100; Rudé, 'The London "Mob" in the Eighteenth Century' (n. 2 above), pp. 13–16.
125. Rogers, pp. 91–100.
126. E. P. Thompson, 'Patrician Society, Plebeian Culture', *Journal of Social History* 7 (1974): 382–405, and 'Eighteenth-Century English Society: Class Struggle without Class?' *Social History* 3 (1978) 133–65.
127. Pearl (n. 8 above). p. 5; in his analysis of the 'December Days' of 1641, however, Brian Manning suggests that the 'mob' was not controlled by political leaders (*The English People and the English Revolution, 1640–1649* [London, 1976], pp. 71–98). Stevenson, *Popular Disturbances in England*. p. 84.

as a significant problem in London in the early eighteenth century, these changes suggest that the growing fears of social upheaval encapsulated in the new name for rioters, the 'mob', would eventually be justified.

Chapter 7

BATH: IDEOLOGY AND UTOPIA, 1700–1760

R. S. Neale

[from R. F. Brissenden and J. C. Eade (eds.), *Studies in the Eighteenth Century*, Vol. III (Canberra, 1976)]

Whereas most towns identified closely with a particular region or locality, Bath was first and foremost a cosmopolitan centre, catering for the medical, recreational and aesthetic needs of the nation's élite. As a consequence of this the spa enjoyed an exceptional level of investment in its cultural fabric and facilities, so that it became a work of art in its own right. To understand Georgian Bath, therefore, the urban historian must employ the tools of analysis associated with other academic disciplines. Ronald Neale's essay is a stimulating if controversial attempt to do this, as he evaluates the work of the city's most famous architect, John Wood the elder. In an overtly Marxist interpretation he portrays Wood's approach to design as a Christian reaction against a rapidly developing capitalist market economy. This is a view the author takes further, and places in a much broader context, in his major study of the city, Bath 1680–1850: a Social History *(1981). Readers of Neale's essay might ask themselves how his interpretation squares with Wood's well-documented role as a building entrepreneur, heavily involved in the world of finance; and question whether Neale provides adequate evidence, other than that by inference, of the architect's disenchantment with capitalism. The most recent and substantial study of Wood,* John Wood: Architect of Obsession *(1988), is by two architectural historians, Tim Mowl and Brian Earnshaw. Like Neale they place considerable emphasis on using Wood's writings to understand his buildings, but they eschew social analysis and portray Wood as a proto-Romantic driven by a visionary, if flawed, sense of history.*

To talk about Bath is to talk about eighteenth-century England. But I am not prepared or able, like some historians, to talk about an

England or a Bath that was objectively real or really there. I can only speak about Bath in the light of my own experience of its surviving buildings, mortgages, leases, newspapers, estate and corporation records, and a variety of other manuscripts, plans, prints, pamphlets, scraps of paper. I will do so with the aid of a conceptual apparatus in which the main parts are ideas about the relationships between society, men, and creativity and knowledge put forward by Karl Marx, Karl Mannheim, and Jean Duvignaud and insights derived from the art historians Erwin Panofsky and Rudolf Wittkower. I shall attempt to convey the results of my observation of this very small whole piece of the world through the inadequate metaphor of a language which forces me to speak and write seriatim however much I believe I can see, at one time, this small piece whole – a complex, dynamic and dialectical *gestalt*. What I would like to do is to write this piece of social history in the way Picasso painted Kahnweiler, whereas I can scarcely manage to do it as Hogarth painted Captain Thomas Coram.

It will probably be allowed that architecture is art and, therefore, that architecture in Bath is art. Certainly its architecture is as much a kaleidoscope of individual and collective acts of creation as the Book of Kells or St Peter's in Rome. Moreover, it could not have been built had not Brunelleschi created the Pazzi Chapel in Florence and Palladio published his *Quattro libri dell'architettura*. Art, however, is very rarely the mere representation of an order in society or of a style associated with it. Indeed, art continuously and anxiously opposes and questions order and Bath, I shall argue, was no mere reflection of an age, be it called Rational, Bourgeois, Georgian or Whiggish. Neither was it simply the Renaissance in England. Rather, Bath consisted of personalised atypic responses to disorder and the anomie of a market economy, juxtaposed with collective and personal expressions which served and re-affirmed that newly-developing structure of society. Creative expression in Bath is, in Mannheim's sense, both ideological and utopian.[1]

Any answer to the question, What is the meaning of eighteenth-century Bath? is likely to be attempted at three levels. The objective level identifies historical Bath as an eighteenth-century watering-place and its buildings as lodging-houses. The expressive level looks to the purposes of its architects and builders and concentrates, on the one hand, on the expressed desire of John Wood, the city's leading architect, to re-create a Roman city complete with Forum, Gymnasium, and Circus and, on the other, on an imputed desire to reunite urban man with nature; Wood, it is argued, anticipated the Romantics and modern town planners. The third level is documen-

---

1. Karl Mannheim, *Ideology and Utopia: An Introduction to the Sociology of Knowledge,* London, 1972, pp. 49–87.

tary or evidential, and it too points to something beyond the city itself, to the spirit of the age, to Whiggism and the Age of Reason.[2] There are elements of truth in all these answers, but those relating to the expressive and documentary levels are frequently stated with all the startling clarity of absolutes. Yet, if one pauses awhile to try to penetrate the form and structure of the city, to understand the historical space it occupies as well as the space in which it is situated, and to pass beyond the grey opaqueness of the buildings to men themselves, this startling clarity will be blurred, and brought into sharper focus only by a searching analysis of the beliefs, ideologies, and institutions of its time. I propose to attempt this by concentrating on the work of John Wood (1705–1754) and the first sixty years of the eighteenth century.

In the early eighteenth century Bath had a population of some seven hundred families or three thousand people. Most of them lived within the town walls which formed an irregular polygon with sides about four hundred yards long. The town, situated in a loop of the Bristol Avon, had the river on two sides and the slopes of Lansdown and Beacon Hill to the north and west. It was an isolated urban enclave approachable in wet weather only from the London side. Its citizens worked to provide a rude accommodation for visitors to its baths and apprenticed their sons to the clothing, food, building and personal service trades. The wealthier among them held land outside the walls and kept inns and lodging houses, all built in the vernacular style – mostly three storied with casement and mullioned windows set in large decorated bays, attics, and high gables fronting the street. They were all architectural flourish and asymmetry. Lacking proportion and harmony, they were a collection of mere houses. According to report, they were inconvenient and uncomfortable.

As the century grew older so grew the nation's wealth. The two thousand families who possessed the land and governed it, protected by law against the claims of the Crown and the common man, increased their grip on power and sought social occasions for harmless sensual pleasures. Bath became a resort for gambling, horse racing, drinking, eating, revelling, dancing, and whoring; or at least it did so twice a year, in the spring and the autumn. As the author of *A Step to the Bath* described it in 1700,

2. Walter Ison, *The Georgian Buildings of Bath from 1700 to 1830*, London, 1948; John Summerson, *Architecture in Britain, 1530–1830*, ed. Nikolaus Pevsner, Harmondsworth, 1953, pp. 197–245; Nikolaus Pevsner, *An Outline of European Architecture*, Harmondsworth, 1960, p. 581; John Fleming, Hugh Honour, Nikolaus Pevesner, *The Penguin Dictionary of Architecture*, Harmondsworth, 1966, p. 242; Fritz Baumgart, *A History of Architectural Styles*, London, 1970, pp. 255–6; Colin and Rose Bell, *City Fathers: The Early History of Town Planning in Britain*, Harmondsworth, 1972.

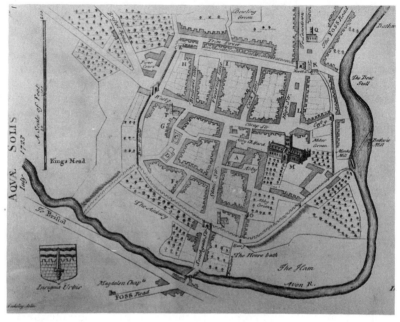

Fig. 1 Map of Bath, 1723; from William Stukeley, *Itinerarium Curiosum* (1724) (reproduced by permission of the Bath Reference Library)

A The King's Bath; B The Queen's Bath; C The Cross Bath; D The Hot Bath; E Gascoin's Tower; F St. Catherine's Hospital; G St. John's Hospital; H Bridewell; I The Playhouse; K St. Mary's; L The Market House; M St. Peter's Cathedral (The Abbey); N St. James; O The Abbey Gate; P St. Michael's; Q St. Michael's Broadstreet.

'tis neither Town nor City, yet goes by the Name of both; five Months in the Year 'tis as Populous as *London*, the other seven as desolate as a Wilderness. it's [*sic*] chiefest Inhabitants are Turn-Spit-Dogs; and it looks like Lombard-street on a Saintsday. During the Season it hath as many Families in a House as *Edenborough*; and Bills are as thick for Lodgings to be Let, as there was for Houses in the *Fryars* on the Late Act of Parliament for the Dissolution of Priviledges; but when the *Baths* are useless, so are their Houses, and as empty as the new Buildings by *St Giles* in the Fields; the *Baths* I can compare to nothing but the *Boylers* in *Fleet-lane* or *Old-Bedlam*, for they have a reeking steem all the year. In a word, 'tis a Valley of Pleasure, yet a sink of Iniquity; Nor is there any Intrigues or Debauch Acted at *London*, but is mimick'd there.[3]

As well as catering to the sensuous needs of men and women Bath also benefited from the pre-scientific state of medicine and the

3. Anon., *A Step to the Bath: with a Character of the Place*, London, 1700, p. 16.

226

continuing belief in magic this encouraged. Dr Oliver, the inventor of the Bath Oliver biscuit, was an astute businessman quite clear about the profitability of magic. He sought to attract customers to Bath by persuading them that a healthy life could be theirs if only they would take the waters inside and out. In his *Practical Dissertation on Bath Waters* Dr Oliver told potential patients that the waters would cure gout, rheumatism, palsies, convulsions, lameness, colic, consumption, asthma, jaundice, scurvy, the itch, scab, leprosy, scrofula, gravel, as well as coldness and pain in the head, epilepsies, most diseases of the eyes, deafness and noise in the ears, running of the ears, palpitation of the heart, sharpness of urine, wounds, ulcers, piles, numbness in any part, and all the special diseases of women including infertility. For good and crucial measure, the waters would also cure the pox – 'If they can't be cured by drinking and bathing here,' wrote Dr Oliver, 'they will never be cured any where'.[4] Yet, according to other reports, the converse was more likely to be true, a visit to 'The Bath' was as like to bring on the pox as cure it!

Sensuous self-indulgence and a desire for magical cures to ease its worst effects were the reason that people flocked to Bath. This influx of visitors caused the first building booms of the century and created in Bath what the eighteenth century and John Wood knew as 'Civil Society', a state of incessant self-regarding and socially disruptive competition.

Although, in these early years, the need to build houses fit for gentlemen in the 'new' Palladian style produced a number of elegant houses and one or two courts designed as wholes, builders were generally more concerned with supplying comfort at a price than with aesthetics. Therefore, local landowners and builders built a house here and another there, added a scatter of public buildings, such as a pumproom, a theatre, and an assembly room, and, in the occasional new street, built according to individual designs. The result was that, in the first quarter of the century, Bath showed every sign of growing piecemeal like any other Cotswold town. And there were good reasons why this should be so. Demand for the services Bath could provide was uncertain, subject to the vagaries of harvest and war. Consequently capital and land were not yet moving freely into real estate development. Moreover, as far as land was concerned, there was another impediment, the problem of tenure. Within the town itself and immediately on its northern, eastern, and southern boundaries land was only available in quite small parcels whether of freehold, copyhold or leasehold land. Where land was potentially available in large blocks controlled by one owner, either corporate or private, the existence of long leases for three

4. William Oliver, *A Practical Dissertation on Bath Waters*, London, 1707, p. 70.

lives meant that any potential for development on a grand scale would be frustrated unless those life-hold leases could be brought into the ambit of a market economy and turned into leases for terms of years. Only on the western side of the town was there real development potential. There lay three large blocks of land. First, ninety acres of common land held in trust by the Corporation for the benefit of the freemen of the city and, therefore, undeveloped for the whole of the eighteenth century. Second, a large area of low-lying meadow, Great Kingsmead and Little Kingsmead, parts of which were thought suitable for development. And, third, the eighty-five acre Barton estate owned by a commercially-minded absentee landlord Robert Gay, a successful barber-surgeon in London. On this estate the problem of life-hold lease had been long since settled. Since it was to be the main site for development there can be little doubt that the first creative acts transforming Bath were constrained and shaped by the uneven penetration of capitalist agriculture into this part of Somerset.[5]

All I have said about the function of tenure in setting the boundaries for action illustrates the importance for the eighteenth century of private property and of the Lockeian notion of absolute property which gave agrarian capitalist practice ideological sanction.[6] This notion, absolute property, meaning freedom to use to the extent of destroying, was a philosophic bludgeon used with almost equal effect against the Crown as against copyholders, life-holders, customary tenants, and all foolish communitarians. It was the kingpin in the ideological scaffolding within which Bath was built. It, too, had west country origins.

But, there was more to property law than that and more than one pin in the scaffolding. In the three-quarters of a century preceding the development of Bath, property owners, secure in law against the Crown and the common man, had employed their lawyers and the Court of Chancery to good effect to develop a system of land law that was flexible and functional rather than absolute and categorical. They produced the settled estate in which, in its classic form, the nominal possessor was in fact only a life tenant. Seisin, or, for the want of a better word, ownership, was vested in trustees. With the development of the principle of equity of redemption as applied to mortgages, those with seisin who were also mortgagors were deemed merely to have an estate in land, while mortgagees

---

5. See my 'Society, Belief, and the Building of Bath, 1700–1793,' in *Landscape and Society, 1500–1800*, ed. C. W. Chalkin and M. Havinden, London, 1973.
6. See John Locke, *Two Treatises of Government*, I, 39; also C. B. MacPherson, *The Political Theory of Possessive Individualism: Hobbes to Locke*, Oxford, 1962; Harold Perkin, *The Origins of Modern English Society, 1780–1880*, London, 1969, pp. 51–3.

had a right to an income from it. Some major consequences of these developments were: settled estates encumbered with all kinds of legal commitments were almost certain to remain intact for several generations; titles to property were more certain and inalienable; the rights of mortgagees were protected by law. Therefore, settled estates and conveyances by way of lease flowing from them were good mortgage investments – a 4 per cent mortgage on Pulteney's estate in Bathwick was as safe as holding government stock. It also offered a better return. The significance of these legal developments for building in Bath arises from the fact that it was a city of small fortunes. As even piecemeal development at £300 to £500 per house was expensive, widespread mortgage facilities and institutions and people with experience in mortgages were essential. Moreover, since most surrounding estates were settled, little land could be bought for building purposes and almost all building was on land let on leases for ninety-nine years. These leasehold titles, secure in law, could be re-let by developers in the form of building sub-leases into which were written building controls and conditions. All leases and sub-leases could be used as mortgage security. The combination of settled estate, building leases and sub-leases, and widespread mortgaging also made it possible to plan and carry through capital-intensive development projects like the Circus and the Royal Crescent, which cost at least £100 000 to complete.[7] In fact, whatever else it might be, Bath is a monument to the credit-raising ingenuity of the eighteenth century, for a very high proportion of the two million pounds invested in its construction, an amount almost equal to that invested in fixed capital in the cotton industry, was raised on mortgages secured by leases of land from settled estates.

Therefore, the initial decision of a landowner either to build himself or to grant building leases was crucial. He not only provided the site but, through the development of the concept of absolute property and with the assistance of developments in property law, he also supplied first class collateral for raising finance from hundreds of cautious small investors. In this way the market economy of agrarian capitalism, as well as determining the strength of demand for the good things Bath supplied and the site and sequence of development, also made it possible to tap reservoirs of capital in such a way as to enable a creative developer like John Wood to translate his image of man and nature into architectural

7. R. S. Neale, 'The Bourgeoisie, Historically, has played a Most Revolutionary Part', in *Feudalism, Capitalism, and Beyond*, ed. Eugene Kamenka, Canberra, 1974; A. W. B. Simpson, *An Introduction to the History of the Land Law*, Oxford, 1961.

forms. Thus Bath was both product and symbol of the achievement of agrarian and commercial capitalism, an existential expression of the social and economic structure of society and its dominant ideology. It was also, by mid-century, one of the principal resorts in England, providing opportunities for respectable social emulation and containing, as it were, the social forces which alone gave it its being. However, every expansion of the physical facilities necessary for this purpose widened the area, physically and socially, into which capitalist practice penetrated. In the end Bath was doomed by the very success of its capitalist citizens and the expansion of civil society.

So to the work of John Wood. I realise that to concentrate on his work and, therefore, on the thirty year period after 1727, is to simplify the milieu into which Wood entered and to do injustice to other early eighteenth-century architect-builders like Killigrew, Strahan, and Greenway. My justification is that Wood *was* a giant among provincial architects and *did* give a new dimension and meaning to Bath. As well, he and his son, also John Wood, were responsible for planning and supervising the building of property with a capital value of some £400 000[8] or about one-fifth of the domestic building carried out in Bath in the eighteenth century.

John Wood was born the son of a mason in 1705. Whether he was born in Bath or Yorkshire is still uncertain. As a young man he worked as a surveyor in London and Yorkshire where, in 1725, he drew up plans for rebuilding Bath as a Roman city. Having unsuccessfully sought the assistance of several landowners in implementing his projected schemes, he entered in 1726 into a contract for digging dirt in the cut at Twerton, which was part of the improvement of the Avon between Bath and Bristol. In 1727 he was contracting surveyor for the development of Chandos Court for the Duke of Chandos. In 1728, and without capital, he began building Queen Square as an independent undertaker or architect-developer.

As an architect-developer Wood had to reconcile two contrasting parts of his being; capitalist and member of civil society, and creative artist. His books suggest that he understood perfectly that without success as a capitalist he would be unable to create. There was an additional problem. He was a deeply religious man, but as a struggling capitalist and artist he catered for the high consumption demands of a self-indulgent clientele 'in a sink of iniquity'. Thus he could neither succeed as a capitalist nor create anything unless he continued to produce what satisfied this market in the context of and according to the conditions of agrarian capitalism already described. Indeed, this seemed the only market that would enable

8. Particulars of Fee Farm Rents, 1787; A Particular of Perpetual Fee Farm Rents, 1771, Guildhall Archives, Bath; Wood Box.

him to do anything at all. Consequently his career is marked by one compromise after another; Queen Square, North Parade, and the Exchange building in Bristol are only three of them. Wood was also fully conscious of the socially disruptive nature of this 'civil society' in which he so actively participated. Writing in and of an age yet to be blessed by Adam Smith's invention of the hidden hand, he wrote, 'Reason as well as Experience sufficiently demonstrates that without Law there can be no Government; and without Government, mankind cannot long subsist in Civil society with one another'.[9] I shall attempt to argue that the tensions produced by the contradictions of this state of 'disorder' in the milieu of Bath are evident in his work and I shall suggest that they were the source of the prodigious energy he displayed in designing and carrying through his projects in the face of opposition, legal difficulties, capital shortage, labour deficiency, and economic depression. They may also account for the fact that he was a prickly sort of man. In any case, his were certainly atypical responses to the 'disorder' of civil society in early eighteenth-century Bath and to the anomie of a developing market economy. Fortunately for him and for posterity, they brought him recognition as a valued participator in the new society. A study of his work, which was both a protest against that society as well as a way of adjusting to it, may take us nearer to the expressive or documentary meaning of Bath.

John Wood, astronomer, antiquarian, and mythologist, as well as architect and capitalist, was what learned men have described as 'self taught' by which they mean he was untutored within the rigid bounds of formal subject learning. His contribution to building apart, he is thought unworthy of serious consideration. Consequently architectural historians and the myriad popularisers of their work have largely ignored or dismissed Wood's writings as a farrago of nonsense. They seem either to contemporise Wood's Bath by making it relevant to twentieth-century town planning or to place it neatly within the context of a linear history of building or architectural styles. The notion that they might try writing history rather than histories scarcely touches their work. The social historian, however, *must* look at Wood's writings as well as his buildings, for his books, *The Origin of Building; or, The Plagiarism of the Heathens Detected* (1741), *An Essay towards a Description of Bath* (1742 and 1749), and *A Dissertation upon the Orders of Columns* (1750), show how Wood, whose work shaped Bath so much in his own image, saw the world and his own place and the place of his buildings in it. If we wish to try to 'read' the early eighteenth century as Wood 'read' it and as he tried to write it in stone, and not as we see it

9. John Wood, *An Essay towards a Description of Bath*, 1765, repr. Bath, 1969, p. 353.

now through the clutter and destruction of the last two hundred and fifty years, we must read these works to learn the language of his polemic signs – those signs which, in Duvignaud's terminology, are a group of activities with a double function: recognising that there is an obstacle (either of participation or expression) to be overcome; and the real or imagined attempt to overcome the obstacle. These functions endow the work of art with a dynamic value of which perhaps even the artist himself is unaware.[10]

We begin this part of our inquiry by taking a look at the landscape in and around Bath. We shall try our best to see it as Wood saw it and from that try to understand his perception of nature, towns and buildings, and, thereby, to comprehend the origins of the polemic signs used by him in his work as architect.

As Wood saw it Bath was but the core of an earlier city the size of Babylon built originally by Bladud, descendant of a Trojan prince, about 480 B.C. Bladud, under the name of Abaris, High Priest of Apollo, had spent eleven years in Greece as 'a Disciple, a Colleague, and even the Master of Pythagoras'.[11] He was, as might be expected, a devotee of a heliocentric system of the planets from which the Pythagorean system was probably derived. This Bladud/Pythagorean system was the reason for the great size of Wood's antique Bath; for, by enlarging it to a triangle with sides fifteen miles by ten by eight he incorporated Stanton Drew. At Stanton Drew there was an impressive circle of standing stones which Wood carefully measured and showed to be a model of the Pythagorean planetary system built by Bladud for use in the Stanton Drew university for British Druids. Wood drew attention to the use of circles in this work and pointed out that the chief ensign of Druidism was a ring. Moreover, the Temple of the Moon at Stanton Drew was identical with the Temple Cyrus ordered the Jews to build in Jerusalem.

Nearer to the surviving core of the city Wood noted the existence of five hills with characteristics of small mountains. Their names meant: Mars' Hill, the Moon's Hill, the Sun's Hill, the King's Hill, the Holy Hill. Hills the elevation of which was such, 'that their Summits command a Country so exceedingly beautiful, and of such vast Extent, that the Eye that views it, and the Mind that considers it with Attention, can never be enough satisfied'.[12] From the tops of these hills Wood reported seeing no sign of the impact of agrarian capitalism, no glimpse of the Bristol slave trade, and no sound of manufacture from the thickening cluster of woollen towns which had

10. See Jean Duvignaud, *The Sociology of Art*, London, 1972, p. 51.
11. Wood, *Essay*, p. 40.
12. Ibid., p. 54.

crept like Triffids to the boundaries of the city – Wood was no Defoe. Instead, he set his *Essay towards a Description of Bath*, his account of his own contribution to the city, against a portrayal of a fantastic historic landscape peopled with Druids, Greeks, and cultivated Britons engaged in building temples, altars, castles, palaces, and forums, all in the antique style. Their forums had a particular fascination for Wood for they applied them to the most noble purposes and in them 'convened the People, held their solemn Assemblies, sacrificed to their Gods, delivered their Orations, and proclaimed their Kings'.[13] The city was also a place where the Britons, 'placed all their other Idols about the hot Fountains, so as to make the City appear as the grand Place of Assembly for the Gods of the Pagan World'.[14] It was a city dedicated by a Pythagorean to Apollo, a God whose chief quality, 'was Divination; whose Musick was the Harmony of the Spheres; and to whom the *Britons* . . . paid the highest Honours'.[15]

Even as Wood looked at what was really there he saw through the eyes of a Greek. Hippocrates had said that cities 'that face the East, and are sheltered from the westerly Winds, RESEMBLE the SPRING; . . . the Inhabitants have good Complexions; and the Women, besides being very fruitful, have easy Times'. As Wood observed, Bath faced east, was sheltered from the westerlies, and, receiving the beams of the rising sun must be admitted to be, 'in a SITUATION that RESEMBLES the SPRING; ever Youthful, ever Gay'.[16]

In short, Wood looked at the Bath landscape with the eyes of a man steeped in the antique style of the Renaissance in which verisimilitude had little part. Consequently, in his eyes, Nature itself was antique. Therefore Man, as Nature, was antique. But antique with a difference. Wood enlarged classical antiquity to include pre-Roman Britain and the pre-Hellenic Holy Land. The point of this was to establish connection and continuity between Jewish, Hellenic, and British culture in order to anglicise and puritanise the antique as part of his attempt to overcome his fear of paganism. Wood, as a young, inexperienced and largely self-taught architect building in a new style for a sensual, albeit puritanically developing society, felt threatened by the pagan origins of the Palladian style. Whereas the artists and architects of the High Renaissance, influenced by Ficino, had achieved a relaxed synthesis of antique form and Christian content, Wood was an architectural late starter, a provincial and

13. Ibid., p. 48.
14. Ibid., p. 57.
15. Ibid., p. 53.
16. Ibid., pp. 56–7.

puritanical Briton, who continued to be plagued by Christian doubts about pagan forms similar to those of the proto-Renaissance. It was the observation of attempts to resolve these doubts which led Panofsky to formulate the 'principle of disjunction'. This principle claims that, 'wherever in the high and later Middle Ages a work of art borrows its form from a classical model, this form is almost invariably invested with a non-classical, normally Christian, significance'.[17] The principle is equally true for Wood in the eighteenth century. It is my contention that, in consciously seeking to reconcile paganism and puritanism, Wood opened up to his secular art emotional spheres which had hitherto been the preserve of religious worship and transformed his buildings in a secular 'sink of iniquity' into symbols of religious and social harmony. His building projects are polemic signs adapted from the antique to indicate a social and religious utopia at odds with the society in which he lived and worked. Unfortunately for Wood it was a utopia unlikely to be achieved because the increasing strength and diversification of the agrarian and commercial capitalism (in which he was such an active and activating agent) was destroying, in its ideal form, what he set out to build.

Evidence for this assertion about the polemic nature of Wood's architecture is set out in his first book published in 1741. It was entitled, *The Origin of Building: or, the Plagiarism of the Heathens Detected* and contained,

> *An* ACCOUNT *of the* RISE and PROGRESS of ARCHITECTURE, *from the Creation of the World to the Death of King* Solomon*; and of its Advancement in* Asia, Egypt, Greece, Italy, *and* Britain, *'till it arriv'd to its highest Perfection.* WHEREIN *the Principles of* Architecture, *the proper* Orders *of* Columns, *the* Forms and Proportions *of* Temples, Basilicas, Churches, *and other celebrated* Edifices, *as well Antient as Modern, are Explained, and Demonstrated to have their Rise from the Works of the Jews, and not* Greecians, *as suggested by* Pagan Writers, *and their* Followers.[18]

In the body of the book Wood argued that beauty in building and classical architecture were brought into the world at God's command with the building of the Tabernacle. God *was* the Divine Architect. He worked only with 'perfect harmony, and the most delightful proportion'. Above all others he preferred and expressed himself in the circular form. Since, in his *Essay on Bath*, Wood also em-

---

17. Erwin Panofsky, *Renaissance and Renascences in Western Art*, London, 1970, p. 84.
18. Advertisement for *The Origin of Building: or, The Plagiarism of the Heathens Detected*, London and Bath, 1741, in *A Description of the Exchange at Bristol*, Bath, 1745, p. 37.

phasised the importance of circles and circular movement in the Bladud/Pythagorean heliocentric system and in the construction of the Druidical university at Stanton Drew, the threefold and unifying symbolism of the circle should be plain. It was Jewish and, thereby, Christian first, then British and Greek; the polemic sign of God, and, therefore, of absolute beauty; of absolute beauty, and, therefore, of God. In this manner Wood re-synthesised for himself antique form and Christian content and freed himself from threatening pagan associations. In doing so he released his creative genius to incorporate religious polemic signs in every building he designed.

God as absolute beauty was unknowable except through Man as made by God in his own image. But this was sufficient for Wood, who considered Man a good starting-point from which to move towards a comprehension of God. He wrote,

> In the works of the Divine Architect of all things, we find nothing but perfect figures, consisting of the utmost *Regularity*, the sweetest *Harmony*, and the most delightful *Proportion*: And as his works universally tend to a circular form, and are as universally constituted of three different principal parts, so those three parts generally carry with them, in the whole, and severally, the properties of *Use, Strength, and Beauty*; to illustrate which, the figure of a Man, created in the image of GOD, is the most notable example.
>
> The parts of Man are mostly circular; and of the infinite number with which he is composed, there is not one superfluous, or that do not answer some particular use, conducive to his existence.
>
> Man consists of three principal parts, namely, the head, the trunk, and the limbs; all the parts, in their utmost extent, are comprehended in a square, or in a circle; and so exact is the mechanism of his whole structure, that all the parts mutually assist each other, and contribute to the *Strength* of the whole.
>
> Man is a complete figure, and the perfection of order.[19]

Man so comprehended was God. Thus Wood's architecture, which can be thought of as a re-creative imitation of nature and of Man, was also a re-creative imitation of God. The symbolic representation of this idea of the omniscience, essence, and beauty of God, and of his unity with Man as his most perfect work embodying order, proportion and harmony, is the Vitruvian figure referred to by Wood in the previous extract. This is a naked man, arms and legs diagonally outstretched with the points of his feet and hands touching the circumference of a circle and the perimeter of a square. Palladio's religious architecture derived from this concept and he employed abstracted versions of the Vitruvian figure in their construction. Wood, a disciple of Palladio, also worked with the concept

---

19. *Origin*, p. 71.

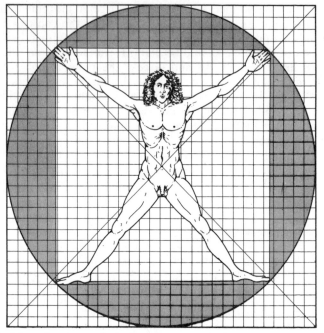

Fig. 2a Vitruvian figure, from Cesariano's edition of Vitruvius (Como, 1521)

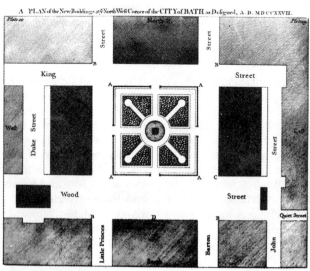

Fig. 2b Queen Square, Bath; from Wood's *Essay towards a Description of Bath* (1765)

and used versions of the Vitruvian figure as polemic signs in his secular architecture. (cf. Figures 2a and 2b for Wood's use of the figure).

Before we explore Wood's use of the circle and of the Vitruvian figure as polemic signs in his building, two other aspects of the Judaeo-Christian content he gave to antique forms must be described. They concern windows and the principal orders of columns. Windows were Tabernacles. For example, Wood described the windows in Belcomb Brook Villa as a model of the 'Octostyle Monopterick Temple of *Delphos*', and those in Titanbarrow Logia as 'dressed so as to become compleat Tabernacles'.[20] We are already acquainted with the significance of the Jewish Tabernacle in his account of the origin of building. It appears likely that Tabernacle windows acted as polemic signs pointing to God as the Divine Architect and served to remind Wood himself of his denial of the pagan origins of antique forms. Such necessarily repeated reminders suggest a continuing uncertainty and tension. Wood's views about the orders of columns are more fully documented. The evidence shows the complexity of their symbolism, while the fact that he published a third book solely on columns indicates the importance he attached to it. The principal orders, Doric, Ionic, and Corinthian, had a threefold symbolism. First, they represented Nature in general and trees in particular; all pillars were imitation trees. Thus, when describing the Corinthian order at Titanbarrow Logia, Wood wrote,

> And all the mouldings and sofits in the whole front, proper to be carved, are to be fully enriched, that nothing may be wanted to decorate the order, which, as it represents nature in all her bloom, requires the greatest profusion of ornament to embellish it that can be put together with propriety and elegance.[21]

Secondly, the three orders were, 'the most lively Symbols of the Robust Man, of the Grave Matron, and of the Sprightly young Girl'.[22] Consequently, the north side of Queen Square, built in the Corinthian order and symbolising a sprightly young girl as well as Nature in all her springlike glory, is described by Wood as soaring above the other buildings with a sprightliness which gives it the elegance and grandeur of a palace. And this in a city itself likened by Wood to spring, youthfulness and gaiety. So to the third symbolic meaning of the orders of columns which flows only from the fusion of all three orders considered as a total re-creative imitation of Man made in God's image. When the three orders are placed upon one

---

20. Wood, *Essay,* p. 238.
21. Ibid., p. 240.
22. John Wood, *A Dissertation Upon the Orders of Columns,* London, 1750, p. 27.

another, Wood wrote, 'a Harmony will, in many Cases attend the Composition beyond any Thing that can be produced by Columns of unequal Altitudes sustaining one another'. However, by making the shafts of the columns of each order of one and the same diameter at bottom

> the Delicacy and Stateliness of one entire Column above the other
> becomes still more Conspicuous. For as the Orders advance towards
> Virginal Beauty and Elegance, the Columns increase in their
> Altitude, and thereby one Order receives a Majesty above the other,
> even in Miniature upon Paper, which words can scarely describe.[23]

One could almost imagine the impossible and believe that Wood had not only seen Botticelli's *The Birth of Venus* and equated Venus with the Corinthian order, but also understood Botticelli's portrayal of divine or transcendent love. Certainly no one who looks at Wood's Bath knowing what Wood tried so desperately to say can ever again look at the orders of columns and see merely pillars – he should at least see Venus or the Three Graces, and pretend he can see God.

So, what are we to make of Wood as he worked to assemble his contribution to Bath as a total polemic sign consisting of circles, squares, Vitruvian figures, Tabernacle windows, the orders of columns, all expressed harmoniously according to the idea of unity in diversity, of three in one, and built in and for a market economy? Principally, Wood contrived to put a frame rather like a proscenium arch around the urban environment of civil society with the purpose of enhancing Man's awareness of himself as made in God's image, and, thereby, his awareness of God.

Look first at the plan for Queen Square (Figure 2b). This square was a novelty in Bath; it let far more light and air into its surrounding houses than reached those in Chandos Court or Beaufort Square, or those in the courts of early eighteenth-century Edinburgh. But the enlargement of the space enclosed does not alter the fact that what Wood planned was an enclosure and not a street or an isolated block of houses. Further, all the surrounding houses were to face into the central area of this enclosure which was designed as a perfect square and intended to be perfectly level. At the centre of the square was to be a perfect circle radiating four diagonals, each ending in smaller circles. The whole geometrical design looks like an abstract Vitruvian figure. This visual impression should be borne in mind when one reads what Wood wrote about the purpose of the enclosure, which he persisted with in spite of the heavy expense involved. He wrote,

23. Ibid.

I preferred an inclosed Square to an open one, to make this as useful as possible: For the Intention of a Square in a City is for People to assemble together; and the Spot whereon they meet, ought to be separated from the Ground common to Men and Beasts, and even to Mankind in General, if Decency and good order are necessary to be observed in such Places of Assembly; of which, I think, there can be no doubt.[24]

Clearly, Wood intended the enclosure as an environmental determinant of good order. It was to be a place in which a chosen few would be able to assemble apart from the bustle of every day things, the animal kingdom, and the generality of men – apart, that is, from civil society. As these few contemplated the north side of the square their spirits would soar in the manner already described. Nature, except in the shape of a green turf and formal shrubs, was expressly excluded. There were to be no forest trees in the square, only low stone walls and espaliers of elm and lime. The fact that the exquisite chapel dedicated to the Virgin Mary and built in the Doric order as part of the whole development scheme attracted a very high demand for building sites in the neighbourhood, suggests that many of his customers, even in the midst of iniquity, fancied the form, if not the substance of his own social and religious beliefs.

When Wood began his next development in the Parades in 1739 he turned the square inside out, and thus the houses of the Grand and South Parades and of the South Parade parallel with it became the central square form, while the associated places of assembly were opened up to the surrounding countryside. Nevertheless, his main concern was to create paved open areas for the practice of public walking and talking, activities which distinguish men from beasts. He hoped to render these activities more congenial in the South Parade by letting in the winter sunshine and developing the open space as a forum. For St James' Triangle, the open space in front of the Grand Parade, he designed a formal garden in the shape of a Vitruvian figure. As in Queen Square this open space was important since, while he thought of the houses on the Grand Parade as outward looking, he also intended that they should be viewed from *across* that formal garden. In this way Nature, except in its antique and formal shape, was still kept at a safe distance and provided only a subdued background to his man-centred buildings. Moreover, whatever aesthetic appeal Nature had was derived from its antique and religious associations. The principal natural feature to be seen from the Grand Parade was Solsbury Hill. In Wood's mythology this had been the site of the Temple of Apollo. He wrote,

24. Wood, *Essay*, p. 345.

If those Works had still existed; their Tremendous Look, from the *Grand Parade*, must have inspired Mankind with a Religious Awe as often as they should consider that the Great God of Heaven and Earth was Adored by them'.[25]

It is in the design of his third great work, the Circus, that Wood gave fullest expression to the ideas he published in 1741. He planned the Circus as two perfect circles, one inside the other. The outer circle of buildings is 318 feet in diameter, which is virtually identical with the present circumference of the chalk wall at Stonehenge, which measures 320 feet from crest to crest, and with the north-south dimension of Queen Square which is 316 feet. Wood's design also incorporated a threefold expression of his idea of the trinity and of unity in diversity; he cut the outer of the two circles into three equal segments, made three approaches to the centre circle, and piled the three principal orders of columns one on top of the other. This piling of the orders had the further symbolic meaning already described. Combining virginal beauty, elegance, and altitude they generated a majesty beyond words. Since a circle of buildings throws the eye more towards the centre and seems to enclose the space within more effectively than a square of buildings, so the Circus, enclosing a smaller area than Queen Square, was even more inward looking than it. Moreover, the Circus was built without any incline on a level ledge cut into the hillside. It was also designed to be totally devoid of natural vegetation. Only its southernmost entrance let in the sun and a distant view of Beechen Cliff. It was designed as pure space enclosed by three equal segments of a perfect circle. Since, as I have argued, Wood's architecture sprang from tension involving a sense of the awfulness and omniscience of God, which he infused into the antique form with which he worked, this austerity of the Circus and the deliberate exclusion of forest trees and of all nature is an integral part of the Circus as a total polemic sign. In designing the Circus Wood was not concerned to unite town and country or to plan towns; rather, in the midst of the corruption of civil society and in its interest, he worked to glorify God by writing *The Whole Duty of Man* in stone. Subsequently his son financed it with the help of loans from local Quakers who had close ties with the West Indian slave and sugar trades.[26] Thus, Wood's utopia, like Marx's capital, came into the world, 'soiled with mire from top to toe, and oozing blood from every pore'.[27]

25. Ibid., p. 351.
26. See mortgages in Wood Box, Guildhall Archives, Bath, especially Indentures, 10 October 1771 and 11 January 1779.
27. Karl Marx, *Capital*, 2 vols., London, 1962, II, 843.

Other historians have offered different explanations of Wood's Bath; for, with the aid of a rather naive deterministic biographical approach to history, which emphasises simple causal relationships between environment and action, it is possible to explain Wood's achievement in terms of the existence and influence of a style. Such 'stylistic' explanations are generally made with one eye firmly on the linear history of architecture and town planning. They are sometimes adequate for their purpose. However, I have emphasised that Wood's creative responses to his circumstances were atypical. Atypical responses cannot be explained by general causes. Objective conditions such as the existence and character of agrarian capitalism and its ideology, the demands of a wealthy clientele, the nature of land law and the structure of landownership, the developing puritanism of society, the existence of a style and the availability of technology, the enduring character of Whig patronage, and the circumstances of personal biography can set the boundaries of objective possibilities and shape conditions for creativity. They can neither determine nor explain its form; there were at least ten architect/builders in early eighteenth-century Bath, but only one John Wood. And therein lies a deal of the difficulty we have in attempting to see Bath as Wood saw it and meant it. His finished works do not obviously spring, soar, or uplift; indeed, one might well question whether strictly classical architectural forms could ever do so. Furthermore, few of Wood's customers in civil society, then or since, had enough grasp of the language of his polemic signs to enable them to read these appearances into his buildings and to grasp his message. Writing in 1749 Wood seemed to have understood this himself. Following a devoted and detailed description of the three country houses he had built he wrote,

> These modern Instances shewing us in Miniature how happily *Bath* is situated for the execution of beautiful Works in Architecture; let the contiguous Building of the City now Demonstrate the Great Regard that hath been lately shewn to display the Free Stone of the Country to as much Advantage as can be well expected in a Place where the Houses, in general, are applied to such Uses as Bring them down almost to the Rank of common Inns.[28]

If this was the view of the author of many of them it is little wonder that while many people could see a generalised beauty in Bath, particularly when the city sparkled white on a clear spring morning, most missed the point of Wood's Bath. Smollet, himself a moralist, nevertheless made his Matthew Bramble dismiss the Circus as 'a pretty bauble; contrived for shew' and let his Lydia Melford, a

---

28. Wood, *Essay*, p. 240.

lovesick modern miss, delight in it as a sumptuous palace in an earthly paradise,[29] a view endorsed in the twentieth century by the doyen of English architectural historians, Sir John Summerson, who finds it, 'quaintly beautiful – as if some simple-minded community had taken over an antique monument and neatly adapted it as a residence'.[30]

But something of Wood's utopian vision forces itself upon us, for, although we may look at Wood's Bath without a knowledge of his polemic signs, the dynamic aesthetic quality they imparted to his works gives them strength to speak for themselves. Naturally the context in which they speak is different. Wood's building influenced the designs of his contemporaries and successors, Palladians all. Since, however, they were less tortured than he about the pagan origins of their style and were more in tune with the vagaries of the market, they built in a lighter vein. Their buildings act as foils to his. Then they appear to us scarred by our own and Victorian vandalism, distorted by the filter of romantic nature, and encroached upon by forest trees and motor cars. Nevertheless, the effect of his polemic signs is to force us to consider seriously his views about the way in which urban men ought to live – views which Burley Griffin's successors have ignored to Canberra's cost. And views which Bath itself is fast forgetting. The polemic signs of Wood's twentieth-century successors in Bath, Bath City Council, city architects, development companies, and city planners point only to the anomie of sub-urban living and the wasteland of the market. Concern for absolute property, whether corporate or private, whether of the retail grocer or of the car owner dominates decision making. John Locke, too, is still with us, as, indeed, he was with John Wood. The difference is that John Wood created the Circus; his twentieth-century successors merely build. Even the dream of utopia eludes them.

29. Tobias Smollet, *The Expedition of Humphry Clinker,* ed. L. M. Knapp, London, 1972, pp. 35, 39.
30. Summerson, *Architecture,* p. 235.

Chapter 8

SCIENCE, PROVINCIAL CULTURE AND PUBLIC OPINION IN ENLIGHTENMENT ENGLAND

R. Porter

[*British Journal for Eighteenth-Century Studies*, 3 (1980)]

Roy Porter has been one of the most prolific historians writing on eighteenth-century England during the last decade or so, and has been particularly concerned to place developments in science and medicine in their social context. In this thought-provoking article he challenges the notion that eighteenth-century science was driven by the utilitarian requirements of industrialization, arguing instead that it was one element in a broader Enlightenment culture, and was motivated by the pursuit of fashion and status rather than economic efficiency. Of especial interest to readers of this volume is the way the author portrays science as part and parcel of the wider provincial 'urban renaissance', explored here in the essays of Alan Everitt, Ronald Neale, and Peter Borsay. However, Porter argues that this cultural resurgence was highly derivative, slavishly imitating London tastes and values. Does he overstate the influence of the metropolis, perhaps a little too influenced in his conclusions by the overtly cosmopolitan resort of Bath, and too little by the more regionally orientated county towns and provincial capitals? The works of Alan Everitt, John Money and, more recently, Jonathan Barry, all emphasize the local input and context of eighteenth-century urban culture.

1. INTRODUCTION

Why did science become an important feature of provincial life in eighteenth century England? As recently as twenty years ago, this might have seemed a non-question. Science was widely believed to have sunk into torpor between the age of Newton and the nineteenth century triumphs of Davy and Dalton, Faraday and Darwin. Popular culture was little studied, for within the Namierite vision of politics 'the stage' was reserved for 'the great actors', with the people 'offstage, supernumeraries who are doubtless to be occasionally addressed, and relied upon for shouts and choruses'.[1] And the provinces were ignored by a historiography whose field of vision extended little further than London and aristocratic estates.

Fortunately these neglected terrains are now coming under cultivation. The work of Read, Chalklin and Borsay in particular has directed attention to 'the rise of the provinces' as part of a major 'English urban renaissance' which had massive consequences *before* the age of heavy industrialization.[2] In a parallel trend, historians have also been recently discovering how sub-gentry strata of society participated far more, and exerted a much greater voice, in Georgian public life than previously assumed. Nicholas Rogers, E. P. Thompson, and George Rudé above all have stressed the authentic vitality of 'plebeian' protest, demonstrating how, in political and economic confrontations like elections, riots and strikes, they could assert considerable negotiating power within the traditional legitimations of a moral economy.[3] Lower class fractiousness forced upon their betters a degree of reciprocity – the mercy of pardons in the theatre of the law, the license to revel in a traditional festive calendar,[4] the enjoyment of common rights. John Brewer and John Money[5] have traced the rise of petit bourgeois clubs, and friendly and debating societies, consolidating surges of political radicalism whipped up by the Wilkite movement. And, perhaps above all,

1. The characterization is that of R. J. White, *The Age of George III* (London, 1968), 25–26. For Namier's own words, see the Preface to *The Structure of Politics at the Accession of George III* (London, 1929).
2. D. Read, *The English Provinces, c. 1760–1960* (London, 1964); C. W. Chalklin, *The Provincial Towns of Georgian England* (London, 1974); P. Borsay, 'The English urban renaissance: the development of provincial urban culture', *Social History*, ii (1977), 581–603.
3. N. Rogers, 'Aristocratic clientage, trade and independency: Popular politics in pre-radical Westminster', *Past and present*, no. 61 (1973), 70–106; G. Rudé, *Wilkes and Liberty* (Oxford, 1962); *The Crowd in History* (New York, 1964); *Paris and London in the Eighteenth Century* (London, 1970); E. P. Thompson, 'Eighteenth century English society : class struggle without class?', *Social History*, iii (1978), 133–65; 'The moral economy of the English crowd in the eighteenth century', *Past and present*, no. 50 (1971), 76–136; *The Making of the English Working Class* (Harmondsworth, 1968); 'Patrician society, plebeian culture', *Journal of Social History*, vii (1974), 382–405.
4. For battles over plebeian sports, see R. W. Malcolmson, *Popular Recreations in English Society, 1700–1850* (Cambridge, 1973).
5. J. Brewer, *Party Ideology and Popular Politics at the Accession of George III* (Cambridge, 1976); J. Money, *Experience and Identity: Birmingham and the West Midlands, 1760–1800* (Manchester, 1977).

J. H. Plumb has been exploring the emergence of a consumer voice, exercised via the power of the pocket, in context of the extension of the commercial market.[6]

And, thirdly, since the 1960s, scholarship has been focussing for the first time on a ferment of scientific activity in eighteenth century England. This has been discovered in those very two areas I have been discussing so far. On the one hand, thanks to the researches of Musson and Robinson, Schofield, Thackray and Shapin, and others, we now know far more about the expansion of science within the provinces. Gentlemen's clubs arose in market towns like Spalding in the first half of the century, leading later to the rural science associated with agricultural societies, like the 'Bath and West', which in turn gave a leg-up to the Royal Institution. And at a slightly later date, major urban growth encouraged the formation both of *ad hoc* groupings of scientists, manufacturers, medical men, dissenters, as in the Lunar Society, and also the first properly-constituted public bodies such as the Literary and Philosophical Societies, the most famous of which became the Manchester, founded in 1781.[7]

And, on the other hand, science became much more widely diffused through Georgian society *via* the commercialization of leisure, the entrepreneurship of knowledge, and the rise of professional communications popularizers. Big markets developed for scientific text-books, scientific poetry[8] and scientific encyclopaedias,[9] for science books directed at ladies,[10] and others for children.[11]

6. J. H. Plumb, *The Commercialization of Leisure in Eighteenth Century England* (Reading, 1973); 'The public, literature and the arts in the eighteenth century', in P. Fritz and D. Williams (eds.), *The Triumph of Culture* (Toronto, 1972); *The Pursuit of Happiness* (New Haven, 1977); 'The new world of children in eighteenth century England', *Past and present*, no. 67 (1975), 65–95; 'Political man', in J. L. Clifford (ed.), *Man versus Society in Eighteenth Century Britain* (Cambridge, 1968), 1–22, esp. p. 1.

7. A. E. Musson and E. Robinson, *Science and Technology in the Industrial Revolution* (Manchester, 1969); R. E. Schofield, *The Lunar Society of Birmingham* (Oxford, 1963); S. Shapin and A. W. Thackray, 'Prosopography as a research tool in history of science: the British scientific community 1700–1900', *History of Science*, xii (1974), 1–28, which contains a good further bibliography. M. Berman, 'The early years of the Royal Institution, 1799–1810, a re-evaluation', *Science Studies*, ii (1972), 205–40.

8. W. P. Jones, *The Rhetoric of Science* (London, 1966); M. H. Nicolson, *Mountain Gloom and Mountain Glory* (Ithaca, N.Y., 1959); *idem, Newton demands the Muse* (Princeton, N.J., 1946).

9. A. Hughes, 'Science in English encyclopaedias 1704–1875', *Annals of Science*, vii (1951), 340–70; viii (1952), 323–67; ix (1953), 233–64.

10. G. D. Meyer, *The Scientific Lady in England 1650–1760* (Berkeley, 1955). J. R. Millburn, *Benjamin Martin, Author, Instrument maker, and 'Country Showman'* (Leyden, 1976), 71–73.

11. See Plumb, 'The new world of children' (ref. 6).

Museums of scientific apparatus and natural history were formed. Owning scientific instruments or displaying natural history cabinets became parts of a gentleman's equipage. Gentlemanly education was now expected to contain some rational scientific and medical knowledge.

Provincial and popularized science were interwoven by the new figure of the scientific lecturer.[12] Starting initially with the experimental performances of Jurin, Hauksbee, Whiston, Desaguliers, Ditton, and others in London early in the century, lecturers then took to the roads, spreading out with their apparatus and demonstrations into the provinces. James Jurin lectured in Newcastle in 1710. William Whiston in Bristol in 1724. James Ferguson – a typical Scot who had taken the high road South to London and become a foremost text-book populariser of science – lectured in Bath and Bristol in the 1760s and 1770s. Benjamin Martin, James Arden, Henry Moyes, John Warltire, and others brought science to the Western counties. By the end of the century few towns of any significance had not been milked by itinerant lecturers, offering courses of six, a dozen, or more, lectures over a period of a few weeks, supplementing their income meanwhile by selling copies of their books and apparatus, offering medical nostrums, performing land surveys, or giving private tuition.

2. THE PROBLEM

Where before there was ignorance, something like an orthodoxy has now sprung up. The answer commonly given to my original question, is that science emerged as an important function in the regions

---

12. For intinerant lecturers see F. W. Gibbs, 'Itinerant lecturers in natural philosophy', *Ambix*, vi (1960), 111–17; Musson and Robinson, op.cit., (ref. 7), which deals thematically with the movement of science from London to the provinces; M. Rowbottom, 'The teaching of experimental philosophy in England, 1700–1730', *Actes du XIe Congrès International d'Histoire des Sciences*, iv (Warsaw, 1968), 46–53; I. Inkster, 'A note on itinerant scientific lecturers, 1790–1850', *Annals of Science*, xxv (1978), 253–6; F. J. G. Robinson, 'A philosophic war: an episode in eighteenth century scientific lecturing in North East England', *The Archaeological and Antiquarian Society of Durham and Northumberland*, no. ii (1970), 101–118; P. J. Wallis, 'British philomaths – mid eighteenth century and earlier', *Centaurus*, xvii (1973), 301–14; O. Pedersen, 'The philomaths of eighteenth century England', *Centaurus* viii (1963), 238–62. Generally helpful is ch. VII of T. Kelly, *A History of Adult Education in Great Britain* (Liverpool, 1962). For particular lecturers see Millburn, op. cit. (ref. 10), on Martin, and E. Henderson, *Life of James Ferguson* (Edinburgh, 1867).

because the provinces were the cradle of 'modernization' and 'industrialization'. Provincial science is thereby seen as a function of the emergence of industrial society. Thus Schofield has argued that science was the expression of the entirely new world of regional industrialization:

> The association of Lunar members and their activities shows a conscious shaping of their world and a deliberate application to solve the problems of industrializing England that fits ill the picture of classic harmony and Augustan balance which is, somehow, at the same time also regarded as characteristic of eighteenth-century England. Polite society, by state and custom established, might still be concerned with land and title, they might still spend their time disputing in an unrepresentative Parliament, discussing literature and the arts in London coffee shops, and drinking and gambling at Whites; but the world they knew was a shadow. Another society, in which position was determined by an ungenteel success, was creating a different world more to its liking. The French War and political repression delayed the formal substitution of new for old, but it was the new society that provided power to win the war, it was their world that they stabilized. The Lunar Society represents this 'other society' pushing for place.[13]

But this 'two nations' account is inadequate in two ways. Firstly, it is indiscriminate. Science undoubtedly 'emerged'. But so did lots of other things, including the provincial theatre, music-hall, water-colours, Dissent, politics, sport, quackery, Methodism. In many towns, quacks, conjurors and showmen like Katterfelto competed for audiences against scientific lecturers, and Money has noted that 'the casual spectator and the partially informed can be forgiven if they failed to differentiate' between them.[14] In some places, scientific popularization, societies and even research throve; in some, it had a halting life; elsewhere, hardly any at all. Why the differen-

---

13. Schofield, op.cit. (ref. 7), 440.
14. Money, op. cit. (ref. 5) 130, 131, 152. 140. Money shows the intimate relations in the West Midlands between the appeal of showman-quacks and rising Freemasonry, both of which surface in Gustavus Katterfelto: p. 40: 'Free-mason, quasi-scientific wonder-worker and quack, who came to England from Prussia in 1782 and rapidly became notorious as an astronomer, balloon aviator, and lecturer on the "Philosophical, Mathematical, Optical, Magnetical, Electrical, Physical, Chemical, Pneumatic, Hydraulic, Hydrostatic, Proetic, Stenographic, Blaencical, and Caprimantic Arts". Katterfelto, whose usual repertoire was a shrewdly-judged mixture of genuine chemical and electrical demonstrations and sensational tricks with his "Most Wonderful Solar Microscope and Royal Patent Delineator" and other devices, was a frequent visitor to Birmingham, where he addressed himself particularly to "all the different Clergy and Preachers, Doctors, Gentlemen, Freemasons, and all Religious Persons" ' Cf. A. Temple Patterson, *Radical Leicester: a History of Leicester, 1780–1850* (Leicester, 1954), 6.

tials? And who were the audiences, the enthusiasts for science? Were they the same men, or different, from those who frequented the clubs and taverns, who were the political radicals, who attended Church or Chapel, who owned, or worked in, factories? We need a more discriminating theory than one of 'emergence' – a litmus to reveal the differentials of scientific activity between (in some places) Church and Chapel, entrepreneur and physician, differences in popularity – cooperation? competition? – between the philosophical society, the library, and the stage. Obviously, to grasp this would require exhaustive local research, which has hardly yet begun to be done.[15] But as a hazardous short-cut, one can at least begin to explore these questions through interpretation of the interests and professed motives of those involved.

This is doubly worth doing because – this is my second point – current historiography contains many assumptions about the emergence of provincial science which are at best half-truths. The first of these is the 'two nations' theory: the assumption that science, being a 'modern' and 'progressive' form of knowledge, self-evidently would be patronized by any major industrial town (it being assumed that such towns were inherently 'progressive' as distinct from the dissipated, fashionable Great Wen of London).[16] Hence the issue is reduced to one of relative temporal priorities – was *this* town a leader or a laggard? But aside from begging questions, this view is undercut by the facts. For it is not true that science automatically developed in context of provincial urbanization – witness places like Nottingham, Sunderland, or the slightly special cases of Plymouth and Portsmouth. Neither did science, once established, automatically flourish, as the disappointed hopes of many literary and philosophical societies testify. Hence precisely what functions science was fulfilling within its urban contexts remains a problem.

The second misleading way of contextualizing provincial science lies in placing it within a Whiggish history of the progress of education. In this reading, lit and phils become the prophets of provincial universities, itinerant lecturers the outriders of university extension and the WEA:[17] 'the [lit and phil] Societies were committed first

---

15. Exceptions would include Shapin and Thackray, op.cit. (ref. 7).
16. This contrast is present throughout Schofield, op. cit. (ref. 7), and programmatically in B. Simon, *The Two Nations and the Educational Structure, 1780–1870* (London, 1974), see esp. p. 24ff.
17. For examples of this kind of prolepsis see the otherwise very informative T. Kelly, *A History of Adult Education in Great Britain* (Liverpool, 1962), esp. p. 101f. See also N. Hans, *New Trends in Education in the Eighteenth Century* (London, 1951), 158f., where he discusses the supposed role of eighteenth century provincial scientific societies in disseminating science 'among the masses'. Or J. W. Adamson, *English Education, 1789–1902* (Cambridge, 1930), 40f. Or, in the context of discussing provincial science, E. Pawson, *The Early Industrial*

and foremost to education'.[18] But absorbing the history of science within the history of education begs more questions than it solves, particularly when, the idea of the history of education as un-problematic, unfolding, improvement is itself unquestioned.

The third set of half-true explanations are those which equate the rise of eighteenth century provincial science with the glories of Dis-senting culture.[19] The role of Dissent in the pre-history of the Manchester Lit and Phil, and of Priestley in the Lunar Society, have been rightly high-lighted.[20] Yet once again historians have produced caricatures. Aristotelian Oxbridge Anglicans, indifferent to science, are set over and against progressive, enlightened, tolerant provincial rational Dissenters.[21] Seeing provincial science as a Dissenters' preserve is factually untrue (in places like Bath, Bristol,[22] Derby, and Leeds it was at least as much in the hands of Anglicans: even in Manchester, only three of the founding members of the Lit and Phil were Unitarians). Presenting Anglicans and nonconformist cul-ture as if they were utterly polarized is also a false hypostasis.[23]

The most popular – and explicit – assumption about the roots of provincial science is that it marched forward as a trinity, with in-

Revolution (London, 1979), 181: 'By the last third of the [eighteenth] century, there were evening classes in London and throughout the provinces designed entirely for adult mechanics and craftsmen'. At least with regard to science, this statement is highly dubious. Itinerant lecturers were hardly directing their atten-tion either to mechanics, or to trade education.

18. G. W. Roderick and M. D. Stephens, 'Private enterprise and technical education: the Liverpool Library and Philosophical Society', in *Scientific and Technical Education in Nineteenth Century England* (Newton Abbot, 1972), 134–45, p. 134.

19. A. Raistrick, *Quakers in Science and Industry* (London, 1950); I. Grubb, *Quakerism and Industry before 1800* (London, 1930); E. D. Bebb, *Noncon-formity and Social and Economic Life, 1660–1800* (London, 1935). R. V. Holt, *The Unitarian Contribution to Social Progress in England* (2nd), revised ed., (London, 1952) chs. 2 and 6.

20. H. McLachlan, *Warrington Academy, its history and influence* (Chetham Society, Manchester, 1943), p. 126: the Manchester Lit. and Phil. 'largely owed its foun-dation and its original character indirectly to the influence of' the Warrington Academy.

21. For this kind of view see Schofield, op.cit. (ref. 7), 11; H. McLachlan, *English Education under the Test Acts* (Manchester, 1931); D. M. Turner, *History of Science Teaching in England* (London, 1927); J. W. Ashley-Smith, *The Birth of Modern Education* (London, 1954).

22. M. Neve, 'Science in a commercial city: Bristol 1820–1860', in I. Inkster and J. Morrell (eds.), *Essays in the Social History of British Science 1780–1850* (London, 1980).

23. A. Thackray, 'Natural knowledge in cultural context: the Manchester model', *American Historical Review*, lxxix (1974), 672–709. Thackray shows how many Manchester Dissenting families were seeking to assimilate themselves to Anglican culture. The scientific and mathematical teaching of Dissenters Academies closely resembled that of eighteenth century Cambridge.

dustry and technology, under the banner of Utility.[24] In the words of J. H. Plumb:

> by 1815, every provincial town of importance had its society supported by both the local aristocracy and the local manufacturers . . . No other aspect of English cultural life had such whole-hearted middle class support, because the intention was completely and avowedly utilitarian – the search for useful knowledge which would maintain England's industrial supremacy.[25]

Or, as Christopher Hill has put it, 'scientific advance in the eighteenth century came from the societies established in the Midlands and North of England by craftsmen and industrialists – the Lunar Society of Birmingham, the Manchester Literary and Philosophical Society'.[26]

But the story is once again more complicated than that. It is not even true that by 1815 all important provincial towns had their lit and phils – even places as large as Bristol, Leeds, Sheffield, Norwich, Hull and Birmingham did not. Thus Edward Baines could write in 1817 of Leeds that

> Philosophical researches are not much cultivated in Leeds: still less do literary pursuits engage the attention of its inhabitants. An attempt was made in 1783 to establish a Society for the discussion of literary and moral subjects, but after being continued for several years it was entirely given up.[27]

---

24. This view is the theme of Musson and Robinson, op. cit. (ref. 7); see Schofield, op.cit, (ref. 7), pp. 438–9: the 'Lunar Society might well be called a pilot project or advance guard of the Industrial Revolution'. See also A. and N. Clow, *The Chemical Revolution* (London, 1952), 614: 'Never before in history was there such an advantageous syncretism of pure science and advancing industry as in the Lunar Society'.
25. J. H. Plumb, *England in the Eighteenth Century* (Harmondsworth, 1951), 167. Of course such a view becomes more plausible if one were to interpret 'useful' in the very broad (non industrial-technological) sense in which it was frequently used in the eighteenth century. See Roy Porter, 'The Industrial Revolution and the rise of the science of geology', in M. Teich and R. M. Young (eds.), *Changing Perspectives in the History of Science* (London, 1973), 320–43. The issue as to whether science did in fact aid technology and industry is a separate one, and is hotly debated. For a recent survey see A. Rupert Hall, 'What did the Industrial Revolution in Britain owe to science?', in N. McKendrick (ed.), *Historical Perspectives. Essays in English Thought and Society in Honour of J. H. Plumb* (London, 1974), 129–51, and A. E. Musson (ed.) *Science, Technology and Economic Growth in the Eighteenth Century* (London 1972), esp. pp. 62f.
26. C. Hill, *Reformation to Industrial Revolution* (Harmondsworth, 1978), 242. It is not clear that any component of this statement is true.
27. Quoted in E. Kitson Clark, *The History of 100 Years of Life of the Leeds Philosophical and Literary Society* (Leeds, 1924), 2.

This means the very founding of local scientific institutions is itself not self-evident but a problematic issue. Furthermore, the role of manufacturers – not to mention craftsmen – in such institutions is not so great as it has been taken to be. And also a glimpse at the ideology underpinning such societies, and at their activities, shows far more was at stake than industrially useful knowledge. The very name, '*Literary* and *Philosophical*' should alert us to the fact that, in the founders' minds, there were goals more pressing than technical expertise, industrially applied science, or the training of mechanics.

THE PLACE OF THE ENLIGHTENMENT

My contention is that the reasons why the connexions between provincial urban growth, popular aspirations and the emergence of science are still inadequately understood; and why we lack a differentiated and discriminating history of the rise of science in the provinces, is that historians have too often ignored provincial *consciousness*.[28] The key fact about provincial opinion in the eighteenth century is that – unlike later – it repudiated its own provinciality.[29] Painfully aware that they existed in the shadow of the metropolis, provincials' prime aim was to assimilate metropolitan culture and values. Provincial culture was more imitation than innovation. The *gradus ad Parnassum* from rudeness to refinement was in effect the mental journey from provinciality to London. As was claimed in 1761, two generations back the inhabitants of counties distant from London had been 'a species almost as different from those of the metropolis as the natives of the Cape of Good Hope'. Now at least the more 'respectable' provincials might be improved by the percolation of London styles and *mores*: 'the several great cities, and we might add many poor county towns, seem to be universally inspired with an ambition of becoming the little *Londons* of the part of the kingdom wherein they are situated'.[30] No wonder a Newcastle address to the metropolitan rulers had stated, 'Our eyes are upon you; we . . . imitate your fashions, good and evil, and from you we fetch

28. The major exception to this generalization is the work of Steven Shapin. See his 'The social uses of science', in G. S. Rousseau and Roy Porter, *The Ferment of Knowledge* (Cambridge, 1980).
29. Unlike in the nineteenth century: for which see Read, op.cit. (ref. 2).
30. Quoted in Read, op.cit. (ref. 2), 18–19.

and frame our customs'.[31] The first sentence – full of ambiguous resonance – of the *Strangers' Guide and Assistant to Bath* (1773) runs, 'The City of BATH is situated in the North East part of the county of Somerset, upon the River AVON, about 107 miles from London'.

To some degree provincial towns took the London air because – as already indicated – they were colonized by London impresarios. But the impulse chiefly came from the pacesetters of the provincial community aping metropolitan institutions and values. Provincial towns named their pleasure gardens Ranelagh and Vauxhall. Theatres were called Drury Lane. John Wood the Elder laid out grounds in Bath 'in imitation of the Ring, in Hyde Park, near London'.[32] Burghers adopted Handel as the staple of regional musical life hard on his oratorio triumphs in London.[33] The citizens of Edinburgh took elocution lessons from the Irish-born Thomas Sheridan to smooth away their Scotticisms and mimic the metropolis.[34] Edinburgh, Bath, Cheltenham and Bristol all built new towns imitating metropolitan neo-classicism and abandoning vernacular architecture and materials.[35] Reading societies and clubs were set up early in the century in market towns like Peterborough and Boston to imbibe *The Spectator*. Allan Ramsay's Easy Club in Edinburgh sold Augustan taste to the Scots. Always the eye was on the capital. 'The theatrical performances here,' announced the *Bristol Guide* of 1801, 'are little (if any) inferior to those in London'.[36] 'The Bath theatre,' wrote the Revd John Nightingale in 1819, 'is little inferior, in elegance and attraction, to those of the metropolis'.[37] Even the Bath Penitentiary for Reformed Prostitutes modelled itself proudly on the London original.

In a word, provincial elites were attempting to bring Enlightenment to their own doorsteps. It is my contention that understanding

---

31. Quoted in P. Clark and P. Slack, *English Towns in Transition*, 1500–1700 (London, 1976), 156.
32. J. Wood, *An Essay towards a Description of Bath*, 2 vols (2nd ed. London, 1749), ii, 439–40.
33. E. D. Mackerness, *A Social History of English Music* (London, 1964), ch. iii; For music in Leicestershire, see J. Simmons, *Leicester Past and Present*, i (London, 1974), 120; for Derbyshire see S. Taylor, 'Musical life in Derby in the 18th and 19th centuries', *Journal of the Derbyshire Archaeological and Natural History Society*, n. s., vol. xx (1947), 1–54.
34. For some of the tensions involved in this selling a birthright for a mess of pottage, see D. Daiches, *The Paradox of Scottish Culture* (London, 1964); D. Craig, *Scottish Literature and the Scottish People, 1680–1830* (London, 1961).
35. *Cf.* Chalklin, op. cit. (ref. 2); A. J. Youngson, *The Making of Classical Edinburgh, 1750–1840* (Edinburgh, 1966).
36. *The Bristol Guide* (Bristol, 1801), 122.
37. Rev. J. Nightingale, *The Beauties of England and Wales*, vol. xiii (London, 1813), 427.

provincial Enlightenment aspirations will put provincial science's development in perspective. But the Enlightenment itself is still a black hole in English historiography. Because, despite the recent advances in historiography which I have been discussing, the Enlightenment in England has continued to suffer almost total neglect.[38] This is partly because general Enlightenment historians such as Peter Gay insist on the essential unity of the Enlightenment, which is then defined largely in terms of the French experience in the age of Voltaire.[39] The Enlightenment is thus seen as a systematic, comprehensive, radical – even – revolutionary critique of the roots of the *ancien régime*, spearheaded by a militant secularism whose motto was *écraser l'infâme*.[40] Clearly, eighteenth century England did not wage battles such as these. But English elites – the equivalents of the philosophes – did not need to. They lived in a state which, as the French philosophes applauded, already embodied the Enlightenment in its constitutionality, representative government, freedom of person, religion, property and speech. Hence, English Enlightenment priorities – nicely dubbed by Henry May, 'The Moderate Enlightenment'[41] – focussed chiefly upon individual and voluntary-group action within established society. Educated and propertied elites were most concerned to establish the validity of egoistic individualism, the liberty to improve one's lot and pursue happiness through knowledge, industry, enterprise, the free use of capital, science, skill. But desiring to secure the peaceful enjoyment of these, they were also committed to public harmony and order, a stability which would partly flow from individual progress, and which partly was to be imposed by the exercise of rationality, moderation, politeness and humanitarianism. For many provincials, science could play a large part in both of these quests.

To provincial eyes, Enlightenment values offered a leg-up from rusticity, associated with barbarity and riot, towards metropolitan – indeed, cosmopolitan – urbanity. Provincials themselves came to rebel against the stigmas of rusticity, parading as lords of taste and fashion over their own rural hinterland. Enlightenment moral philosophy taught that man was a rational being, born for thought, discourse, friendly sociability, decency and good order. To be civil and urbane, men must live in cities and towns. The country was for

---

38. One exception is J. Redwood, *Reason, Ridicule and Religion: The English Enlightenment 1660–1750* (London, 1976).
39. P. J. Gay, *The Enlightenment: an Interpretation*, 2 vols (London, 1967–70).
40. For lengthier discussion of Enlightenment historiography see Roy Porter, 'The English Enlightenment', in Roy Porter and Mikulas Teich, *The Enlightenment in National Context* (Cambridge, 1981).
41. H. May, *The Enlightenment in America* (New York, 1976).

the beasts, but the town was for men.[42] Only in towns could man achieve taste, elegance, society, knowledge, science. Towns were foci of improvement and light; beyond them was superstition, disorder, and what Marx was later to dub the 'idiocy of rural life'.

Enlightened aspirations then demanded that rustic behaviour in towns must be elevated into a refined London tone. Looking back in 1801 on the development of Bath, Richard Warner bemoaned that 'the sports which sufficiently satisfied our ancestors of the sixteenth and seventeenth centuries' had been,

> the pranks of mountebanks, the feats of jugglers, tumblers, and dancers, the jests of itinerant *mimes* or mummers, and the dangerous amusement of the quintane, diversified occasionally by the pageant and the masque, or the *elegant* pastime of bull-baiting, cock-fighting, cock-scaling, pig-racing, bowling, football, grinning through a horse-collar, and swallowing scalding hot frumenty . . . But as national manners gradually refined, the ideas of elegance were proportionally enlarged, and publick amusements insensibly approximated to the taste and splendour which they at present exhibit; balls, plays, and cards, usurping the place of those rude athletick sports, or gross sensual amusements, to which the hours of vacancy had before been devoted. This improvement in manners and opinions produced the erection of the first Assembly-Room in Bath in the year 1708.[43]

In this context, provincials embraced Enlightenment values because they spelt out culture. And – I shall claim – it was because science

42. These beliefs were well articulated by John Wood the Elder, the Bath architect, for which see Ron Neale, 'Society, belief and the building of Bath, 1700–1793', in (ed.), C. W. Chalklin and M. A. Havinden, *Rural Change and Urban Growth, 1500–1800* (London, 1974), 252–80. For Enlightenment respect for urban culture see C. E. Schorske, 'The idea of the city in European thought, Voltaire to Spengler', in (eds.) O. Handlin and J. Burchard, *The Historian and the City* (Cambridge, Mass., 1966), 95–114. See also R. M. Wiles, 'Provincial culture in early Georgian England' in P. Fritz and D. Williams (eds.), op. cit. (ref. 6), 49–68, and R. Williams, *The Country and the City* (London, 1973).

43. R. Warner, *History of Bath* (Bath, 1801), 349. Compare the similar view in respect of Birmingham expressed by Matthew Boulton (qu. in Money, op. cit. (ref. 5), 90):

> All well regulated states have found it expedient to indulge the people with amusements of some kind of other, and certainly those are most eligible that tend to improve the morals, the manners, or the taste of the people, and at the same time to prevent them from relapsing into the barbarous amusements which prevailed in the neighbourhood in the last century when Birmingham was as remarkable for good forgers and filers as for their bad taste in all their works. Their diversions were bull baitings, cock fightings, boxing matches, and abominable drunkenness with all its train. But now the scene is changed. The people are more polite and civilized, and the taste of their manufactures greatly improved. There is not a town of its size in Europe where mechanism is brought to such perfection, and we have also made considerable progress in some of the liberal arts.

was a branch of *culture*, rather than because it primarily meant industrial utility, or Dissent, or the education of youth or employees, or even the advancement of research, that provincials embraced science. The prominence given to the cultural value of science by its eighteenth century ideologues is too often passed over by historians. But it was overwhelmingly present. Appealing to provincial culture vultures, Benjamin Martin the itinerant lecturer insisted that

> Knowledge is now become a fashionable thing, and philosophy is the science à la mode: hence, to cultivate this study, is only to be in taste, and politeness is an inseparable consequence.[44]

– which perhaps echoes Locke's belief that 'a gentleman must look into [natural philosophy] to fit himself for conversation'.[45]

Indeed the appeal of provincial science through the century was first and foremost not to manufacturers and mechanics, but to gentlemen and ladies[46] and to those who wished snobbishly to ape gentlemanly pursuits and status. This cries out from the popularizing works put out for amateurs and children. Thus Martin's *General Magazine*[47] had as its sub-caption: 'The young gentleman's and lady's philosophy'. Newbery's best-selling *The Newtonian System of Philosophy* was subtitled *Adapted to the capacities of young gentlemen and ladies*, and specifically referred to its readers as 'young gentry'.[48] It is also inferable in the relatively high fees generally charged for lectures by itinerant men of science. A guinea, for a course of half a dozen lectures, was common, or half a crown for a single lecture. Such prices seem to indicate that lecturers expected an audience at the high end of the market. The fact that little evidence survives of really cheap (e.g. 6d) scientific lectures in the eighteenth century suggests that scientific lecturers perhaps did

---

44. Millburn, op. cit. (ref. 10), 44.
45. Locke, quoted in M. L' Espinasse, 'The decline and fall of Restoration science', *Past and Present*, xiv (1958), 71–89, p. 76.
46. See Meyer, op. cit. (ref. 10). Compare this poem by Henry James, 'Addressed to the ladies who attended Mr Booth's lecture', in *Poems on several occasions* (London, 1749), 25–26.
    Thrice happy few! that wisely here attend
    The Voice of Science, and her Cause befriend!
    Let others, heedless of their youthful Prime,
    Squander on empty Joys their fleeting Time.
47. Millburn, op. cit. (ref. 10), 70f. Millburn comments: 'This was not a magazine for artisans and tradesmen. Like his courses of philosophical lectures in the 1740s, it was directed primarily at "the gentry", particularly those who wished to keep up with recent developments in the sciences'.
48. See the unpublished paper by J. Secord, 'Newton in the nursery: Tom Telescope and the philosophy of tops and balls'. Secord notes that later editions of Newbery's children's science books evidently moved down market, in the early nineteenth century. Words like 'young gentlemen and ladies' were abandoned for 'young persons', and lower class people appear in the drawings. My im-

not seek, or get, audiences from below the ranks of the comfortably-off.[49] Certainly, surviving attendance lists from Dr Warwick's Sheffield lectures at the turn of the nineteenth century indicate a high-class clientele of medical men, manufacturers, minor gentry and professional people. Warwick offered his lectures 'at the express solicitation of a Society of Gentlemen'.[50]

This appeal to the gentleman amateur, to the professional man rather than the tradesmen, and to the ethic of politeness, was obviously calculated to enhance the self-respect of provincial elites. As Thomas Henry coaxed in Manchester,

> In proportion as a nation acquires superior degrees of [knowledge] her state of civilization advances

and achieves 'greater refinement'. 'The natural tendency of a cultivation of polite learning is to refine the understanding, humanize the soul, enlarge the field of useful knowledge'. Henry's argument, doubtless to win over Manchester industrialists and merchants to the infant Lit and Phil, concluded that 'a taste for polite literature, and the works of nature and art, is essentially necessary to form the

pression is that most eighteenth century scientific popularization was either appealing to a socially select market, or to those who sought to identify themselves with the same. See P. Oborne, 'Social attitudes in children's literature 1750–1820' (unpublished), who notes how many of the characters appearing in late eighteenth century children's books are titled (e. g., The Duke of Galaxy). James Ferguson's *The Young Gentleman's and Lady's Astronomy* (London, 1768), was couched as a dialogue between Neander and Eudosia. Oborne has noted the prominence of Enlightenment attitudes in this literature – e. g. kindness to animals, or hostility to slavery. Musson and Robinson have shown the concern of Boulton and Watt that the education of their sons should be 'genteel'. Op. cit. (ref. 7) 201.

49. As a yardstick of comparison, the Edinburgh petty-bourgeoisie of the 1820s were prepared to pay 7/6 or 10/6 for lecture courses. Phrenological lectures at that period were offered to working men at 1d or 2d a time. See Steven Shapin, ' "Merchants in philosophy": The politics of an Edinburgh plan for the diffusion of science, 1832–36', in I. Inkster and J. Morrell (eds.), *Essays in the social history of British Science, 1780–1850* (London, 1980).

50. M. Brook, 'Dr Warwick's chemistry lectures and the science audience in Sheffield (1799–1801)', *Annals of Science*, xi (1955), 224–37. Warwick charged two guineas for his course. Brook comments that the audience was 'small, and confined largely to the professional middle class, with some representative of the commercial middle class, and a very strong representation of Dissenters, which was probably due in part only to the denominational allegiance they shared with the lecturer'.

It is possible that science was not popularized so far down the social scale as many forms of culture. Artisan audiences for science are probably a nineteenth century development, with the rise of mechanics' institutes (though they themselves were remarkably middle class) and of popular (counter) science movements like phrenology.

gentleman', and he quoted Addison's view that learning gave a gentleman 'a kind of property in everything he sees'.[51]

The wider implications were that forming one of the attributes of a gentleman, science also served as a public social badge. In a provincial town, science could serve as an intellectual curtain, segregating the polite and the rational from the mob. Benjamin Martin, the itinerant lecturer, played on this effect in his evident appeal to audience snobbery:[52]

> I remember, as my goods were once carrying into my lecture-room, at a certain town, the rabble crouded about the door, to know what it was; and one wiser than the rest immediately cries out, *'Tis a ZHOW come to town*; and what do we give to zee't? A GUINEA, replies the other. Z-----nds, says the fellow, this is the D-----l of a *Zhow*; why *Luck-man-zshure*, none but the *gentlevauke* can see this. And to say the truth, there are many places where I have been, so barbarously ignorant, that they have taken me for a magician; yea, some have threaten'd my life, for raising storms and hurricanes: nor could I shew my face in some towns, but in company with the clergy or gentry.

But at the same time, the appeal to the cultural medicine of science might be a way to refine the tone of the elite themselves and to entice members of the petty bourgeoisie into hegemonic Enlightenment culture.[53] When Thomas Henry advocated natural philosophy as preferable to 'the tavern, the gaming table, or the brothel' presumably he had an eye at least to some of the general Manchester populace[54] as well as to the more raffish and uncouth members of the elite.[55] Similarly, arguing for the setting up of a literary and philosophical society for Newcastle, William Turner emphasized science's ornamental role, no less than its utilitarian aspects:

> Might they [lit and phil societies] not be expected to increase the pleasures and advantage of social intercourse, by providing an easy method of spending the evening agreeably and usefully; may then not this be a means of checking the first formation of dissipated habits, of banishing from our table the coarser pleasures of intemperance, and

51. Thomas Henry, 'On the advantages of literature and philosophy in general, and especially on the consistency of literary and philosophical with commercial pursuits.', *Memoirs of the Manchester Literary and Philosophical Society*, i (1785), 7–29, p. 7 and 9. Erasmus Darwin sought *'gentlemanlike* facts' for the Derby Philosophical Society (see Musson and Robinson, op. cit. (ref. 7), 192).
52. Quoted in Millburn, op. cit. (ref. 10), 41.
53. For elements of these beliefs see S. Shapin and B. Barnes, 'Science, nature and control: Interpreting mechanics' institutes', *Social Studies of Science*, ii (1977), 31–74.
54. Or at least to mollifying their masters.
55. Henry, op. cit. (ref. 51), 14.

of substituting for the always trifling and frequently destructive pursuits of the gamester the rational and manly entertainments of literature and philosophy.[56]

I have been arguing that the industrially utilitarian aspects of provincial science have been overstressed. The reason is because the gaze is too readily fixed on formal institutions.[57] In the provinces such institutions were not formed until the last twenty years of the eighteenth century. That was the period of the greatest industrialization. Hence it is presumed that provincial science and industrialization are intimately related. But that is a partial truth based on a false perspective.[58] The founding of formal scientific societies was the climax of a very long, cumulative, tradition of scientific lecturing, instruction, teaching, showmanship, gentleman's clubs, medical societies, etc.[59] In these developments which got under way in towns in the pre-industrial urban renaissance, a tradition of provincial science was growing up which the lit and phils inherited, and that was the tradition of science as rational culture within a broad Enlightenment civility. The towns visited by the lecturers show an initial concentration upon the gentry centres and resorts of Southern England – Bath, Bristol, Reading, Oxford, Aylesbury, Cambridge, Norwich, etc.[60] Certainly lecturing expanded into the industrializing towns of the Midlands and North in the second half of the century; certainly it may slowly have moved down-market; but later developments remained within the style of metropolitan polite lecturing which had become well-established, with the same content of polite learning and the same appeal to gentlemanly Enlightenment interests.

This view is substantiated by the promotion of Enlightenment liberal attitudes towards natural knowledge *in* the lit and phils.

---

56. William Turner, *Speculations on the Propriety of Attempting the Establishing a Literary Society in Newcastle upon Tyne* (Newcastle, 1793), 3.
57. This point is made in Inkster, op. cit. (ref. 12).
58. One of the chief reasons for this dubious perspective is that so many authors have chosen to commence their books at about 1780, thereby leading them to attribute major changes directly to industrialization. E.g., H. J. Perkin, *The Origins of Modern English Society* (London, 1969); J. Roach, *Social Reform in England, 1780–1880* (London, 1978).
59. In many towns, such as Newcastle, medical societies precede scientific societies, and suggest thereby the crucial role of the medical profession in stimulating provincial science.
60. Thus Ferguson is known to have lectured as follows: 1748, London; 1753, Norwich; 1755, Cambridge; 1761, Chelmsford; 1762, Derby; 1763, Bristol; 1767, Bristol, Bath; 1767, Liverpool; 1770, Newcastle; 1771, Bath; 1772, Derby; 1774, Bristol, Bath, London. Early in his career Martin probably lectured in Gloucester, Salisbury, Newbury, Oxford, Chichester, Bath, Reading, York, Scarborough, Ipswich. In 1747 he lectured in Birmingham for the first time.

Thomas Henry's opening paper to the Manchester Lit and Phil in 1781, 'On the advantages of Literary and Philosophical Societies in general' illustrates the point.[61] Of course, Henry argued that science possessed industrial utility. But his emphasis was that for the improvement of the manufacturing arts, the beneficent hand of liberal natural philosophy was needed. 'Practical knowledge should be united to theory, in order to produce the most beneficial discoveries.' 'Liberal science'[62] as Thomas Barnes similarly argued, would crown 'commercial industry'; or in Rudolf Erich Raspe's words:[63]

> It is only in the wisest and most enlightened ages, that we find some philosophers and wise men, stepping down from the giddy heights of their exalted station of learning, into which the barbarous ignorance of the vulgar and their own conceit had placed them, in order to fix, to rectify, and to improve the arts.

But at least as prominent was Henry's concern to show how science was quintessentially a gentlemanly pursuit:

> Affluent circumstances and abundant leisure give the Gentleman great advantages over his inferiors, in the more refined studies. The cold and heavy hand of poverty chills and represses the efforts of genius; wealth cherishes, and if I may be allowed the metaphor, manures and pushes it forward into maturity . . . The importance of the Gentleman will still rise higher, his mind be enlarged, and his pleasures be increased, if, to the accomplishments of the polite scholar, he add the knowledge of the philosopher.[64]

Henry held out his hand to encourage the man of business to join in this gentlemanly pursuit; for science would 'enlarge his understanding at the same time that it affords him the most rational amusement'.[65]

---

61. Henry, op. cit. (ref. 51), 7.
62. Thomas Barnes, 'A plan for the improvement and extension of liberal education in Manchester', *Memoirs of the Manchester Literary and Philosophical Society*, ii (1785), 16–29; *idem*, 'On the affinity subsisting between the arts, with a plan for promoting and extending manufactures by encouraging those arts on which manufacturers principally depend', *Manchester Literary and Philosophical Society Memoirs*, i (1785), 72–89.
63. Rudolf Erich Raspe, *Travels through the Bannal of Temeswar . . . described in a series of letters to Professor Ferber* (London, 1771), xii.
64. Henry, op. cit. (ref. 46), 9–10. Compare the ideas of William Turner in Newcastle as expressed in his *A General Introductory Discourse* (Newcastle, 1802), 5, where he argued that the advantage of science lay in its giving 'dignity to the possession of wealth', and reducing 'the snares and dangers with which it is surrounded', and that science would 'provide a constant source of rational and innocent amusement'.
65. Henry, op. cit. (ref. 51), 19.

CONCLUSIONS

I have been contending that we obtain a much needed more balanced understanding of the growth of provincial science by seeing it within a long-developing tradition, nurtured by the urban renaissance, within Enlightenment values of rational politeness, than if we view it primarily within the utilitarianism of industrialization, or the ethic of Dissent. The popularization of provincial science had more to do with cultural status than with factories, more to do with adjusting social relations than with refining engines. This point is confirmed into the nineteenth century by the indifference of many lit and phils to questions of direct utility and their extensive coverage of antiquarian and literary topics;[66] their bans on investigations which might interfere with matters of trade;[67] and their frequent failure in directly utilitarian enterprise.[68] It is further underlined by the continuation of similar traditions of polite learning well into the Victorian period, even in industrial areas – for example, the Yorkshire Philosophical Society;[69] or by the vogue amongst the middle classes of Victorian England for establishing naturalists' clubs, and antiquarian and archaeological societies.[70]

I believe that this recontextualizing helps us when we try – as has hardly been done hitherto – to explain the *relative* development of science in various provincial towns. Once we shift the focus of attention from Industrialization to Enlightenment, it is less surprising that the town which possibly drew the largest audiences for science lectures,[71] and which then possessed the first formal Philosophical

66. Cf. E. Kitson Clark, op. cit. (ref. 27), and Neve, op. cit. (ref. 22). If, furthermore, as many economic and technological historians assert, provincial science actually contributed little to industrial growth, then the case for a cultural interpretation of provincial scientific activity is strengthened.
67. Lit and phils had to avoid touching on various scientific and technical matters lest they be thought to be interfering with trade, and unfairly advantaging particular manufacturers. Thus William Turner, speaking of the activities of the Newcastle society in the previous year, stressed that 'all practical questions were studiously avoided'. *Historical Sketch of the Transactions of the Literary and Philosophical Society of Newcastle Upon Tyne* (Newcastle, 1807).
68. This is the argument of Porter, op. cit. (ref. 24).
69. Or see the article by J. B. Morrell, 'Economic and ornamental geology: the Geological and Polytechnic Society of the West Riding of Yorkshire, 1837–1853', in I. Inkster, and J. B. Morrell, op. cit. (ref. 22). A. D. Orange, 'The British Association for the Advancement of Science: the Provincial background', *Science Studies*, i (1971), 327; *idem, Philosophers and Provincials* (York, 1973).
70. See D. E. Allen, *The Naturalist in Britain* (London, 1976). For nineteenth century aspects of science within polite values see S. F. Cannon, *Science in Culture: The Early Victorian Period* (New York, 1978).
71. Ferguson had no fewer than 118 subscribers to one of his courses in Bath. Quoted in Millburn, op. cit. (ref. 10), 52.

Society, was not Birmingham, or Manchester but Bath. Because historians of science have so largely ignored Bath, it is worth dwelling on it for a moment.

Bath, as is well known, supported the great astronomer, William Herschel, in the 1770s. But many Bathonians besides Herschel cultivated science. In the field of natural history, for example, Ralph Schomberg, William Falconer, John Walcott, and Caleb Parry were active.[72] And fashionable visitors took a polite interest. These 'people of fashion . . . when so disposed, attend lectures upon the arts and sciences, which are frequently taught there in a pretty superficial manner, so as not to teize the understanding, while they afford the imagination some amusement'.[73] Furthermore, there was a knot of serious-minded, self-improving residents, with ambitions for establishing regular scientific institutions, focussing in the 1770s and '80s upon the Quaker, Edmund Rack, and his friends. And the outcome of these were the two Bath Philosophical Societies, one founded in 1779 by Rack, and the other in 1799.

And yet the very Enlightenment values which brought Bath science into existence also explains why it never became more than a small part of Bath culture, and why it remained rational amusement rather than (say) becoming a research centre. The serious Quaker leaders like Rack were marginal men who were attempting to win cultural prestige through promoting science. But being mere petits bourgeois in an aristocratic milieu they never won cultural authority.[74] As a paid secretary Rack could galvanize the Bath and West Society, the agricultural improvement society founded in 1777, into success. But though quartered on Bath, that was hardly an urban institution – it embodied the hopes of the landowning society of the Western counties. Its ties with Bath as such were ultimately contingent. But men like Rack and William Matthews had no power to convert Pump Room society to steam engine values. Rack's sober

72. Hugh Torrens, 'Geological communications in the Bath area in the second half of the eighteenth century', in L. J. Jordanova and Roy Porter (eds.), *Images of the Earth* (Chalfont St Giles, 1979); and Torren's contributions on the Bath Philosophical Societies to A. J. Turner, *Science and Music in Eighteenth Century Bath* (exhibition catalogue, Bath, 1977).
73. [O. Goldsmith,] *The life of Richard Nash of Bath* (London, 1762), 46.
74. Almost no research has been done on the tensions which existed in Bath between different groups of visitors, or between visitors and townsfolk. Bath citizens, for example, were not permitted to subscribe to the Upper Assembly Rooms (cf. *New Bath Guide* (Bath, 1821), 161). Similarly, the Bath poor were specifically banned from the facilities of the Mineral Hospital. After Nash's death, fashionable society itself became split between the Upper and Lower Rooms, with two M. C.'s and the public culture splintered into innumerable private coteries. For the lack of a solid trading basis in Bath see R. Warner, op. cit. (ref. 43), 344.

utilitarian Quaker piety reproved fashionable gentlemanly idle Bath even as he courted it.[75]

But neither could its fashionable population support a lasting, and distinctive cultural achievement. For they were too mobile. They came to Bath as a 'temporary residence' for 'diversion',[76] above all for gambling,[77] for fashion, for amours, the marriage market, society. 'The goddess of pleasure has selected this city as the place of her principal residence.'[78] Other parts of Enlightenment culture – novels, the theatre, assemblies, music – were available and more readily gave pleasure than science. The achievement of Nash as Bath Godfather lay in disciplining the idle into a genteel, clockwork round. Tea-table frivolity and the circulating library set the cultural tone. Aside from architecture, only perhaps in music did the demands of the fashionable stimulate an inventive, quality, artistic tradition, deploying the talents of Herschel, Linley, and then, *par excellence*, Rauzzini.[79]

But why didn't the medical community play master of ceremonies to scientific activity in Bath? For physicians were to be crucial in sowing polite scientific culture in other provincial centres like Sheffield and Manchester.[80] And in Bath they were many and influential. One must hazard conjectures. In many areas medical practitioners supported literary and philosophical institutions to stake their claims and consolidate their own cultural pre-eminence as professional men. Their status was perhaps insecure. They perhaps had time on their hands. Bath, however, was different. Its physicians were busy,

---

75. Edmund Rack's 'A disultory journal of events &c at Bath' (Bath Reference Library R69/12675) for 1779 well expresses his own love and hate feelings towards fashionable Bath society. For published expression of Rack's views and values see his *Poems on several subjects* (Bath, 1775), and his *Mentor's letters* (Bath, 1778). For a contemporary view of Rack as a petty bourgeois social climber see [?P. Thicknesse] *Edmund: An eclogue* (n. p., n. d.). 8:
   When from the land of Essex first I came,
   Propell'd by vanity and thirst of fame,
   Eager I strove in wild ambition's fits
   To elbow in, and shine among the wits. (etc.)
76. P. Egan, *Walks through Bath* (Bath, 1819), 71.
77. Goldsmith, op. cit. (ref. 73), 50f.; Wood, op. cit. (ref. 42), ii, 442.
78. *The New Bath Guide* (Bath, 1821), 137. Cf. A. Barbeau's comment, *Life and Letters at Bath in the XVIII Century* (London, 1904), 111: 'there was little desire for literary or scientific knowledge and little interest in higher subjects generally'. Charles Wesley dubbed Bath 'the headquarters of Satan'.
79. See Wood, op. cit. (ref. 42), ii, 437–8. Perhaps surprisingly painting led a rather chequered existence in Bath. See T. Fawcett, *The Rise of English Provincial Art* (Oxford, 1974), 131–8.
80. See Thackray, op. cit. (ref. 23): p. 685: 'the medical profession as guardian of the polite virtues in an industrializing world'.

rich.[81] Many already enjoyed prestigious positions with the various Bath hospitals and charities. They aimed to adapt themselves to genteel society through literature and politeness. They did not need – unlike elsewhere – to dig an oasis of their own amid a cultural desert. Furthermore, Bath doctors were divided amongst themselves. From mid-century, bitter wars raged in print between established physicians, such as William Moyses, William Falconer, and William Oliver, and more marginal men trying to crash the charmed balneological circle, like Charles Lucas, William Baylies, James Graham and their supporters such as Philip Thicknesse.[82] The members of the faculty were deeply enough split in their ambitions to preclude scientific cooperation.

Prima facie, Manchester might seem the prime case of science arising out of the needs of manufacturers. But, as Arnold Thackray has shown,[83] we see not manufacturers and industry demanding useful science, but ornamental scientific culture being promoted by groups of affluent but marginal men – medical practitioners[84] and Unitarians above all – attempting to exercise intellectual overlordship through essentially Enlightenment values. Manchester's scientific emergence under the umbrella of the Enlightenment values of a cultural elite may help to explain parallel developments in other industrial towns. Newcastle developed a reasonably thriving lit and phil chiefly through Unitarian intellectuals like its founder, William Turner.[85] The course of the Newcastle Literary and Philosophical Society also reminds us that science was one part, but one part only, of improving (though ultimately conservative), rational culture. For it seriously split only a decade after it was formed, between a faction which claimed that the main purpose of the Society was to be a

81. J. L. Murch, *Bath Physicians of Former Times* (Bath, 1882). For some of their literary activities see G. S. Rousseau, 'Matt Bramble and the sulphur controversy in the XVIIIth century', *Journal of the History of Ideas*, xviii(1967), 57–89.
82. For the balneological wars see Rousseau, op. cit. (ref.81), and C. F. Mullet, 'Public baths and health in England, 16th–18th century', *Supplement to the Bulletin of the History of Medicine*, no. 5 (Baltimore, 1946), 1–85. Perhaps the same kind of explanation will account also for why Churchmen did not lead Bath culture into sober and improving channels, as 'Liberal Anglicans' were to do elsewhere (e. g. in nineteenth century Bristol: though cf. Neve, op. cit. (ref. 22). For one thing, Bath was hardly a deeply religious centre. But it was also centrifugal in its religious affiliations, with Unitarians, Methodists, Quakers, and the Countess of Huntingdon's Connexion jostling alongside orthodox Anglicans.
83. Thackray, op. cit. (ref. 23).
84. Medical practitioners were the largest group in the Derby Philosophical Society. See Musson and Robinson, op. cit. (ref. 7), 193.
85. The Newcastle Lit and Phil had its way paved by a Philosophical and Medical Society – as so often medical practitioners were the initiatory spirit in scientific innovation. See R. S. Watson, *The History of the Literary and Philosophical Society of Newcastle-Upon-Tyne (1793–1896)* (London, 1897), 30f.

library; and those who were more committed to scientific pursuits. What many members wanted was evidently a broad access to culture rather than science *per se*.[86] The reason why other major industrial centres such as Leeds lagged far behind Manchester in establishing similar societies may be because they lacked similar professional and intellectual marginal men striving to exercise a dominant role in urban life through cultural hegemony.[87] Leeds merchants were generally Anglican, and had already well developed their own non-scientific gentlemanly interests – e.g. in land, building and the visual arts.[88] The promoters of the Leeds Philosophical and Literary Society (when it was eventually founded in 1822) chiefly stressed its role in developing politeness, virtue, responsibility and 'the cultivation of those noble powers, which alone exalts man to an infinite height above the brutes and assimilate him to the image of his Maker'.[89]

Indeed, one can argue that in well-established affluent mercantile and industrial towns, where the plutocrats had already put down some roots into polite culture, orienting intellectual pursuits towards science was not of particular moment. Thus Bristol had quite strong literary and theatrical connexions,[90] and it developed its own school of painting. For this reason, perhaps, the promotion and patronage of science did not find institutional form till the 1820s, and never

86. For this battle see the *Reports* of the Newcastle Lit and Phil compiled by its first secretary, Anthony Hedley, and deposited in the archives of the Society.
87. Ian Inkster's researches on Sheffield have indicated the centre role of medical 'Marginal men' in boosting scientific development. See his 'Marginal men: aspects of the social role of the medical community in Sheffield, 1790–1850', in (eds.) J. Woodward and David Richards, *Health Care and Popular Medicine in Nineteenth Century England* (London, 1977), 128–63; *idem*, 'Culture, institutions and urbanity: the intinerant science lecturer in Sheffield, 1790–1850', in S. Pollard and C. Holmes (eds.), *Essays in the Economic and Social History of South Yorkshire* (Sheffield, 1976), 218–32; *idem*, 'The development of a scientific community in Sheffield 1790–1850: A network of people and interests', *Transactions of the Hunter Archaeological Society*, x (1971), 99–131; *idem*, 'Studies in the social history of science in England during the Industrial Revolution' (Ph. D. dissertation, Sheffield, 1977). There is no disputing the role of medical men in bringing polite culture to Sheffield, as elsewhere – as is well brought out in W. S. Porter's *Sheffield Literary and Philosophical Society: A centenary retrospect, 1822–1922* (Sheffield, 1922). Precisely how far and in what ways medical men were 'marginal', however, requires further study.
88. The same argument might apply to Exeter, Norwich, York, etc., which already had good cultural institutions (though ones to which science was marginal). For Leeds see R. G. Wilson, *Gentlemen Merchants: the Merchant Community in Leeds, 1700–1830* (Manchester, 1971). For York, R. G. Heape, *Georgian York* (London, 1937). Wilson argues that Leeds merchants were successfully assimilating themselves into the landowning class.
89. Quoted in Kitson Clark, op. cit. (ref. 27), 5.
90. Fawcett, op. cit. (ref. 79). Generally on Bristol culture see B. D. G. Little, *The City and County of Bristol: a Study in Atlantic Civilization* (London, 1954).

developed powerful momentum.[91] Liverpool may be the same.
Liverpool certainly lagged behind Manchester in science.[92] Yet this
was not because Liverpool lacked all enlightened taste. Rather it
went into buildings, into libraries, the theatre, the Athenaeum. The
American traveller, Louis Simond, wrote in 1811:[93]

> the public buildings of Liverpool are more numerous, and in a better
> style of architecture. There are several literary establishments, with
> respectable libraries, in large and convenient apartments, and well
> attended by the inhabitants of this great commercial town, who are
> not nearly so exclusively merchants as those on the western continent.

Liverpool's amenities were adequate without science. It is perhaps
symptomatic that Liverpool's leading intellectuals (including Dissenters) found literary pursuits more congenial than scientific ones.
William Roscoe wrote the life of Lorenzo de Medici (1795). James
Currie, though friendly with the Manchester and Warrington Dissenting scientists and medical practitioners, 'had a preference for
belles lettres to scientific experimentation', and wrote the life of
Burns.[94] Science was perhaps the favoured Manchester pursuit because Manchester had hitherto lacked both a medical society and
congenial openings for the exercise of taste and literary talents.

Birmingham is of course the crucial test-case, for the Lunar
Society was clearly the luminary of eighteenth century provincial
science. Yet social understanding of the Society has been ill-served
by historians. Schofield put the society firmly in context of the In-

91. The small group of men surrounding Thomas Beddoes at the Pneumatic Institution never attracted elite patronage from the town, and remained a marginal
and radical minority.
92. On Liverpool see F. Vigier, *Change and Apathy; Liverpool and Manchester
during the Industrial Revolution* (Cambridge, Mass., 1970); R. Brooke, *Liverpool as it was during the last quarter of the eighteenth century 1775–1800*
(Liverpool, 1853); for a contemporary comment, see *Monthly Magazine*, vol.
VIII (August, 1799), 535–6: 'Outlines of the plan of the library and news-room
at Liverpool'. For science in Liverpool see J. Fulton, 'The Warrington Academy
(1757–86), and its influence upon medicine and science', *Bulletin of the Institute
of the History of Medicine*, i (1933), 50–80; G. W. Roderick and M. D.
Stephens, 'Nineteenth century ventures in Liverpool's scientific education', *Annals of Science*, xxviii (1972), 61–86.
93. L. Simond, *An American in Regency England* ed. C. Hibbert (London, 1968),
70. There was a contrary view as well. Liverpool was 'the only town in England
of any pre-eminence that has not one single erection or endowment for the
advancement of science, the cultivation of the arts, or promotion of useful
knowledge . . . The liberal arts are a species of merchandise in which few of
the inhabitants are desirous to deal unless for exportation'. Quoted in Vigier,
op. cit. (ref. 92), 78.
94. Currie was instrumental in founding the first – short-lived – two Liverpool
Philosophical societies (1779, 1782). He himself abandoned them for a literary
society. See R. D. Thornton, *James Currie, the Entire Stranger and Robert
Burns* (Edinburgh, 1963), 164f.

dustrial Revolution,[95] but he hardly inquired into the relationship to Birmingham culture. From the other end, Money has written a history of the cultural identity of the West Midlands which hardly mentions the Lunar Society.[96] But the social balance is the critical question. The West Midlands were the home *par excellence* of industrialization through small masters and workshops. But the Lunar Society did not emerge out of that society. It was a mixture of gentlemen, like Day and Edgeworth, rich physicians, Dissenters, and the grandest manufacturers of the region – Boulton and Wedgwood. Such men self-consciously located themselves within Enlightenment culture, and pursued Enlightenment projects like the abolition of the Slave Trade. As manufacturers, Boulton and Wedgwood were acutely aware that in Birmingham, the 'Grand Toy Shop of Europe', prosperity hinged upon taste and fashion.[97]

The Lunar example perhaps shows a wedge driven between an elite Enlightenment which fostered science and a very different, lower level of Enlightenment culture – that of the prudential, self-help, self-interest, of the small master class.[98] The latter was more interested in music, fellowship, theatre, book clubs, the tavern and debating society politics than in science.[99] When the French Revolution came, not only was the Birmingham mob quite happy to raze Priestley's house, but more importantly, no native Birmingham tradition of science quickly rose out of the ashes.[100]

These last few pages have been speculations, and much further research is necessary. But I trust that they have offered concrete examples of the case I have been arguing, that the rise of eighteenth century English provincial science cannot be understood simply as a kind of automatic response to the growth of industrialization. The

95. Schofield, op. cit. (ref. 7), 4. See also for the same view, Clow and Clow, op. cit. (ref. 24), 61. Of course, it is somewhat contentious, and perhaps misleading to talk of the Lunar Society of *Birmingham* at all. It did not arise out of one town. It coordinated an elite spread out across the West Midlands.
96. Money, op. cit. (ref 5).
97. For Lunar members in the forefront of the Enlightenment see Desmond King-Hele, *Erasmus Darwin, Doctor of Revolution* (London, 1977).
98. This brings to mind the distinctions which Robert Darnton has taught us to make between High Enlightenment and Low Enlightenment culture. 'In search of the Enlightenment: Recent attempts to create a social history of ideas', *Journal of Modern History* (1971), 113–32; 'The High Enlightenment and the low life of literature in pre-Revolutionary France', *Past and Present*, no. 51 (1971), 81–115; *Mesmerism and the End of the Enlightenment in France* (Cambridge, Mass., 1968).
99. For the deep divides between Anglican and Dissenter, which led in Birmingham to the establishment of rival libraries, see C. Parish, *History of the Birmingham Library* (London, 1966).
100. Money, op. cit. (ref. 5), 83f.

growth of provincial scientific culture – and its particular contours, its light and shade – can be much better understood in context of the Enlightenment.

Chapter 9

MONEY, LAND AND LINEAGE: THE BIG BOURGEOISIE OF HANOVERIAN LONDON

Nicholas Rogers

[*Social History*, 4, no. 3 (1979)]

Nicholas Rogers has made a number of astute and finely researched contributions to the study of society and popular politics in London in the first half of the eighteenth century. In this imaginative essay he seeks to explore the structure and character of the City élite through a close examination of the aldermanic bench. His broad conclusion is that by the mid-eighteenth century the leading bourgeoisie are becoming increasingly dynastic and London orientated, as they find themselves able to operate socially and politically on an equal level with the nation's rural leaders without having to abandon the metropolis. Rogers's thesis has come under fire from Donna Andrew, who in 'Aldermen and the big bourgeoisie of London reconsidered', Social History, *6, no. 3 (1981), argues that aldermen are not typical of London's big bourgeoisie, and that there still existed considerable hostility between trade and polite society which prevented the mixing of urban and rural élites. Rogers replies to these points in the same issue of* Social History. *Doubts about the validity of equating London's leading bourgeoisie with the City aldermen also surface in Henry Horwitz's ' "The mess of the middle class" revisited: the case of the "big bourgeoisie" of Augustan London',* Continuity and Change, *2, no. 2 (1987). Focusing on the early eighteenth century, he discovers a substantial group of prominent businessmen who avoided civic office and who in several important respects behaved differently from the aldermen. Most significantly for Rogers's argument, a much lower proportion of the eldest sons of the non-citizen élite followed their fathers into business, and a much higher proportion migrated out of the City into landed society.*

Money, land and lineage: the big bourgeoisie of Hanoverian London

Hanoverian England has conventionally been described as a cohesive oligarchy in which land conferred both social recognition and political power. Since the publication of Namier's study of the parliamentary élite, it has been customary to emphasize the political pre-eminence of the territorial grandees and the near-monopoly of government which they enjoyed with the greater gentry. Despite the expansion of overseas trade and the emergence of an investing society, the commercial bourgeoisie has been consistently relegated to a subordinate position. Save conceivably for the final decades of the century, merchants and bankers were underrepresented in parliament. In so far as they exercised power, they did so primarily through the mediation of aristocratic patronage.

More recently the client status of the bourgeoisie has been extended to the social sphere. Historians who have wished to emphasize the underlying continuity of the pre-modern period have suggested that the bourgeoisie habitually deferred to the landed aristocracy. The prestige of land, so the argument runs, inhibited the development of a self-confident merchant class and facilitated the emergence of a heterogeneous ruling élite under aristocratic leadership. However unified merchants might have been in functional terms, the summit of their ambitions was to enter landed society. At the same time the prevailing pattern of inheritance, forcing younger sons of the gentry to seek their fortunes in trade or the professions, ensured that urban oligarchies were to a striking degree gentle in origin. This exchange gave Hanoverian England a continued vigour, stability and resilience, producing, in Harold Perkin's words, 'a self-contained system of social movement which left the shape and structure of society precisely as before'.[1]

This neo-Namierite thesis has not, however, won wholehearted acceptance. Marxist historians have implied that the question of mobility is in reality marginal to the question of power. It does not address itself to the structural limitations of aristocratic rule, to the fact that the leadership of the great landed proprietors was circumscribed by the imperatives of an ebullient capitalist economy. 'The Whig grandees,' Eric Hobsbawm has claimed, 'knew quite well that the power of the country, and their own, rested on a readiness to make money militantly and commercially.'[2] Furthermore, they have argued that the partial absorption of business magnates into landed society does not contradict the existence of a merchant class; it only defines its social horizons and the pattern of domination

1. Harold Perkin, *The Origins of Modern English Society 1780–1880* (1969), 62. See also Peter Laslett, *The World We Have Lost* (1965), 46–51.
2. E. J. Hobsbawm, *Industry and Empire* (Harmondsworth, 1969), 32. See also E. P. Thompson, 'The peculiarities of the English', in Ralph Miliband and John Saville (eds), *The Socialist Register 1965* (1965), 317–19.

within the capitalist bloc. Indeed, since aristocratic notations of gentility were substantially modified during the course of the eighteenth century to accommodate mobile sources of wealth, the exchange between land and commerce may have been more reciprocal than orthodoxy assumes. In sum, the symbiosis of land and trade may have been symptomatic of a polite bourgeois culture attuned to the dominant forces in post-Revolution society rather than a reaffirmation of landed status.

If Marxists have questioned the meaning of mobility between land and commerce, non-Marxists have also questioned its incidence. Some historians have speculated that the influx of new wealth into land declined after 1660, that the post-Restoration era heralded an advance in merchant standing and the emergence of oligarchies permanently committed to urban life. Others have asserted the continuing importance of broad acres as a source of prestige, and the *constraints*, demographic or economic, which curbed mercantile ambition.[3] There is, in fact, little consensus about the openness of high society, whether in terms of occupational mobility, marriage or social exclusivity, a situation compounded by a dearth of statistical data and by an inherent tendency to generalize from standard genealogical sources, sources which potentially exaggerate the entry of new wealth to landed society. In these circumstances it is worthwhile examining the evidence of the mid-century London aldermen, and where possible groups of comparable standing, to see what light their family profiles throw on these divergent interpretations.

I

The aldermen were by reputation *la crème de la crème* of the London bourgeoisie. From the fifteenth century onwards there was a close correspondence between big business and civic leadership. The wealthiest citizens of the 1559 subsidy, for example, were almost to a man members of the aldermanic court; and as the hierarchy of merchant syndicates changed during the seventeenth century, the Merchant Venturers giving way to the Levant and East India com-

3. H. J. Habakkuk, 'The English land market in the eighteenth century', in J. S. Bromley and E. H. Kossmann (eds), *Britain and the Netherlands* (1960), 154–73. Cf. Lawrence Stone, 'Social mobility in England 1500–1700', *Past and Present*, XXXIII (1966), 16–55.

panies, so too did London's rulers.[4] In the Civil War decades, admittedly, this pattern was temporarily disrupted. And as the money market matured after 1700, and a new nexus of business contracts emerged, so the City became increasingly divorced from the bankocracy. The disassociation of financial capital from City politics was nevertheless a protracted affair, offset in part by Walpole's determination to wield magnate power against a factious citizen rank and file. And it did not critically affect the composition of the aldermanic court until the radical era.

Nor did the introduction of direct elections in 1714 substantially alter the social character of the City aristocracy, for only the richest citizens could aspire to aldermanic rank. The fees and gratuities of a sheriff, for example, an office which virtually every alderman held, were inadequate to meet the heavy expenses of Old Bailey dinners and other civic functions. It was estimated in 1837 that sheriffs spent at least £2000 beyond their allowances,[5] and in the eighteenth century it was almost certainly higher. An alderman might recover his losses when he rose to the chair, but this depended upon the vacant offices he could sell, over and above the normal perquisites. The total profits of mayoral office varied considerably – in the 1740s from £3000 to £4500[6] – and so the expenses of an elaborate equipage and household could put a dignitary out of pocket. John Barber, the Lord Mayor during the excise crisis, lamented to Swift two months before the expiry of his term that 'fortune has been my foe, for I have no death happened in my year (a fiddler excepted) yet, nor have made £500 in all'; and Charles Ford concluded he was 'something the poorer for his office'.[7] Nor surprisingly, a man worth less than £15 000 in 'Lands, Goods and Separate Debts' could decline to stand.[8] No alderman could rely on making a fortune in civic office; he had to have one before he started.

Most of these fortunes were derived from overseas trade. A select minority were engaged in banking; approximately 20 per cent were wholesalers in the textile and provisioning trades, as was the case with George Nelson, a corn factor dealing in Liverpool and Yarmouth, with extensive provincial contacts. And a handful of

4. Robert Brenner, 'The Civil War politics of London's merchant community', *Past and Present*, LVIII (1975), 53–107; K. G. Davies, 'Joint-stock investment in the later seventeenth century', *Economic History Review*, 2nd ser., IV (1952), 283–301; G. D. Ramsay, *The City of London in International Politics at the Accession of Elizabeth Tudor* (Manchester, 1975), 39–41.
5. B. P. P., 1837, XXV, 82.
6. Guild. MS. 100, fos. 46–7.
7. Harold Williams (ed.), *The Correspondence of Jonathan Swift*, 5 vols (Oxford, 1963–5), IV, 203.
8. 'Insufficiency of wealth' was set at £10 000 in 1640, £15 000 in 1737, £20 000 in 1799 and £30 000 in 1813.

manufacturers attained aldermanic rank, including two of the leading five porter brewers in the metropolis producing between them 94 000 barrels a year.[9] But over half of the seventy-four aldermen who held office during the mid-century decades had commercial interests abroad, in most cases combining them with investments in high finance. Among their number were to be found some of the leading representatives of merchant society: Sir John Barnard, preeminent among the private underwriters of marine insurance; Sir Edward Bellamy, the largest fish-importer; Sir John Williams, reputedly the 'greatest exporter of cloth in England'; and the Eyles brothers, whose interests encompassed the Levant, Iberian, American and West Indian trades.[10] Other important magnates included Sir William Baker, one of the foremost American merchants of the mid-century. He won several lucrative victualling contracts from the government, dominated the Hudson's Bay Company, acquired huge tracts of land in Georgia and South Carolina, and profited immensely from his association with the DeLancey clan in New York. Then there was Micajah Perry, owner of one of the largest tobacco houses in Maryland and Virginia, shipping, according to Walpole's sources, 1500 hogsheads a year.[11] Finally, there were the Beckfords, whose sugar fortunes astonished contemporaries. Richard, for a short time alderman of Farringdon Without, left £21 800 in legacies besides making provision for the payment of five annuities totalling £730. He also left his son his estates in England and Jamaica, the latter worth, with four sugar plantations, a house in Spanish Town, and over 900 slaves, something in the region of £120 000. His brother William's fortune was even greater. Reputedly a millionaire, he owned no less than fourteen plantations, over 1000 slaves, and had a long train of debts owed to him by fellow planters. In addition to these assets he bequeathed to his son

9. Peter Mathias, *The Brewing Industry in England* 1700–1830 (Cambridge, 1959), 23. In 1748 Sir William Calvert's Hour Glass brewhouse on Thames Street produced 55 700 barrels of beer; Humphrey Parsons' Red Lion brewery in Wapping, 39 000. Nelson's provincial contacts are mentioned in the *London Evening Post*, 6/9 August 1757.
10. *H. M. C. Egmont MSS*, I, 130; Geraldine Meroney, 'The London entrepot merchants and the Georgia colony', *William and Mary Quarterly*, 3rd ser., XXV (1968), 230–44.
11. L. B. Namier and John Brooke (eds), *The History of Parliament: The House of Commons 1754–90*, 3 vols (1964), II, 39–41; P. W. Kingsford, 'A London merchant: Sir William Baker', *History Today*, XXI (1971), 338–48; Julian Gwyn, *The Enterprising Admiral. The Personal Fortune of Sir Peter Warren* (Montreal, 1974), *passim*. On Perry, see Elizabeth Doran, 'Eighteenth-century English merchants. Micajah Perry', *Journal of Economic and Business History*, V (1931), 79–98, and Cambridge University, Cholmondley (Houghton) MS. C(H) 29/29/3.

two estates in England and gave the rest of his family £43 500 in money legacies alone.[12]

Few mid-century aldermen were as wealthy as the Beckfords. The only one who scaled their dizzy heights was Sir Samuel Fludyer, a packer and Blackwell Hall factor who also speculated in the drug trade and government finance. In the 1760s he was regarded by the Duke of Newcastle as 'the most considerable trader in the City of London',[13] and when he died in 1768 his fortune was estimated at £900 000. But fortunes of £100 000 or more were not uncommon, on a par with the most eminent merchants. Sir Thomas Lombe, for example, the Derby silk manufacturer whose throwing machines revolutionized the production of thread, computed that his estate, real and personal, amounted to £118 000.[14] Sir Charles Asgil, who headed a banking house in Lombard Street, died at the age of 75 'worth upwards of £160 000'.[15] Sir Robert Ladbroke left over £60 000 in outstanding debts and money, real estate in London and in at least four counties, and a banking partnership, while James Heywood valued his personal fortune at £86 780, not to mention his property in London and Essex and investments in a Cornish copper company.[16] Even the smaller fry had fortunes in tens of thousands. Samuel Turner, for instance, a comparatively inconspicuous West India merchant, left over £25 000 in money, stock-in-trade, and public securities, as well as an estate in Surrey; George Nelson left £20 000 in his trade, a seat at Battle in Sussex and a city residence. Richard Blunt, a distiller, bequeathed £15 000 personaly, his business premises, several freehold messuages in the East End, and a villa in Essex; whereas Daniel Lambert left a personal estate of approximately £18 000, freehold property near Ryegate worth £250 per annum, and a family estate at Perrot's Manor near Banstead, Surrey.[17] Even John Barber, the only printer to achieve aldermanic office, left £30 000 in liquid assets and property in London, Westminster and East Sheen, a fortune derived from successful speculations during the South Sea Bubble, which, as Swift so aptly

---

12. Richard Sheridan, 'Planter and historian: the career of William Beckford of Jamaica and England, 1744–99', *Jamaica Hist. Review*, IV (1964), 38–45; P.R.O. PROB 11/821/59 and 11/959/256.
13. B. L. Add. MS. 32871 fo. 456. See also D.N.B. entry.
14. PROB 11/694/14.
15. F. G. Hilton Price, *A Handbook of London Bankers* (1891), 123.
16. On Ladbroke, see Namier and Brooke, *History of Parliament*, III, 16; PROB 11/992/435; Guildhall MSS. 8674/76, 150, 8674/92, 233, 11,936/91, 426. On Heywood, see PROB 11/1021/317.
17. (Nelson) PROB 11/924/429; Guildhall MS 12, 012, 151; (Blunt) PROB 11/895/2; (Lambert) PROB 11/779/169.

put it, 'enabled him to make a figure in the City'.[18] Indeed, making
a figure was the characteristic hallmark of aldermen; fine equipages,
hoards of silver plate,[19] metropolitan and country residences. In this
respect City aldermen were typical members of the big bourgeoisie,
maintaining two households within close proximity of the capital.

Taken together, the London aldermen reflected a broad cross-
section of the greater merchant community. Among their numbers
were to be found some of the richest commoners of England, men
whose wealth vied with tycoons like Sampson Gideon and the Van-
necks.[20] They represented virtually every theatre of commerce from
the East Indies to the Atlantic seaboard. And they drew their
recruits from some of the rising sectors of the business world:
bankers in Lombard Street and the West End, where the gentry
jockeyed for loans and mortgages; capital brewers, sugar refiners,
and distillers; not to mention wholesalers in the long-established
trades, wool in particular. They were not, furthermore, without
financiers. Although many prominent creditors avoided the hurley-
burley of City politics for the safer havens of a closed borough, at
least a handful joined the aldermanic ranks. Approximately 20 per
cent of all aldermen were at one time or other directors of the three
great monied companies; and an even greater proportion were active
investors in high finance. A review of the stock-holdings of thirty-
two aldermen who held office during the late 1740s reveals that
twenty-two were substantial proprietors, and of the other ten, at
least six were short-time creditors of the government or the East
India Company. Of the stockholders, nineteen had individual holdings of £1000 or more, and nine had cumulative holdings of over
£4000 apiece.[21] What is more, several aldermen became leading

18. Willams (ed.), *Correspondence*, IV, 535; *London Magazine*, IX (1740), 49;
    London Evening Post, 1/3 January 1741.
19. P.R.O., T 47/5, plate tax returns, 1756–63. Of the thirteen aldermen located in
    the returns, all but two owned 500 ounces or more, and seven owned 1000 ounces
    or more. The rate assessments for the mid-eighteenth century also reveal that 80
    per cent of the aldermen's business premises and/or residences were rated at £50
    per annum or over; 46 per cent were rated at £100 per annum or over.
20. Sampson Gideon's fortune was in the region of £350 000; Gerrard Vanneck left
    approximately £240 000. Clearly the richest aldermen could rival these fortunes,
    while their colleagues could match a more typical representative of the merchant
    élite. In 1727 Defoe believed £25 000 was a good fortune, sufficient to support
    a merchant in comfort and status. See Richard Grassby, 'The personal wealth of
    the business community in seventeenth-century England', *Economic History
    Review*, 2nd ser., XXIII (1970), 228.
21. *A List of the Names of the Governor and Company of Merchants of Great-Britain
    trading to the South Sea . . . who are Qualified to Vote . . . Dec. 25, 1747* (1747);
    *A List of the Names of all Such Proprietors of the Bank of England . . . March
    5, 1749* (1749); and East India stock and bond ledgers 1743–53, India House,
    L/AG/14/5/9, 69–72, 252–5, 328–33.

critics of the bankocracy, the clique of interlocking business syndicates which dominated the financial world. Of course the aldermanic élite is not a perfect sample of the greater bourgeoisie. The cosmopolitan plutocracy of London which featured prominently in the leading insurance companies and speculated in government and allied securities is conspicuously absent.[22] But aside from this immigrant élite, comprised principally of Dutch, Jewish and Huguenot merchants, they did reflect the most prominent sectors of the heterogeneous but composite merchant-financier bloc at the apex of London society. A random sample of the merchants and eminent tradesmen who publicly supported the Bank of England during the financial crisis of 1745, for instance, corresponds strikingly with the occupational profile of the aldermanic court.[23]

II

There are grounds, then, for suggesting that the record of the mid-eighteenth-century aldermen is of more sociological significance than might first appear; that their family histories will represent, in broad terms, the fortunes of their class. What, in fact, does the record reveal?

It indicates, in the first place, an important shift in élite recruitment. Prior to the Hanoverian era a high proportion of great

22. This is not a severe handicap because the cosmopolitans are not a group that one normally associates with 'gentrification'. They intermarried a good deal, retained their cultural identities for two to three generations, and, coming from centres like Amsterdam and Geneva, were pre-eminently urban creatures. To have included them would have skewed the trends among the indigenous merchant élite.

23. Occupational profile of the London aldermen, 1738–63, and the Bank of England supporters of 1745.

	Aldermen (74) (%)	Bank supporters (138) (%)
Merchants, bankers, financiers	63	58
Manufacturers	9	8
Wholesalers	20	20
Other	8	7
Unknown	—	7

The Bank supporters are taken from a 10 per cent random sample of the signatories mentioned in the *London Evening Post*, 26/28 September and 28 September/1 October 1745. The occupations are principally derived from the City directories of the Guildhall, the British Library, and the Institute of Historical Research, London. I have also used the stock ledgers of the East India company 1743–8 (India House, L/AG/14/5/9, 69–72) and the list of government short-term creditors for 1745 mentioned in the Exchequer records (E401/2095).

merchants, whether civic dignitaries or not, were born outside of London. Of the 438 merchant grandees located by W. K. Jordan in the period 1480–1660, only 9 per cent were Londoners: of the 172 mayors holding office during the same period a mere 8 per cent.[24] The proportion of London-born merchants increased as the century progressed, albeit unevenly, but it still did not compare with the pattern of Hanoverian recruitment. During the post-Restoration decades, for example, a quarter of London's aldermen were actually born there.[25] Over half hailed from areas outside London and the home counties, principally from the Midlands and the south-west, and although merchants and tradesmen provided a significant proportion of the personnel, the gentry and yeomanry returned one third. By contrast, the background of the Hanoverian aldermen was conspicuously commercial and London-based. Gentry recruitment fell from 27 per cent to 22 per cent, while men of yeoman stock dwindled to insignificant proportions. Scions of the provincial bourgeoisie also declined in numbers, especially from the Midlands, a symptom, perhaps, of the growing attraction of careers in the expanding industrial and commercial centres of that region. They were replaced by men already well entrenched in London society: sons of merchants and first-rate tradesmen, in some cases citizens who had featured prominently in the first phase of the financial revolution and had held important civic offices. Indeed, a striking number of mid-eighteenth-century aldermen helped to perpetuate what can only be described as a city patriciate, bound by interlocking ties of kinship. Sir John Eyles was the son of an alderman and the nephew, brother and cousin of three others. Humphrey Parsons was the son of a Lord Mayor and the son-in-law of Sir Ambrose Crowley, the ironmaster and former alderman and sheriff. Sir Francis Child's grandfather had held the City chair in 1698; he succeeded his brother as alderman of Farringdon Without. Richard Levett, Joseph Hankey and Robert Alsop were all sons of aldermen. Richard Hoare was the grandson of the well-known Tory banker of Queen Anne's reign, Sir Richard, member for the City from 1710–15 and Lord Mayor 1712–13. And George Heathcote, although born in Jamaica, was the nephew of Sir Gilbert, Sir Richard's protagonist, and the cousin-by-marriage of one of his own colleagues, Sir John Eyles. Approximately a third of the Georgian aldermen were related

---

24. W. K. Jordan, *The Charities of London 1480–1660* (1960), 308–18. Jordan's figures may be low. The evidence for Elizabethan and early Stuart London suggests that 20–25 per cent of the aldermen were born or bred in the metropolis. See Peter Clark and Paul Slack, *English Towns in Transition 1500–1700* (Oxford, 1976), 119, and R. G. Lang, 'Social origins and social aspirations of Jacobean London merchants', *Economic History Review*, 2nd ser., XXVII (1974), 28–47.
25. See Appendices A and B.

to former City dignitaries or to their fellow members. Compared to their seventeenth-century counterparts they constituted an indigenous élite, solidly grounded in London merchant society, although supplemented by continuing recruitment from the gentry of the south-east and west.

It might be argued that the traditions of service in City circles accentuated the burghal character of its élite. London patriciates were not unknown; they had emerged at other times in the City's history. What seems to be an important change in merchant recruitment may in fact be peculiar to the civic élite; a sociological anomaly. Compelling as this argument appears, it ought to be rejected. The apprenticeship indentures of three leading livery companies, the Grocers, Goldsmiths and Fishmongers, show that recruitment from London and the home counties increased substantially in the years 1690–1750.[26] Furthermore, a survey of the social provenance of Bank directors reveals a high proportion who were born and bred in the London world of commerce.[27] Similarly over half the London merchants in parliament during the heyday of Whig oligarchy hailed from the metropolis. Of the hundred active in business in 1750 or thereabouts, only 14 per cent came from the gentry, while 16 per cent emanated from the provincial bourgeoisie.[28] If kinship affiliations were more evident among the aldermanic élite than among the merchant class as a whole, their overall records were not dissimilar.

There are good reasons, therefore, for maintaining that the eighteenth-century witnessed a significant shift in the recruitment patterns of the London commercial élite. Hitherto businessmen had thrown their net wide, both geographically and socially, even though kinsmen normally had first priority. The high profitability of trade in the post-Restoration decades, however, intensified the competition for apprenticeships, narrowing the social base of recruitment to the eclipse of the yeomen and lesser tradesmen. Certainly neither they nor the parish gentry could afford the high premiums demanded by London merchants, which for a reputable house amounted to over £500 by 1750. Moreover, the price of a junior

---

26. W. F. Kahl, 'Apprenticeship and the freedom of the London Livery Companies 1690–1750', *Guildhall Miscellany*, VII (1956), 17–20.
27. According to my calculations 43 per cent of the mid-century Bank directors (1739–64) hailed from London, usually from merchant-banker stock. See W. Marston Acres, 'Directors of the Bank of England', *Notes and Queries*, CLXXIX (1940), 38 *et seq.*
28. These figures are derived from Romney Sedgwick (ed.), *History of Parliament: The House of Commons 1714–54*, 2 vols (1976) and Namier and Brooke, *History of Parliament*. I should like to thank Silva Basmajian for helping me compile the data.

partnership – as high as £5000 in a second-rate firm[29] – probably deterred even the minor gentry from setting up their sons in London commerce. A share in a provincial house was a more amenable target. At the same time new avenues of mobility emerged. The expansion of the state after 1690 provided a broader range of careers for younger sons of the gentry, whose numbers probably declined during the late-seventeenth and early-eighteenth centuries and whose chances of inheriting property correspondingly increased.[30] The army, navy and church became increasingly gentry preserves, while the professions commanded a growing clientele. The bar attracted a regular inflow of younger sons – in the mid-century decades their numbers proportionately rose[31] – and the medical profession became popular. In the years 1765–74 no less than 40 per cent of the Apothecaries' apprentices were sons of esquires and gentlemen. The premiums their fathers paid were high; rarely did they fall below £100.[32] But seldom did they reach the spectacular sums demanded by the greater merchants.

If the inflow of gentlemen into merchanting declined markedly during the eighteenth century, intermarriage between landed society and the commercial magnates of London increased. In the Stuart era this was largely a matter of snapping up bourgeois daughters, preferably heiresses; a hefty portion, or better still a fortune, helped to discharge incumbrances and allowed younger sons the opportunity of becoming gentlemen of leisure. This practice continued in the eighteenth century. Approximately 4 per cent of all noble marriages were to daughters of businessmen, a figure roughly comparable to the seventeenth century. In the case of City families, marriage with the peerage probably decreased; only four daughters, three of them heiresses, married noblemen, although several sisters of aldermen did so too. But marriage with gentry families rose. Of the daughters of London aldermen who married, 60 per cent joined the gentry in the Restoration decades as against 68 per cent in the mid-eighteenth century. Not all of these husbands were of ancient lineage. John Olmius, for example, who married the daughter of Sir William Billers, was the grandson of a Dutch merchant and the only

29. Edward Hughes, *North Country Life in the Eighteenth Century. The North West 1700–1750* (Oxford, 1952), 107. See also Namier and Brooke, *History of Parliament*, II, 34, 291–3.
30. J. P. Cooper, 'Inheritance and settlement by great Landowners', in Jack Goody, Joan Thirsk and E. P. Thompson (eds), *Family and Inheritance: Rural Society in Western Europe 1200–1800* (Cambridge, 1976), 226, 232.
31. Paul Lucas, 'A collective biography of students and barristers of Lincoln's Inn 1680–1804: a study of the "aristocratic resurgence" of the Eighteenth Century', *Journal of Modern History*, XLVI (1974), 227–61.
32. Guildhall MS. 8207, apprenticeship indentures of the Apothecaries Company, 1765–74.

son of a deputy-governor of the Bank of England. In 1737 he bought the former seat of the Dukes of Buckingham and Albemarle, entered parliament, and plagued the Whig grandees for a peerage. When he proposed to set up a volunteer regiment during the Forty-Five, presumably to ingratiate himself with the government, he was told by the Lord Lieutenant of Essex that 'such offers did not become any private gentleman, but only the very prime of the nobility'.[33] But there is no knowing how typical Olmius was. Sir John Eyles's daughter married an MP who hailed from an old Devonshire family; Sir Thomas Lombe's, a family who had frequently represented Nottinghamshire. All the indications are that aldermanic daughters married old landed gentry as well as new.

Yet the most revealing feature of bourgeois marriages in the Hanoverian era, and one which historians have overlooked, is the rising proportion of businessmen marrying daughters of the gentry. Whereas Restoration aldermen were largely endogamous, sustaining a weft of familial and business contacts among the upper crust of London society, their Hanoverian counterparts showed an increasing disposition to marry landed families. While London unions still predominated and reflected a wide range of business affiliations, approximately 40 per cent of all marriages were with the gentry. Sir Richard Glyn's second wife came from a prominent Northumberland family. Two other bankers, Edward Ironside and Thomas Rawlinson, married into the west-country gentry. Robert Willimot married the Surrey branch of his colleague, Daniel Lambert's family. Sir George Champion wedded the daughter of Sir Joseph Andrews of Kempton Park; Sir John Williams, the daughter of the Speaker of the House of Commons; while William Bridgen, a lace merchant, successfully courted an aristocratic widow, Lady Belomont. Nor was the aldermanic record idiosyncratic. Links with landed society are also evident in the marriages of the merchants and financiers in parliament. Although London-based marriages again predominated, gentry matches came a close second.

The rising incidence of marriages between London businessmen and the daughters of the gentry reflected the importance of the Season, that annual gathering of high society which flourished during the eighteenth century.[34] In the Stuart era the London bourgeoisie had comparatively few opportunities to meet the landed aristocracy. Parliament met infrequently; the Court was socially exclusive; the focal point of gentry life remained the county

---

33. Sedgwick, *History of Parliament*, II, 307.
34. The Season became a more formal affair during the nineteenth century, with a well-defined calendar of fixtures. The social protocol also became more elaborate, a symptom, no doubt, of a crisis of identity among the quality. See Leonore Davidoff, *The Best Circles: Social Etiquette and the Season* (1973).

community. The relatively narrow orbit in which Stuart merchants moved is indicated by their choice of marriage partners. Usually they came from a finite group of acquaintances in the City, or, where they had strong landed roots from their county of origin.[35] But with the emergence of the Season, when the gentry flocked to town to contract marriages and mortgages, to cultivate the right connections, to gamble, gourmandize, and to do the social rounds, so the choice of eligible partners widened. Parliamentary matches, in particular, became more frequent. This was not surprising. The Hanoverian aldermen had more kin in parliament when they embarked on their careers than did their Stuart counterparts. Even where they lacked such advantages, the expansion of an urban genteel culture facilitated their entry into polite society.

The complementary feature of this process was the advance in mercantile respectability. A gentleman might take a London bride out of necessity. Like the archetypal rake of James Miller's *Politeness*, who married money to recover his fortune after an uproarious Grand Tour, he might derive 'the awkward City Mien and Dress' and loathe 'the nauseous smell of sad Cheapside'.[36] But to marry one's daughter to a businessman denoted a distinct shift in social attitudes. The change can be chronicled through cultural pacemakers like Addison and Defoe, who urged the gentry to renounce their disdain for new wealth, but it emerges most clearly in popular hand books on social precedence. In the early editions of Chamberlayne's *Angliae Notitia*, first published in 1669, a tradesman was 'not capable of any Honourable Estate' and a gentleman so apprenticed irrevocably blotted his pedigree. But within thirty years Chamberlayne, secretary to successive noblemen, was beginning to capitulate to social pressures. By 1700 he was prepared to admit 'that if a Gentleman be bound an Apprentice to a Merchant, or other Trade, he hath not thereby lost his Degree of Gentility'. Seven years later his son conceded that merchants were 'of best Repute in England . . . to become a Merchant of Foreign Commerce hath been allowed no Disparagement to a Gentleman born, especially to a younger Brother'.[37] It was left to Defoe to complete the equation: if a man did not lose his gentility by trade, then trade could make gentility.[38]

35. J. R. Woodhead, 'The Rulers of London: The Composition of the Courts of Aldermen and Common Council of the City of London 1660–1688' (M.A. thesis, University of London, 1961), 47–8. On the endogamous character of the gentry and the importance of local ties and affiliations in the seventeenth century, see C. W. Chalklin, *Seventeenth-century Kent* (1965), 193–4 and Lawrence Stone, *The Family, Sex and Marriage in England 1500–1800* (New York, 1977), 61–2.
36. William Irving, *John Gay's London* (Cambridge, 1928), 232.
37. Helen S. Hughes, 'The middle class reader and the English novel', *Journal of English and Germanic Philology*, XXV (1926), 366–8.
38. Daniel Defoe, *The Compleat English Tradesman*, 2 vols (3rd edn, 1732), I, 305–11.

Indeed, by the mid-eighteenth century gentlemen-merchants were no longer a misnomer; manuals even indexed genteel trades in a society in which rank, fortune and demeanour were finely calibrated. Breeding and conspicuous consumption vied with birth on the social scale, and in the last analysis, money, whether derived from rentals, marriage, merchanting or stocks and shares, counted for more than ancient lineage.

Changing social attitudes and the development of the London Season, then, facilitated the links between landed and commercial society. Yet if City aldermen sometimes sought marriage outside business circles and were prepared to add a little aristocratic *cachet* to their pedigrees, they were not necessarily transient members of urban society, anxious to leave the counting-house for the country seat. Those with strong landed ties before they began their careers admittedly showed a willingness to be reabsorbed into the gentry. Thomas Harley, for example, a prominent wine merchant and government contractor, the fourth son of the Earl of Oxford, returned to his native Herefordshire late in life. He became a Member of Parliament for the county, the ultimate honour for a landed commoner, and Lord-Lieutenant of Radnorshire. Similarly John Blachford, a Cripplegate sugar refiner whose father was a gentleman of Fordingbridge, bought Bowcombe Manor on the Isle of Wight and re-established contact with leading representatives of the local gentry. A bachelor, he left his estate to a cadet branch of the family in Osborne, not to his nephews in City trade.[39] But the majority of aldermen identified strongly with the City, leaving bequests to civic colleagues, business associates and local charities. Thirty-one regularly subscribed to the growing number of hospitals.[40] Over twenty left money to London charities in an age not noted for its philanthropic legacies. Eight left doles to their parish poor. Even aldermen with landed roots, such as William Benn and Charles Ewer, who both hailed from the Hertfordshire gentry, acknowledged City friendships in their wills. Benn gave mourning rings to the common-councilmen of Aldersgate and Bishopsgate wards as well as to the mayor, aldermen and other civic dignitaries; Ewer to 'the members of the Club of Grocers at Pope's Head, Cornhill'.[41] In fact very few aldermen did not recognize London links in some way. Most trustees and executors outside family circles were Londoners: principally bankers, merchants and lawyers. And old City hands requested that they be buried in family vaults deep in the merchant quarter.

39. PROB 10 Box 2259.
40. I owe this information to Donna Andrew, who is currently revising for publication her University of Toronto doctoral dissertation on London charities in the eighteenth century.
41. PROB 11/817/211 (Benn); PROB 11/718/182 (Ewer).

The social orientation of the aldermen did not, of course, preclude the possibility that their families would be assimilated into gentry society. Contemporaries recognized that the transmission of new wealth into land could take time, that aldermen in particular, would be unlikely to break with a lifetime of associations. 'The first money getting wretch,' Defoe assured his genteel readers, would never lose 'the smell of the Exchange'.[42] It was his posterity who had the chance to become complete gentlemen, and much depended on how the *arriviste* prepared for the family homecoming.

Without doubt aldermen smoothed the path for their heirs. Although few had received a polite education themselves, perhaps ten out of a total of seventy-four,[43] they did not necessarily deprive their sons of the opportunity. Of the thirty-four who had male heirs, six sent them to Westminster, two to Eton, while the Beckfords provided tutors for their offspring, legitimate and illegitimate. Ten aldermen also sent their sons to Oxbridge, followed in most cases by a short stint at the Inns of Court, and at least four packed them off on a Grand Tour. To summarize: approximately half educated their sons in a manner befitting landed gentlemen. Thus culturally equipped, aldermanic heirs were often in a better position to move in the best circles than their fathers.

Aldermen who inherited landed estates, moreover, frequently showed a keen sense of dynastic continuity. Sir John Williams entailed Tendering Hall, Suffolk, on his son's heir. Sir William Billers, whose father had acquired Thorley in Hertfordshire during the 1690s, took care not to overburden the family estate with money legacies.[44] Aldermen whose kin were already ensconced on the land even used their fortunes to shore up the family inheritance. Charles Ewer purchased his ancestral home in Hertfordshire so that it remained in the family. So too did Sir Daniel Lambert, whose ancestors had owned Perrot's manor, Banstead, since the sixteenth century.[45]

But most aldermen did not come from long-established landed families, nor did they inherit sizeable estates. If they wished to facilitate the transfusion of City money into land they had to acquire

42. Daniel Defoe, *The Compleat English Gentleman* (ed. Karl D. Bulbring, 1890), 257–8.
43. The ten I have located are Richard and William Beckford, William Calvert, Edward Davies (?), Marshe Dickenson, Richard Glyn, Edward Gibbon, Thomas Harley, George Heathcote and Richard Hoare. The wealthiest provincial merchants also sent their sons to Oxbridge. See W. G. Hoskins, *Industry, Trade and People in Exeter 1688–1800* (Manchester, 1935), 122n, and R. G. Wilson, *Gentlemen Merchants: The merchant community in Leeds 1700–1830* (Manchester, 1971), 209.
44. PROB 11/742/265.
45. (Lambert) PROB 11/779/163.

a suitable property, by marriage or purchase. An important minority did just this. Sir Richard Glyn, a Lombard Street banker, acquired an estate in Surrey by marrying a merchant heiress and bought another in Dorset for his second son.[46] Sir Crisp Gascoyne, a London brewer and verderer of Epping Forest, built up his family holdings in Essex, purchasing the lands of the ancient chapel and hospital of Ilford and consolidating his father-in-law's estate at Bifrons, near Barking.[47] A further four purchased property in their native counties, or at least in the counties that they identified with their lineage, including Thomas Harley, who lavished huge sums on Berrington Hall. Other large estates were acquired by William Baker, who bought a 3000 acre seat at Bayfordbury in Hertfordshire, and by William Whitaker, who purchased Loughton Hall, with its 1300 acres of parkland, from the Earl of Rochford.[48] Finally there was William Beckford, who erected a magnificent Palladian mansion at Fonthill, Wiltshire. With its giant portico and five wings, it was the architectural wonder of the county, surpassing Stourhead and Standlynch as the last word in mercantile opulence and high fashion.[49]

Yet the aquisition of estates large enough to sustain the leisured life of a country gentleman was more characteristic of the years 1690–1720 than it was of the mid-century decades. Although some contemporaries believed merchant land-hunger was insatiable, most aldermen appear to have settled for modest seats, retaining much of their wealth in trade or in public securities.[50] By and large they went in for riverside villas or medium-sized mansions within close proximity of the capital, embellished no doubt with canals, fish-ponds, pleasure grounds and gardens, commanding a fine prospect of the Thames. Estates of this kind had traditionally been purchased by the merchant class, and indeed, despite Defoe's statement to the contrary, had frequently changed hands within the London bourgeoisie.[51] Although bedecked with the trappings of gentility, they

46. Roger Fulford, *Glyn's 1753–1953* (1953), 38–9.
47. See entry in *D.N.B.* and *V.C.H. Essex*, V, 193–4.
48. *V.C.H. Essex*, IV, 119.
49. Nikolaus Pevsner and Judy Nairn, *The Buildings of England. Wiltshire* (Harmondsworth, 1963; 2nd edn 1975), 46, 246–7.
50. Very few aldermen bought estates of over 300 acres and I have found little evidence of a major diversion of wealth from commerce and high finance to landed property (although a fair number dabbled in the London property market). These conclusions are based on the evidence of wills, fire insurance policies and the Middlesex Land Registry.
51. Defoe, *The Compleat English Gentleman*, 263–4. See also *V.C.H. Essex*, VI, 189, 219, 249, 269 and the Rev. Henry Hunter, *The History of London and its Environs* (1811), II, 124, 537. For a typical country villa on sale during the 1770s, see the *Daily Advertiser*, 9 July 1774. The paper announced the auction at Leadenhall Street of 'A very valuable Estate, suitable for a Merchant or any

were not pure derivatives of landed culture. Rather they were an integral aspect of an urban genteel culture which merchants and gentry shared, along with pleasure gardens, coffee-houses, balls, concerts and fashionable spas like Bath, Epsom and Tunbridge Wells. From these merchant-aldermen commuted to London, reproducing their own version of the gentry's amphibious life-style. Occasionally they simply rented suitable residences. Mount Mascal, for example, a small seat south-east of Blackheath near the London-Maidstone road, was successively leased by aldermen Billers, Calvert and Ladbroke.[52] Those that did buy estates, moreover, did not always settle them on their heirs. Henry Bankes asked his trustees to sell his real estate and re-invest the proceeds in the funds. Samuel Fludyer recommended that his seat at Lee, Kent, be added to his personal stock; the only realty he specifically left his eldest son, who was to be 'maintained and educated as such', was a house in Downing Street. Likewise Sir Charles Asgill had few scruples about disposing of his mansion at Richmond, whose value, he calculated, was £5000; 'yet I think,' he continued, 'it will sell for a great deal more or lett [*sic*] and furnished for £300 per annum'.[53] In no sense did he regard it as a family heirloom.

Hanoverian aldermen, then, did not necessarily facilitate the entry of their sons into landed society by purchasing suitable estates. Although those of landed origin harked back to their roots, and although some merchant princes lavished their fortunes on magnificent seats, many chose to remain within the commercial world, purchasing small retreats or residential villas near London. Compared to their Restoration brethren, who bought proportionately more land outside the home counties, they were a distinctly metropolitan group.[54] Possibly fewer opportunities came their way, for it does seem likely that the property market narrowed a little after 1720, as mortgages became available and stricter settlements

genteel Family, in a most delightful and healthy situation at Layton, near Walthamstow, in Essex, about five miles from Town, being on a rising ground, and commands a fine prospect: consisting of a spacious and substantial Brick Mansion, Wings adjoining, with a large Court yard, Coach-yard, two excellent six-stall stables, and other stabling for eight horses, Four Coach Houses, large Kitchen and Pleasure Gardens, with fine shady Walls, Shrubberies handsomely laid out, the Walls and Garden well stocked with choice Fruit-trees, Fishponds and Canal . . . likewise a good Farm Yard detached from the Mansion with a large barn &c. The whole containing 33 acres and a Half of rich pasture land, Part Freehold and Part Copyhold, the Property of the late Captain Moore deceased.'

52. David Hughson, *pseudonym* (Edward Pugh), *London*, 6 vols (1805), V, 147–8.
53. PROB 11/1169/423.
54. Approximately 40 per cent of the post-Restoration aldermen held land outside a twenty-five mile radius of the capital. The corresponding figure for the mid-eighteenth-century aldermen was 19 per cent, for their merchant counterparts in parliament, 28 per cent.

more frequent. Perhaps, too, demographic fortune inhibited the acquisition of larger estates. Mid-eighteenth-century aldermen were not blessed with sons. Of those who married, as many as 45 per cent died without male issue. What land purchases might record, in other words, are not changing aspirations so much as economic and demographic constraints. Yet in the last analysis this explanation is not really adequate. Recent research on patterns of landownership in Lincolnshire and East Anglia has revealed a comparatively dynamic market, and we now know that the incidence of female or indirect inheritance was inordinately high, reaching 40 per cent among gentry families. As the record of Indian nabobs well illustrates, London merchants had ample opportunity to buy creditable estates had they so desired.[55] Furthermore, there is no evidence that fertility substantially affected land purchases. Property arrangements in the eighteenth century were normally conducted in anticipation of heirs. In any case, there is no obvious correspondence between the purchase of a landed estate and the survival of male progeny. Nor does the distribution of landed estates among the mercantile élite in parliament, where the rate of direct male inheritance was higher differ markedly from that of the aldermen. In both cases the majority purchased property within easy access to the capital; a trend complemented by the emergence of daily coach services to residential satellites such as Barking, Bromley, Camberwell, Clapham, Hackney, Highgate and Hampstead.[56] The commuting City gent had arrived.

55. James M. Holzman, *The Nabobs in England. A Study of the Returned Anglo-Indian 1760–1785* (New York, 1926), 26, 123–30. Holzman shows that nabobs rarely had fortunes of more than £20 000, yet they purchased estates far and wide. On the demography of the gentry, see Stone, *Family, Sex and Marriage in England*, 66–7. On the current reappraisal of the eighteenth-century land market see Christopher Clay, 'Marriage, inheritance and the rise of the large estates in England, 1660–1815', *Economic History Review*, 2nd ser., XXI (1968), 503–18; J. V. Beckett, 'English landownership in the later seventeenth and eighteenth centuries: the debate and its problems', *Economic History Review*, 2nd ser., XXX (1971), 567–81; and B. A. Holderness, 'The English land market in the eighteenth century: the case of Lincolnshire', *Economic History Review*, 2nd ser., XXVII (1974), 557–76.

56. *A Complete Guide to all Persons who have any Trade or Concern with the City of London* (1752), 99–123. Residential villages first emerged in the late seventeenth century and grew in popularity with the creation of turnpikes during the years 1713–18. By 1773 there were thirty-seven daily suburban services leaving the City and also the West End. Six years later there were hourly coach services from the City to Hackney, a suburb popular with London financiers. See F. M. L. Thompson, *Hampstead. Building a Borough 1650–1964* (1974), 18–26; Ian Nairn and Nikolaus Pevsner, *The Buildings of England. Surrey* (Harmondsworth, 1960), 49–50; Eric Pawson, *Transport and Economy: The Turnpike Roads of Eighteenth Century Britain* (1977), 330–2.

The shift towards suburban living and smaller estates cannot, therefore, be solely attributed to the vicissitudes of demography and land-ownership. It reflected, above all, changes in social aspiration. The rise of merchant status, the emergence of a polite but not exclusively landed ruling-class culture, the facility with which merchants married the quality, the increasing security of non-landed investments, all curbed the obsession with broad acres. Only among the nabobs, a group who lacked the social esteem of the eminent merchants, and the planters, a Caribbean gentry class whose sons received a polite education in the universities and public schools, did the commitment to landed gentility remain total. A review of the careers of aldermanic heirs adds weight to this view. Despite their large fortunes and country seats, an important number remained active in London trade. Humphrey Parsons' heir assumed control of the family brewery. George Nelson's continued as a corn factor. Heywood's son became a hardwareman. Richard Sclater advised his executors to apprentice his only son to a chemist and arranged a partnership for him in the family firm when he came of age.[57] Turner's son remained in overseas trade, Blakiston's in wholesaling. Bankers, above all, trod in their father's footsteps. Although most inherited large estates, singularly few abandoned business altogether, a practice that continued well into the nineteenth century. Aldermen who lacked sons, moreover, sometimes brought their nephews and heirs into their firms. Such was the case with William Benn, Richard Blunt, Sir William Calvert, Charles Ewer and Sir Daniel Lambert.

Spectacular fortunes and polite schooling, of course, inevitably disposed some heirs to join the leisured élite. The Beckford heirs became men of letters. Their cousin, who also derived his fortune from sugar and slaves, became an *aficionado* of the hunt, writing books on dog-kennels, scent and Greek hare-hunting. Barnard's son became a well-known art collector, resident in Berkeley Square, while Marshe Dickenson's heir, who inherited the family estate at Dunstable and substantial investments in the funds, re-entered the Bedfordshire gentry.[58] Ten sons, including William Beckford's heir,

57. PROB 11/808/150. The career patterns of aldermanic sons are derived from a search of the City directories of the 1770s and 1780s and from miscellaneous biographical material.
58. For the Beckfords see the entries in *D.N.B.* For Barnard, see John Pye, *Patronage of British Art, an Historical Sketch* (1845; 1970 facsimile), 145–6, and Gerald Reitlinger, *The Economics of Taste* (1961), 30. For Dickenson, *V.C.H. Bedfordshire*, II, 69.

also followed their fathers to parliament.[59] But even here, the attractions of Westminster did not sever their connections with commerce. Rawlinson and Ladbroke remained in banking and finance. The Fludyer brothers retained an interest in their family concerns. And William Baker's heir, despite his genteel education and magnificent estate, continued to be active in the Hudson's Bay Company and at the meetings of North American merchants. Only late in life, when he represented Hertfordshire, did he finally integrate with county society.

There are grounds, then, for suggesting that the quest for landed status became less compulsive as the century progressed. As new sources of stable investment emerged and merchants rose in respectability, so green-acred gentility lost some of its attractiveness. Land still remained the primary source of permanent political influence, but it was not the only reliable source of income, nor a necessary prerequisite of social acceptability. Indeed, to influential City families, total withdrawal from business might well have entailed a loss of political leverage and social influence; and it is hardly surprising that the heirs of London aldermen and big creditors, having watched their fathers rub shoulders with the parliamentary élite and entertain judges and peers, should sometimes prefer a *rentier* existence within the *beau-monde* to county standing. Some merchants would, of course, continue to hanker after landed pre-eminence. Sir Richard Carr Glyn, for example, who followed his father as a banker and alderman, told his son to nurture his connections with Dorset so that his progeny could easily assimilate into gentry society. His grandson's fortune, he anticipated, would 'be ample and sufficient to give him consequence in life and in the county' without entering the family business, and he hoped that an education at Westminster and Christ Church, Oxford, followed by a stint in 'the Guards or the Law and Parliament',[60] would smooth his social ascent. But fewer and fewer businessmen thought this way. Continuing contact with the City did not proscribe men from high society, although much depended upon the type of business one was engaged in and the prestige of one's patrons. If London families were eventually absorbed into landed society, it was sometimes through fortuitous circumstances rather than design, for few, over a period of three or four generations, could withstand the hazards of female

---

59. The ten sons were William Baker, William and Richard Beckford, Samuel Brudenell Fludyer and his brother George, Bamber Gascoyne, Edward Gibbon, Sir Richard Carr Glyn, Robert Ladbroke and Walter Rawlinson. Seven were heirs.
60. Fulford, *Glyns 1753–1953*, 69.

or indirect inheritance. In 1750 the age of permanent City dynasties was beginning.

III

We have seen that the big bourgeoisie of London did not necessarily travel the traditional route to social recognition. Pre-eminent in finance and overseas commerce, in close touch with high society through marriage and parliamentary membership, they enjoy a certain autonomy within the ruling class. The question that must be confronted is whether their situation was idiosyncratic or common to the great merchants as a whole. Perhaps, after all, the declining importance of landed prestige pertained only to the merchant princes and bankocrats of the metropolitan world, and was not reproduced elsewhere.

Certainly the provincial bourgeoisie could not detach itself so readily from landed society. Its political influence depended to a great extent upon regional affiliations, even allowing for the pressure that the outports could bring to bear upon ministers and parliament, and towns that lacked formal representation sometimes found it difficult to hold their leading families. Only six of the thirteen eminent merchant houses in Leeds continued in business during the course of the eighteenth century.[61] Furthermore, if a provincial merchant wished to stabilize his fortune by diversification, land remained an obvious choice. Few were in a position to invest huge sums in public securities, largely because an intimate knowledge of the money market and reliable London contacts were required.[62] Local ventures were a safer bet, and these, whether concerned with mining, mortgages, transport or property, were bound up with the land.

A variety of factors thus encouraged the aspiring merchant of the outports and manufacturing centres to integrate with landed society. Yet the migration of provincial wealth to the countryside was both partial and protracted. The leading families of Norwich showed no disposition to found landed dynasties; nor did many of their Bristol counterparts. The same was true of the Glasgow tobacco lords and the great merchants of Hull, in spite of the fact that the richest pur-

61. R. G. Wilson, *Gentlemen Merchants*, 19–20, 215.
62. Wilson, *Gentlemen Merchants*, 225. On the overwhelming preponderance of London investors in the funds see P. G. Dickson, *The Financial Revolution in England* (1967), ch. 11, and Sir John Clapham, *The Bank of England, a History*, 2 vols (Cambridge, 1944), I, ch. 8.

chased estates in neighbouring counties.[63] As with the London merchants, land was an important supplementary source of investment as much as a status symbol; rarely did it lead to a dramatic exodus from trade. Although some families gravitated to the countryside after a period of three or four generations, most merchants combined business with gentlemanly pleasures, commuting between elegant town houses and nearby country villas. For by the mid-eighteenth century no social gulf separated the gentry from the provincial bourgeoisie. Refinement was not the exclusive preserve of landed culture. Merchants employed fashionable architects, portrait artists and statuaries; rubbed shoulders with the gentry at the local assembly rooms and spas; joined them at the races and the hunt; and invited them to share in the annual round of civic convivialities. Drawn principally from well-established urban families resembling at times extended kinship groups,[64] the merchant élites of the Georgian era enjoyed a status not accorded to the captains of industry, whose profit-making inhibited the pursuit of pleasure, and whose petty-bourgeois origins created formidable social barriers. The acceptance of the merchant grandee but not the factory-master, in fact, underscored both the flexibility and limitations of Hanoverian polite culture.

Yet in the last analysis the civilities which characterized the relations between the landed and commercial aristocracy simply reinforced their basic class affinities. Both the landowner and merchant benefited from the development of capitalist agriculture and the concomitant expansion of unregulated industry upon which Britain's overseas trade rested. At a more personal level merchants relieved landed expenditures with mortgages and loans and joined enterprising landlords in promoting turnpikes, navigation schemes and agricultural improvements. As distinct but overlapping fractions of the capitalist class, they had a large stake in Britain's age of manufacture, and the cultural adjustments I have recorded merely register that fact. Those who argue to the contrary, who contend that landed prestige determined the durability of their alliance, have to account for the substantial redefinition of gentility and the complex exchange of land and money that confounds simple formulas

63. Penelope J. Corfield, 'The Social and Economic History of Norwich 1650–1850: A Study in Urban Growth' (Ph.D. thesis, Univ. of London, 1976), I, 236–7; R. H. Quilici, 'Turmoil in a City and an Empire: Bristol Factions 1700–1775' (Ph. D. thesis, University of New Hampshire, 1976), 142–4; T. M. Devine, *The Tobacco Lords* (Edinburgh, 1975), ch. I; Gordon Jackson, *Hull in the Eighteenth Century* (1972), 115.

64. Wilson, *Gentlemen Merchants*, 203–4, 212–13, 231–2; Devine, *Tobacco Lords*, ch. I; Walter E. Minchinton, 'The merchants in England in the eighteenth century', in Hugh G. J. Aitken (ed.), *Explorations in Enterprise* (Cambridge, 1965) 291.

of social emulation. They also have to account for the subtle trans-mutations of aristocratic culture, the way in which dynastic marriages were challenged by bourgeois notions of individualism and domesticity, and the commercialization of leisure which eroded the aristocracy's monopoly of conspicuous consumption.[65]

Of course honorific distinctions could still command respect in Hanoverian society. Within the circle of privilege the English nobility enjoyed an extraordinary *cachet*. Until the younger Pitt ex-panded its ranks, it was a closed, largely endogamous, self-confident clique, pre-eminent in parliament and cushioned from the embar-rassment of poverty by royal doles. Yet it is worth emphasizing that its continued supremacy principally rested on its ability to act as brokers for the bourgeoisie. As Horace Walpole reminded the young Marquis of Rockingham in 1752, it was his lordship's patronage of the woollen industry that would mark him out.[66] In other words, the esteem of the peerage did not contradict the fact that the dominant ethos of society was bourgeois and plutocratic. This did not mean that money alone talked; as we have seen, it had to be suitably decanted to taste. But the great merchants had little difficulty in fulfilling this requirement; business rarely impeded the social round. Attuned to a polite culture which largely accepted them on their own terms, they formed part of the heterogeneous but unified ruling class of the Hanoverian era. Indeed, when the industrial and professional middle class challenged the Georgian order, demanding a rationalization of the state and the economy, the merchant princes, bankers and financiers were by and large still located in the establishment camp.

APPENDIX A   The provenance of the London aldermen

	1660–89 (84)	1738–63 (74)
	%	%
London	25	45
South-east	20	10
South-west	18	13
East	7	4
Midlands	19	3
North	2	2
Elsewhere	1	7
Unknown	5	16

65. Stone, *The Family, Sex and Marriage in England*, chs. 6–8; J. H. Plumb, *The Commercialization of Leisure in Eighteenth-Century England* (Reading, 1973).
66. Michael W. McCahill, 'Peers, Patronage, and the Industrial Revolution 1760–1800', *Journal of British Studies*, XVI (1976), 93.

APPENDIX B   The social origin of the London aldermen

	1660–89 %	1738–63 %
Gentry	27	22
Yeomen	6	1
City business	23	46
Provincial business	12	7
Other	10	4
Unknown	23	21

Sources: J. R. Woodhead, *The Rulers of London, 1660–1689* (1965); company records of the Great Twelve, where accessible; C.L.R.O., apprenticeship indentures deposited with the Chamberlain's court; City of London Guildhall, Stocken MSS. and MS. 12 012. The Stuart cohort excludes those aldermen who declined office and the Crown nominees of the 1680s.

Chapter 10

BIRMINGHAM AND THE WEST MIDLANDS, 1760–1793: POLITICS AND REGIONAL IDENTITY IN THE ENGLISH PROVINCES IN THE LATER EIGHTEENTH CENTURY[1]

J. Money

[*Midland History*, 1 (1971)]

> *In his article John Money develops a theme also explored in Alan Everitt's contribution to this volume, that of the relationship between an urban centre and its locality. Both authors stress the vital role which a town could play in moulding the identity of its attendant region: but whereas Everitt is dealing with what by the eighteenth century were well-established local units, the county and its community, Money investigates an industrializing area and its urban capital which were still rapidly evolving entities. In the case*

---

1. This is a revised version of a paper read at Seattle, Washington, on 7 March 1970, to the Pacific North-West Section of the Conference of British Studies. It is originally derived from my 'Public Opinion in the West Midlands, 1760–1793' (Cambridge, unpublished Ph.D. dissertation, 1967). In the footnotes to the text, I have used the following abbreviations:

Aris	*Aris' Birmingham Gazette.*
Assay Office Papers	The Boulton and Watt Collection, the Assay Office Library, Birmingham. My thanks are due to the Assay Master for permission to quote from papers in his keeping.
BRL	Birmingham Reference Library.
Garbett-Lansdowne Letters	Four volumes of photostat copies of letters, chiefly from Samuel Garbett to the Earl of Shelburne, later Marquis of Lansdowne, in the Birmingham Reference Library.
Hist. Parl.	Sir Lewis Namier and John Brooke, *The History of Parliament, the House of Commons, 1754–1790* (3 vols., London, 1964).
Jopson	*Jopson's Coventry Mercury.*
Langford, *Birm. Life*	J. A. Langford, *A Century of Birmingham Life*, a Chronicle of Local Events, 1741–1841 (2 vols., Birmingham. 1868).
Swinney	Swinney's *Birmingham and Stafford Chronicle.*
U.B.H.J.	*University of Birmingham Historical Journal.*

*of Birmingham and the West Midlands, therefore, the relationship
between town and region is more fluid and dynamic, not least, as
Peter Large has shown ('Urban growth and agricultural change in
the West Midlands during the seventeenth and eighteenth centuries',
in P. Clark (ed.),* The Transformation of English Provincial
Towns 1600–1800 *(London, 1984)), because the region at this time
was engaged in a process of agricultural and industrial rationalization which was redefining the economic roles of the urban and rural
sectors. Money examines especially the function of politics in the
evolving relationship between Birmingham and its locality, and
places particular emphasis on widening popular involvement in the
political process. He develops these ideas further in 'Taverns,
coffee-houses, and clubs: local politics and popular articulacy in the
Birmingham area, in the age of the American Revolution',* Historical Journal, *14, no. 1 (1971), and his major study,* Experience and
Identity: Birmingham and the West Midlands 1760–1800
*(Manchester, 1977). Money's work raises the broader question as
to how far other expanding industrial centres, such as Manchester,
Leeds, and Sheffield, were creating powerful new regional blocks
during the eighteenth century and reshaping the human geography
of England.*

The West Midlands, by which has been understood the counties surrounding Birmingham, was one of the regions of England in which
the problems of life and work in manufacturing towns were first met.
From the whole experience of West Midlanders during the thirty
years which preceded the outbreak of the Revolutionary Wars in
1793, both with regard to the major events of national history, and
to their own local pre-occupations, there emerged a growing sense,
not only of the region's own special identity, but also of the contribution which it had to make to the wider development of society.
The most conspicuous single feature of this experience was the growing size and significance of Birmingham itself; but the town was not
yet the obvious centre of the region which it later became. Birmingham is situated, not at the hub of any previously recognizable area
of its own, but at the meeting point of the three counties of Warwickshire, Worcestershire and Staffordshire. As it grew, so there
developed a balancing tension between the new centre and the older
influence and example of the county towns and cathedral cities of
the region.[2] Although the novelty of the situation created by the

2. For Birmingham's earlier relationships with other West Midlands centres, see
   M. J. Wise, 'Birmingham and its Trade Relations in the early Eighteenth
   Century', *U.B.H.J.*, II no. 1 (1949), 53–79. For the early history of industrial
   development in the West Midlands, see W. H. B. Court, *The Rise of the Midlands
   Industries, 1650–1838* (London, 1938, reprinted, Oxford, 1953).

growth of Birmingham is inescapable, this must be seen in a proper perspective if the experience of those who lived and worked in this part of England during the later eighteenth century is to be properly recaptured.

The comprehensive study of changing ideas and developing identity within a regional community like the West Midlands over a long and eventful time span entails the handling of a vast and diffuse body of evidence and the pursuit of any number of local themes, important both in themselves and for the contribution they made to the coherent sum of the region's experience. In the space here available, it will therefore not be possible to do more than sketch briefly some of the issues involved. Within these limits, the discussion which follows will be particularly concerned with the political implications of the West Midlands' growing sense of its own identity.

Examples of the reciprocal relationship which existed between Birmingham and its surroundings, and of the ways in which the different parts of the region were becoming aware of what they had in common are not hard to find. Nothing which happened to them during the later eighteenth century captured the imagination or retained the attention of West Midlanders for such long periods of time as the fact that their home country was becoming the principal crossing point in a new system of communications and transport. The building of the canals made the interdependence of different parts of the region impossible to ignore. It made the region as a whole increasingly aware of its relationships with other parts of England. It produced a continuous exchange of views on a subject both indigenous to the region and important to the nation at large, an exchange which reflected not merely the rise of one centre but rather the need for particular interests in different places to learn to co-operate with each other, and with more distant areas, for the sake of mutual advantage. Quite apart from the material benefits conferred by the canals themselves, the various activities connected with their construction thus exerted considerable influence on the emerging self-consciousness of the West Midlands.[3]

This was not all. The successful promotion of a canal navigation needed more than the co-operation of private interests. It also required an approach to the legislature on the one hand and the

---

3. For Birmingham's own local network of canals, which linked the town to the longer navigations and thus with other areas of the country, see *VCH Warwicks.*, VII, 33–7. For Midlands waterways in general, see Charles Hadfield, *The Canals of the West Midlands* and *The Canals of the East Midlands* (both Newton Abbot, 1966). The stimulus which the canals gave to a growing sense of regional identity received typical recognition in the 'account of canals' with which Samuel Aris launched his new 'miscellany' supplement in *Aris*, 30 November 1772.

acquiescence, if possible the positive approval, of a large part of the general public on the other. For example, Josiah Wedgwood and his fellow backers of the Trent and Mersey canal had to do four things:[4] to recruit support from the different towns which would be affected, to present the scheme so as to generate informed public discussion, to coax the landowners into agreeing to the necessary invasion of their property and to develop political connections strong enough to ensure a safe passage for the requisite Act of Parliament. They showed themselves equally adroit at all four. During the early summer of 1765, the navigators worked hard to recruit support. The active interest of Liverpool was essential, and Thomas Bentley, who was in contact with Sir William Meredith, Member of Parliament for the port, advised a concerted approach to its Mayor, John Tarleton. Accordingly, great importance was attached to formal overtures to the Mayor and Corporation of Liverpool from their counterparts in the inland cities and towns which would have a stake in the canal. The Mayor and Corporation of Newcastle-under-Lyme, who also enlisted the patronage of the Marquis of Stafford, led the way, and Wedgwood was anxious to see Lichfield and Birmingham follow suit. The Trent and Mersey proposals were given extensive coverage in the newspapers. The *St James' Chronicle* carried two articles a week on the canal and became the London mouthpiece for the group. In the provinces, the press campaign was based on the papers which circulated from Liverpool, Manchester, Chester, Derby, Nottingham and Birmingham.[5] Wedgwood, however, was well aware that the dangers of thrusting the scheme too importunately before the public were every bit as great as those of neglecting to do so at all. The courtship of public approval was a delicate business, best conducted 'by degrees and by stealth as it were', for,

4. For Wedgwood's canal activities, see Eliza Meteyard, *The Life of Josiah Wedgwood* (London, 2 vols., 1865–66), especially I, chapters IX, X; K. E. Farrer ed., *Wedgwood's Letters to Bentley* (2 vols., privately printed, 1903), I, *passim*, and Anne Finer and George Savage eds., *The selected Letters of Josiah Wedgwood* (London, 1965), 30–4, 39–40. The Liverpool edition of Bentley's *View of the Advantages of Inland Navigation*, together with further correspondence on the Trent and Mersey Canal, is reprinted as an appendix to K. E. Farrer ed., *The Correspondence of Josiah Wedgwood, 1781–1794* (privately printed, 1906).

My thanks are due to the firm of Josiah Wedgwood and Sons Ltd., and particularly to Mr Billington, curator of the Wedgwood Museum, for allowing me to consult unpublished material in the collection at Barlaston. References to this have been identified by the abbreviation *Barl.* The John Rylands Library, Manchester, also has a collection of MS. copies of Wedgwood correspondence, English MSS. 1101–1110, which has been identified below as *Ryl. Eng. MSS.*

5. Wedgwood to Erasmus Darwin, 3 April and n.d. April 1765 *(Barl.)*, Wedgwood to Thomas Bentley, 27 April 1765 *(Ryl. Eng. MSS.* 1101, p. 68).

> If the individuals of this Public shd. once perceive that instruction is
> offered them *without their asking for it*, they are sure to be
> refractory, and counteract rather than coincide with any measures
> intended for their benefit.[6]

Thomas Bentley's *View of the Advantages of Inland Navigation* was
crucial to the success of the Trent and Mersey proposals, but
punctilious care was taken over the drafting of the pamphlet during
the late summer of 1765 lest inelegancies of style, a misplaced word
or an unintentional innuendo should create the wrong impression
among the fastidious, anger the owners of property or should
prejudice the scheme's chances with the politicians.[7]

Besides the effort to rouse the various provincial towns and cities
and to make friends in the right places, what is striking about all
this is the highly sophisticated awareness of public reactions to which
it bears witness and the attention paid to the mobilization of
opinion. It was not that the equally important business of constructing a lobby within the 'Structure of Politics' was neglected, far from
it; but this was seen as secondary to the main objective. The
proposals for the Trent and Mersey canal were to be vindicated by
public controversy, after which those who persisted in opposing
them would stand revealed as retrogressive obscurantists. The passage of the necessary bill through an enlightened legislature would
be the logical conclusion of a rational argument. Though canal
navigation was not a matter of national politics – at least, not in the
eighteenth century's conventional understanding of the term – it was
becoming a matter of wide concern, and in the appeal by the
navigators to informed public discussion can be seen the genesis of
a relationship between politics and public opinion more characteristic of nineteenth-century England than of the age of oligarchy.

Improvements in communications multiplied Birmingham's connections with a wider world. Extensions of the postal services, both
to and from London, and across country, 'by which means correspondence between this town and many other commercial parts in
both kingdoms will be greatly accelerated', were noticed by the
Birmingham Gazette on 4 July 1768. By 1777, fifty-two coaches,
carrying up to six passengers in each, left Birmingham for London
every week; in addition, sixteen went to Bristol, four to Coventry,

---

6. Wedgwood to Erasmus Darwin, 13 April 1765 *(Barl)*. In the appendix on canals
   in Farrer ed., The *Correspondence of Josiah Wedgwood, 1781–1794*, 227–8, the
   texts of this letter and that of Wedgwood to Darwin, 3 April 1765, have been
   elided and are printed as one letter dated 3 April 1765.
7. For the drafting of the pamphlet, see *Wedgwood's Letters to Bentley*, 1, 48–69,
   letters between August and November 1765. See particularly pp. 55, 56, 62, 68–9,
   Wedgwood to Bentley 26, 27 September, 15 October, 18 November 1765 for
   Darwin's strictures on style.

and four to Sheffield.[8] By the end of the American War, the town had its own links with the world, and was no longer so dependent on London for its news. Indeed, as far as commercial matters were concerned, the Midlands were a nerve centre whose reactions were far quicker than those of the capital. When Joseph II of Austria issued an edict in 1784 prohibiting the entry of British goods into his domains, Birmingham knew of it months before the news made any impact in London. As Samuel Garbett complained to the Earl of Shelburne:

> This Edict was printing in July, was published the 15 September, and Administration admit the latter end of October that they have no account of it but from the middle of their own kingdom.[9]

In fact, it was only after correspondence between Garbett, acting for the Birmingham Commercial Committee, and Dr Percival in Manchester, and after an express memorandum thence to the Treasury, that the matter began to be taken seriously.[10] Even then, the 'official' view remained one of polite disbelief. The indignation of the Birmingham men at the diplomatic persiflage and masterly inactivity of the central government showed very clearly in Garbett's angry letter to Matthew Boulton in February 1785:

> I have not the smallest doubt that Mr Rose's attention to this business is like his answer, and like the attention of the Minister in Vienna, who sent no account of the edict. The whole affair is 'Sir, your most obedient and most humble servant etc. etc.'.[11]

The affair of the Imperial Edict was but one episode in the development of the manufacturers' organizations which culminated in the formation of the General Chamber of the Manufacturers of Great Britain in the early months of 1785 in order to oppose Pitt's Irish Commercial Treaty. The detailed history of this has been written elsewhere[12] and no new purpose would be served by giving an

---

8. Langford, *Birm. Life*, I, 224. Since the estimate doesn't mention services to Liverpool or Manchester, it probably by no means accounts for all passenger movements.
9. *Garbett-Lansdowne Letters*, I, Garbett to Shelburne, 7, 9, 30 October, 2 November 1784. Garbett first got wind of the edict from a letter sent from Prague the previous July to the Birmingham firm of Oakridge and Marindin.
10. *Garbett-Lansdowne Letters*, I, Garbett to Shelburne, 14, 26 October 1784 and respective enclosures.
11. *Assay Office Papers*, Garbett Box, Garbett to Boulton, 14 February 1785.
12. See J. M. Norris, 'Samuel Garbett and the Early Development of Industrial Lobbying in Great Britain', *Econ. Hist. Rev.*, II, x (1957–58), 450–60. On the second major episode in the history of the General Chamber of Manufacturers, see Witt Bowden, 'The English Manufacturers and the Commercial Treaty of 1786 with France', *American Historical Review*, XXV (1919–20), 18–35, and W. O. Henderson, 'The Anglo-French Commercial Treaty of 1786', *Econ. Hist. Rev.*,

abridgement here; but it is impossible to read much of the correspondence of those involved without noticing the repeated challenge to existing ideas and to the automatic hegemony of London which it expressed. This was particularly so in the case of Samuel Garbett. Garbett preferred not to join the leaders who were meeting in London unless he absolutely had to, and therefore avoided some of the limelight. Nevertheless, he deserves to be remembered with Wedgwood and Boulton as one of the General Chamber's prime movers for his untiring efforts to mobilize the suspicious ironmasters of the West Midlands were crucial to its success, as least as far as the Birmingham area was concerned.[13] Indeed, the considerable local difficulties which Garbett had to overcome led him to an attitude to the Chamber's future just as sanguine as that of his better known colleagues, if not more so. He thought that a direct request that Parliament suspend its discussion of the Irish proposals until it had heard from the General Chamber was an essential step towards securing the 'station we are entitled to'.[14] Wedgwood, on the other hand, feared that the new organization might provoke adverse reactions by exceeding its brief:

> We may no doubt publish our resolutions and propositions voluntarily to the public, but I always understand it to be our idea that we should wait to be called on before we do anything that could, even by our enemies, be construed into giving information immediately to Parliament itself.[15]

No doubt Wedgwood, writing from London, was more aware of the finesse required in the handling of a delicate situation than Garbett, working among the men of the Black Country. But what was the point of expressing opinions if there was no way of bringing the politicians to the point? 'Depend upon it,' wrote Garbett, 'The Chamber sinks if, when the delegates meet, they go no further than wording good resolutions at a tavern to put into newspapers'.[16] Mere propaganda would not be enough to jolt the hesitant Midlanders into action. The General Chamber must not be deterred by Parliament's refusal to hear it as a body, nor by the obsolete pro-

II, x (1957–58), 104–12. More general accounts are in Paul Mantoux, *The Industrial Revolution in the Eighteenth Century* (Revised edition, London, 1961), 390–2, and Witt Bowden, *Industrial Society in England towards the end of the Eighteenth Century* (2nd edition, London, 1965), 160–93.

13. On Garbett's career and his rôle as 'the commercial intermediary of Birmingham *vis-à-vis* the government of the day', see P. S. Bebbington, 'Samuel Garbett, 1717–1803, a Birmingham Pioneer' (Birmingham, M.Comm. Thesis, 1938). Other references are taken from *Assay Office Papers*, Garbett Box.

14. Garbett to Boulton, 3 April 1785.

15. *Assay Office Papers*, Wedgwood Box, Wedgwood to Boulton, 4 April 1785.

16. Garbett to Boulton, 9 April 1785.

cedural devices which were being resuscitated to avoid hearing
individual members of it. Even if the Chamber was not prepared to
petition as a body, it should take the initiative and call the Minister's
bluff by delivering petitions from its individual members. Once this
was done,

> The ground will be completely gained for Birmingham and other
> places also to petition, taking notice of the representations that you
> as *delegates* have laid before the House of Commons. In this mode,
> the character of the Chamber will be established, and this too will be
> done whether the petition is received or rejected. The world will form
> its opinion of the General Chamber of Manufacturers by the manner
> in which they treat the little shuffling device that was probably
> concerted to prevent your petitioning. But if any minister can support
> himself after refusing a petition from such persons, we shall see our
> situation is become desperate, and rouze accordingly.[17]

Certainly the General Chamber of Manufacturers, which was only
a few weeks old when Garbett urged this course of action on Boulton early in April 1785, had no ancient credentials in the legal or
constitutional sense of the word, and certainly the pushing provincials who formed it could not claim to represent any historic interest.
As a coherent force, 'the manufacturing interest' was very new, and
its representative body had therefore to establish its own credentials
by challenging both Parliament and the Minister in the forum of
Public Opinion. Garbett did not think that Pitt would dare to send
eminent men back to the country to report that they had been
fobbed off with, as he put it, 'the flimsy operation of an insignificant
form'. Therefore he urged the members of the Chamber to press
their petitions as individuals. As his letter explained, once this was
done, Birmingham and the other manufacturing districts involved
could designate the petitioners as their delegates, thus providing
them with credentials enough, and establishing the Chamber on
ground which the Minister would not dare to question. At the same
time, the whole campaign could be supported by further petitions
from each of the particular districts involved. These were hardly orthodox politics by the standards of the day — but then Samuel
Garbett didn't have much time for 'what is called Politics by those
who guide the affairs of this country'.[18]

---

17. Garbett to Boulton, 11 April 1785. 'The little shuffling device' was Pitt's refusal
    to countenance petitions either from the General Chamber as a body or from
    individual members of it on the grounds that the new organization was not, in
    the strict sense of the term, a legally constituted body.
18. *Garbett-Lansdowne Letters*, I, Garbett to Lord Rawdon, n.d. ? May 1784. The
    aggressive line advocated by Garbett early in 1785 requires some further expla-
    nation in the light of J. M. Norris' overall account of the political tactics of the
    General Chamber ('Samuel Garbett and Industrial Lobbying', pp. 456–7), which

'What is called Politics . . . '. The structure of society in Garbett's day was of course dominated by its more traditional elements, and politics was largely a matter of relationships between members of an established order conducted with little or no direct regard for a wider public. It may be, however, that historians have accepted this stereotype of eighteenth-century politics and society too easily and have applied it too broadly. The experience of West Midlanders during the later part of the century provides ample evidence at all social levels that the meaning of politics was already changing. As the energy which was devoted to their own public affairs shows, West Midlanders were acquiring a marked sense of their own identity, were beginning to challenge the leadership of London and were being led through a multitude of different channels towards a general notion of politics which was a good deal more comprehensive than that accepted by the establishment at Westminster. The activities of the General Chamber of Manufacturers foreshadowed the kind of sustained and concentrated extra-parliamentary pressure directed at particular objectives which was to play such an important part in the history of the next century. Wedgwood in 1780 was expressing views on 'General and Particular Representation' – whether a Member of Parliament should regard himself as a general representative free to follow his own discretion or as a delegate acting under particular instructions from his constituents – which ran counter to the hallowed idea of Virtual Representation, reflected the potter's practical experience of delegated responsibility in

it appears to contradict. Faced with the need to determine its attitude to party-politics, with which Parliamentary discussion of the Irish proposals had become entangled, the Chamber divided into two main groups. Wedgwood and the Lancashire men favoured an alliance with the opposition and joined Lord Sheffield and William Eden in public agitation against the ministry. The Birmingham men looked askance on this association with party, and preferred to rely on persuasion and personal influence at Westminster. On the face of it, therefore, Garbett had second thoughts about his earlier militancy; but the change was more apparent than real. To the understanding of Garbett's attitude, which remained consistent throughout, the distinction between politics and party-politics, and that between two notions of 'Public Opinion' and its rôle, are both crucial. At no time did Garbett wish to jeopardise the political position of the irreplaceable Pitt, for 'we cannot expect to find so good a minister in his room amongst those who oppose him'. (To Boulton, 25 February 1785, *Assay Office Papers*, Garbett Box). Despite his exasperation in April, Garbett had no intention of getting embroiled in party-politics. The forum to which he appealed was that of 'eminent men', leaders in their own right, and the purpose of the appeal was to authenticate and reinforce the lobby, not to replace it. There was a decisive difference between real 'Public Opinion' in this sense of the phrase, and the kind of agitation which the Manchester men were advocating, agitation which, far from serving the ends of the Chamber would only obscure them, and whose overtones of potential social disruption were profoundly inimical to Garbett's essentially conservative mind.

Turnpike and Navigation business, and endorsed the theories of Dr John Jebb of the Society for Constitutional Information.[19] Nor would any account of that society be adequate which found no place for Joseph Priestley and his friend William Russell, or which overlooked the rôle of lesser men, such as those listed in the Society's minutes on 29 June 1792 as its Midlands distributors of 'Mr Paine's letter to Mr Secretary Dundas' and other printed material: the Revd John Edwards, who succeeded Priestley at the Birmingham Old Meeting House; Mr Thomas Francis, also of Birmingham; the Revd Mr Rowe of Shrewsbury; Mr Fox of Derby; the editor of the *Leicester Herald*, and the Revd Mr Corrie of Bromsgrove.[20]

It might be objected that these examples relate to particular groups of men with particular interests rather than to any general consciousness, that the activities of the Society for Constitutional Information were a matter of the converted preaching to the converted and making precious few proselytes, and that the real state of West Midlands opinion is better shown by the region's apathy during the County Association movement between 1779 and 1785, which obliged Priestley to admit to Christopher Wyvill that 'What you call a *pause of astonishment* is in this part of the country a *pause of indifference*'.[21] There were, however, reasons for this, and the region was not so much indifferent to the idea of reform in principle as unimpressed by the particular reforms proposed by Wyvill and the associated counties. There are indeed signs that when Wyvill wrote to Boulton and Garbett on 31 January 1785 to solicit their

---

19. Wedgwood to Bentley, 20 May 1780, *The Selected Letters of Josiah Wedgwood*, 250–1. This kind of questioning of current assumptions in the West Midlands was, of course, part of something much bigger. The theoretical and practical problems which concerned Jebb and Wedgwood in 1780 and Garbett in 1785 – the responsibilities of delegates, the sources of their authority, the relationship between a representative assembly and its wider constituency, the right to be heard of particular communities or interests within that constituency – all focused on the distinction between Virtual and Particular Representation. Though the emphasis differed in each case, this was being re-examined on both sides of the Atlantic. In America, the predicament of the Colonists forced the distinction into prominence, so that the notion of Particular Representation, originally a seventeenth century idea based on medieval forms of attorneyship, became capable of new development (see Bernard Bailyn, *The Ideological Origins of the American Revolution* (Cambridge, Mass., 1967, 161–75). In England, the concerns of Wedgwood, and of others like him, produced similar results. The experience of these men, while obviously not the same as that of the Colonists, was equally novel.

20. Public Record Office, Treasury Solicitor's Papers, TS 11/962, Minutes Book of the Society for Constitutional Information, 1792–1794. For Richard Phillips of the *Leicester Herald*, see A. Temple Patterson, *Radical Leicester* (Leicester, 1954), 67–73.

21. Joseph Priestley to Christopher Wyvill, 14 February 1782, Christopher Wyvill, *Political Papers* (York, 1794–1808), IV, 157.

help in obtaining a petition from Birmingham in support of Pitt's forthcoming reform bill, he was to some extent justified in 'having understood from several friends how much you are disposed to give every important assistance to the cause of Political Reformation'.[22] The Birmingham leaders remained cautious however. They kept their own counsel, and regarded Wyvill's enthusiasm as rather naive and premature. On 31 January 1785, when Wyvill was writing to Boulton, *Aris' Birmingham Gazette* printed an address from 'A Real Reformer'. Several broadsheet copies of this, still in mint condition, survive among the papers of Matthew Boulton. It is reasonable to assume that Boulton had some hand in the printing and circulation of the address and in its insertion in the Birmingham paper, and that it contained proposals which he endorsed – proposals enclosed in a letter which he had recently received from a Mr Deane of Broseley in Shropshire.[23] Deane's letter urged Boulton to have the proposals published, and cast serious doubts on the reform plans of Pitt and Wyvill. The address from 'A Real Reformer' did the same. After subscribing to the principle of reform, it was highly critical of the expected plan to double the county representation, to leave the boroughs untouched, and merely to enfranchise the larger of the manufacturing towns. Such half measures would simply reduce places like Birmingham and Manchester to the status of Old Sarum, and would leave the representation of the nation as disproportionate as ever. Instead, the address made seven proposals of its own: that boroughs with less than a specified number of voters should be absorbed into the county constituencies; that at General Elections, polling should take place on the same day throughout the kingdom, should be limited in duration according to the size of the constituency, and that voters should be polled in their own parishes; that candidates should be qualified by a specified period of residence in their constituencies; that voters should be similarly qualified; that the representation of the commercial and manufacturing part of the nation should be increased by enfranchising those who could show that they earned more than a specified minimum in trade and industry; that votes should be cast by ballot, and that voters should be registered in their home parishes and be checked at the hustings. 'A Real Reformer's' misgivings were justified, and the Birmingham leaders, who in any case were far more directly occupied at the time with their opposition to Pitt's proposed Irish Commercial Treaty and anxious to keep their objectives in this respect free from any imputation of party political motives, displayed no further interest in the reform movement.

22. Wyvill to Boulton, 31 January 1785, *Political Papers*, IV, 458.
23. *Assay Office Papers*, P. Deane to Boulton, 28 January 1785.

Quite apart from these general shortcomings, both the proposals of the associated counties, and the reform bill which Pitt laid before Parliament in 1785, failed to provide a more attractive alternative to the very satisfactory arrangement which had recently been worked out between Birmingham and the representation of Warwickshire. The way in which this came to pass illustrates very clearly the shortcomings of that commonplace among eighteenth-century historians recently questioned by Professor J. H. Plumb: that there were

> Two worlds of politics in the eighteenth century – a tight political establishment, linked to small groups of powerful managers in the provinces, who controlled parliament, the executive, and all that was effective in the nation, and outside this an amorphous mass of political sentiment that found expression in occasional hysteria and impotent polemic, but whose effective voice in the nation was negligible.[24]

The people of the West Midlands were no mere political spectators. Birmingham itself may not have sent its own representatives to Westminster, but the town could exert considerable political influence in the counties and boroughs of the surrounding region. The interest of Matthew Boulton was a valuable electoral asset both at Lichfield and Bridgnorth.[25] Besides the virtually direct control of one of the Warwickshire members which Birmingham established in 1774 and deliberately exerted from 1780 onwards, the town's leaders could muster an impressive lobby of members for other Midlands constituencies when the occasion demanded it.[26] Though connections of this kind were much more seriously cultivated during the later eighteenth century, they were no new thing. It was Sir Richard Newdigate, Member of Parliament for Warwickshire, who, in 1692, secured for the gunsmiths of Birmingham a major contract from His Majesty's Board of Ordnance.[27]

The mutual understanding between the local gentry and the manufacturers of Birmingham found a well established forum in the

---

24. See his essay 'Political Man' in James L. Clifford ed., *Man Versus Society in Eighteenth Century Britain, Six Points of View* (Cambridge, England, 1968), 12.
25. *Assay Office Papers*, letter from Thomas Anson and Thomas Gilbert requesting Boulton's vote and interest at Lichfield, n.d., 1768; letter from Thomas Anson and Sir John Wrottesley, 1 July 1802, asking for Boulton's presence during their forth-coming canvass of Lichfield, and several papers on the Bridgnorth election of 1802, when Boulton and Watt helped to mobilize Birmingham voters at short notice on behalf of Isaac Hawkins-Brown and J. Whitmore.
26. *VCH Warwicks.*, VII, 275–6 lists them. See also J. M. Norris, 'Samuel Garbett and the Early Development of Industrial Lobbying in Great Britain' and Eric Robinson, 'Matthew Boulton and the Art of Parliamentary Lobbying', *The Historical Journal*, VII (1964), 209–29.
27. *VCH Warwicks.*, VII, 85, 273.

Birmingham Bean Club, founded soon after the Restoration as a loyalist dining club in which the leaders of the town and the land-owners of the surrounding country districts could meet on equal terms and enjoy free and confidential discussion of matters of mutual interest.[28] By the later eighteenth century, Bean Club members were being drawn from a wide area surrounding Birmingham, an area which included large parts of existing county divisions, but which conformed to the boundaries of none of them.[29] The club was by then involved in many different aspects of Birmingham life. Its members were prominent among the Street Commissioners appointed under Birmingham's Improvement Act in 1769; they were active in the foundation and administration of the General Hospital; later, many of them were active supporters of the Sunday School movement; Samuel Aris of the *Birmingham Gazette* and his successor James Rollason were both Bean Club members.[30] Though an organized and coherent 'Birmingham Interest' did not become a clearly identifiable factor in Warwickshire politics until after the 1774 election, Bean Club members played an important part in its development. The club's county stewards in 1769–70 were Lord Craven and Thomas Skipwith,[31] who was elected Member of Parliament for Warwickshire on 29 March 1769. Sir Charles Holte, the victor in the county election in 1774, was steward of the Bean Club in the same year, and in 1780–81 and 1781–82, Sir George Shuckburgh and Sir Robert Lawley, Warwickshire's two new members, succeeded each other in the same office. It was a Bean Club member, Thomas Gem, who initiated the measures taken before the 1780 election to maintain and consolidate the advantages gained in 1774, measures which secured the nomination and return of Sir Robert Lawley as peculiarly 'The Member for Birmingham'.[32]

In its reactions to wider events, the Bean Club showed itself to be increasingly conservative from the 1770s onwards. When Mat-

---

28. Sir J. B. Stone, *Annals of the Bean Club*, BRL 345313, p. 1.
29. Bean Club members can be identified from notices of club meetings in *Aris* and, more extensively, from W. K. R. Bedford, *Notes from the Minutes Book of the Bean Club, 1754–1836* (1889), BRL 131399. This gives brief details of early meetings and a continuous record of membership, elections, officials and the more important resolutions of the club from 1772 onwards. By the 1780s, the membership was being drawn from places as far apart as Bridgnorth, Stone, Stoke (Herefordshire, not Stoke-on-Trent), Appleby (Leicestershire). Burton-on-Trent, Malvern and Daventry.
30. Nine of the Street Commissioners listed by Langford, *Birm. Life*, I, 190, appeared in the Bean Club membership records during the ten years following 1769. The original Hospital committee, appointed on 24 December 1765 (Langford, *Birm. Life*, I, 155) likewise contained several Bean Club members.
31. *Aris*, 4 August 1769, 3 September 1770.
32. See particularly *HMC Dartmouth III*, 252–3, Gem to the Earl of Dartmouth, 14 September 1780, and in general, *VCH Warwicks.*, VII, 276.

thew Boulton was organizing his address in support of the Ministry's American policy early in 1775,[33] he made a list of 'Names to petition of the inhabitants of the town and neighbourhood of Birmingham to North America'. Twenty-three of the eighty-seven names which Boulton assembled appeared also in the minute book of the Bean Club before 1782.[34] After the American War, the club fast became a hotbed from which the loyalist associations of the 1790s sprang up as naturally as weeds. Edward Carver, County Steward of the Bean Club in 1789, was president of the Birmingham Church and King Club founded in November 1792, and the Birmingham Association for the Preservation of Liberty and Property had at least five Bean Club members on its committee.[35] The Bean Club's attitude was no more than might be expected from a body which included among its members the country gentlemen of the district, the magistrates and the clergy of the established church. This, however, does not mean that the club simply represented forces opposed on principle to the progress and development of society. Through a club which had existed for nearly a century before 1760, the association between the established ranks of society and the tradesmen who were aspiring to leadership in the growing towns was firmly linked, in Birmingham at least, to the traditions of the eighteenth-century constitution. Those traditions came under increasing stress from 1760 onwards, particularly during the American War, and this was reflected by signs of strain within the Bean Club.[36] The conventional

33. On this, see Brian D. Bargar, 'Matthew Boulton and the Birmingham Petition of 1775', *William and Mary Quarterly*, 3rd series, xiii(1956), 26–39, *VCH Warwicks.* VII, 275, is mistaken in associating Boulton with the conciliatory petition which was presented at the same time.
34. The list is in *Assay Office Papers,* America Box. The names were Joseph Carles, Henry Clay, Richard Conquest, James Cooke, Edward Davis, William Dickenson, Thomas Faulconbridge, Samuel Ford, John Fothergill, Thomas Gem, John Gimblett, John Goodall, Richard Goulden, Joseph Green, Thomas Ingram, Thomas Lutwyche, James Male, Thomas Rock, John Meredith, Thomas Orton, Edward Palmer, Thomas Tomlinson and D. Winwood. There are three more 'possibles', John Simcox, John Birch and James Duker (?Dickson) Budd.
35. *VCH Warwicks.*, VII, 282–3: Joseph Carles, The Revd Dr Spencer, Sir Robert Lawley, The Revd Charles Curtis, The Revd George Croft. Cf.: Donald E. Ginter, 'The Loyalist Association Movement in 1792–3 and British Public Opinion', *The Historical Journal*, IX (1966), 179–90, especially p. 187: 'From one point of view the Reeves Associations were so effective as to be a most unreliable gauge of public opinion. For the most part the associations were composed of men from a single neighbourhood, accustomed to frequent social and political intercourse. The associations were specifically designed to make it exceedingly difficult for individuals to avoid membership by remaining in the background.'
36. A number of signs suggest that the affairs of the Bean Club did not run smoothly during the 1770's. The club's association with Boulton's address in support of the Coercive Acts in 1775 ran counter to the Bean Club's links with the War-

formulae of Liberty and Independence, in which the club's proceedings had hitherto been enshrined, were no longer able to accommodate the serious divergences of opinion which lay beneath the rhetoric. Nevertheless, within the limits of the constitution as they understood it, Bean Club members had, by the 1790s, gone some way towards finding viable solutions to the problems created by the growth of Birmingham. The club was not simply a bastion of reaction. It was a conservative institution closely associated through its membership with the whole development of society in the Birmingham area. As such, it was in many respects a precursor of the attachment of the middle classes to the aristocratic constitution which was more widely achieved after 1832, and it embodied in microcosm the merits as well as the defects of that conjunction.

'Two worlds of politics' there have always been; but the influence which unrepresented Birmingham could exert in the constituencies of the West Midlands, the lobby of Members of Parliament which the town could command and the social relationships which existed between country gentlemen and Birmingham manufacturers all show that, in this part of England at least, those two worlds were never finally separated from each other. Indeed, from the time of the Seven Years' War onwards, the links between them were being mul-

---

wickshire MPs. Boulton, who was apostrophized for his pains as a 'toad-eating sycophant', had taken the part of the 'despicable dimunative [*sic*] junto' which was defeated in the 1774 election. Sir Charles Holte, the victor on that occassion, was an independent, whose sympathies were Whig if anything. Although he did present Boulton's address in 1775, Thomas Skipwith was very definitely in the Rockingham camp and voted consistently against the ministry right through the war. His rather surprising transfer to a safe Rockingham seat at Steyning in 1780 suggests that, contrary to appearances, he had disagreed with at least one important group among his Warwickshire constituents. If this was so, the bone of contention was probably American policy, and the Bean Club may well have been involved. The club's own minutes and records also hint at dissension. Stone states that the Bean Club did not meet between 11 August 1775 and 22 August 1777; yet Bedford records minutes during the intervening period and *Aris* advertised meetings on 3 June and 5 August 1776. The nomination of Myles Swinney, whose *Birmingham and Stafford Chronicle* had been distinctly sympathetic to the colonists during the previous two years, was turned down by the Bean Club on 22 August 1777, along with that of Dr Withering. On 22 August 1778, John Gough of Perry Hall was blackballed for holding rival dinners at the same time as Bean Club meetings, and a resolution was passed making members' attendance at Bean Club anniversaries compulsory on pain of expulsion. Clearly, something was disturbing the oldest establishment clique in Birmingham. See *Assay Office Papers*, undated note from Lady Aylesford to Boulton soliciting his interest on behalf of her son, Lord Guernsey, the original 'Lordly' candidate in the 1774 election for Warwickshire; John Mordaunt (who replaced Guernsey on the hustings) to Boulton, 11 November 1774; MS. copy in 'America' box of 'Veritas' to the *London Evening Post*, 7–9 February 1775; *Hist. Parl.*, II, 634; III, 442–3; W. Cobbett and J. Wright, *Parliamentary History*, XVIII (1774–77), 182; Bedford, *Minutes, passim*, and Stone, *Annals of the Bean Club*, p. 8.

tiplied rather than diminished, and new connections of a different kind began to appear alongside those provided by such longstanding institutions as the Bean Club. The results became particularly conspicuous when the escapades of John Wilkes and the dispute with the American Colonies provided for the first time a series of issues on which the emerging self-consciousness and nascent radicalism of the new manufacturing districts could concentrate their energies. This concentration produced a downwards extension of articulacy to levels of society which had not been reached consistently, except in London, since the early years of the century, when the struggle for political mastery had entailed frequent appeals to a large electorate and the stability of Walpolean politics and society was yet to be achieved.[37]

In the older provincial centres, especially those whose parliamentary franchises were comparatively open still, and where politics were dominated by longstanding feuds between rival interests, the effects of new developments merged with local traditions which were still very much alive. In the West Midlands, the possible results of this can be seen in the contrasting examples of Coventry and Worcester. Both had wide franchises; both were notorious for the corruption and violence of their election contests; in both, politics were dominated by the battle between Freemen and Corporation, and in both, popular response to Wilkes was caught up in the local quarrel. There the similarities ended. In Worcester, the popular cause continued to be associated with Wilkes and played an important part in shaping the political consciousness of Birmingham and the Black Country. In Coventry too, there was plenty of evidence of Wilkite sympathy until late in 1768, when it was permanently distorted out of all recognition by the local fight between the city's True Blue Freemen and their Whiggish, Occasionally Conforming, Corporation. Sir Richard Glyn, a London banker who was backed by the Ministry in the Coventry by-election in December 1768, made skilful play with the susceptibilities of the Freemen, and the shouts which accompanied his election – 'High Church – Glyn and Liberty – Now or never', made an ironic contrast to the usual slogans of the day.[38]

In the areas of new growth, unenfranchised, and with their own traditions as yet unformed, circumstances were different, for the new

---

37. I have given a more detailed account of what follows in 'Taverns, Coffee Houses and Clubs: Local Politics and Popular Articulacy in the Birmingham Area in the Age of the American Revolution', shortly to be published in *The Historical Journal*. I have therefore reduced references here to a minimum, except in the case of the new material.

38. For Coventry, see *Hist. Parl.*, I, 401; T. W. Whitley, *The Parliamentary Representation of the City of Coventry* (Coventry, 1894), 165–8, and *Jopson, passim*. The rôle of Worcester will be apparent from what follows.

articulacy could express itself without being so directly influenced by older preconceptions. Nevertheless, the new towns took their cues as much from the existing provincial centres as they did from London, and from wherever the specific impetus came in each individual case, the result was the same: the appearance in the provinces of institutions and modes of association among the common people which had previously been confined to the capital, and the creation of a public which was both literate and politically active. The Robin Hood Debating Society, already notorious in London in 1750, had at least two imitators in Liverpool by 1768, and the pages of Cowburne's *Liverpool Chronicle*, alive with political debate, helped to form the opinions of thousands of men and women actively interested in the politics of the day. In the West Midlands, the Birmingham Robin Hood Free Debating Society, which first published its order sheets and resolutions early in 1774, met in Sam Wickens' Long Room at the Red Lion Inn to discuss a surprising range of questions, moral, philosophical, parochial, political, economic, and facetious. Though the rough and tumble of its meetings made it the butt for satirical comment in the papers and for the invidious attention of the more exclusive and perhaps more decorous Amicable Debating Society, its example was followed in Wolverhampton and Walsall, and it seems to have attracted the attention of the parent society in London. Of Birmingham's two newspapers, *Aris' Birmingham Gazette*, first published in 1741, was already recognized as one of the leading provincial papers, while Myles Swinneys *Birmingham and Stafford Chronicle* took a more adventurous line. Swinney, who also ran a subscription club where books, pamphlets, and the London daily papers were available to his readers,[39] first raised the eyebrows of the respectable in 1772 when he printed Voltaire's *Thoughts on Religion* in the columns of *The Warwickshire Journal*, one of the three prototypes launched during the crowded years 1769–70 from which the *Birmingham and Stafford Chronicle* was derived in 1773. In 1775, the *Chronicle* supported Birmingham's conciliatory petition at the start of the American War, and crossed swords with Aris' *Gazette*, the mouthpiece of Matthew Boulton's countermeasures in favour of the Coercive Acts. Between 1778 and 1781, Swinney collaborated with J. W. Piercy of *Piercy's Coventry Gazette* in a joint venture which incurred the wrath of the rabidly Tory *Jopson's Coventry Mercury* for its opposition to Lord North and its support of the Coventry corporation during that city's election contest in 1780, one of the most violent and corrupt of the entire century. Even in 1793, when the two Birmingham papers had drawn closer together to face the threat of revolution, Swinney's

39. *Aris*, 10 February 1772.

paper was still sufficiently conspicuous as the most active opinion forming organ in the Midlands for John Brooke, one of the local magistrates, to urge the Home Office to acquire a controlling interest in it, especially as there was a chance that it might fall into the hands of 'Violent supporters of Priestley and Paine'.[40]

Nor were the diverse roots of popular articulacy confined only to such tangible forms of expression as the local newspapers. They must be sought in the entire range of activity which characterized the life of a growing manufacturing town. Birmingham's artisans could not but be infected by the enthusiasm generated by the aspirations of what Burke called 'The Great Toy Shop of Europe' to social and cultural status, as well as to political recognition. Thus, as the one form of entertainment equally attractive to all tastes and to all sections of society, the Theatre played an important part in shaping the consciousness of the common people. The united reign of Industry and Art, 'The Drama's useful scenes', were welcomed, not merely as an inducement to rich tourists to spend their money in the town, but also as a reward for 'Th'industrious artisans's o'er laboured day'. The Birmingham Robin Hood Free Debating Society returned a favourable answer to the question 'Is the Exhibition of Plays likely to be serviceable or detrimental to the town of Birmingham either in respect to Temporals or to Morals?'[41] The pantomime at Swann's Amphitheatre in February 1788, featuring 'THE TAYLORS JOURNEY TO BRENTFORD ELECTION', and 'The Peregrinations of a Certain Great Character', or the Adventures of 'THE BONNIE LADDIE or HARLEQUIN JEW' with scenery to match, including Newgate prison in flames, illustrates the way in which the two episodes during the previous twenty years which had most involved the common people – the Middlesex Election and the Gordon Riots – had been absorbed into the stock of vulgar comedy. Similarly, while the middle classes enjoyed concerts, cards and dancing in the genteel surroundings of the Vauxhall Gardens or the Assembly Rooms of the Royal Hotel, the working people of the town formed themselves into clubs and cliques like the Birmingham Musical and Amicable Society, founded in 1762, devoted not only to mutual providence and benefit, but also to beer, song and sociable discussion. It was such societies, together with the Masonic Lodges, the Ancient and Noble Order of Bucks, or the Society,

40. Introduction to *Voltaire's Creed Proved Insufficient for Man's Salvation* (Birmingham, 1771), BRL 62409; *VCH Warwicks.*, VII, 210; Joseph Hill, *The Bookmakers and Booksellers of Old Birmingham* (Birmingham, privately printed, 1907), 73; *Swinney*, 2 February 1775 (in America Box, *Assay Office Papers*), and 24 December 1778 (when it was also printed by J. W. Piercy in Coventry); *Jopson*, 20 November 1780, 15 January 1781; Public Record Office, Home Office Papers, H.O. 42/25, John Brooke to Evan Nepean, 7 June 1793.
41. *Aris*, 16, 23 May 1774.

presumably of Welshmen, which honoured the memory of Caractacus at the Bowling Green House, Longnor, Shropshire, in September 1777, which provided the background for men like John Freeth, tavern and coffee-house keeper, book-club promoter, election poet and ballad monger extraordinary. They acted as an equivalent among the artisans to the assemblies, concerts and oratorio festivals at which more polite society could meet informally, and at which social and political attitudes would be tacitly reinforced. Particularly important for the development of the latter was the fact that Birmingham was not merely a centre of influence, but a point of confluence as well, where ideas and opinions originating over a wide area might be exchanged, and might affect each other. Because so many of them were recent immigrants from the surrounding country districts, Birmingham people represented in themselves the divided sympathies of the West Midlands, drawn as they were by the opportunities offered by the town, yet leaving behind them interests and loyalties in their original homes. Thus, though Birmingham was itself unrepresented in Parliament, it constituted a reservoir of potential voters who were wooed at election times by candidates from constituencies as far apart as Worcester, Leicester, Newcastle-under-Lyme, and even Lincoln. The affairs of these must have bulked large among the talking points in Birmingham's taverns and coffee-houses, particularly in the Leicester Arms at the corner of Bell Street and Lease Lane, where John Freeth played host to the Birmingham Book Club, and made his house the recognized meeting place for opponents of the ministry.

Between 1768 and 1774, the Birmingham papers were rife with reports of petitions in redress of grievances, of gestures of sympathy and solidarity with the hero of the day, and of rumours of Wilkite campaigns in the region which they served. Many of these proved to be groundless, but they all kept interest in local politics very much alive. In 1769, Warwickshire came close to joining the petitioning movement which followed the Middlesex election,[42] and the prospect gave 'Aemilius' a chance to point out in Aris' *Gazette* of 23 October that, as a commercial town, Birmingham could 'never prosper unless the general liberties and rights of the people are preserved inviolate', and to urge all parties 'to oppose with vigour any invasion of the constitution'. Across the county boundary in Staffordshire, activity was more restrained, but even though ministerial influence was expected to prevent a petition, the freeholders showed signs of forsaking their usual subservience, and of presuming to instruct their

42. *Aris*, 25 September, 9, 16, 23, 30 October 1769; George Rudé, *Wilkes and Liberty, a Social Study of 1763 to 1774* (Oxford, 1962), n. 3 to p. 133.

Members of Parliament, 'a right,' said Aris' paper, 'the immediate exertion of which, though perhaps not altogether consistent with good manners, is, however, highly necessary.'[43] In particular, attention was focused on Worcester, where during 1773 and 1774, during two by-elections and the general election of the latter year, Sir Watkin Lewes fought what was one of the major campaigns mounted in the provinces by the Wilkites on behalf of the Independent Freemen against the formidable combination of Dean and Chapter, Corporation, Peer and Nabob which controlled the city's politics. In the Black Country towns, Worcester Freemen formed clubs to support Lewes, and in Birmingham, John Freeth invited the friends of Sir Watkin, and all who were concerned to restore 'a distracted state to the tranquil order and pursuit of public measures which may be conducive to the prosperity and happiness of a brave and free people' to meet at the Constitutional Society at the Leicester Arms Tavern.[44]

The most significant result of all this was indirect. Sir Watkin's cause at Worcester was fundamentally hopeless, and though he improved his position in each of the three polls which he stood, he filled the last place every time. However, as with other Wilkite gestures in the region, such as the enquiry of the burgesses of Wenlock into the conduct of their Members of Parliament in June 1769, so with Lewes' campaigns: it was not so much the factual outcome which was significant so far as the political awareness of Birmingham people was concerned, as the noise which they made. In Wenlock, represented by thirteen members of the same family, not counting relatives, between 1529 and 1885, 'The free, safe, and peaceable exercise of their rights' meant the burgess' freedom to return a Forester, as they had done time out of mind. The readers of *Aris' Birmingham Gazette*, however, were told that 'The spirited conduct of the Burgesses of Wenlock . . . would . . . convince the elected that they are the ministers, and not the masters of the electors.'[45] Similarly, the actual result of the Worcester election was not the end of the matter. The cause of the Independent Freemen had been well publicized from the beginning. Several aspects of it appealed very strongly to those who lived and worked in an increasingly important, though unrepresented, manufacturing region. For those people, the fact that the Worcester contest had been fought under the full panoply of the Wilkite Radical programme – that such support had actually materialized – must have served to offset the memory of rumours from other places which had proved groundless.

43. *Aris*, 13 November 1769.
44. *Aris*, 8, 22 August, 3, 10 October 1774.
45. *Aris*, 26 June 1769; *Hist. Parl.*, II, 450.

It was the independent cause in Warwickshire which was the real gainer from Lewes' campaign. Warwickshire elections had been uncontested since the early years of the century, and though a *modus vivendi* had been reached between gentry and aristocracy, it was the latter, specifically the Earls of Warwick, Aylesford, Craven and Hertford, whose influence had hitherto been paramount in county politics.[46] There had been rumblings of discontent with 'Lordly Power' in March 1769, when the death of William Bromley created a vacancy in the Warwickshire membership. The return of Thomas Skipwith on this occasion, despite the threatened candidatures of the Hon. Mr Craven and Lord Beauchamp, the eldest son of the Earl of Hertford, was hailed as a blow for independence,[47] and later in the year, dark references were made to suspected measures taken by 'The Great' to prevent the county from petitioning after the Middlesex election.[48] Nevertheless, no really purposeful moves had been made because there was as yet no hint that the other incumbent member, Sir Charles Mordaunt, might resign his seat. Sir Charles' intention to retire was not made known to the county at large until 10 October 1774. Only then therefore did the prospect of a contest become real, for only then could the Independents decently mount a campaign and avoid the odium which would have damned any attempt to oust a sitting member in a county undisturbed in living memory. By that time, there remained only three days before the nomination meeting in Warwick, and another week after that before the poll began. Yet in the event, the freeholders of Hemlingford Hundred, virtually Birmingham and its vicinity, outweighed the rest of the county, defeated John Mordaunt, the 'Lordly' candidate, and sent Sir Charles Holte to join Skipwith in the next Parliament. Thus, after a last-minute campaign, were demonstrated for the first time the political implications of the growing population of north-western Warwickshire. It could hardly have happened if the people of Birmingham had not already been alerted by events elsewhere, so that their potential political energy could be redirected at

---

46. *Hist. Parl.*, I, 399–400.
47. *Aris*, 13, 20 March 1769. Birmingham's first improvement Act was causing considerable controversy in the town, but, whatever their differences on local affairs, Birmingham voters were agreed that, in the words of John Freeth's 'Epigram on the Bill Now Depending for Removing Public Nuisances',

The Greatest Nuisances that we want
Fairly from the land shove,
Are worse than any town complaint,
And every day are seen above.

48. *Aris*, 30 October 1769.
49. *Aris*, 7, 14, 21, 28 November 1774; 16 January, 16 October 1775.

short notice to the affairs of the home county. John Freeth's Constitutional Society with its Worcester connections may have disappeared, but even as it did so, the Independent Constitutional Society of the Freeholders of Warwickshire was meeting at the Swan Inn to celebrate Holte's victory, and to lay plans for its consolidation.[49]

That Birmingham opinion was indeed sufficiently responsive to transmit reactions in this way between different constituencies, and that local politicians had to take account of the fact, was further shown soon after the General Election. Some of Holte's more zealous supporters were duped by misleading propaganda from Leicestershire, where a by-election was pending. The crucial issue in this was one on which the opinions of Sir Charles' Birmingham friends were particularly sensitive, namely the alignment of the Dissenting interest in Leicestershire, which both candidates were wooing, one with intentions rather more honourable than the other. Two of Holte's supporters, John Rickards, a dissenting Birmingham attorney,[50] and a Mr William Sadler of West Bromwich, inserted notices in *Aris' Birmingham Gazette* which were doubtless well meant, but which committed Sir Charles' goodwill to the wrong side in the neighbouring county. Holte's reputation in the Birmingham area could have been seriously damaged had he not corrected the error personally as soon as the real situation in Leicestershire became clear. His tactfully phrased, but hasty notice in the *Birmingham Gazette* on 12 December 1774 showed that he was well aware of the danger.[51]

These interactions within a group of West Midlands constituencies may not have been paralleled by immediate alterations in the way the affairs of the nation were conducted at Westminster, but they do show how the substructure of politics was beginning to change in one of the developing regions of England, where older communities were being affected by their proximity to a new centre with markedly different characteristics, and with its own political traditions still to be formed. The Warwickshire election of 1774 and the circumstances which produced its unexpected result did not *ipso facto* signal the appearance of a fully fledged 'Birmingham interest'. Despite the near unanimity of 1774, the serious divisions caused by the American War had to be resolved before the town's leaders could put themselves at the head of the body of opinion which had hailed Skipwith in 1769 and which returned Sir Charles Holte five

---

50. John Rickards' name appeared frequently among those present at meetings of the general assembly of subscribers to the Old Meeting House. See *Old Meeting House, Register of Resolutions of the General Assembly of Subscribers, 1771–1791*, BRL 641586.
51. *Hist. Parl.*, I, 322; *Aris*, 28 November, 5, 12 December 1774.

years later. Nevertheless, it was the victory of Sir Charles Holte which established the bridgehead from which Birmingham's claim to a pre-emptive nomination of one of the Warwickshire members could be developed. In 1780, steps were taken prior to the county meeting to ensure a nomination acceptable to Birmingham, and by the time of the 1784 election, the newly formed Birmingham Commercial Committee was taking the lead in the town's deliberations.[52] Thus was the accommodation achieved between a growing manufacturing town in the forefront of the Industrial Revolution and the established structure of English politics.

52. For the Commercial Committee, see *An Account of the Manner in which a Standing Commercial Committee was Established at Birmingham for the Purpose of Watching Over, and Conducting the Public Interests of that Town and Neighbourhood* (Birmingham, 1784), BRL 27082. For the Commercial Committee's leadership in the 1784 election, see *Aris*, 9 February, 29 March, 5 April 1784. It was the Commercial Committee which called the town together to address the king in support of his dismissal of the Fox-North Coalition, and it was the same body which met to discuss action to be taken on the dissolution of Parliament. The older authorities in Birmingham stood pointedly aloof.

Chapter 11

SOCIAL CLASS AND SOCIAL GEOGRAPHY: THE MIDDLE CLASSES IN LONDON AT THE END OF THE EIGHTEENTH CENTURY

L. D. Schwarz

[*Social History*, 7, no. 2 (1982)]

The study of the social geography of the pre-modern town has been dominated by the differing theories of Sjoberg and Vance. However, John Langton's 'Residential patterns in pre-industrial cities: some case studies from seventeenth-century Britain', Transactions of the Institute of British Geographers, *65 (1975), has questioned the value of such rigid models in the context of the complex residential patterns found in British towns. This is a conclusion which also emerges from Leonard Schwarz's essay. He undertakes an inventive analysis of the spatial distribution of the middle class in late eighteenth-century London using the tax assessment returns of 1798 (it must be emphasized that two-thirds or more of the capital's population were considered too poor to be liable for payments). Schwarz discovers a clear tendency for the wealthier and less well off to concentrate in different areas of the city, but this does not lead, as Sjoberg would argue, to a simple division between a richer centre and a poorer periphery. Moreover, any tendency towards segregation was only a* tendency, *since all parishes accommodated a significant sprinkling of the various tax-paying categories. In fact, Schwarz's tax group III, people of middling incomes (many of whom were shopkeepers) were spread fairly evenly across London, which leads him to speculate that their political attitudes may have varied according to the social complexion of the area that they occupied. The author's move from income to class analysis, and social to political geography, is an issue to consider while reading this piece.*

The importance of the middling classes – or 'middling order' – in eighteenth-century metropolitan politics, whether in the City of London, in Westminster or Middlesex itself, is undisputed. In the City, public opinion was formulated not by, the prosperous aldermen, the directors of the great joint-stock companies, the rich merchants and the thriving financiers . . . but by the lesser merchants, the tradesmen, the master-craftsmen and the host of minor intermediaries who formed the majority in the popular organs of City government and who thronged the meetings and clubs where political opinion was formulated.[1]

Describing the Westminster election of 1749 Nicholas Rogers makes a case for 'a rough correlation between the genteel character of the Court vote and the *petit bourgeois* character of their opponents',[2] although this pattern was still heavily overlaid by ties of clientage, deference and dependency, which were all gradually to weaken in the course of the century. Wilkes received his support in Middlesex principally from 'the smaller property-owners of the county' – not from all of them by any means, but from those 'in the populous commercial parishes lying to the east and north of the City'.[3]

Considering their importance, it is surprising that the middle classes have not been examined more closely, though such an examination is rendered particularly difficult by the absence of convenient sources. In this respect the eighteenth century is unfortunate compared with the seventeenth century with its Hearth Tax or the sixteenth century's Subsidy Assessment. Fortunately, there is a comparatively concise source that refers to London in 1798: the returns sent to the government by the collectors of assessed taxes in that year. I have analysed these returns to provide a general outline of the social structure and distribution of incomes in London,[4] and found that the wealthiest group, with incomes exceeding £200 a year, formed no more than 5 per cent of the population, while those with middling incomes formed another 20 per cent. This article will examine the top 25 per cent in more detail. The first section will provide a brief résumé of the source involved; the rest of the article will discuss certain relationships that emerge when the various London parishes are examined in more detail.

1. L. Sutherland, *The City of London and the Opposition to Government, 1768–74* (1959), 6–7.
2. N. Rogers, 'Aristocratic clientage, trade and independency: popular politics in pre-radical Westminster', *Past and Present*, LXI (1973), 83.
3. G. Rudé, 'The Middlesex Electors of 1768–69', *English Historical Review*, LXXV (1960), 609, 615.
4. L. D. Schwarz, 'Income distribution and social structure in London in the late eighteenth century', *Economic History Review*, XXXII, 2 (1979), 250–9.

I

The term 'assessed taxes' comprised those taxes collected not by the land tax commissioners nor the Excise, but by the 'Commissioners for Assessed Taxes': in 1798, when the government asked the local commissioners for information about their individual regions they were collecting taxes on windows, horses, carriages, manservants, dogs, clocks and watches. The information requested by the government has survived for only a very few parts of the country, but among those parts London is very well represented, with returns from parishes which together accounted for some 75 per cent of the population of London in 1801.[5] The collectors – there appears to have been at least one for each parish, sometimes more – were asked to divide the houses in their areas into two groups: those that had retail shops in them, and those that did not. Each of these groups was then further subdivided, specifying houses with lodgers, houses whose owners found it difficult to pay their assessed taxes, houses where the owners had been excused some or all of their assessed taxes, and houses where warrants had been issued compelling the owners to pay. Furthermore, all houses were divided into five categories, depending on the total amount of assessed tax they paid each year: those paying less than £1 per annum, those paying more than £1 and less than £2, from £2 to less than £5, from £5 to less than £10, and those paying more than £10. Of course the assessed taxes were evaded, but the categories employed are sufficiently broad to allow for some evasion. The taxes were, however, fairly heavily progressive, so it is impossible to move directly and accurately from the amount of assessed taxes paid to an estimate of annual income. Fortunately, some of the collectors provided impressionistic accounts of income according to the amount of taxation paid, from which a rough indication of median incomes, the midpoint in the scale, can be attained. It is shown in Table 1. While this table would make no pretence at considerable accuracy, it does suggest that, roughly speaking, classes III and IV, whose income was thought by the various collectors to range between £70 and £200 a year, and with median incomes of £79 and £128, can be considered as middle class, at least as far as their incomes were concerned, while class V, earning over £200 a year would quite probably be upper class. Whether those in tax categories I and II with incomes of £61 and £66 a year should be considered middle class is open to

5. P. R. O., PRO/30/8/280–1. The detailed statistics are in L. D. Schwarz, 'Conditions of Life and Work in London, *c.* 1700–1820, with special reference to East London' (Oxford University, D. Phil. thesis, 1976), 343–57.

TABLE 1. Median incomes according to the amount of assessed tax paid annually[a]

Amount of tax	Income per annum
I. Under £1 tax	£61
II. £1–under £2 tax	£66
III. £2–under £5 tax	£79
IV. £5–under £10 tax	£128
V. £10 and over tax	over £200

[a]There is a graph in Schwarz, 'Income distribution', 253.

doubt, and for the original estimate of the size of the London middle classes, where the intention was to compare the results with Patrick Colquhoun's estimate of the 'comfortable' middle classes, they were not specifically considered,[6] although some allowances were made. In this paper, however, they are included, not because persons with incomes exceeding £60 a year were intrinsically 'middle class' – a skilled artisan could earn as much – but because, comprising some 10 to 12 per cent of London's population, they formed a group between the 'comfortable' middle classes of the higher tax categories and the two-thirds or more of London's population too poor to be liable to assessed taxes at all, while they merged with neither of them. For convenience they will be referred to as lower-middle class – to refer to their incomes and *not* to make implications about class consciousness or related factors. Similarly, classes IV and V are referred to as upper-middle class.

Needless to say, aggregate figures impose a deceptive unity on the various parts of London. This is well illustrated by Table 2, which compares several parts of the metropolis: three wealthy parishes in Westminster, eighteen wealthy and small wards of the 'City Within' (the most prosperous part of the City of London) and fifteen predominantly poor parishes in the Tower Division of the East.[7] Over half the taxed houses in the Tower Division found themselves in tax classes I and II, compared with a quarter in

6. Ibid., 256, n.1. If included, the London middle and upper classes formed 30 per cent of the population; excluded they formed 25 per cent.
7. Westminster: St Anne, Soho; St George, Hanover Square; St Paul, Covent Garden. City Within: wards of Cripplegate, Dowgate, Castle Baynard, Cordwainer, Candlewick, Coleman Street, Bridge, Walbrook, Langbourn, Broad Street, Bread Street. No data on lodgers from wards of Vintry, Billingsgate, Farringdon Within, Lime Street, Tower, Aldgate and Cheap. Tower Division: St Katherine's, St George-in-the-East, Shadwell, Mile End, Ratcliffe, Christ Church Spitalfields, East Smithfield, Limehouse, Bow. No data on lodgers from Bethnal Green, Shoreditch, Wapping, Whitechapel, Norton Falgate and Poplar.

TABLE 2   Distribution of buildings in each taxation class, Westminster, City Within, Tower Division

Taxation class	Westminster	City Within	Tower
I. Under £1	15	5	29
II. £1–under £2	10	8	26
III. £2–under £5	24	29	31
IV. £5–under £10	30	34	10
V. £10 and over	20	24	4
Total	99	100	100
Number	7 082	6 954	12 795

TABLE 3   Proportion of shops and residential houses with lodgers

	Westminster	City Within	Tower
Percentage of shops with lodgers	69	53	38
Percentage of houses with lodgers	52	35	39

Westminster and less than one in seven in the City Within. On the other hand, less than one in seven of the houses in the Tower Division were in the highest tax categories IV and V, compared with over half those in Westminster and the City Within.

The balance between houses and shops was also very different. For every 100 shops, there were in Westminster a little over 100 residential houses without shops in them; in the City Within there were 245 and in the Tower Division 187. As Table 3 demonstrates, these three areas were also different in their pattern of taking lodgers. The rest of this article is concerned with exploring these differences: not only the differences between the three areas of London, but more generally the difference between the wealthy and the poorer parishes in the metropolis, as a whole.

II

When the figures for the individual parishes are analysed in some detail, the first and most obvious conclusion to emerge is that in

319

parishes where a high proportion of the houses paying assessed taxes were in tax class I there was also a high proportion in class II; where the proportion of houses in class IV was high, so also was the proportion in class V. However, as the proportion of houses in classes I and II increased, the proportion in classes IV and V fell very steadily and markedly. In parishes where there were many taxpayers with incomes of around £66 a year or less there were therefore few who earned much more than £100; conversely, where there were many earning more than £100 there were few taxpayers with incomes below that figure. This was clearly residential segregation, but as yet it was only valid to a certain degree. In the first place, whether they earned £60 or £200 a year, all those paying their assessed taxes lived near to those not paying any assessed taxes at all. Wealthy and poor taxpayers were all equally likely to have an equivalent proportion of houses not liable for assessed taxes in their parish. The chances of a wealthy taxpayer, living in a wealthy parish, finding poorer *taxpayers* around him were less than one in five, but (excluding the city for which such data are unavailable) he was quite as likely as his poorer counterpart to have as many unassessed *houses* in his parish.[8]

On the other hand, he was by no means as likely to suffer an equivalent number of the very poor. The greater the proportion that the wealthiest taxpayers, in classes IV and V, formed of the total number of assessed houses in their parish, the greater their share in the total population. That does not mean that they totally dominated even the wealthiest of parishes. Nowhere did they form much more than half the population, usually very much less.[9] In this respect London was similar to the other large cities of Europe: in Paris in the 1840s – albeit a later period – there was not a single *arrondissement* where the bourgeoisie formed a majority of the population;[10] in Dublin in 1798 the middle classes formed between 6 per cent and 36 per cent of the population of their respective parishes.[11] Further

---

8. Spearman correlation coefficients; buildings by amount of tax paid (significant at 95 per cent level). See table on p. 321.
9. Assuming – improbably – an average family size of six, they came to 54 per cent in Covent Garden and 52 per cent in St George the Martyr; on average, for the six wealthiest parishes outside the City, they came to 34 per cent.
10. A. Daumard, *La Bourgeoisie parisienne, 1815–1848* (Paris, 1963), 181–5, 210–11; P. H. Amann, *Revolution and Mass Democracy* (Princeton, 1975), 16, suggests, however, that the bourgeoisie enjoyed a narrow majority in one *arrondissement* out of twelve.
11. Except in one parish, where they formed 45 per cent: N. T. Burke, 'Dublin 1600–1800. An Essay in Urban Morphogenesis' (Dublin University Ph.D. thesis, 1973), 447–52. (I am indebted to Dr D. Dickson for this reference.) Over the whole town they came to 22 per cent. The source is Whitelaw's census of Dublin in 1798; it is not clear how Whitelaw decided who belonged to the upper and middle classes and who did not.

This table forms part of note 8 on p. 320.

Tax categories	I	II	III	IV	V	I & II	IV & V	Percentage of buildings excused tax
I	1.00							
II	0.8140	1.00						
III	n.s.	n.s.	1.00					
IV	−0.8703	−0.8984	−0.2881	1.00				
V	−0.8484	−0.8229	−0.4200	0.8466	1.00			
I and II	0.9518	0.9302	n.s.	−0.9291	−0.8709	1.00		
IV and V	−0.8880	−0.9051	−0.3951	0.9535	0.9461	−0.9387	1.00	
Percentage of buildings excused tax	n.s.	0.3743	n.s.	n.s.	n.s.	n.s.	n.s.	1.00

By I is meant the proportion that the houses in tax class I formed of all the houses paying tax, II is the proportion that houses in class II formed of all those paying tax, and so on.

321

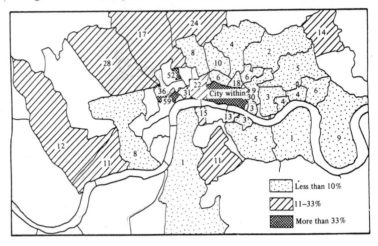

Fig. 1 Proportion that taxpayers in categories IV and V form of the population of their respective parishes.

research will probably uncover a similar pattern in other large cities. The process of residential segregation was sufficiently recent, towns were not yet sufficiently large, transport too poor and the demand for labour-intensive services too great to permit their total domination of areas larger than a few squares or streets.

Nevertheless, as Figure 1 shows, the area that was particularly heavily influenced by the higher income group was rather large, comprising the City Within, parts of Westminster, with a definite clustering around the central, western and north-western parts of London. Middle-class, or rather upper-middle-class *domination*, had not yet taken place, but a tendency towards *segregation*, even on the relatively large scale of the parish, was becoming a reality. And when class III, the lower end of the comfortable middle classes, is included, there is a marked picture of bourgeois influence over the City, large parts of Westminster, and the north-west. It is probable that in no other major European city of the time was so large a proportion of the built-up area subjected to such heavy middle-class pressure. As a corollary, the 'comfortable' middle classes of tax categories III, IV and V were rather thin on the ground elsewhere (Figure 2). But in these areas the 'insecure' lower-middle class in tax categories I and II were heavily in evidence. In the twelve wealthiest

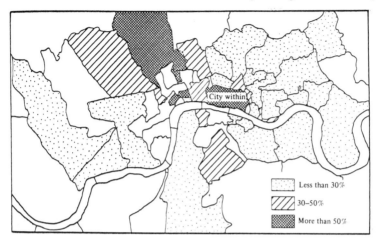

Fig. 2 Proportion that taxpayers in categories III, IV and V form of the population of their respective parishes.

parishes outside the City they formed less than 3 per cent of the population; in the fifteen poorest parishes they formed 20 per cent.[12]

Distinct – or at least distinguishable – upper- and lower-middle classes are, of course, well-known phenomena of mid-nineteenth-century Britain[13] as well as of eighteenth-century London, as manifested, for instance, by the support for Wilkes in the 1760s, or in the mid-1790s by the agitation of the more democratic representative chamber of the City of London, Common Hall, against the war: an agitation staunchly opposed by the more select Common

12. The poorest parishes are taken as being those where fewer than 15 per cent of the houses liable for assessed taxes were in tax categories IV and V; the wealthiest parishes were those with more than 50 per cent of the taxed houses in this category. To have divided the 59 parishes into three nearly equal sections would have produced some geographical absurdities, putting into separate categories adjoining parishes where the proportion of houses in classes IV and V was different by only a fraction of 1 per cent; hence this division. Fifteen parishes had fewer than 15 per cent of their houses in tax classes IV and V, 19 had between 16 per cent and 49 per cent, while 12 had more than 50 per cent in this category.
13. See, for example, R. S. Neale, 'Class and class consciousness in early nineteenth-century England: three classes or five?' in R. S. Neale (ed.), *Class and Ideology in the Nineteenth Century* (1972); J. Foster, *Class Struggle and the Industrial Revolution: Early Industrial Capitalism in Three English Towns* (1974), ch. 6; R. J. Morris, *Class and Class Consciousness in the Industrial Revolution, 1780–1850* (1979).

Council.[14] The tax data do not, of course, provide a means of telling whether, in sociological terms, tax categories I and II can be called 'lower-middle class' or 'labour aristocracy', or indeed whether such terms have very much meaning when applied to London at the end of the eighteenth century. However, even by purely statistical criteria, tax categories I and II did not merge with the rest of the untaxed population. Had they done so, it would be expected that, statistically, as categories I and II increased as a proportion of the population from parish to parish, so would the proportion of the population untaxed, but in fact the latter proportion showed no particular tendency either to increase or to decline.[15] Similarly, as the number of wealthy householders in tax classes IV and V declined, the number of householders in classes I and II increased very drastically, but the proportion of houses untaxed showed only a minimal, statistically insignificant tendency to fall.[16]

The householders in the low tax classes I and II, paying less than £2 a year assessed taxes, did not, in fact, dominate their parishes. They had to coexist with tax class III, paying between £2 and £5 a year in taxes, whose median incomes were a little over £80 a year. The members of tax class III spread themselves remarkably evenly across London, forming about a tenth of the population everywhere, irrespective of the wealth or poverty of their parish, and stubbornly refusing to correlate themselves with any of the variables that could be thrown at them. The Tower Division for instance had four times as many householders in tax classes I and II as in classes IV and V; in Westminster the picture was reversed with twice as many householders in classes IV and V as in classes I and II. Nevertheless, while in Westminster householders of class III formed 24 per cent of all those householders liable to pay assessed taxes, in the Tower Division they formed 31 per cent. The outcome was a total taxpaying population that was spread fairly evenly across London. The Tower Division had proportionately almost as many taxpayers as the wealthy parts of Westminster, but in the Tower Division lived a very

14. For Wilkes, see G. Rudé, *Wilkes and Liberty* (Oxford, 1962), 81, 85–7; for the 1790s, see G. Rudé, *Hanoverian London* (1971), 243; J. Ann Hone, 'Radicalism in London, 1796–1802: convergence and continuities', in J. Stevenson (ed.), *London in the Age of Reform* (Oxford, 1977), 89; J. Dinwiddy, 'Robert Waithman and the revival of radicalism in the City of London', *Bulletin of the Institute of Historical Research*, XLVI (1973).
15. Proportion of population in tax classes I and II correlated with proportion of population not liable to taxes: R. Spearman = −0.1972 (sig. 76 per cent).
16. Proportion that houses in tax classes IV and V formed of all the houses paying tax correlated with: (*a*) proportion of taxable houses in classes I and II: R. Spearman = −0.9387 (99 per cent sig.); (*b*) proportion of houses excused assessed taxes: R. Spearman = −0.2760 (91 per cent sig.).

different bourgeoisie (if bourgeoisie they can be called) from their
more comfortable, if politically radical, counterpart in Westminster.

The Westminster taxpayers may have been more comfortably
situated than those in the Tower Division; they were also more
likely to be letting their rooms to lodgers.[17] The parishes with a high
proportion of wealthy taxpayers in 1798 had, in 1801, an average of
two persons more per house, and this difference cannot entirely be
accounted for by arguing that wealthy families may have been
larger. If he wished to live in a poor area, a prospective householder
could choose from among a number of small houses and had little
reason to pay more rent than he might consider reasonable; it was
otherwise if he wished to move into a wealthier area. And this was
especially the case for a shopkeeper, seeking the wealthier customers of the more salubrious parts of London. As Adam Smith
commented:

> There is no City in Europe, I believe, in which house-rent is dearer
> than in London, and yet I know no capital in which a furnished
> apartment can be hired so cheap. Lodging is not only much cheaper
> in London than in Paris; it is much cheaper than in Edinburgh, of the
> same degree of goodness; and what may seem extraordinary, the
> dearness of house-rent is the cause of the cheapness of lodging. The
> dearness of house-rent in London arises, not only from those causes
> which render it dear in all great capitals, the dearness of labour, the
> dearness of the materials of building, which must generally be
> brought from a great distance, and above all, the dearness of
> ground-rent . . . but it arises in part from the peculiar manners and
> customs of the people which oblige every master of a family to hire a
> whole house from top to bottom. A dwelling-house in England means
> everything that is contained under the same roof. In France,
> Scotland, and, many other parts of Europe, it frequently means no
> more than a single story. A tradesman in London is obliged to hire a
> whole house in that part of the town where his customers live. His
> shop is upon the ground-floor, and he and his family sleep in the
> garret; and he endeavours to pay a part of his house-rent by letting
> the two middle stories to lodgers. He expects to maintain his family
> by his trade, and not by his lodgers. Whereas at Paris and
> Edinburgh, the people who let lodgings have commonly no other
> means of subsistence; and the price of lodging must pay, not only the
> rent of the house, but the whole expence of the family.[18]

17. Spearman correlation coefficients: proportion of taxed buildings in classes IV and
    V correlated with (*a*) proportion of taxed shops taking lodgers = 0.4452 (99 per
    cent sig.); (*b*) proportion of houses taking lodgers: not significant; (*c*) persons
    per house = 0.4587 (99 per cent). Proportion of taxed buildings in classes I and
    II correlated with (*a*) proportion of taxed shops taking lodgers = 0.3951 (98 per
    cent sig.); (b) proportion of houses taking lodgers: not significant; (*c*) persons
    per house = −0.4097 (98 per cent sig.).
18. A. Smith, *Wealth of Nations*, I (1776), ed. Cannan, 131–2.

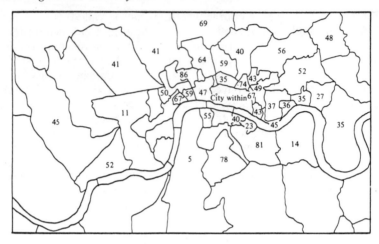

Fig. 3   Assessed taxpayers as a proportion of the population of their parishes.

To a considerable extent, the larger proportion of lodgers in a wealthy parish is simply a reflection of the greater number of shops there. One-eighth of all the shops in the fifteen poorest parishes took

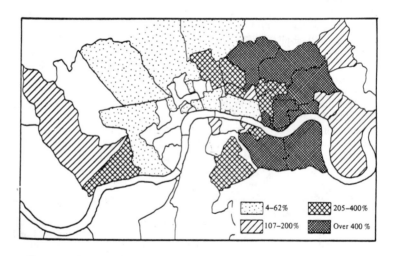

Fig. 4 Number of taxpayers in categories I and II for every 100 in categories IV and V.

TABLE 4 Proportion of shopkeepers and other householders taking lodgers, by amount of assessed tax paid[a]

	shopkeepers %	*other householders* %
I. Under £1	50	46
II. £1–under £2	56	53
III. £2–under £5	59	53
IV. £5–under £10	67	51
V. £10 and over	50	32
Mean	60	48
Number	11 372	19 703

[a]Shops in this context are defined as selling goods; 'workshops' that did not sell to the public are therefore excluded.

lodgers, compared with over one-third of the shops in the nineteen intermediate parishes, and well over half of those in the twelve wealthiest parishes. Almost three-quarters of the third- and fourth-class shops in the wealthiest parishes took lodgers, compared with about 40 per cent of similar shops in the poorest parishes.[19] In those parishes where only a few houses were excused assessed taxes, and the floating population of London was therefore putting particular pressure on the assessed taxpayers to take lodgers, it was the shop-keeper who was the more likely to take them.[20] Taking lodgers certainly eased financial problems; it was the smaller taxed shops, most of which were in the poor parts of London, that were excused some or all of their assessed taxes, not the shops that were rated more highly. According to Table 5, as many as one-third of the shops paying less than £1 a year in taxes were excused some or all of this, compared with less than one in thirteen of those paying between £2 and £5, and one in fifty of those paying more than £5 a year.

On account of both their wealth and their numbers, shopkeepers were a particularly important group in London society, comprising as many as 37 per cent of those paying taxes. More significant is that as many as 73 per cent of those shops that paid their taxes were in tax categories III, IV and V, compared with 57 per cent of other houses; however great an allowance is made for shops that were not

19. For the definition of poor and wealthy parishes, see above, n. 12.
20. Spearman correlation: proportion of houses excused tax with (*a*) proportion of shops taking lodgers = −0.4092 (95 per cent significant); (*b*) proportion of other houses taking lodgers = −0.2746 (90 per cent significant).

TABLE 5   Class of shops excused taxation, wholly or in part

Class	Per cent
I. Under £1	30.0
II. £1–under £2	17.0
III. £2–Under £5	7.6
IV. £5–under £10	2.1
V. £10 and over	1.3
Average	1.3
Number	10 775

taxed at all, this still leaves between a third and a half of London's shopkeepers as middle class, at least as far as their incomes are concerned, compared with a maximum of 30 per cent for London's population as a whole.[21] Depending on family size, shopkeepers liable for assessed taxes formed between 9 and 11 per cent of London's population. If a quarter of London's shopkeepers were not liable for assessed taxes, then as a group shopkeepers – taxed and untaxed – formed between 11 and 14 per cent of the population: a remarkably high proportion by the standards of the present day, and a reflection of the small-scale artisan mode of production so prevalent in London. This is not to deny the existence of many small chandlers' shops, whose owners lived on the breadline,[22] but to warn against exaggerating their numbers. 'Shopocracy' was not an empty term, and the importance of shopkeepers in metropolitan politics is not difficult to explain. When Pitt imposed a tax on shops in 1785, protests from London were the principal cause of the tax being abolished only a few years later.[23] After all, more than one-third of those earning more than £75 a year were shopkeepers.

III

By the end of the eighteenth century there was, therefore, a considerable degree of social segregation in London. The more 'comfortable' middle classes were situated in the western and central

21. See Appendix B. The figure of 30 per cent includes the lower middle class in tax categories I and II.
22. Not to mention street sellers.
23. S. Dowell, *A History of Taxation and Taxes in England*, III (1884), 16–19; J. Ehrman, *The Younger Pitt. The Years of Acclaim* (1969), 258–61.

parts of the metropolis, while maintaining a relatively low profile in the east and the south. The area of their influence was large – proportionately larger than in any other European city of the time – a significant factor when considering the nature of politics in London. This picture of developing residential segregation requires two major qualifications. In the first place, the wide spread of manufacturing in London considerably lessened the extent to which poor areas were deprived of their bourgeoisie. Silkweaving, for instance, was in the east, as was shipbuilding; watchmaking was conducted in Clerkenwell in the north, while tanning and brewing were for the most part in the south; the luxury trades concentrated in Westminster and in the City. The absence of a central business district led to a wide spread of purchasing power and of shopkeepers across London: shops comprised 24 per cent of all taxed buildings in the poorest parts of the metropolis, 30 per cent in the wealthiest parts, and 27 per cent in the intermediate. Tax class III, the lower end of what, for convenience, can be called the 'comfortable' middle class, was spread fairly evenly across London, and almost half the members of class III were shopkeepers.

The second qualification concerns the wealthy areas themselves. Nowhere did the wealthy taxpayers in classes IV and V form much more than half the resident population of their parish (usually very much less) and even when class III is included, it is rare to find them in a majority. This was a reflection of a pattern of middle- and upper-class concentration in squares and avenues, a pattern which also goes some way to account for the absence of any connection between the wealth of a parish and the density of its population.[24] The reasons for such a juxtaposition of wealth and poverty are not hard to find, and were common to many pre-industrial towns, especially regional or national capitals. Wealthy areas, with their intensive and seasonal demands for labour, generated their own poor hinterlands. The wealthy required servants, porters, cooks and washerwomen in abundance; their presence attracted retailers, craftsmen, prostitutes, writers, criminals and many others. The resulting under-employment was exacerbated by the seasonal nature of demand: the aristocracy resided in London for a few months during the Season, but left town at the end of spring; the lesser gentry, in their turn, spent a part of each year in their county towns. Middle-class demand fluctuated, while even a large manufacturing sector – and eighteenth-century London was the largest manufacturing town in Europe, if not the world – was not immune to considerable seasonal fluctuations in demand as well as supply, es-

24. The Spearman correlation coefficient of density of population per hectare with proportion of taxed buildings in classes IV and V is insignificant, even at the 50 per cent level of confidence.

pecially during the winter.[25] Low incomes, overcrowding – in a word, slums – was inevitable; estate developers sought to hold back the growth of slums with careful leases, imposing town squares, parks, gates and beadles, but to prevent an area from becoming a slum was difficult, sometimes impossible. It is no accident that some of the greatest overcrowding in London was to be found around Holborn, strategically placed between the City and Westminster, and within convenient reach of both, by foot. Nor is it accidental that St Giles, Soho came to be so notorious: it bordered a particularly wealthy area, so it housed the local criminals and casual labourers.

It is doubtful whether the process of social differentiation could have gone very much further, given these constraints. The detailed social geography of London depended not only on morphological factors and varying leasehold agreements, but also on London's social structure, the nature of the demand and supply of labour and commodities, as well as the housing market. These factors are readily acknowledged in a general fashion when an entire town is under consideration, but sometimes ignored when considering parts of a town, such as individual estates or parishes.[26]

IV

There are two general conclusions that can be drawn from this study. One relates to the study of social geography, the other to the study of social class. Discussions of the social pyramid in pre-industrial English towns have tended to confine themselves to extremes. The wealthiest and the poorest strata of the population are carefully pointed out to the curious reader, the remainder are dismissed. The same is true of descriptions of the social geography of these towns, with only the wealthiest and the poorest parishes

25. Schwarz, 'Conditions of Life', ch. 3. Eighteenth-century London was similar in this respect to the later nineteenth century: G. Stedman Jones, *Outcast London* (Oxford, 1971), ch. 2. For an analysis of the effects of fluctuations on the labour market, thereby creating a permanent labour surplus, see W. Beveridge, *Unemployment: A Problem of Industry* (1909), 78–81.
26. D. Cannadine, 'Urban development in England and America in the nineteenth century: some comparisons and contrasts', *Economic History Review*, XXXIII (1980), 309–25, and *Lords and Landlords: The Aristocracy and the Towns 1774–1967* (Leicester U. P., 1980), 301–416, attacks this approach but does not extend his criticisms to a consideration of the precise nature of income distribution and wealth as a factor in urban geography.

being mentioned.[27] Historians of eighteenth-century England have worked a great deal on the economic background of individual towns and on the development of their economies.[28] There has been some work on the economic background of urban England and on the contribution of towns to economic growth;[29] rather less on the occupational structure of towns,[30] and least of all on the overall distribution of incomes and of social classes within towns, a surprising omission when the volume of publications on this topic for the seventeenth century is borne in mind.[31] No doubt this is due, in part, to the lack of suitably concise sources, and to the difficulties involved in manipulating the poor rate and the land tax registers, but considering the interest shown by geographers in the social geography of contemporary towns, this omission is surprising.

There are two important geographical theories, by Sjoberg[32] and Vance,[33] that seek to account for the social geography of preindustrial towns. Both suffer from the drawback of concentrating on the urban élite, and even within that context they suffer from serious

27. See for example, P. Clark and P. Slack, *English Towns in Transition, 1500–1700* (Oxford, 1976), ch. 8: 'The social structure' – based on a great deal of recent research, and reflecting this approach. A few summaries of the Hearth Tax present the data in such a manner that the middle ground can subsequently be calculated: for example W. G. Hoskins, *Industry, Trade and People in Exeter, 1688–1800* (Manchester, 1935), 122; *Victoria County History: Cambridge*, IV (1953), 274–80.
28. This is part of the stock-in-trade of current British economic history, and no urban history is complete without it. A list is superfluous: see the survey in the introduction to P. Clark (ed.), *The Early Modern Town, A Reader* (1976).
29. H. C. Darby (ed.), *A Historical Geography of England* (Cambridge, 1973), 381–8, 458–64; M. J. Daunton, 'Towns and economic growth in eighteenth-century England', in P. Abrams and E. A. Wrigley (eds), *Towns in Societies* (Cambridge, 1976), 245–77; E. A. Wrigley, 'Parasite or stimulus, the towns in a pre-industrial economy', ibid., 295–309; L. A. Clarkson, *The Pre-Industrial Economy of England, 1500–1750* (1971), 47, 119–23; Clark and Slack (eds), op. cit.
30. Clarkson, op. cit., 88–9 summarizes most of them.
31. Analyses of the subsidy assessment of 1523–5 and the Hearth Tax of the 1670s are well known. For a few examples of their use, J. F. Pound, 'The social and trade structure of Norwich, 1525–1578', *Past and Present*, XXIV (1966); W. T. McCaffrey, *Exeter, 1540–1640* (Harvard, 1958), 247–51; W. G. Hoskins, *Industry, Trade and People in Exeter, 1688–1800* (Manchester, 1935); P. Corfield, 'A provincial capital in the late seventeenth century: the case of Norwich', in P. Clark and P. Slack (eds) *Crisis and Order in English Towns, 1500–1700* (1972). The volumes of the *Victoria County History* regularly summarize these two sources.
32. G. Sjoberg, *The Pre-Industrial City* (Glencoe, 1960).
33. J. E. Vance, 'Land assignment in the pre-capitalist, capitalist and post-capitalist city', *Economic Geography* XLVII (1971), 101–20.

disadvantages.[34] Sjoberg's theory is the best known. In his 'pre-industrial city' the wealthy and powerful live near the centre of the city, the poor and powerless on the periphery. It is not difficult to discover such cities; it is the question of why this should be the case that is important. Sjoberg, whose research ranged over several continents and several millennia, concluded that pre-industrial urban élites were based on status rather than on wealth. They tended to regard money making as a subsidiary occupation, and did not live in the centre of the city because it was a place of business or of exchange, but in order to perform their various administrative, religious, political, ceremonial and educational activities.[35]

Vance, on the other hand, argues, perhaps somewhat euphemistically, that there was no economic rationale for intra-urban locational economies in the pre-industrial city. In the middle ages, cities were occupationally zoned, but not zoned in any predetermined or locationally determined order, thus leading to a multi-nucleate city. In the medieval city, land had no value except in so far as it happened to be assigned to a particular craft, from which it followed that because

> a man used rather than possessed land, his valuation of it was a
> functional rather than a capitalized one. In such a context, locations
> were not relative but absolute; to exist within a gild area was
> necessary for the proper practice of a trade and for the receipt of the
> social beneficence of that organization. In a true sense the value of
> land in the Middle Ages was the value of social association.[36]

The fall from grace started in the sixteenth century, when gilds declined and class zoning became apparent. Fashionable houses began to be built on the outskirts of the city, while the poor were left, increasingly, with the housing stock of the central area.

Langton has tested both these models against the available statistics on the distribution of wealth in seventeenth-century Newcastle, Exeter and Dublin,[37] finding that on the whole the residential patterns of these cities 'go a considerable way to corroborate Sjoberg's

34. For criticisms of Sjoberg, see L. Mumford in *American Sociological Review*, XXVI (1961); O. C. Cox in *Sociological Quarterly*, V (1964) and P. Burke, 'Some reflections on the pre-industrial city', *Urban History Yearbook* (1975), 13–21.

35. Sjoberg, op. cit., 95–103.

36. Vance, op cit., 103.

37. J. Langton, 'Residential patterns in pre-industrial cities: some case studies from seventeenth-century Britain', *Transactions of the Institute of British Geographers*, LXVI (1975), 1–27. There is no such article on eighteenth-century England, although R. J. Langton and P. Laxton, 'Parish registers and urban structure: the example of late eighteenth-century Liverpool', *Urban History Yearbook* (1978), 94–9, is one of the few to make — or at least to announce the intention of

hypothesis [as] does the prevalence of a sharp decline in wealth away from the peaks towards the walls or the outskirts of the cities'.[38] Not surprisingly, however, he considered Sjoberg's explanation of this phenomenon to be unsuitable. The urban élites of seventeenth-century England could hardly be accused of regarding the pursuit of financial gain as being far less important than their ceremonial and administrative functions. Emrys Jones has examined seventeenth-century London, using data on the distribution of wealth in the City in 1635 and 1695,[39] and has similarly found the models of both Vance and Sjoberg to be unsuitable. The City of London did indeed have an inner core, albeit a commercial core, but one must not ignore Westminster, a second centre of wealth. 'We can,' he concludes, 'faintly discern a new and more intricate model: a commercial core and an administrative/legal core, both of which would eventually lose their residential functions, separated by a sector which would become a retail link.'[40] A century later, this process had not gone very much further in London. Suburbs were developing, and there was greater social segregation. On the other hand, the metropolis remained essentially a twin-centred city, suburban development existing alongside inner-city élites. Furthermore, the élites continued to reside side by side with the poor.[41]

Historians of social class, in their turn, have perhaps not devoted sufficient attention to social geography. While an analysis of the geography of income distribution will naturally not provide any 'answers', it is nevertheless an important background. This paper has not purported to provide an extensive analysis of social class in late eighteenth-century London. Far too little is known at present about the varied groupings of the London bourgeoisie – the traders, manufacturers, shopkeepers, financiers, professional men, to mention but a few. The transition from incomes to social class is difficult.

making — such a survey relating to the eighteenth-century. There are maps in F. Vigier, *Change and Apathy. Liverpool and Merseyside during the Industrial Revolution* (M. I. T., 1970), and a description of Dublin in 1798 in Burke, op. cit., 447–52.

38. Langton, op. cit., 9–10.
39. E. Jones, 'London in the early seventeenth century: an ecological approach', *London Journal*, VI (1980), 123–33.
40. Ibid., 131–2.
41. It would be interesting to compare the social geography of this period with that of 50 or 100 years earlier, but this is unfortunately extremely difficult, even to the extent of connecting the assessed tax data with the picture put together for the City by Professor D. V. Glass in *London Inhabitants within the Walls, 1695* (London Record Soc., 1966), and discussed most recently by Emrys Jones, op. cit. For 1798, the assessed tax data was given by wards, whereas the 1801 census gives population by parish : the two overlap to some extent in the City Without, but not in the City Within. However, practically every ward of the City Within has characteristics common to the wealthy parishes of the West End.

This paper has concentrated primarily on incomes, making an occasional transition when it appeared suitable. In the light of the assessed taxes, however, it may be suggested, albeit somewhat speculatively, that one of the crucial elements in the London bourgeoisie will emerge as being those who earlier in this paper have been referred to as tax class III: a group with 'middling' incomes, half of them shopkeepers, and a group, moreover, that spread itself fairly evenly across the metropolis. In the poorer areas, the members of this group would be the natural leaders of the community, dispensing poor relief, supervising the poor rate, directing the local constables and managing the workhouse. This does not imply that their loyalties necessarily ran in any particular direction. In the wake of the Gordon riots, armed associations for the defence of property arose all over the metropolis: not only in Westminster or the City, but also in the poor parishes of Bethnal Green, Christ Church Spitalfields and Shoreditch – whose principal inhabitants offered to patrol the street by rotation, ten or fourteen at a time, carrying arms.[42] Of course, what the principal inhabitants of Shoreditch meant by the 'defence of property' may have been somewhat different from the meaning attributed to it by the principal inhabitants of Mayfair. During the 1790s it was crucial to the London Corresponding Society whether such 'principal inhabitants' joined their ranks or joined those of their opponents. The nature of the loyalist response has not been examined in very much detail at the local level. The importance of small shopkeepers and employers to the London Corresponding Society is demonstrable[43] and the similarities between its membership and the Parisian sans-culottes are striking.[44] But at what point in the social scale did membership of the LCS cease – and was this point different in the various parts of London? When Horne Tooke, the 'acquitted traitor' of 1794 stood for election to Parliament in Westminister in 1796, he collected 2819 votes,[45] so presumably support for Tooke extended a considerable distance up the social scale. But how much support would Tooke have obtained outside Westminster?

The London middle classes need to be carefully differentiated and examined at the regional level, not only for traces of radicalism, but also for their attitudes towards authority and property. After all, the

---

42. L. Radzinowicz, *A History of English Criminal Law*, II (1956), 209, for the associations in general. For Shoreditch, P. R. O., HO 42/189, James May (parish clerk) to Lord Sidmouth.

43. J. Walvin, 'English Democratic Societies and Popular Radicalism, 1791–1800' (York University Ph.D. thesis, 1969).

44. G. A. Williams, *Artisans and Sans-Culottes* (1968), 4–5, 71, 73.

45. A. Stephens, *Memoirs of John Horne Tooke*, II (1813), 227. Charles James Fox had 5160 votes, Sir Alan Gardner (government candidate) 4814.

forces of law and order, supposedly embodied by the middle classes, did not spring out of the ground, articulate and suspicious, when the Chartists converged on to Kennington Common in 1848.

APPENDIX A. DISTRIBUTION OF PARISHES

Parishes in the poorest group (total percentage of fourth- and fifth-class houses in parentheses): *under 15 per cent* – Bermondsey (5.9%), St Katherine (7.4%), Rotherhithe (8.3%), St George's East (8.8%), Shadwell (10.2%), Mile End (10.6%), Ratcliffe (11.6%), Clerkenwell (12.8%), Christ Church Spitalfields (13.6%), East Smithfield (14.3%).

15–49 per cent – Cripplegate Without (16.4%), Old Street (16.6%), Limehouse (21.2%), Chelsea (22.0%), Kensington (27.3%), Christ Church Surrey (28.0%), St Sepulchre Middx (29.6%), Bow (30.3%), Lambeth (30.6%), St Olave Surrey (32.1%), Rolls Liberty (40.4%), St Pancras (41.8%), Farringdon Without (43.9%); in the City Within: ward of Aldersgate (39.8%).

50 per cent and over – St Clement Danes (53.5%), St Marylebone (70.2%), St Paul Covent Garden (73.2%), St Anne Soho (71.1%); in the City Within: wards of Cripplegate Within (50.3%), Dowgate (52.1%), Castle Baynard (53.9%), Cordwainer (54.1%), Candlewick (54.8%), Coleman St (57.4%), Bishopsgate Within (64.3%), Bridge (66.4%), Walbrook (67.1%), Langbourn (69.5%), Broad Street (70.5%), Bread Street (79.8%).

The detailed figures, from which the conclusions of this paper have been drawn, are in my thesis, 343–57.

APPENDIX B: SHOPKEEPERS

Demonstrating the extent to which shopkeepers were a relatively wealthy group involves two assumptions: the size of a family, and the number of shops that did not pay taxes. For instance, if it is assumed that 20 per cent of London's shops did not pay taxes, then the number of shops increases from 16 930 to a little over 21 000; in the parishes for which data have survived there was a population of some 675 000 in 1801. With an average family size of four this becomes 170 000 families; 150 000 of them were not shopkeepers, but only 35 000, or 24 per cent, were liable for assessed taxes. If family size is increased to six, there were still only 38 per cent paying taxes. It is only on the assumption that half the shopkeepers did not pay assessed taxes – which, it will be suggested, is extremely unlikely – and that the average London family contained as many as six members – also unlikely – that the proportions of shopkeepers and others not liable for assessed taxes become equal (Table 6).

There are three reasons why it is unlikely that as many as half London's shopkeepers escaped liability to assessed taxes. First of all, their premises were of greater value than those of the other householders. Second, evasion of basic taxes was more difficult for shopkeepers. Third, only about one-quarter of the shops in the City of London appear to have been excused the assessed tax, and the source for this evidence includes the poor parishes of the City Without, which in 1801 contained some 57 per cent of the City's population, so it cannot be argued that the source that gives this information is biased towards a particularly wealthy area.[46]

46. The same volume of the Chatham papers that summarizes the tax returns contains in addition what purports to be 'an account of the number of shops showing the Rent paid by the possessors of the same' in the City of London and in Westminster (P. R. O., PRO/30/8/281, f. 144). The source of this information is not provided, but presumably it is the same collectors who provided the figure already used in this paper. The difference between these figures and the tax figures is that the former are supposed to cover all the parishes in the City of London and Westminster and, presumably, to include all shops, whether liable for assessed taxes or not. The figures for Westminster cannot be compared with the detailed returns, as the latter have survived for only half the Westminster parishes; however, the surviving tax returns for the City of London cover areas with almost 90 per cent of the city's houses in 1801. There are, according to the general figure, one-third more shops in the City than there are shops paying assessed taxes. We must make an allowance for the area not included in the detailed tax returns; as 87 per cent of the houses in the City are included and only 13 per cent not, it is reasonable to make an allowance of 13 per cent. This leaves one quarter of the shops in the City not paying assessed taxes, compared with almost half the City's residential houses. Not surprisingly, the smallest houses tended not to contain shops.

TABLE 6 Proportions that shopkeepers and others formed of total population

| | No allowance | | 20% allowance Family size | | | | 50% allowance Family size | | | |
| | | | 4 | | 6 | | 4 | | 6 | |
	Houses	Shops	Houses	Shops	Houses	Shops	Houses	Shops	Houses	Shops
Untaxed	—	—	76.0	20.0	61.2	20.0	73.7	50.0	55.0	50.0
I. Under £1	20.8	11.9	5.0	9.5	8.0	9.5	5.5	5.9	9.4	5.9
II. £1-under £2	18.3	16.9	4.4	13.6	7.1	13.6	4.8	8.4	8.2	8.4
III. £2-under £5	28.9	36.7	6.9	29.4	11.2	29.4	7.6	18.3	13.0	18.3
IV. £5-under £10	20.8	25.5	5.0	20.4	8.1	20.4	5.5	12.7	9.4	12.7
V. £10 and over	11.3	9.1	2.7	7.2	4.4	7.2	3.0	4.5	5.1	4.5
Total	100.1	100.1	100.0	100.1	100.0	100.1	100.1	99.9	100.1	99.9
Number of families	35 434	16 930	147 587	21 162	91 338	21 162	134 890	33 860	78 640	33 860

Chapter 12
VOLUNTARY SOCIETIES AND BRITISH URBAN ELITES 1780–1850: AN ANALYSIS

R. J. Morris

[*Historical Journal*, 26, no. 1 (1983)]

Robert Morris has published widely on class and the nineteenth-century town. He sees a close relationship between the emergence of the middle class and the rise of the modern city, and has written that 'the middle class created the towns as social units from the economic and material structures which they controlled'. ('The middle class and British towns and cities of the Industrial Revolution 1780–1870', in D. Fraser and A. Sutcliffe (eds), The Pursuit of Urban History *(London, 1983), p. 304.) This line of argument is evident in the article reproduced here, which explores a vital organ of middle-class power, the voluntary society. Of particular interest are Morris's observations about why the urban bourgeoisie used such organizations to exert their influence, notably his thesis that they utilized the voluntary sector to bypass the state. Recent work has revealed the strength of the middling groups and of voluntary societies in the late seventeenth- and eighteenth-century town. This raises the general question whether the processes analysed by Morris in this article are exclusively a phenomenon of the Industrial Revolution, or whether they could be traced back to an earlier point in time.*

I

Whilst it would be wrong to claim that voluntary societies in Britain were new in the period 1780 to 1850, the growth of large industrial and urban populations was accompanied by an increase in the foundation and prosperity of such societies. These societies were diverse in their purpose, form, size and membership.[1] Edward Baines, junior, one of the self-appointed tribunes of the industrial middle class, in 1843 described recent developments as follows:

> I might dwell upon many institutions and associations for the diffusion of knowledge, and for the dispensing of every kind of good, which have arisen within the present or last generation and which have flourished most in the manufacturing towns and villages – such as mechanics institutes, literary societies, circulating libraries, youth's guardian societies, friendly societies, temperance societies, medical charities, clothing societies, benevolent and district visiting societies – forty nine fiftieths of which are of quite recent origin.[2]

Baines might have added to his list several trades unions, radical discussion groups, Societies for the Suppression of Vice, philosophical societies, and even brass bands, chess clubs and gardening societies, all of which were part of the same major social development. The 1780s formed a suitable start for this study as that decade witnessed an increase in the formation of voluntary societies, an increase which continued beyond 1850. By that date an important portion of the voluntary societies had begun to reassess their relationship with the state. Although neither date marked a sharp break in continuity, they did mark a change in trend.

The important voluntary societies created in this period were concerned with a variety of activities ranging from poor relief, medical aid, moral reform, public order, education and thrift, to the diffusion of science and culture and the organization of leisure. The group upon which this article concentrates had three distinctive features. The membership was mainly drawn from the middle class and most societies were dominated by the elite of that class. Very few of the gentry or members of the aristocracy were involved except as patrons, and except in the metropolitan-based societies of Edinburgh and London, where these societies had ambitions for national in-

---

1. The most comprehensive study so far is by M. B. Simey, *Charitable effort in Liverpool in the nineteenth century* (Liverpool, 1951); S. Yeo, *Religion and voluntary organisations in crisis* (1976) is a valuable counterpoint to this article. In many ways his study of Reading looks at the end or perhaps the transmutation of the process described in its beginnings in this article: see my review, *Social History*, III, 2 (May, 1978), 263–5. There are many excellent studies of particular sectors of voluntary activity, for example David Owen, *English philanthropy, 1660–1960* (Harvard, 1960); M. Tylecote, *The mechanics institutions of Lancashire and Yorkshire before 1851* (Manchester, 1957); B. H. Harrison, *Drink and the Victorians: the temperance question in England, 1815–1872* (1971); B. Abel Smith, *The hospitals, 1800–1948* (1964); E. J. Cleary, *The building society movement* (1965); T. W. Laqueur, *Religion and respectability, Sunday schools and working class culture, 1780–1850* (Yale, 1976).
2. Edward Baines, junior, *The social, educational and religious state of the manufacturing districts* (London and Leeds, 1843), pp. 28 and 62.

fluence. Wage-earners were less likely to take part in voluntary societies. When they did they took part in fewer societies. They were most likely to join benefit or friendly societies. When they did join a society, it was likely to be more important to them than any single voluntary society would be for those of higher status.[3] Unlike voluntary societies in twentieth century Britain which tend to act as pressure groups upon government in addition to promoting their own social activities, the major societies of this period were designed to achieve their aims without reference to government aid or authority. It was this feature which made the period 1780–1850 so distinctive. Thirdly, these societies, like the power of the middle class elite which controlled them, were urban-based.

This group of voluntary societies will be shown to have been involved in several interlocking social processes which were vital to the distribution and mediation of power within British towns. They were part of the continuous recreation of urban elites in conditions of rapid social and economic change. They were the basis for the formation of a middle-class identity across the wide status ranges, and the fragmented political and religious structure of the potential members of that class. They enabled the elite to assert their economic and cultural authority within that middle class. They enabled the middle class, under the supervision of the elite, to assert their identity and authority against and over the working classes. This was accompanied by a developing attitude to the use of state power. In the early part of the period the use of state power was minimal. Movements like the Trustee Savings Banks and the Societies for the Suppression of Beggars used the state to provide a legislative framework, or to provide police and legal power at local government level. By 1830, most societies avoided even this minimal use of state authority, an attitude which was modified around 1850.

These societies must be sought in particular provincial localities if their unity and fortunes as a coherent social development are to be demonstrated. Attention has been paid here to three towns. Leeds was the seventh largest town in the kingdom. Its mixed economy was dominated by the manufacture and merchanting of woollen textiles, and over the period an engineering industry serving railways and textiles emerged from the machine building shops of

---

3. T. Bottomore, 'Social stratification in voluntary organisations', in D. V. Glass (ed.), *Social mobility in Britain* (1954), pp. 349–82; N. Babchuck and Alan Booth, 'Voluntary association membership: a longitudinal analysis', *American Sociological Review*, 34 (1969), 31–45; James Curtis, 'Voluntary association joining: a cross national comparative note', *American Sociological Review*, 36 (1971), 872–9; Erich Goode, 'Class styles of religious sociation', *British Journal of Sociology*, XIX (1968), 1–16.

the large mills.[4] Newcastle had a long history as a coal exporter, and as a salt, glass and pottery producer. Its merchant leaders had a long tradition of ruling one of the wealthiest of provincial centres. They also had long experience of conflict with wage labour, notably the miners and keelmen.[5] Edinburgh was the town of the professional man (the lawyer, the medical man and the professor), noted for its printing industry and worried by the poverty of its migrant and casual labour force.[6] All three were service centres for the surrounding countryside. None had extreme rates of population growth.[7] None was dominated by one industry alone. All these towns generated dozens of organizations which shared the defining characteristics of voluntary societies. They were organized groups of people formed to further a common interest. Membership was neither mandatory nor acquired by birth.

The great majority of their active members were unpaid.[8] The similarities rather than the differences of the voluntary organizations which developed in these three different towns were significant for middle class formation.

The reasons for the timing and expansion of each society in each place were specific, but two general sorts of pressures can be discerned. Many foundations were part of a response to a specific urban crisis. In the winter of 1799–1800, Leeds like most of Britain was affected by typhus which was in part a consequence of food scarcity. As a direct result of this epidemic Dr Thorpe, a leading

4. W. C. Rimmer, 'The industrial profile of Leeds, 1740–1840', and 'Occupations of Leeds, 1841–1951', both in *Publications of the Thoresby Society*, 50 (1967). For a fuller discussion of both the economy and voluntary societies of Leeds see R. J. Morris, 'Organisation and aims of the principal secular organisations of the Leeds middle class, 1830–1851' (Oxford D.Phil., 1970).

5. E. Mackenzie, *A descriptive and historical account of the town and county of Newcastle upon Tyne* (Newcastle, 1827); Thomas Oliver, *A new picture of Newcastle upon Tyne* (Newcastle, 1831); S. Middlebrook, *Newcastle upon Tyne: its growth and achievement* (Newcastle, 1950); W. L. Burn, 'Newcastle upon Tyne in the early nineteenth century', *Archaeologia Aeliania*, XXXIV (1956), 1–55; N. McCord, 'The government of Tyneside, 1800–1850', *Transactions of the Royal Historical Society*, 5th series, XX (1970), 5–29.

6. Edinburgh because of its political history had characteristics of both a metropolitan and provincial urban centre: T. C. Smout, *A history of the Scottish people, 1560–1840* (1969), pp. 366–78; L. J. Saunders, *Scottish democracy, 1815–1840* (Edinburgh, 1950), pp. 81–96; J. Stark, 'Inquiry into some points of the sanatory state of Edinburgh . . . ', *Edinburgh Medical and Surgical Journal*, LXVII (1847), 1–43.

7. Population Growth Rates, 1801–51; Leeds 224%, Newcastle 166%, Edinburgh 135%; compare Brighton 836%, Bradford 682%, Preston 471%. Source: B. P. P., *1851 Census of Great Britain*, 1852–53, LXXXV, 76–7.

8. D. L. Sills, 'Voluntary societies', *International encyclopedia of social sciences*, XVI (1968), 360–1; K. Little, *West African urbanisation* (Cambridge, 1966), pp. 85–102.

local physician, began a campaign which resulted in the opening of a fever hospital, the House of Recovery on the north-east edge of town in 1804. This was supported by annual subscriptions, 'affording a ready and safe asylum to the poor, but also security to the more opulent, by the reception of their apprentices and servants when attacked by fever'.[9] In Edinburgh, the economic distress of 1812 resulted in an increase in street-begging and led to the creation of the Edinburgh Society for the Suppression of Beggars.[10] The Leeds Mechanics Institution was founded in response to different influences but in the view of its promoters one of the factors which sustained middle-class elite support for the Institution in its difficult first twenty years was the threat of working class radicalism in 1832 and Chartism in 1839–42.[11] The savage economic depression of 1842 was another stimulus to action. In Leeds, that year produced not just obvious responses like a soup-kitchen but also more thoughtful contributions like the garden allotment schemes started by several mill-owners.[12] This simple model of specific crisis and response would provide a partial account of most societies but would be misleading for others. What the incidents of 1799–1800, 1812, 1832 and 1842 did was to concentrate anxieties about disease, street begging, radicalism and poverty which already existed. Such incidents provided a motive for selecting from the variety of ideas and examples of action by voluntary societies which were current at any given time.

In many places, a potent influence on the nature and timing of voluntary society activity was the stimulus of action taken in other towns. A campaign to found a new society frequently cited examples from other places. Edinburgh's tactics for the suppression of begging were justified by reference to similar measures being taken in Bath, Hull, Liverpool and Hamburg.[13] For the founders of the Edinburgh Lancastrian School, the examples of London and Liverpool were far more important than the rioting which took place as the school was being planned.[14] Fashion and the influence of innovations in other urban centres were important. For many other societies emulation

---

9. Dr Hunter, 'On continued fever in Leeds', *Edinburgh Medical and Surgical Journal*, XV (April, 1819), 234–45.
10. *First report of the Edinburgh Society for the Suppression of Beggars, instituted 25 January 1813* (Edinburgh, 1814).
11. R. J. Morris, 'Organization', pp. 245–337.
12. *Leeds Mercury*, 12 and 19 March 1842, and *Leeds Mercury*, 18 June 1841.
13. *Report of the committee appointed by the commissioners of police to inquire into the practicality of suppressing the practice of common begging and relieving the industrious poor* (Edinburgh, 1812).
14. *Report of the ordinary directors of the Edinburgh Lancastrian School Society* (Edinburgh, 1813); *Observations upon the propriety of establishing a Lancastrian School in Edinburgh* (Edinburgh, 1811).

was the only short run influence operating. A large number of mechanics institutions were founded after the establishment of the London Institution in 1824.[15] A different sort of influence was brought by the English tours of Scotsmen like John Dunlop in 1830–1 which left a rash of anti-spirits societies in their wake.[16]

The members of middle class urban elites responded to such fashions, to the examples of other towns and to crises of the types described above in the context of longer term social and economic changes. These created a series of pressures, challenges and opportunities which must be outlined, albeit in a schematic form, for they were the context in which those with economic and social power sought to defend, justify and extend that power.

Mid-eighteenth century Britain was a stable society in the sense that those with material and ideological power were able to defend this power in an effective and dynamic manner. Population was rising slowly and recent agricultural improvement and investment meant that food supply was assured. The rate of technological change was enough to ensure the prosperity of an expanding foreign trade without serious social dislocation. The conflicts which did occur were essentially reconcilable. Factions among aristocratic and merchant elites fought for power at national, county and urban level, but within an agreed set of rules. The labour consciousness of groups like the West Country clothiers and the miners and keelmen of north east England were contained within price and wage disputes. The violence of the bread riots was limited by a notion of 'fairness' common to aristocracy and people, and the willingness of the authorities to control the actions of middlemen as well as those of the 'mob'.[17] Sources of conflict were revealed by the continuing need to reorganize agricultural production through enclosure and incidents in which those in authority failed to meet the legitimate expectations of lower status groups, provoking violent reaction as in

15. J. F. C. Harrison, *Learning and living, 1790–1960: a study of the English adult education movement* (1961), pp. 59–61; John Tidd Pratt, *The history of savings banks* (1830); H. O. Horne, *A history of savings banks* (Oxford, 1947).
16. B. H. Harrison, *Drink and the Victorians*, p. 104.
17. P. Deane and W. A. Cole, *British economic growth, 1668–1959* (Cambridge, 1972), pp. 40–97; A. H. John, 'Aspects of English economic growth in the first half of the 18th century', *Economica*, New Series, XXVIII (1961), 176–7; Eric Kerridge, *The agricultural revolution* (1967), pp. 328–48; S. and B. Webb, *The history of trades unionism, 1666–1920* (1919), p. 33; J. M. Fewster, 'The keelmen of Tyneside in the 18th century', *Durham University Journal*, L (1957), 24–33 and 66–75; E. P. Thompson 'The moral economy of the English crowd in the 18th century', *Past and Present*, L (1971), 76–136; R. B. Rose, 'Eighteenth century price riots and public policy in England', *International Journal of Social History*, IV (1961), 275–9; E. F. Genovese, 'The many faces of moral economy', *Past and Present*, LVIII (1973), 161–8; E. P. Thompson, 'Patrician society, plebian culture', *Journal of Social History*, VII (1974), 382–405.

the Newcastle riots of 1740.[18] Open conflict of this kind was always limited because those with authority always had adequate material and ideological resources to contain opposition.

In the twenty years after 1780, this consensus structure was broken. The forces which became apparent in those years offered a developing challenge to all forms of social authority. Several material and ideological factors acted together. The rate of population increase accelerated, so that food prices rose, and supplies came to depend on imports and marginal land. The price of grain doubled in twenty years without a corresponding increase in wages.[19] The increasing pace of technological change, coupled with the result of population pressure in the labour market meant that many groups like the handloom weavers, nailmakers and keelmen experienced sharp falls in status and prosperity. Over the whole period an increasing number of employers and wage earners faced new conditions of work and work discipline and a general increase in the intensity of work. Wage labour suffered an increasing loss of control of workplace-situations to capitalist discipline; the clock towers which rose above the mills of Lancashire and Yorkshire were one symbol of this.[20] Added to this was the new concept of individuality promoted by writers as different as Adam Smith and Tom Paine, which steadily destroyed the moral and ideological imperatives of the hierarchical aristocratic Christian and paternalistic values celebrated by Archdeacon Paley.[21] Worst of all were the moral teachings of Malthus. Population increase combined with technological change produced a rapid growth in urban population. The size and density of this population, its need for food and work and the large numbers of recent migrants produced new problems. The

18. E. P. Thompson, *Whigs and hunters, the origins of the Black Act* (1975); George Rudé, *The crowd in history, 1730–1848* (New York, 1964), pp. 33–45; E. Mackenzie, *Newcastle upon Tyne*, pp. 52–3.

19. B. R. Mitchell and P. Deane, *British historical statistics* (Cambridge, 1962), pp. 488–9; R. S. Tucker, 'Real wages of artizans in London, 1729–1935', *Journal of the American Statistical Association*, XXXI (1936). The decline was clearest in the London figures. The evidence of other series, few of which span all these crucial years, suggests that the expectations of most wage-earners received a sharp check in the 1790s, even if their real wage did not fall below that obtained around 1780.

20. D. Bythell, *The hand loom weavers* (Cambridge, 1969); J. Fewster, 'The keelmen of Tyneside'; W. H. B. Court, *The rise of the midland industries, 1600–1830* (Oxford, 1938), p. 202; E. P. Thompson, *The making of the English working class* (1963), pp. 234–68; E. P. Thompson and E.Yeo, *The unknown Mayhew* (1971); S. Pollard, *The genesis of modern British management* (1965), pp. 160–208; E. P. Thompson, 'Time, work discipline and industrial capitalism', *Past and Present*, XXXVIII (1967), 56–97; John Myerscough, 'Recent history of the use of leisure time', in Ian Appleton (ed.), *Leisure research and policy* (Edinburgh, 1974), pp. 3–16.

21. William Paley, *Moral and political philosophy*, book 3, part 2, chs. 1 and 5, in *Works* (1851), pp. 155–60.

early generation of town-dwellers faced the task of adapting ways suited to rural and small town life to the life of large urban centres.

The pressure on food supplies and the increased extent of urban migration, together with technological, workplace and ideological change worked together to disrupt many crucial social relationships. The dangerous but mutually understood clash of riot and military force became less successful as a method of balancing the claims of ruling class and common people. The rulers having understood Adam Smith, felt less able to allow interference with market prices, and in any case the increase in imports meant that the ruling-class control over food supplies was itself reduced.[22] The ruled as they read Tom Paine began to make political claims, like the 'five or six mechanics . . . conversing about the enormous high price of provisions', in late 1791 who formed the Sheffield Constitutional Society.[23] It was clear that during the 1790s many groups of labourers and artisans found that the old power structure was increasingly unable to ensure them their basic 'right', a minimal food supply. Discontent over food, with a little help from Paine and the example of the French, developed into a fundamental questioning of the whole power structure of British society, political and economic, through a changing network of radical societies and publications.[24] Thus the conflict became more dangerous because its political content made it irreconcilable. At the same time the pressures which produced this conflict showed in many other ways. The Church of England failed to maintain its authority. The new urban centres failed to maintain existing literacy rates in the early years of the century, despite the increasing need for literacy created by urban and industrial change. The extent, cost and awareness of poverty rose, and scant evidence suggests that urban death-rates also rose in the first thirty years of the nineteenth century.[25] At the same time the increasing prosperity of many sections of the urban middle class, coupled with the deteriorating environment of the larger towns, meant that those with the power, money and education to tackle these problems were isolating themselves in suburbs away from the immediate impact of the failures of urban industrial society.[26]

22. L. Radzinowicz, *A history of English criminal law*, IV (London, 1965), 105–55; E. P. Thompson, 'The moral economy'.
23. Gwyn Williams, *Artizans and Sans-Culottes* (London, 1968), p. 58; Henry Collins, 'The London Corresponding Society', in J. Saville (ed.), *Democracy and the labour movement* (1954), pp. 103–34; F. K. Donelly and J. L. Baxter, 'Sheffield and the English revolutionary tradition, 1791–1820', *International Review of Social History*, XX (1975), 398–423.
24. E. P. Thompson, *The making of the English working class* (1963), pp. 17–185.
25. W. R. Ward, *Religion and society in England* (1972); K. S. Inglis, *Churches and the working class in Victorian England* (1963); E. R. Wickham, *Church and people in an industrial city* (1957); M. Sanderson. 'Literacy and social mobility in the industrial revolution in England', *Past and Present*, no. 56 (1972), pp. 75–

Thus the major manufacturers and shopkeepers and their professional allies were faced with the double task of gaining and asserting authority in the new situations which urban and industrial growth were continually providing, and of defending their social, economic and political power and privilege from threats of disease, food scarcity, crime, public disorder, labour organization and radical ideological and political action. A growing network of voluntary societies was part of the response to this situation. The nature of the need for authority and the challenge to authority changed with the development of the economy, so that the voluntary societies responded to this changing situation as well as to their own successes, failures and innovations.

II

The characteristic institutional form of the nineteenth-century voluntary society was that of the subscriber democracy. Money was collected from members. The funds were distributed and activities organized by a committee and officers elected by the subscribers at the annual general meeting. One subscription, one vote, was the general rule and uncontested elections the normal practice. Normally the result was rule by an oligarchy selected from the higher status members of the society. The president was often a high-status local leader, often a major industrialist, the secretary usually a solicitor, and the treasurer perhaps a local merchant or banker. The committee included a number of hard-working regular attenders. Such an arrangement was normally a perfect compromise between the middle class striving for self respect and independence and the reality of hierarchical society with its massive inequalities of wealth and power, even within the middle class. Such societies devised elaborate hierarchies of patrons, vice-presidents, trustees and grades

104; R. S. Schofield, 'Illiteracy in pre-industrial England', in Egil Johansson ed., *Literacy and society in historical perspective – a conference report*, Educational Reports, no. 2 (Umeå University, 1973); M. W. Flinn, *Introduction to the report on the sanitary condition of the labouring population of Great Britain*, by Edwin Chadwick (Edinburgh, 1965), pp. 13–14.

26. M. W. Beresford, 'Prosperity Street and others', in M. W. Beresford and G. R. J. Jones, *Leeds and its region* (Leeds, 1967), pp. 186–97; A. J. Youngson, *The making of classical Edinburgh* (Edinburgh: 1966).

27. *First report of the Leeds Benefit Building and Investment Society* (Leeds, 1850). I am grateful to Mr S. K. Walker, Manager of the Leeds Building Society, for showing me the early records of the Society.

of membership to acknowledge this. The Leeds Benefit Building and Investment Society had a structure carefully graded to secure trust as well as active participation from its membership.[27] The patrons included local councillors, JPs and MPs from across the north of England. One was Richard Cobden. The trustees, those who legally held the considerable assets of the Society, were local capitalists of moderate social status. Services were provided by named bankers, a solicitor, a surveyor, a manager, treasurer, secretary and auditor. Unpaid administrative services were undertaken by members in the form of president, stewards and committee. At the bottom of the hierarchy came the members themselves. The Newcastle Botanical Gardens proposed a finely graded membership, permanent subscribers £10 and then 10s. 6d. per year, annual subscribers £1. 1s, ticket holders 10s. 6d. per year, young persons at boarding school with their teachers, 5s. each, and 'the working classes . . . at certain times, without paying an admission fee' – all to be regulated by a committee and trustees.[28] In the Leeds Mechanics Institution a similar division between members who elected the 'working man' section of the committee, and the subscribers, proved unacceptable to the majority of members and had to be modified in the early 1840s to allow the expansion of the institution.[29] The need for financial support, and in many cases for men of property and probity to act as trustees, in whom the property of the society could be vested, meant that patronage was welcomed by many members of lower status. When the Newcastle Literary, Scientific and Mechanical Institution was founded in 1824, George Younger, carver and gilder, proposed that 'gentlemen' should be allowed to join at the next meeting to 'add weight and stability to the society'.[30] There were rare occasions when the democracy of the meeting broke through. This happened in 1836 when the Leeds Temperance Society split over the introduction of an exclusive teetotal pledge. Such a pledge was resisted by the high-status committee members who had founded and sponsored the society. Despite pleas from the platform that 'the speakers on one side should properly consider what is due to the respectability and station in life of their opponents . . . men who have been originators and supporters of many of the most charitable and benevolent institutions', the general meeting voted

28. *Prospectus of the proposed botanical and zoological gardens* (Newcastle upon Tyne, 1838), Wilson Collection, vol. 6, fo. 1398. This collection is in Newcastle-upon-Tyne Central Library.
29. Fredric Hill, *National education: its present state and prospects* (London, 1836), p. 195.
30. *Tyne Mercury*, 2 March 1824, Wilson Collection, vol. 2. fo. 336; G. Crossick, 'The labour aristocracy and its values: a study of mid-Victorian Kentish London', *Victorian Studies*, XIV (1976), 301–28 notes the survival of the need for patrons amongst the fiercely independent artisan societies of Kentish London.

for the teetotal pledge, and the committee left the society clearly disturbed by the rejection of their social authority.[31]

Each voluntary society was based upon a local community, but most were also related in various ways to national movements, groups or identities. Members, subscribers and money for a society or a branch, all came from one town or district, and funds were usually spent and activities based upon that same district. The link to a wider national movement took a variety of forms. The Bible and Missionary societies were branches of London-based organizations. They collected money, organized sermons and meetings, and in some cases distributed bibles and arranged local evangelizing, but they remitted most of their money to London. In 1849, The Leeds Religious Tract Society met for its forty-fifth annual meeting to hear of the foreign operations of the parent society from Shanghai to Bechuanaland, and of the distribution of 42 000 copies of the *Monthly Messenger* to the inhabitants of Leeds including 2000 to the frequenters of the Casino and 19 000 during the recent cholera epidemic. The Leeds Auxiliary of the British and Foreign Bible Society had distributed its share of bibles to the local population but met to be chided by the Rev. C. J. Glyn, vicar of Witchampton, Dorset, a deputation from the parent society, for not raising enough cash for the central body.[32] The National and the Lancastrian School societies had more local independence but they relied upon the central society to inspire policy and supply literature, including the teaching manuals. The central society also employed permanent lecturers and officials, and organized lobbies and petitions to government. The Edinburgh Society looked to London both for the training of its teachers and the system of teaching and discipline to be used in the schools founded in Edinburgh. The annual meetings of the Newcastle and the Leeds Societies were both attended by Lieutenant Fabian, RN, agent for the parent society who made similar speeches on aims and policy on each occasion.[33] Other societies lacked even the co-ordination of a central parent society and were connected only in so far as each urban centre tended to copy and follow the example of others. Thus the Edinburgh Society for the Suppression of Begging was clearly following the example of Bath and other places, whilst the Newcastle Society for the Suppression of Vagrancy and Mendicity founded in 1831, quoted the

31. *Report of the public meeting of the Leeds Temperance Society held in the Music Hall, Tuesday 21 January 1836* . . . (Leeds, 1836).
32. *Leeds Mercury*, 24 November 1849; C. Silvester Horne, *The story of the L. M. S., 1795–1895* (1894).
33. *Report of the ordinary directors of the Edinburgh Lancastrian School Society* (Edinburgh, 1813); British and Foreign School Society, *Manual of the System of Teaching* (1816); *Leeds Mercury*, 14 September 1839; 'Annual general meeting of the British and Foreign School Society, Newcastle', in Wilson Collection, vol. IV, fo. 866.

examples of Bristol, Cheltenham, again Bath and others.[34] Wider national identities of this kind were often strengthened by the periodical literature which grew around many of the voluntary societies and which gave the local reader-subscriber the sense of being part of a larger movement with interests in common. Thus the *Mechanics Magazine* and *Chambers Edinburgh Journal* were a focus of the reading of those in the mechanics institutes. The religious organizations were the best provided with literature. The reader of the *Edinburgh Missionary and Philanthropic Register* in Edinburgh learnt of the doings of the Glasgow City Mission, the Greenock Seaman's Friend Society and the itinerating libraries of Jamaica.[35] Whether formally or informally organized, the voluntary societies were networks of people in similar situations solving like problems and fulfilling like needs in an independent manner but conscious of each other's existence. This was part of the process of creating class, sectarian and other forms of group consciousness on a national basis, and thus overcoming the individuality of the nineteenth-century towns with their community loyalties and politics.

The origin of the nineteenth-century voluntary society as an organizational form must be sought in three places. Some of the features of the annual general meeting, and the relationship between subscribers and committee or promoters, came from the Joint Stock Companies which had promoted canals, public utilities and trading ventures in the eighteenth-century. The practice of financing the buildings of voluntary societies through proprietary members or shareholders was also derived directly from Joint Stock practice.[36] But the major organizational sources of the societies were the non-conformist chapel and the public house. With the chapels, the property was usually held by trustees, with varied but ill-defined rights for the congregation, especially the pew rent-payers, the neo-subscribers. They might elect or reject a minister, or perhaps inspect the accounts. In the trust deeds of High Bridge Chapel in Newcastle, an especially independent-minded congregation of Scotch Presbyterians, the deeds, papers and accounts of the chapel were inspected with ritual solemnity:

34. For Edinburgh, see above footnote 13; 'Meeting for the foundation of the Newcastle Society for the Suppression of Vagrancy and Mendicity, 27 January 1831', Wilson Collection, vol. III, fos. 689–90.

35. *Scottish Missionary and Philanthropic Register*, vol. XII (Edinburgh, 1831).

36. A. B. Dubois, *The England business company after the Bubble Act, 1720–1800* (New York, 1938), pp. 115–16 and 346–66; G. H. Evans, *British corporation Finance, 1775–1850: a study of preference shares* (Baltimore, 1936); B. C. Hunt, *The development of the business corporation in England, 1800–1867* (Harvard, 1946); William Albert, *The turnpike road system in England, 1663–1840* (Cambridge, 1972), pp. 93–119.

the said trustees . . . shall yearly upon the first day of January from the hour of ten in the forenoon to the hour of one in the afternoon of the said day, produce and shew forth . . . unto the congregation of the time being who shall then be assembled within the said chapel . . . all and every other deeds, evidences and writings touching . . . on the said premises heretofore mentioned . . . also all and every of the books of account . . . and permit and suffer the said congregation or any of them, then and there to peruse, read over, inspect and examine the same without any interruption, hindrance or molestation whatsoever.[37]

But the display of the accounts was not to become a new sacrament or the Protestant answer to the display of holy relics upon the saint's day. It was to become the annual general meeting of the voluntary society. These chapels were the base from which many voluntary societies emerged. Many chapels supported a varied structure of voluntary societies. By 1800 Norfolk Street Chapel in Sheffield supported a Wesleyan Library, a poor fund for its own congregation and a Benevolent Society (which was non-sectarian). In 1830, there was a Wesleyan Home and Foreign Mission Society and a Sunday School (late in this example) and later still a Band of Hope. Some were little more than a committee of the chapel. Others like the Benevolent Society, lost their sectarian identity and gained general support in the town.[38]

For many generations, the public house had been focus for community, class, trade and other interest groups, who had met with little formality or structure to their proceedings. Such groups were a crucial base for voluntary societies. The Building Societies and the Loan Clubs emerged from the public house in the 1840s. The Friendly Societies, the most numerous of all the voluntary societies, never became detached from their public-house origins despite the building of Oddfellows Halls and the like in many of the larger towns. The discussion society, and the public and subscription libraries all had origins in the public house or replaced similar public house functions. The drinking club, whether in a public house or private rooms had a place in the life of most eighteenth-century urban elites. In Manchester in 1720, Aikin recalled,

> there was an evening club of the most opulent manufacturers, at which the expense of each person was fixed at four pence half-penny, viz, four pence for ale and half-penny for tobacco. At a much later

37. P. R. O. C 54 8717 (II); E. Mackenzie, op cit., 387.
38. Rev. T. Alexander Seed, *Norfolk Street Wesleyan Chapel, Sheffield* (Sheffield, 1907); S. Yeo, *Religion and Voluntary organization*, places major emphasis on chapel-based organizations in late nineteenth-century Reading.

period, however, a sixpennyworth of punch and a pipe or two were esteemed fully sufficient for the evening's tavern amusement of the principal inhabitants.[39]

Such meetings were supplemented by meetings in the counting-houses of the leading merchants or later by dinner parties, but as the economy and society of the major cities became increasingly complex and differentiated, and the problems affecting the elite more pressing, and indeed the number of men who claimed a share in local power more numerous, such informal groups were no longer adequate, and the Chamber of Commerce, the Benevolent or Stranger's Friend Society and the Sunday School Union took over. The process still left many societies and clubs in the ale house and the chapel, and others retaining some connexion. Thus in 1839, the Natural History Society of Northumberland, Durham and New-castle-upon-Tyne held its annual general meeting at the Literary and Philosophical Society Building, erected in 1826, but retired to dine at the Queen's Head, tickets 15s. each.[40]

The model of voluntary society development in Figure 1 is offered for analysis of the development of voluntary societies as a social phenomenon as well as the analysis of the development pattern of particular sectors of voluntary activity. Each society identified its initial aims. It then acted in terms of available resources, knowledge and values, and then expanded, adapted or disappeared according to its success in attracting cash from subscribers and the response from those whose behaviour was meant to be influenced. The situations to which the voluntary societies responded were not themselves static, so that the changes which took place in the mechanics institutions in the 1830s were not only a response to the internal problems of the institutions but also to the greater urgency felt by their promoters as labour organization and working class radicalism became more effective.

The manner in which this model operated may best be seen in terms of voluntary poor relief. The care of the poor by the agencies of state and church was disrupted by increased rural–urban migration, by population pressure in times of harvest failure, by periodic trade slumps and by the harassing thoughts of Parson Malthus. A major sector of voluntary societies in most towns was directed towards devising and operating solutions to the poverty problem. The poverty caused by periodic trade slumps was

---

39. Quoted in James Croston (ed.), *The history of the County Palatine and Duchy of Lancaster by the late Edward Baines*, 5 vols. (Manchester, 1889), vol. 2, 121.
40. Wilson Collection, vol. 7, fo. 1555; B. H. Harrison, 'Pubs', in H. J. Dyos and M. Wolff (eds.), *The Victorian city* (2 vols., 1973), I, 161–90.

countered by special town funds, usually collected by the mayor and corporation, thinly disguised as a committee for the relief of the poor. In Leeds, such funds were collected at least seventeen times between 1800 and 1850. The device of the voluntary committee raised *ad hoc* for the crisis had several advantages.[41] The statutory leaders of the community, the corporation, could include the full range of social leaders in the temporary committee without compromising the exclusive nature of a closed corporation or vestry. It also sidestepped the problems caused by the incongruence of the settlement laws and the cyclical poverty of a commercial industrial economy which wanted to keep its workforce alive and healthy without dispersing them to home parishes.

Malthus had provided a major ideological problem for the middle classes by teaching that the indiscriminate charity of the old poor law and the traditional alms-giver would only increase poverty, in the short run by driving up the price of food, and in the long run by encouraging an increase in population.[42] Yet the distress and discontent caused by the poor harvest of 1779–1800 or the trade slump of 1812 made extensive poor relief imperative if social disorder and the destruction of a potential labour force was to be avoided, and traditional Christian values still demanded help for the poor, although few men had the confidence of the old tory vicar of Yarnton near Oxford, Rev. Vaughan Thomas, who attacked the 'charlatannerie of political and statistical empires' (Malthus) and championed 'this great scheme of charitable jurisprudence' (the Old Poor Law).[43]

There was a wide variety of attempts to unravel this particular knot of social and moral imperatives. The Leeds Benevolent or Stranger's Friend Society was founded in 1789 by a group associated with the Wesleyan methodist church. Like the society formed in London about the same time, it was soon taken over by an evangelically inclined but non-denominational group. Members subscribed money to the society and placed recommendations in the box on the wall of the Old Chapel. This weekly committee checked the recommendations and sent a visitor to the 'object' of charity. He reported on the real need of the case, and another visitor was sent with the grant which he handed over after checking yet again on need.[44] The visiting system and the concept of deserving and undeserving pov-

---

41. R. J. Morris, 'Organization', pp. 95–145; *Leeds Mercury*, 15 July 1837.
42. T. R. Malthus, *An essay on population* (2 vols., Everyman edition, 1958), II, 38–69.
43. Rev. Vaughan Thomas, *Memorials of the malignant cholera in 1832* (Oxford, 1835), IX; *Rev. Vaughan Thomas, On the visitation of prisoners, an assize sermon preached at St Mary's Oxford, 3rd March 1825* (Oxford, 1825).
44. J. M. Gardiner, *History of the Leeds Benevolent or Strangers Friend Society, 1789–1889* (Leeds, 1890).

Voluntary societies and British urban élites 1780–1850: an analysis

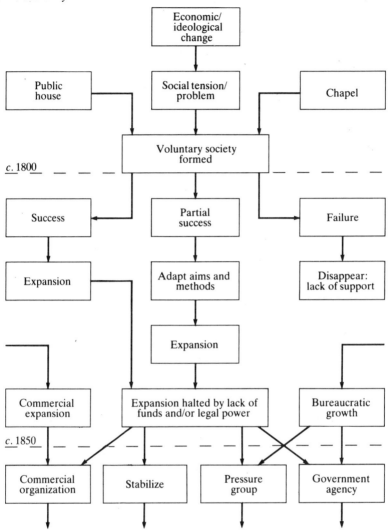

Fig. 1 The development of voluntary societies, 1780–1850. Note: (i) The dates indicate broad time bands. (ii) The scheme was designed for the analysis of all sections of voluntary activity 1780–1850, but it should prove equally appropriate for other waves of voluntary society formation; for example a series formed 1700–10 in conditions very similar to those of the late eighteenth century; the reaction of the eighteenth-century Edinburgh élite to their disturbing position of controlling a national capital without government authority; and by 1850 new social tensions, notably concerned with housing and casual labour created another wave of voluntary societies, but unlike earlier waves these could not operate with the same innocence of the possibilities of government action.

353

erty was used and in part evolved by the voluntary societies and became major tactics for resolving the conflict of values created by Malthus. The Edinburgh Society for the Suppression of Beggars founded in 1812 added another element to the visiting system. Alarmed by the recent increase in street begging, which was not only distasteful but prevented charity reaching 'deserving objects', it sought cooperation from the commissioners of police. After suitable publicity, the Society investigated all applications for relief, gave some food and cash, found others work, provided children with suitable education and sent others back to their home parishes. This left the field clear for the police to prosecute anyone caught begging in the streets, for the public could be sure, claimed the society, that the man was begging from choice, not necessity.[45] Several tensions were set up by these modes of operation, for the societies became increasingly involved in influencing the life-style of those they helped. In another Edinburgh society, the visitor was

> required earnestly to recommend cleanliness to those he visits . . . exhort them to attend a place of worship, to send their children to Sunday School, and to ascertain whether or not they possess a copy of the Holy Scripture that they may be supplied.[46]

Such activities, especially in the context of the north of England, soon awoke denominational jealousies. In 1832, all the funds for Leeds were collected by the Stranger's Friend committee with the aid of Anglican and Catholic subscriptions. By 1842, funds were collected by the Church District Visiting Society for the Anglicans, by a Catholic Benevolent Society as well as the Stranger's Friend, still claiming to be non-sectarian but in practice protestant dissenters.[47] The increasing fragmentation of voluntary effort for the relief of poverty itself caused problems. In 1850 Leeds opened the Charitable Enquiry Office to check applications for relief. This was an information service which prevented the duplication of case visiting work, and reduced the possibility of deception caused by people going from one society to another for help.[48] Other tensions arose from the reluctance of the respectable artisans and operatives to accept charity. This was countered by providing relief in return for labour on public works projects like the roads in Holyrood Park, Edin-

---

45. *First report of the Edinburgh Society for the Suppression of Beggars* (Edinburgh, 1814)
46. *Seventeenth annual report of the Edinburgh Benevolent or Strangers Friend Society* (Edinburgh, 1832).
47. *Leeds Mercury*, 1832–42, *passim*: R. J. Morris, 'The first urban immigrant: the Irish in England, 1830–1851', *The Institute of Race Relations Newsletter*, 3 March 1969, 133–8.
48. *Leeds Mercury*, 9 March and 11 May 1850.

burgh, which were built by men working under the Association for the Relief of Industrious Labourers and Mechanics.[49] The final problem, as in all the voluntary societies, was inadequate funds for fulfilling the societies' aims. In Leeds the 1842 relief fund run by a joint committee of the Stranger's Friend and the Church District Visiting Society ran out of funds well before the end of the depression. An attempt was made to fill the gap by introducing a soup kitchen. This was a cost-conscious decision made on the advice of their quaker chairman, Robert Jowitt who called it 'one of the most efficient means of relief'.[50] The real end to this process was the change in the poor law in 1845 and 1847 which made it much easier for the resident but non-native labour force to gain settlement rights in the towns which normally gave them work.[51] After that date the urban poor law accepted a greater part of the burden which had once belonged to the voluntary poor relief funds, although voluntary action retained its place as a means of overriding the constraints of the poor law in times of crisis such as the Lancashire cotton famine in 1862, and the unemployment in London in the winters of 1886 and 1887, which led to rioting in Trafalgar Square and the West End.[52] The Charity Organization Society in the 1850s recognized that state agencies with their greater authority and financial resources must undertake the bulk of poor relief work, for that society, despite itself, was as much a pressure group upon government as an initiator of social action.[53] The same process of action, reaction and adaptation, was apparent in the response to the need for urban literacy by the school societies, to the need for industrial skills by the mechanics institutions, and to the need for improved medical skill and knowledge to tackle urban health problems in the voluntary hospitals and medical societies. Many of the societies made, adjusted, and changed the aims, constitution, membership, and content of their activity in the light of experience. Temperance switched from a moderationist to a teetotal pledge; the mechanic's

---

49. *Report of the Association for the Relief of the Industrious Labourers and Mechanics* (Edinburgh, 1816). In Scotland the voluntary society was even more important, because the Scottish Poor Law, even after its formal establishment in 1844, gave no aid to the able bodied poor. R. Mitchison, 'The making of the Old Scottish Poor Law', *Past and Present*, no. 63 (1974), pp. 58–93; Audrey Paterson, 'The poor law in 19th century Scotland', in D. Fraser (ed.), *The New Poor Law in the nineteenth century* (1976), pp. 171–93.
50. *Leeds Mercury*, 12 and 19 March 1842.
51. M. E. Rose, *The English Poor Law, 1780–1930* (Newton Abbot, 1971), 192–3.
52. R. A. Arnold, *The history of the cotton famine* (1864), pp. 104–5, 118–23, 210–11, 313, 355–6, 416–17, 491–8; G. Stedman Jones, *Outcast London: a study of the relationships between classes in Victorian society* (Oxford, 1971), pp. 291–5.
53. C. L. Mowatt, *The Charity Organization Society, 1869–1913* (1961), pp. 5 and 116.

institutions moved away from practical scientific education for artisans to day-schools for teenage boys and entertaining lectures and books for adult members.[54] In both these cases change was brought about by the pressure of the mass of the membership on the elite, and the elite's need to stay in contact with those they sought to influence.

III

This creation and development of voluntary societies was part of, and eased the progress of, many of the social processes outlined at the beginning of this article. Within the voluntary societies the elite and their followers from the rest of the middle class looked for solutions to the problems of urban society, both the specific crisis of epidemic, riot and economic slump, and the longer term trends which worried those with power and authority. The focus of action was not only the direct threats like radicalism, trades union influence, crime and disease, but also the need to organize leisure, to ensure access to national literary and scientific culture and to counter the effects of transciency, personal isolation and the divisive influence of diverse interests and class tensions in the growing towns.[55] In doing this the voluntary societies enabled the middle classes to move towards the creation of a consciousness and cohesion amongst themselves and become a middle class. In the voluntary societies the middle classes began to overcome two major problems which hindered effective middle class action. Their ideology was incoherent, ill-developed and often contradictory, especially between the utilitarian and evangelical strands in middle class thought. Secondly the middle classes were bitterly divided, between parties, especially whig and tory, between status groups, especially the urban elites and the radically conscious sections of the petite bourgeoisie, and above all between sectarian religious groups.[56]

54. *Report of the public meeting of the Leeds Temperance Society held in the Music Hall, 21 January 1836* (Leeds, 1836); J. W. Hudson, *The history of adult education* (1851), pp. 92–5; B. H. Harrison, *Drink and the Victorians*, p. 38.
55. James Walvin, *Leisure and society, 1830–1950* (1978), pp. 2–10 and 45–57; Peter Bailey, *Leisure and class in Victorian England: rational recreation and the contest for control, 1830–1885* (1978), pp. 35–55; H. E. Meller, *Leisure and the changing city, 1870–1914* (1976); Robert H. Kargon, *Science in Victorian Manchester: enterprise and expertise* (Manchester, 1977), pp. 1–85.
56. Derek Fraser, *Urban politics in Victorian England* (Leicester, 1976), pp. 25–111 and 279–85; Frank Bechhofer and Brian Elliott, 'Persistence and change: the

The creation of voluntary societies also enabled the urban middle class elite to seek dominance over the industrial towns without the use of main force, not just by direct ideological influence, such as the propaganda against strike action based upon political economy, but also by reproducing in the voluntary societies forms of behaviour and social relationships which represented a paradigm for their ideal industrial society (as is shown below in the example of the Leeds Loan Society). The organization of consent which they continually sought was not only the consent of the subordinate classes to a beneficial domination but the consent of the fragments of a potential middle class to cooperate with each other in seeking and sustaining this domination.[57]

The years between 1790 and 1820 had shown the increasing inadequacies of the aristocratically controlled state in matters which were vital to the interests of the middle classes. Failures in the management of finance, foreign trade and public order had been demonstrated by Pitt's income tax, the lengthy crisis over the orders in council and above all by the events of Peterloo.[58] Such events provided increasing motivation amongst the middle class elite to seek control of the major agencies of the state, but the urban elites and the owners of industrial capital had neither the means nor the desire for the rapid and possibly violent capture of the state. Instead they avoided or minimized their need to use state power and created a network of voluntary societies.[59]

The formation of a network of voluntary societies was a carefully chosen response to the pressures and needs outlined above. There were many alternative social responses available through the family, the business, the community and the state. Indeed, many of these contributed to the same purposes and social changes as the voluntary societies. Government intervention was expected, requested, and refused in the case of the Yorkshire and West Country clothiers, 1804–9, the framework knitters of the East Midlands in 1812, and

petite bourgeoisie in industrial society', *Archives Européenes de Sociologie*, XVII (1976), 74–99; for a preliminary report on my own work on this aspect of the middle class see *Social History Society Newsletter*, I, no. 1 (Spring, 1976) 5.

57. Antonio Gramsci, *Selection from the prison notebooks*, edited and translated by Q. Hoare and G. Nowell-Smith (1971) pp. 53–60, 132, 160–70.

58. Asa Briggs, *Age of improvement* (1959), pp. 162–92; Donald Read, *Peterloo, the massacre and its background* (Manchester, 1958).

59. 'There can, and indeed must be hegemonic activity even before the rise to power, and one should not count on the material force which power gives in order to exercise effective leadership . . . In forms and by means, which may be called 'liberal' – in other words through individual, 'molecular', 'private' enterprise (i.e. not through a party programme worked out and constituted according to a plan, in advance of the practical and organisational action)': Antonio Gramsci, *Prison notebooks*, pp. 59–60.

the handloom weavers in 1834. At the same time, parliament dismantled a wide range of controls over wages, prices, apprenticeship and trades unions.[60] The label 'laisser faire' like its alternative 'Benthamism' is inadequate to describe the changes of 1780–1850.[61] The state proved capable of devising many new agencies, like the factory and education inspectorate and the improvement and police commissions of local government. Although improvement commissions and like bodies made substantial contributions to the solution of urban problems, recent studies of urban politics have shown the danger inherent in the use of such state agencies. Sectarian and party divisions were important in delaying progress in the provision of clean water supplies to Leeds as well as in delaying the provision of adequate burial ground facilities.[62] The simple profit motive in individual enterprise, partnerships, and joint stock companies, created many viable alternatives, which provided water, cemeteries and education for the growing towns. Many of the problems tackled by the voluntary societies had been dealt with by the social relationships of family, neighbourhood and occupational grouping for many centuries before 1780. This continued in traditional and newer ways. The lodgers and co-residing kin of Preston contributed to family income, reducing poverty, and gaining themselves an introduction to urban society. Mayhew's costermongers enforced a common morality on each other, provided entertainment, and raised subscriptions for each other, without any formal organization. Many survivals of rural community behaviour like 'riding the stang' and 'rough music' controlled urban social relationships.[63] For the wealthy, the family and the extended neighbourhood still

60. R. Wilson, *Gentlemen merchants: the merchant community in Leeds, 1700–1830* (Manchester, 1971), pp. 102–4; E. P. Thompson, *The making of the English working class* (1969), pp. 517 and 544–5.

61. I prefer to reserve the term 'laisser faire' to refer to a group of doctrines which justified policy (or lack of it) towards a limited range of economic relationships, especially in foreign trade and labour relationships. This element in middle class ideology does not usefully contribute to an explanation of the use of voluntary societies in preference to the state; see also A. V. Dicey, *Lectures on the relationship between law and public opinion* (1905), pp. 62–209; A. J. Taylor, *Laisser faire and state intervention in nineteenth century Britain* (Economic History Society, 1972), pp. 32–38.

62. Fraser, *Urban politics*, pp. 92–3, 155–60.

63. M. Anderson, *Family structure in nineteenth century Lancashire* (Cambridge, 1971), pp. 43–52; H. Mayhew, *London labour and the London poor* (4 vols., 1861), I, 4–61; F. Engels, *The condition of the working class in England*, translated by W. O. Henderson and W. H. Chaloner (Oxford, 1958), pp. 100–2 and 140; George Walker, *The costume of Yorkshire in 1814* (Leeds, 1885), p. 65; J. Lawson, *Letters to the young on progress in Pudsey* (Stanningley, 1887), p. 66; E. P. Thompson, '"Rough music": le charivari anglais', *Annales*, 27ᵉ Année (1972), 285–312.

operated as it had done in the eighteenth century, through balls, race meetings, assemblies, dinner parties and visits to cousins, to ensure capital supply, arrange marriages, and discuss politics and social policy. Exceptional individuals were able to sustain paternalistic relationships with wage labour and the poor. Many enlightened coal-owners and owners of country mills provided housing and schools for their labour force. In Leeds, the Marshalls, owners of several large flax mills, ran their own factory schools and sponsored friendly societies, as well as contributing to the local network of voluntary societies.[64] But such alternatives proved increasingly inadequate between 1780 and 1850. Urban dwellers turned to formal organizations with rules, stated aims and activities, free from both the state and the profit motive.

There were several reasons why voluntary organizations should have been favoured by the urban middle classes during these decades. Joining an association entailed mild formal but limited commitment. This suited a situation in which migration rates and town size meant that significant numbers of people had the need and motivation to cooperate together but lacked the degree of trust and shared values created by kin and communal ties. The extreme flexibility of the voluntary society was attractive in the face of great uncertainty and rapid change. Individuals could withdraw, policies could change and new organizations be founded in a matter of weeks. This avoided the slow development of state action, and the waste of resources consequent on government commitment to policies which proved impracticable or unacceptable to those whose cooperation was essential for their success. Nineteenth-century Britain developed the bulk of its educational, poor law and hospital system by using the experience of voluntary organizations and the tactics and values evolved through those organizations as a guide for state action. Other schemes like the Society for the Suppression of Vice, the phrenological movement and the Owenite communities faded when their impracticability and their incongruence with scientific and social reality emerged.[65] The urban elite was divided by

64. Francis Hill, *Georgian Lincoln* (Cambridge, 1966), pp. 1–52; Leonore Davidoff, *The best circles: society, etiquette and the season* (1963), pp. 13–36; S. Pollard, *Genesis of modern management*, pp. 160–208; Ray Pallister, 'Educational investment by industrialists in the early part of the 19th century in County Durham', *Durham University Journal*, LXI (1968), 32–38; R. Boyson, *The Ashworth cotton enterprise* (Oxford, 1970), pp. 84–140; W. G. Rimmer, *Marshalls of Leeds, flax spinners, 1778–1886* (Cambridge, 1960), pp. 104–5, 194, 216–17.
65. Steve Shapin, 'Phrenological knowledge and the social structure of nineteenth-century Edinburgh', *Annals of Science*, XXXII (1975), 219–43; S. Pollard, 'Nineteenth century cooperation: from community to shopkeeping', in A. Briggs and J. Saville (eds.), *Essays in labour history* (1960), pp. 74–112; W. H. G. Armytage, *Heavens below: utopian experiments in England, 1560–1960* (1961),

political, religious and status differences. Voluntary action meant that difficult questions could be avoided about the relationships of the 'out-groups', whigs, dissenters, catholics and lower status masters and shopkeepers, to state agencies.[66] Thus different sectarian groups competed together to provide a fragmentary elementary education system within a voluntary framework, at a time when education was regarded as a crucial means of controlling the way in which the working classes thought about the world around them, and yet religious disputes made direct state organization of education impossible.[67] The voluntary associations provided an expression of social power for those endowed with increasing social and economic authority, but excluded from the effective exercise of state power by religious restrictions, franchise limitation, and often by the lack of any appropriate state agency.[68] The aristocracy had a minimal involvement in the societies described here, and did not generate a network of voluntary societies of their own. They had adequate class organizations in parliament, their family alliances, the law courts and the church. A third attraction of voluntary societies was the manner in which they allowed the middle class to tackle crucial social problems without ever fully facing the contradictions in their own value systems and social situation. The evangelical and utilitarian competition for middle-class attention took place between rival voluntary societies, not as a disruptive contest for the resources of the state. The values of the market place through which wealth was amassed and the paternalistic Christian values through which social authority was legitimated were reconciled by allocating market values to economic organizations, like the firm and the landed estate, and allocating paternalistic values to the dominant voluntary societies. Engels commented on this with well known bitterness:

pp. 77–167; J. F. C. Harrison, *Robert Owen and the Owenites in Britain and America* (1969), *passim*; Ian Donnachie, 'Orbiston, a Scottish Owenite community 1825–8', in J. Butt, *Robert Owen, prince of cotton spinners* (Newton Abbot, 1971), pp. 135–67; R. G. Garnett, 'Robert Owen and the community experiments', in S. Pollard and J. Salt, *Robert Owen, prophet of the poor* (1971), pp. 39–64; R. G. Garnett, *Cooperation and the Owenite socialist communities in Britain, 1825–45* (Manchester, 1972).

66. See *Historical Journal*, 26, no. 1 (1983), pp. 106–8 (the original source of this chapter) for an example of this in the Leeds committees for the relief of the poor.

67. R. Johnson, 'Educational policy and social control in early Victorian England', *Past and Present*, no. 49 (1970), pp. 96–119; R. Colls, '"Oh happy English children": coal, class and education in the North East', *Past and Present*, no. 73 (1976), pp. 75–99.

68. S. N. Eisenstadt, 'The social conditions for the development of voluntary association – a case study of Israel', *Scripta Hierosolymitama*, III (1956), 104–25, looks at a similar situation in pre-1948 Israel; the elite withdrew from voluntary associations once they had state power.

Englishmen are shocked if anyone suggests that they neglect their duty towards the poor. Have they not subscribed to the erection of more institutions for the relief of poverty than are to be found anywhere else in the world? Yes, indeed – welfare institutions! The vampire middle classes first suck the wretched workers dry so that afterwards they can, with consummate hypocrisy, throw a few miserable crumbs of charity at their feet.[69]

But all this gave time for the slow resolution of these contradictions or, even better, avoided the need to resolve them at all. Finally the voluntary societies enabled useful action to be taken by a community when government or profit seekers were unable or unwilling to act. The committee of the proposed Newcastle Botanical and Zoological Gardens made a virtue of necessity:

It has been particularly desired that this institution should be – free from all appearance of personal speculation or individual advantage – one immediately connected and wound up with the town, and which from the benefit it contemplates to all classes, it would be the pride, as well as the interest, of the inhabitants generally to support.[70]

The unity of those societies sponsored by the urban elites derived from the image of an 'ideal' society towards which they worked. This ideal was in direct opposition to the threatening image of the working classes held by many of the elite. The middle class, especially its wealthiest and most influential members, might have been increasingly isolated from the working class by the growth of suburbs and by the social distance created by the inequalities of wealth and capital; but this did not mean they were ignorant of, or uninterested in the working classes. Contact was extremely specialized and the media which informed the bulk of the middle classes was a distorting lens of great power. Street begging made a profound and disturbing impact in many towns:

Nothing can be more harassing than to have a claim of either real or pretended distress made upon one at every corner of a street, and such claims often persisted in with a degree of pertinacity, meant and calculated to coerce the passenger, in some measure to compliance.[71]

Here in the context of a face-to-face relationship and individual decision-taking were all the anxieties of the moral problem posed for the middle classes by the conflicting imperatives of Malthus and

69. Engels, *Condition of the working classes*, p. 313.
70. *Prospectus of the proposed botanical and zoological gardens* (Newcastle upon Tyne, 1838), Wilson Collection, VI, fo. 1398.
71. *Report of the committee appointed by commissioners of police to inquire into the practicability of suppressing the practice of common begging and relieving the industrious and destitute* (Edinburgh, 1812); *First report of the Society for the Suppression of Beggars instituted 25 January 1813* (Edinburgh, 1814).

Christian charity. The sense of distaste and physical threat was much wider than this. The impact of these encounters was supplemented by a variety of reports on the conditions and doings of the working classes. Newspaper reports of crime and disorder, the reports of the voluntary societies themselves, reports of propagandists and parliament on the health, education, poverty and housing of working people, built up a compelling stereotype of the working classes. Baines junior, the whig newspaper editor, summed up the impact with casual candour. He described the industrial suburb of Holbeck to the south of Leeds:

> the great part of the population was composed of thoughtless youth, some as illiterate as savages . . . drunkenness among young men was a prevailing vice . . . . street brawling a daily occurrence.[72]

Characteristically this threat was identified with the youth culture of the working classes, and many organizations were designed to counter the threat in these terms. Thus the Newcastle Literary, Scientific and Mechanical Institution was welcomed, amongst other things, because 'it will tend to improve the morals of the rising generation, to guard them from seductive pleasures, from drunkenness and dissipation'.[73] The awareness of the working classes as an ideological and political threat tended to be heightened at times of crisis in political and industrial relationships. Against this aspect of behaviour the voluntary societies were equally important. In 1832, Dr Williamson called for support for the Mechanics Institution in Leeds because

> political events had given an unusual excitement to the thinking powers of the great mass of society, the right direction of which chiefly depends on the adoption of an extensive system of education.[74]

It was clear that the leaders of the dominant voluntary societies felt that they were engaged in the creation of a particular set of social relationships which were intended to provide stability and legitimacy for their own power and privilege. The full range of the societies may be seen as a progression designed to create the sort of person who would be the ideal member of a stable, thriving, industrial community. The end product of the process was intended to be a society of independent, hard-working, self-disciplined owners of small units of property, created and directed by an elite which still concentrated wealth and power in their own hands. This ideal and the part played by the voluntary societies in creating it was

---

72. *Leeds Mercury*, 2 May 1835.
73. *Tyne Mercury*, 2 March 1824, Wilson Collection, II, fo. 336; Stanley Cohen, *Folk devils and moral panics: the creation of Mods and Rockers* (1972).
74. *Leeds Mercury*, 22 Sept. 1832.

forcibly expressed in an early handbill of the Leeds Permanent Building Society in 1849:

> Young men are especially recommended to join this society and thus lay the foundation of future comfort and ease. The Temperance movement has removed temptation out of the way of thousands, and the Mechanics Institutes and Reading Rooms have taught them many useful lessons. Let these advantages be further improved by securing a comfortable habitation. The means are within their reach and they are invited to embrace them.[75]

Thus the working man, the problem of the age, was saved from disease and starvation, sobered up, educated, and finally given the means to acquire property and capital. Somewhere along the line he had purchased a Bible, read several tracts, and joined a church or chapel. The partial failure of this plan and the further adaptation of the energies behind it are another story, but by 1850 the different elements of the plan were all in place.

All this occurred, or was intended to occur under carefully controlled conditions. Baines again expressed this clearly when he praised the Sunday schools:

> a kind of spiritual superintendence on the part of 60 000 teachers, generally from the middle class, over 400 000 scholars, generally from the working class . . . the Sunday Schools form a bond of greatest importance between two classes of society.[76]

Although the Sunday schools and the mechanics institutes could not reproduce the relationships of the landed estate, the factory village, or the traditional workshop, they did aim to create a new institutionalized form of paternalism. All the major features of such a relationship were sought and often achieved. Disciplined care of the welfare and behaviour of those with little power was accepted as a duty by those with wealth and authority. The activities of the voluntary societies were designed to create an ideal society of the independent and the respectable, but they were also designed to have that stabilizing and legitimating effect which paternalism always strives to impose upon inequality. The leaders of all the societies reflected with pleasure on the gratitude of those who had received help. Thus the Leeds Friendly Loan Society which provided small loans to help the poor set up in business printed dozens of letters like the following:

> GENTLEMEN - I am happy to say that the loan I received from your society has proved very beneficial to me. . . your loan enabled me to pay the landlord, and remove into a house of less rent, and

---

75. *The Leeds Building and Investment Society*, handbill issued 1846.
76. Edward Baines, junior, op. cit., pp. 24–5.

begin a small shop . . . it has done me a very deal of good, for which I am grateful to the Committee and Gentlemen of the Leeds Friendly Loan Society, and remain
Yours Respectfully,
H. S.[77]

It was a paradigm of the ideal relationship between elite and people towards which the societies were striving.

IV

These were the aims of those who sponsored an important group of the voluntary societies. How successful were they? This question cannot be adequately answered in the final paragraphs of an article, but it is possible to hint at what happened to the ideals outlined above. The behaviour patterns, values and ambitions of the clerks and the lower middle class in the second half of the nineteenth century came very close to their realization. Mr Polly, Kipps and Mr Pooter expressed just that mixture of deference and proud independence which the letter to the Friendly Loan Society suggested.[78] The clear inability of the artisan trades unions of the 1850s to argue their claims in anything but the terms of political economy suggests that intellectual energies had been successfully diverted from devising any alternative.[79] But there are problems in accepting the success of these voluntary societies without question. Recent research has shown that many of the working classes were able to take and use items from the cultural package offered to them without compromising their own class identity or interest. Indeed, elements like the mechanics institutions, savings banks, the volunteers of the 1850s and 1860s, and even the Sunday schools, were taken and reinterpreted within the traditions of the artisan and others in the working classes.[80] Thus 'saving', 'education' and 'temperance' made

---

77. *Second annual report of the Leeds Friendly Loan Society* (Leeds, 1846), p. 9.
78. G. L. Anderson, *Victorian clerks* (Manchester, 1976); Geoffrey Crossick (ed.), *The lower middle class in Britain, 1870–1914* (1977); George and Weedon Grossmith, *The diary of a nobody* (1892); H. G. Wells, *The history of Mr Polly* (1910); H. G. Wells, *Kipps* (1905).
79. R. V. Clements, 'British trades unions and popular political economy, 1850–1875', *Economic History Review*, XIV, 2nd series (1961), 93–104.
80. R. Gray, *The labour aristocracy in Victorian Edinburgh* (Oxford, 1976); Hugh Cunningham, *The volunteer force: a social and political history, 1859–1908* (1975); Geoffrey Crossick, *An artisan elite in Victorian society: Kentish London, 1840–1880* (1978); T. W. Laquer, *Religion and respectability*; Robert Colls, *The colliers rant: song and culture in the industrial village* (1977).

Voluntary societies and British urban élites 1780–1850: an analysis

an occupational group more formidable in labour disputes, for their threats of strike action had resources and self-control to sustain them. The whole concept of 'respectability' became a powerful weapon to gain political support for trades unions and franchise reform from the enfranchised middle classes. Further problems were created by working class 'apathy'. The working class resisted by just not coming to meeting, library or mission. Hole and Hudson realized this in the early 1850s, and Yeo and Meller show that the problem was the same in the 1890s.[81] In the short run the most serious threat faced by the voluntary societies was shortage of cash. A trade slump or a change in fashion could bring a sharp drop in income, or the natural processes of deaths and removals amongst subscribers would steadily reduce income. In any case subscribers were always a minority of the middle classes.[82]

By 1850, one group of voluntary societies after another began to search for aid from the state. In 1845–6, a change in the settlement laws took much of the task of caring for in-migrants to the towns from the voluntary societies. From 1846, the voluntary societies which dealt with primary education were increasingly infiltrated by the state through grants, teacher training and HMIs. The temperance movement turned to the state for legislation to increase their influence, although in this case they were politically unsuccessful.[83] The mechanics institutions after being diverted into the provision of cultural entertainment turned back to their central task of instruction by using the department of science and art grants provided in the 1850s. Others like the building societies became commercial organizations – although the building societies retained traces of their origin by remaining non-profit making agencies.[84]

One response to this was the glorification of voluntary activity as an end in itself, but such a view gradually gave way before the logic of industrial and urban society. In 1867, Baines, who with Edward Miall, had been one of the major protagonists of voluntaryism, admitted defeat: 'we must govern our conduct by the facts and experience, as well as by sacred principles'. He reviewed the progress of the voluntary schools since 1843: 'I am compelled with

81. J. W. Hudson, Ph. D., *The history of adult education* (1851), VII-XII; James Hole, *An essay on the history and management of literary, scientific and mechanics institutions* (1853), pp. 17–25; S. Yeo, 'On the uses of "Apathy"', *Archives Européenes de Sociologie*, XV (1974), 279–311; S. Yeo, *Religion and voluntary organisations* (1976); H. E. Meller, *Leisure*.
82. R. J. Morris, 'Organization' provides details of this, pp. 136, 157–61, 201 and 210.
83. M. Sturt, *The education of the people* (1967); M. E. Rose, op. cit; B. H . Harrison, *Drink and the Victorians*, pp. 196 ff.
84. J. F. C. Harrison, *Learning and living*, pp. 214–15; E. J. Cleary, *The building society movement* (1965).

pain to acknowledge that it has not been satisfactory . . . '. The need to maintain class hegemony was paramount, or as he put it, 'the duty of the wealthier classes to assist in the education of the humbler'.[85] If the aims of the voluntary societies were to be achieved, then the legal power and financial resources of the state were necessary. At the same time, the growing strength of the state bureaucracy created new demands for uniformity, consistency and effectiveness in tackling the problems of industrial society. Thus ambitions within state institutions met realizations of weakness on the part of the promoters of voluntary societies, creating part of the environment for growth in the scope and depth of the social actions of the state.[86]

This essentially marked the end of the first episode in the history of the nineteenth-century voluntary society. The societies went on to increase and diversify but worked within the shadow of state agencies and commercial competition. The voluntary societies became and remained a dominant feature of nineteenth-century British society especially in the towns. This article begins the task of explaining why.[87]

85. Edward Baines, *National education: an address as chairman of a breakfast of the Congregational Union of England and Wales at Manchester, Friday 11 October 1867* (1867).
86. M. Weber, 'Bureaucracy', in H. H. Gerth and C. Wright Mills (eds), *From Max Weber* (1948), pp. 196–44; O. MacDonagh, 'The nineteenth-century revolution in government – a reappraisal', *Historical Journal* (1958), I, 52–67; Gillian Sutherland (ed.), *Studies in the growth of nineteenth century government* (1972).
87. My thanks to Professor M. Anderson, Dr R. Davidson, Dr N. T. Phillipson and Professor T. C. Smout for valuable comments on an earlier version of this paper, and to those who contributed to discussion when the ideas in this article were first put forward at the Urban History Conference in Leicester in 1973.

SELECT READING LIST

The following is a selection from the secondary literature on the English town 1688–1820. Items included in this reader are marked with an asterisk. For a more detailed bibliography see the footnotes to Chapter 1, Introduction.

GENERAL

Clark, P. (ed.), *Country Towns in Pre-industrial England* (Leicester, 1981). Includes an excellent introduction, and essays on seventeenth-century Ipswich, Winchester 1580–1700, and Bath 1660–1800.

Clark, P. (ed.), *The Transformation of English Provincial Towns 1600–1800* (London, 1984). Contains a valuable introduction, and essays on Totnes houses 1500–1800, economic change in Kendal *c.* 1550–1700, migration and towns, urban growth and agricultural change, social relations in Newcastle upon Tyne 1660–1760, urban ritual 1660–1800, urban retailing 1700–1815, church building in eighteenth-century towns, and the civic leaders of Gloucester 1580–1800.

Corfield, P. J., 'A provincial capital in the late seventeenth century: the case of Norwich', in P. Clark and P. Slack (eds), *Crisis and Order in English Towns 1500–1700* (London, 1972).

Corfield, P. J., *The Impact of English Towns 1700–1800* (Oxford, 1982). The best introduction to the eighteenth-century town.

*Everitt, A. M., 'Country, county and town: patterns of regional evolution in England', *Transactions of the Royal Historical Society*, 5th ser., 29 (1979).

Farrant, S., *Georgian Brighton 1740 to 1820* (Brighton, 1980).

Fraser, D., and Sutcliffe, A. (eds), *The Pursuit of Urban History* (London, 1983). Includes essays on popular ritual in Stuart and

Hanoverian London, the writing of urban history before 1800, the middle class and towns 1780–1870, and sexual differentiation among the Birmingham middle class 1780–1850.

George, M. D., *London Life in the Eighteenth Century* (Harmondsworth, 1966).

Hoskins, W. G., *Industry, Trade, and People in Exeter 1688–1800*, 2nd edn (Exeter, 1968).

Jackson, G., *Hull in the Eighteenth Century* (Oxford, 1972).

Life in the Georgian Town, papers given at the Georgian Group symposium 1985 (London, 1986). Contains a general introduction to the Georgian town, and essays on self-improvement societies, the town promenade, religion, resorts, and horse-racing.

McInnes, A., *The English Town 1660–1760*, Historical Association (London, 1980).

Marshall, J. D., 'Kendal in the late seventeenth and eighteenth centuries', *Transactions of the Cumberland and Westmorland Antiquarian Society*, new ser., 75 (1975).

Marshall, J. D., 'The rise and transformation of the Cumbrian market town 1660–1900', *Northern History*, 19 (1983).

Money, J., *Experience and Identity: Birmingham and the West Midlands 1760–1800* (Manchester, 1977).

Neale, R. S., *Bath 1680–1850: a Social History* (London, 1981).

Noble, M., 'Growth and development in a regional urban system: the country towns of Eastern Yorkshire 1700–1850', *Urban History Yearbook* (1987).

Unwin, R. W., 'Tradition and transition: market towns of the Vale of York 1660–1830', *Northern History*, 17 (1981).

Walvin, J., *English Urban Life 1776–1851* (London, 1984).

Wrigley, E. A., 'A simple model of London's importance in changing English society and economy 1650–1750', *Past and Present*, 37 (1967).

POPULATION

Armstrong, W. A., 'The trend of mortality in Carlisle between the 1780s and the 1840s: a demographic contribution to the Standard of Living debate', *Economic History Review*, 2nd ser., 34, no. 1 (1981).

Chambers, J. D., 'Population change in a provincial town: Nottingham 1700–1800', in D. V. Glass and D. E. C. Eversley (eds), *Population in History: Essays in Historical Demography* (London, 1965).

Clark, P., 'Migration in England during the late seventeenth and early eighteenth centuries', *Past and Present*, 83 (1979).

Landers, J., 'Mortality, weather, and prices in London 1675–1825: a study of short-term fluctuations', *Journal of Historical Geography*, 12, no. 4 (1986).

Landers, J., and Mouzas, A., 'Burial seasonality and causes of death in London 1670–1819', *Population Studies*, 42 (1988).

Law, C. M., 'Some notes on the urban population of England and Wales in the eighteenth century', *Local Historian*, 10, no. 1 (1972).

*Wrigley, E. A., 'Urban growth and agricultural change: England and the Continent in the early modern period', *Journal of Interdisciplinary History*, 15, no. 4 (1985).

ECONOMY

Clemens, P. G. E., 'The rise of Liverpool 1665–1750', *Economic History Review*, 2nd ser., 29, no. 2 (1976).

Daunton, M. J., 'Towns and economic growth in eighteenth-century England', in P. Abrams and E. A. Wrigley (eds), *Towns in Societies: Essays in Economic History and Historical Sociology* (Cambridge, 1979).

Everitt, A. M., 'The food market of the English town 1660–1760', in *Third International Conference of Economic History* (Munich, 1965).

*Jones, E. L., and Falkus, M. E., 'Urban improvement and the English economy in the seventeenth and eighteenth centuries', in P. J. Uselding (ed.), *Research in Economic History*, Vol. 4 (Greenwich, Conn., 1979).

Minchinton, W. E., 'Bristol: metropolis of the West in the eighteenth century', *Transactions of the Royal Historical Society*, 5th ser., 4 (1954).

Priestley, U., ' "The fabric of stuffs": the Norwich textile industry c. 1650–1750', *Textile History*, 16, no. 2 (1985).

SOCIAL STRUCTURE AND STANDARDS OF LIVING

Botham, F. W., and Hunt, E. H., 'Wages in Britain during the Industrial Revolution', *Economic History Review*, 2nd ser., 40, no. 3 (1987).

Davidoff, L., and Hall, C., *Family Fortunes: Men and Women of the English Middle Class 1780–1850* (London, 1987).

Earle, P., *The Making of the English Middle Class: Business, Society, and Family Life in London 1660–1730* (London, 1989).

Horwitz, H., ' "The mess of the middle class" revisited: the case of the "big bourgeoisie" of Augustan London', *Continuity and Change*, 2, no. 2 (1987).

Lindert, P. H., and Williamson, J. G., 'English workers' living standards during the Industrial Revolution: a new look', *Economic History Review*, 2nd ser., 36, no. 1 (1983).

Macfarlane, S., 'Social policy and the poor in the later seventeenth century', in A. L. Beier and R. Finlay (eds), *London 1500–1700: the Making of the Metropolis* (London, 1986).

*Morris, R. J., 'Voluntary societies and British urban élites 1780–1850: an analysis', *Historical Journal*, 26, no. 1 (1983).

Ripley, P., 'Poverty in Gloucester and its alleviation 1690–1740', *Transactions of the Bristol and Gloucestershire Archaeological Society*, 103 (1985).

*Rogers, N., 'Money, land and lineage: the big bourgeoisie of Hanoverian London', *Social History*, 4, no. 3 (1979).

*Schwarz, L. D., 'Social class and social geography: the middle classes in London at the end of the eighteenth century', *Social History*, 7, no. 2 (1982).

Schwarz, L. D., 'The standard of living in the long run: London 1760–1860', *Economic History Review*, 2nd ser., 38, no. 1 (1985).

Taylor, A. J. (ed.), *The Standard of Living in Britain in the Industrial Revolution* (London, 1975).

Wilson, R. G., *Gentlemen Merchants: the Merchant Community in Leeds 1700–1830* (Manchester, 1971).

POLITICS AND RELIGION

Curtis, T. C., and Speck, W. A., 'The societies for the reformation of manners: a case study in the theory and practice of moral reform', *Literature and History*, 3 (1976).

De Krey, G. S., *A Fractured Society: the Politics of London in the First Age of Party 1688–1715* (Oxford, 1985).

Ellis, J., 'Urban conflict and popular violence: the Guildhall riots of 1740 in Newcastle-upon-Tyne', *International Review of Social History*, 25 (1980).

Harrison, M., *Crowds and History: Mass Phenomena in English Towns 1790–1835* (Cambridge, 1988).

Holmes, G. S., 'The Sacheverell riots: the crowd and the church in early eighteenth-century London', *Past and Present*, 72 (1976).

Horwitz, H., 'Party in a civic context: London from the Exclusion Crisis to the fall of Walpole', in C. Jones (ed.), *Britain in the First Age of Party 1680–1750* (London, 1987).

McCalman, I., 'Ultra-radicalism and convivial debating-clubs in London 1795–1838', *English Historical Review*, 102, no. 403 (1987).

*Money, J., 'Birmingham and the West Midlands 1760–1793: politics and regional identity in the English provinces in the later eighteenth century', *Midland History*, 1 (1971).

Phillips, J. A., 'The structure of electoral politics in unreformed England', *Journal of British Studies*, 19, no. 2 (1980).

Rogers, N., 'Aristocratic clientage, trade, and independency: popular politics in pre-radical Westminster', *Past and Present*, 61 (1973).

Rogers, N., 'Popular protest in early Hanoverian London', *Past and Present*, 79 (1978).

Rudé, G., *Paris and London in the Eighteenth Century: Studies in Popular Protest* (London, 1970).

Seed, J., 'Gentlemen dissenters: the social and political meanings of rational dissent in the 1770s and 1780s', *Historical Journal*, 28, no. 2 (1985).

*Shoemaker, R. B., 'The London "mob" in the early eighteenth century', *Journal of British Studies*, 26, no. 3 (1987).

Stevenson, J., *Popular Disturbances in England 1700–1870* (London, 1979).

Thompson, E. P., *The Making of the English Working Class* (Harmondsworth, 1968).

CULTURE AND LANDSCAPE

*Borsay, P., 'The English urban renaissance: the development of provincial urban culture *c*.1680–*c*.1760', *Social History*, 2, no. 2 (1977).

Borsay, P., *The English Urban Renaissance: Culture and Society in the Provincial Town 1660–1770* (Oxford, 1989).

Chalklin, C. W., *The Provincial Towns of Georgian England: a Study of the Building Process 1740–1820* (London, 1974).

Chalklin, C. W., 'The making of some new towns *c*. 1600–1720', in

C. W. Chalklin and M. A. Havinden (eds), *Rural Change and Urban Growth 1500–1800* (London, 1974).

Clark, P., *The English Alehouse: a Social History 1200–1830* (London, 1983).

Everitt, A. M., 'The English urban inn 1560–1760', in A. M. Everitt (ed.), *Perspectives in English Urban History* (London, 1973).

Inkster, I., 'The development of a scientific community in Sheffield 1790–1850: a network of people and interests', *Transactions of the Hunter Archaeological Society*, 10 (1971–77).

McInnes, A., 'The emergence of a leisure town: Shrewsbury 1660–1760', *Past and Present*, 120 (1988).

*Neale, R. S., 'Bath: ideology and utopia 1700–1760', in R. F. Brissenden and J. C. Eade (eds), *Studies in the Eighteenth Century*, Vol. III (Canberra, 1976).

Olsen, D. J., *Town Planning in London: the Eighteenth and Nineteenth Centuries*, 2nd edn (New Haven and London, 1982).

*Porter, R., 'Science, provincial culture and public opinion in Enlightenment England', *British Journal for Eighteenth-Century Studies*, 3 (1980).

Reid, D., 'Interpreting the festival calendar: wakes and fairs as carnivals', in R. D. Storch (ed.), *Popular Culture and Custom in Nineteenth-Century England* (London, 1982).

Summerson, J., *Georgian London* (Harmondsworth, 1962).

Taylor, I. C., 'The court and cellar dwelling: the eighteenth-century origin of the Liverpool slum', *Transactions of the Historic Society of Lancashire and Cheshire*, 72 (1970).

INDEX

Index